# MANAGERIAL ECONOMICS

## CORPORATE ECONOMICS AND STRATEGY

# MANAGERIAL ECONOMICS

## CORPORATE ECONOMICS AND STRATEGY

**Thomas H. Naylor**
Duke University

**John M. Vernon**
Duke University

**Kenneth L. Wertz**
University of North Carolina

**McGRAW-HILL BOOK COMPANY**
New York   St. Louis   San Francisco   Auckland   Bogotá
Hamburg   Johannesburg   London   Madrid   Mexico   Montreal   New Delhi
Panama   Paris   São Paulo   Singapore   Sydney   Tokyo   Toronto

This book was set in Times Roman by A Graphic Method Inc.
The editors were Bonnie E. Lieberman, Peter J. Dougherty, and Edwin Hanson;
the production supervisor was Phil Galea.
The drawings were done by VIP Graphics.
The cover was designed by Miriam Reccio.
R. R. Donnelley & Sons Company was printer and binder.

**MANAGERIAL ECONOMICS**

**Corporate Economics and Strategy**

2 3 4 5 6 7 8 9 0  DOCDOC  8 9 8 7 6 5 4 3

ISBN 0-07-045947-9

Library of Congress Cataloging in Publication Data

Naylor, Thomas H., date
    Managerial economics.

    Includes bibliographies and index.
    1. Managerial economics.  2. Corporate planning.
I. Vernon, John Mitcham, date  . II. Wertz,
Kenneth L.  III. Title.
HD30.22.N39  1983     658.4'03     82-8983
ISBN 0-07-045947-9     AACR2

# CONTENTS

# PREFACE

Most textbooks on managerial economics contain chapters on demand analysis, production, cost analysis, the theory of the firm, market structures, and capital budgeting. This text is no exception in that it too contains these core topics. However, there is a fundamental difference between this book and other managerial economics texts: This is the first textbook on the subject to recognize and acknowledge an important new approach to decision making, known as *corporate strategy,* that emerged in the 1970s.

The major premise of this book is that the single most important application of microeconomics to practical business problems is in strategic planning, which lies at the heart of the firm's long-term resource allocation problem. Given a set of corporate goals and objectives, and a set of assumptions about the company's economic, competitive, regulatory, factor-supply, technological, and international environments, strategic planning is a threefold problem: a *portfolio* problem, an *investment* problem, and a *strategy selection* problem. Which businesses should the company be in? What level of investment should be made in each business? Which specific financial, marketing, and production strategies should each business follow? *Corporate economics* is defined as the integration of microeconomics and strategic planning.

To understand the firm's economic and competitive environments, we must consider both demand theory (Chapter 2) and empirical demand analysis and econometrics (Chapter 3). The study of production and cost functions in Chapter 4 is necessary to enhance our knowledge of the factor-supply and technological environments of the firm. The regulatory and international environments can affect the firm through its demand, cost, and production functions.

The firm's factor-input and product-output decisions are analyzed in Chapter 5 using conventional marginal analysis and linear programming. Although relatively few firms employ optimization techniques as strategic planning tools, optimization is a useful conceptual framework through which to view the interdependence of the firm's portfolio, investment, and strategy selection problems.

Having developed the basic elements of microeconomics in Chapters 2 through 5, we apply microeconomics to the firm's competitive environment in Chapters 6 through 8. We formulate and analyze competitive markets in Chapter 6, industrial organization and competitive analysis are the topics of Chapter 7, and Chapter 8 treats antitrust and government regulation.

In Chapters 9 and 10 the microeconomic theory of the firm is extended to include capital investment decisions and decision making under risk and uncertainty.

The final three chapters are concerned with the direct application of microeconomics to corporate strategic planning. After outlining the elements of strategic planning in Chapter 11, we argue that microeconomics, instead of accounting, should be the language of strategic planning. Two different types of strategic planning models, those of competitive strategy and simulation, are described in Chapter 12. Finally, Chapter 13 covers the "politics of corporate economics," which concerns the practical problem of integrating corporate economics and strategy into the decision-making process.

Armed with the analytical tools and the microeconomic conceptual framework outlined in this book, the reader should be able to come to grips with solutions to the three major interdependent problems of business: the portfolio problem, the investment problem, and the strategy selection problem.

Throughout the entire book substantial emphasis is placed on practical examples to illustrate the application of corporate economics to the "real world." Based on the authors' extensive consulting experience with over 200 major corporations, the book attempts to combine microeconomic theory, strategic planning, and the analytical tools used in both fields.

This book is aimed at three different groups: (1) managerial decision makers who use corporate economics to make decisions, (2) corporate economists who specialize in the application of microeconomics to problems of the firm, and (3) advanced undergraduate and beginning graduate students in business and economics who expect to use corporate economics in the future.

The reader who has had a basic course in calculus will find numerous applications in footnotes and appendixes. However, readers who have had only high school algebra should have little difficulty with this book. In several sections some previous knowledge of elementary statistics should prove helpful. Appendixes are included on calculus, optimization, and the simplex method of linear programming. Each chapter has a set of review problems and questions.

We are grateful to the Literary Executor of the late Sir Ronald A. Fisher, F.R.S., to Dr. Frank Yates, F.R.S., and to the Longman Group Ltd., London, for permission to reprint Table III from their book *Statistical Tables for Biological, Agricultural, and Medical Research* (6th ed., 1974).

We are indebted to dozens of graduate students in the Department of Economics and the Fuqua School of Business at Duke University who served as willing experimental subjects for over two years, while earlier drafts of this book were being tested in the classroom. Michele H. Mann provided valuable editorial assistance throughout the development of the book.

We would also like to express our thanks for the many useful comments and suggestions provided by colleagues who reviewed this text during the course of its development, especially to Donald Bumpass, Texas Tech University; Paul Hayashi, University of Texas, Arlington; John Pisciotta, Center of Economic Education, Baylor University; Mark Schaefer, Georgia State University; Charles Stokes, College of Business Administration, University of Bridgeport; John Tomaske, California State University, Los Angeles; Ron Wilder, University of South Carolina School of Business; and Daniel Williamson, California Polytechnic State University.

*Thomas H. Naylor*
*John M. Vernon*
*Kenneth L. Wertz*

# PART ONE

# INTRODUCTION

# CHAPTER 1

# WHY CORPORATE ECONOMICS?

**CHAPTER OUTLINE**

UNCERTAINTY IN TODAY'S CORPORATIONS
    Economic Recessions
    Inflation and Tight Money
    Energy Problems and Supply Constraints
    Government Regulation
CORPORATE ECONOMIC DECISIONS
    Demand Forecasting
    Pricing and Competitive Strategy
    Cost Analysis
    Supply Forecasting
    Resource Allocation
    Government Regulation
    Risk Analysis
    Capital Investment Analysis
    Strategic Planning
    Corporate Development
THE RELATIONSHIP BETWEEN CORPORATE ECONOMICS
AND OTHER FUNCTIONS OF THE FIRM
    Finance
    Marketing
    Production
    Personnel
    Legal

This book is aimed at (1) managerial decision makers who use corporate economics to make decisions, (2) corporate economists who specialize in the application of microeconomics to problems of the firm, and (3) undergraduate and graduate students who expect to use corporate economics in the future as managerial decision makers, corporate economists, or both.

Since the intended audience for this book includes those who specialize in corporate economics and those who merely use some of the tools associated with corporate economics as aids to decision making, we shall use the terms "corporate economist" and "decision maker" interchangeably. Although we recognize that some corporate economists are stereotyped as researchers who make few decisions, we are concerned primarily with the application of corporate economics to decision making. Rather than always referring to corporate economists and decision makers, we will tend to use only one of these designations at a time.

## UNCERTAINTY IN TODAY'S CORPORATIONS

The decade of the 1970s has imposed on corporate executives a degree of uncertainty which has not been seen since the end of World War II. As the external economic environment faced by large and small firms alike has become more uncertain and complex, corporations have been forced to treat economics much more seriously than in the past. During the past 10 years, corporate economists have come into their own as an integral part of the top management team of many large companies. It is appropriate to begin this book on corporate economics by defining some of the forms of economic uncertainty which have been exerting tremendous pressure on corporations, problems which corporate economists are being asked to help solve.

### Economic Recessions

The memory of the 1974–1975 recession still lingers in the minds of many corporate executives who anticipated neither the timing nor the depth of the most serious recession in the United States in over 40 years. Sears Roebuck and General Motors were among hundreds of corporate giants who paid a very high price for not adjusting their corporate strategies fast enough to cope with the rapid deterioration of the economic environment. More recently, in 1980, the automobile industry faced another economic crisis. The industry as a whole, and Chrysler in particular, simply did not switch to smaller, more fuel-efficient cars to meet the rising cost of gasoline and thus avoid a significant reduction in sales and massive layoffs. The whole industry was dealt a severe economic blow, and Chrysler tottered on the brink of bankruptcy for several months.

**Inflation and Tight Money**

In the 1960s, inflation was not a major concern to most American corporate executives. By the late 1970s, double-digit inflation appeared to have become institutionalized in the United States in much the same way that it has in Argentina and Brazil. In response to double-digit inflation the Federal Reserve Board tightened the money supply, thus sending the prime rate of interest to over 20 percent.

Inflation, tight money, high interest rates, the potential collapse of the international monetary system, and cash-flow problems represent a set of interdependent problems which few firms managed to escape during the 1970s. Although we have all felt the impact of these problems, financial institutions (banks, savings and loan associations, and insurance companies) have been particularly influenced by these forces. The demise of Penn Central, Franklin National Bank, and W. T. Grant did not go unnoticed by financial institutions, nor did the fact that there were 13 bank failures in the United States in 1975, the largest number in one year since the end of the Great Depression. Property-casualty insurance companies were particularly hard hit by inflation, a slow economic recovery in 1975 and 1976, and premium levels inadequate to cover large underwriting losses from both property and accident and health insurance.

Banks, insurance companies, and other financial institutions began asking themselves the question, "Do I have an adequate early warning system to enable me to anticipate liquidity problems before they become acute and while I still have a number of viable options available?" Many financial institutions, including some very large banks, were made to realize that their forecasting systems were inadequate to meet these challenges. Since 1974, banks have shown increased interest in macroeconomic forecasting in general and corporate economics in particular.

**Energy Problems and Supply Constraints**

In the fall of 1973, OPEC signaled the beginning of the energy crisis by cutting off the supply of crude oil from the middle east and then setting the price of crude oil at a level most people never dreamed possible. The price of gasoline doubled within a few months, and gasoline shortages emerged at the retail level. The energy crisis exposed the fact that the state of the art of economic planning and forecasting in the United States and other parts of the world was abysmal.

As the memory of the 1973 energy crisis began to fade into the past, the flow of oil from Iran was curtailed not once but twice in 1979. The potential for similar political unrest in virtually every oil-producing country in the middle east is now a strong possibility. Multinational companies and companies which are heavily dependent on relatively unstable countries as their principal suppliers of raw materials have little choice but to improve the quality of their factor supply and factor-price-forecasting capabilities.

The decade of the 1960s was a period of expansion and rapid growth for most American companies. So-called growth companies were characterized by increased sales volume and market share. The merger-acquisition mode of expansion came into vogue during this period as well. There were no supply constraints, nor was there any energy crisis. The only constraint on corporate growth was the rate of growth of the market itself. But by the mid-1970s, American companies began facing a different external environment. In 1974, for the first time since the end of World War II, manufacturing industries encountered shortages in a wide variety of factor inputs in their production processes. Natural gas, coal, petroleum feedstocks, and a broad range of minerals were all in short supply. Indeed, the energy crisis was merely a special case of a more general problem. Although the 1975 recession brought temporary relief, this appears to be a long-run problem. An excessive rate of population growth throughout the world and increased per capita consumption among the more affluent nations are the causes. Our natural resources are being depleted at alarmingly high rates.

We have drilled the shallow oil wells and have developed the surface mines. The next time around, the oil wells will be much deeper and more expensive. Offshore wells will replace conventional wells. Mines will also be deeper than they were in the past. We have skimmed off the cream and have taken the easy profits. Barring some major breakthrough in technology, which seems unlikely, shortages and rising factor input prices are likely to be with us for a long time.

### Government Regulation

During the past 50 years increased government regulation has become a fact of life not only in the United States but throughout the entire world, in capitalist and socialist countries alike. No major industry has managed to escape the ever-extending arms of all levels of government in the United States. (At the time this book was written, it was still too early to determine whether the movement toward deregulation initiated by the Reagan administration will continue.) Although many government regulations are well intended, their side effects frequently are extremely costly.

Consider the following examples. The requirement of pollution-abatement and safety devices on all automobiles increased prices and contributed significantly to the 1974–1975 depression of the auto industry. Federal water-pollution regulations drove many marginal producers of paper out of business and greatly increased the cost of building new paper mills. Artificially imposed price ceilings on natural gas and crude oil had an adverse effect on exploration and drilling activity at a time when we could ill afford reductions in the supply of these critical sources of energy. The recent decontrol of these industries has resulted in a storm of exploration and drilling activities in search of oil and natural gas.

For some industries, increased governmental activity may produce windfall gains. The pharmaceutical industry would reap substantial benefits from the passage of a national health insurance program by Congress. Per capita drug consumption in the United States would probably increase dramatically. On the other hand, national health insurance may be accompanied by government-imposed price controls on drugs.

If one is planning for the future, one cannot avoid taking into consideration the likely impact of pending government legislation and programs. Although we do not know how to predict the behavior of legislative bodies and governmental agencies, corporate economists can help develop strategic plans to anticipate the possible impact of proposed programs on corporate performance.

## CORPORATE ECONOMIC DECISIONS

There are at least 10 major types of decisions with which corporate economists are likely to be involved in a typical corporation. They include:

1 Demand forecasting
2 Pricing and competitive analysis
3 Cost analysis
4 Supply forecasting
5 Resource allocation
6 Government regulation
7 Risk analysis
8 Capital investment analysis
9 Strategic planning
10 Corporate development

### Demand Forecasting

With the advent of national econometric forecasting services such as Chase, Wharton, and DRI, demand forecasting has become an increasingly important function of corporate economists. Over 750 corporations in the United States now have some sort of econometric forecasting model for predicting demand for a variety of different products whose sales are linked to some national econometric model and data base. In some companies the role of the corporate economist is to produce such forecasts. In other companies corporate economists may work with outside consultants who generate the demand forecasts. Alternatively, the corporate economist may serve as an in-house consultant to those in the company who are actually doing forecasting.

Demand analysis and demand forecasting constitute the subject matter of Chapters 2 and 3, respectively.

### Pricing and Competitive Strategy

Pricing decisions have long been within the purview of corporate economists. Indeed, pricing policies are merely a subset of a broader class of corporate economic problems: competitive analysis. Competitive analysis includes the anticipation of the response of competitors to the company's pricing, advertising, and marketing strategies. It also includes evaluations of the impact on the company's sales of alternative marketing strategies employed by competitors. Pricing and competitive marketing decisions require considerable knowledge of specific product markets and industry behavior on the part of the corporate economist. This topic will be addressed in Chapters 6, 7, and 12.

### Cost Analysis

Routine cost analyses are normally handled by the company's cost accountants and industrial engineers. However, some production processes are so complex that they necessitate the assistance of a corporate economist in providing an appropriate conceptual framework for defining certain costs. The specification of corporate planning models usually requires the expertise of an economist to formulate realistic models of production operations. Corporate economists may also be asked to participate in relatively sophisticated cost-benefit studies. Chapters 4 and 5 are concerned with production decisions and cost analysis.

### Supply Forecasting

As the economy of the United States has shifted from the demand-constrained economy of the 1960s to a supply-constrained economy in the 1970s, the importance of forecasting factor input supplies and prices has increased dramatically. Supply forecasting is not a field in which most corporations have a substantial amount of experience. Forecasting energy supplies and prices requires that the corporate economist be very much attuned to the international political scene. Supply models are examined in Chapters 4, 5, and 12.

### Resource Allocation

Some economists would go so far as to define economics in terms of the problem, "How do we allocate scarce resources subject to a set of constraints?" Although our definition of economics tends to be somewhat more eclectic, we would agree that how the firm allocates its scarce resources is a topic worthy of consideration by the corporate economist. Resource allocation is treated primarily in Chapters 5, 9, and 12.

### Government Regulation

Government regulation and antitrust problems have become increasingly complex as the federal government continues to extend its far-reaching arms into almost every phase of business. Whether it is a matter of providing arguments in defense of the company against alleged antitrust violations or of providing support for rate increases for electric utilities, there are endless applications of corporate economics to the entire field of government regulation. In many companies, the corporate economics function evolved out of work which may have originally been concentrated entirely on problems of government regulation. Chapters 7 and 8 are devoted to problems of government regulation, and antitrust issues.

### Risk Analysis

Economists may also be useful to top management in assessing the risks associated with various projects. In addition to providing the appropriate analytical tools for decision problems involving risk and uncertainty, economists may be helpful merely in asking the "right" questions of senior management. Risk analysis is the subject of Chapter 10.

### Capital Investment Analysis

Investments in plant and equipment may involve millions or even hundreds of millions of dollars. The lead time on some capital investment decisions is enormous. For example, a decision today to build a new nuclear power plant may not be fully realized for nearly 15 years. Given such high stakes, extreme care must be taken in choosing among alternative investments. Again, corporate economists may play a useful analytical role in decisions of this type. Chapter 9 is concerned with investment decisions.

### Strategic Planning

In recent years, a number of corporate economists have found themselves heading up the strategic planning function for large corporations. To some extent this is not at all surprising and represents an important springboard for economists who want to move into the executive suite.

The purpose of strategic planning is to provide management with a framework on which decisions can be made which will have a long-term (three to five years or longer) impact on the behavior of the company or business. Strategic planning involves the formulation of long-term goals and objectives for the company and the selection of strategies to achieve these goals and objectives in light of the uncertain external environment in which the firm must operate.

Corporate *objectives* represent a general statement of the direction in which the chief executive officer (CEO) wants to see the company move over the long run. A corporate objective describes a future state of being for the corporation that management can work toward. On the other hand, corporate *goals* refer to a specific achievement to be realized within a definite time period. Goals are much more specific than objectives and typically lend themselves to quantification.

The following examples may serve to clarify the differences between objectives and goals. A statement of objectives might be to achieve a maximum return on investment while maintaining a high level of customer service and a stable work force. A possible set of goals consistent with these objectives might include achieving a return on investment of 20 percent by 1980 with a 10 percent reduction in customer complaints and a 5 percent reduction in employee turnover. Goals are set with the expectation that if they are achieved, they will contribute to the near-term satisfaction of the company's objectives.

Strategic planning is concerned with overall corporate objectives and the selection of strategies to achieve those objectives. A business strategy may involve a commitment to a particular market, a particular mix of products, a specific way of doing business, or a certain manufacturing process. The perspective of strategic planning is global, in contrast to project planning, which focuses on a specific project or activity, and operational planning, which examines the details required to implement a particular strategy within a certain time period.

One of the central themes of this book is that there should be a much closer relationship between microeconomics and strategic planning than is the case in most companies. Indeed, what we shall call corporate economics is the integration of microeconomics and strategic planning.

## Corporate Development

The problem of multidivisional planning is one of managing a portfolio of businesses. Basically, the company has a limited amount of cash and other financial resources. The planning problem is to decide how to allocate the company's scarce financial resources across the set of businesses or divisions which the company owns so as to achieve some predetermined objective or set of objectives.

The problem of corporate development is a logical extension of the problem of multidivisional planning. The necessity of considering the acquisition of new businesses or the divestiture of existing businesses implies some type of imbalance in the existing portfolio of businesses. For some reason management may need to acquire additional businesses or sell some of the poor performers. The idea is to sell those businesses which do not offer future growth potential and buy businesses which offer good growth potential and the possibility of generating substantial amounts of cash in the future. This implies some type of search for additional business options as well as a serious review of the existing businesses to cull those businesses or products which should be deleted from the portfolio. Otherwise, the decision process for corporate development is not fundamentally different from the decision process for multidivisional planning.

## THE RELATIONSHIP BETWEEN CORPORATE ECONOMICS AND OTHER FUNCTIONS OF THE FIRM

Obviously, corporate economics does not exist in a vacuum within the firm but is completely interdependent with many other functions of the firm. In this section, we shall briefly summarize some of the important linkages between corporate economics and the other important functions of the firm.

### Finance

Corporate economists play a supporting role in a variety of different ways with regard to the financial management of a company. Economists may be called on to forecast interest rates, bond yields, and returns on investments as well as overall trends in the economy. Cash forecasting and management are tied closely to the performance of the company and the national economy. New issues of debt or equity may also require consultation from the corporate economist.

### Marketing

Many of the functions of marketing involve direct applications of microeconomic theory. It is therefore not surprising to find that corporate economics is a valuable tool for making pricing decisions, evaluating competitors, designing advertising and promotion programs, and determining the impact of the national economy on sales. Indeed, it is not an overstatement to suggest that market analysis is impossible without a firm foundation in corporate economics.

### Production

Production planning involves sales forecasting, factor-supply forecasting, capital budgeting, decisions about resource allocation, strategic planning, and government regulation—all of which are activities in which the services of a corporate economist may prove to be useful. In addition, economists often collaborate with management scientists to solve problems of inventory control and production scheduling.

### Personnel

Personnel planning and forecasting may also require the analytical skills of a corporate economist. Likewise, wage and salary negotiations may necessitate special studies by the corporate economist.

### Legal

Both corporate economists and corporate attorneys have among their principal concerns the external environment of the firm. The corporate economist should be able to say whether a particular government regulation or legal problem identified by the attorney has economic significance. Or on the other hand, the corporate attorney is expected to monitor the legality of alternative programs, projects, and strategies which may have been proposed by the corporate economist. Monitoring the external environment of a company has become increasingly complex business. To accomplish this goal in an effective manner requires close cooperation between the economists and the attorneys.

### Management Science

The relationship between corporate economics and management science in corporations varies from complementarity to competitiveness. Often the analytical tools and training of corporate economists and management scientists are almost identical. Traditionally, management scientists have tended to specialize in tactical or operational planning rather than strategic planning. Production scheduling, inventory control, waiting line problems, and order allocation problems are examples of typical management science problems.

### Management Information Systems

The term "management information system" (MIS) usually refers to the data processing or computer function of the company. Obviously, economic forecasting, economic analysis, and econometric modeling all require the use of computers. Economic data bases are of considerable importance in the development of demand forecasting models. The MIS department is also responsible for providing the appropriate computer software for economic modeling.

### THE ECONOMIC THEORY OF THE FIRM

The fundamental analytical framework underlying corporate economics is the body of knowledge known as the economic theory of the firm, which consists of three basic elements:

1 Goals
2 Information
3 Decisions

## Goals

A theory of the firm could be formulated to satisfy the goals of any one of the following groups of individuals:

1 Consumers
2 Employees
3 Society
4 Stockholders
5 Managers

Traditionally, microeconomics, with its holistic view of the firm, has treated the firm as a collective economic unit that pursues one or more goals in a completely rational manner. If the firm pursues more than one goal, it is assumed that it assigns weights or priorities to its different goals. This view assumes that the firm, its stockholders, and its managers are one and the same and that they share a common goal—profit maximization.

On the other hand, if the firm's goals were formulated by consumers, one of the goals might be the minimization of the cost of producing a particular set of goods and services. Alternatively, the consumer might be interested in increasing the firm's output of a given product while holding production costs constant.

In a socialist economy the goal of industrial firms is more likely to be production for use rather than production for profit. The goal of Soviet planners, for example, is to provide consumers with specified amounts of goods and services in accordance with a given five-year plan.

A labor leader is likely to view the firm from yet another perspective. To the labor leader, the problem of the firm may be defined in terms of job opportunities, wage increases, fringe benefits, and improved working conditions.

To the extent that the interests of political activists, public officials, and the like are representative of the interests of society as a whole, we are likely to find that their definition of the problem of the firm differs considerably from that of the previously mentioned groups. The importance of the public sector in influencing the firm's regulatory environment has been discussed already in this chapter. Although this book is aimed primarily at corporate managers and corporate economists, it is important that managers and economists understand the goals of the public.

Of the various groups of individuals who have some ax to grind concerning the behavior of business firms in a market economy, stockholders are probably somewhat less difficult to analyze than other special-interest groups. In the case of large corporations in which there is a clear dichotomy between owners (stockholders) and management, one can argue that more often than not stockholders are interested in making money. On the other hand, stockholders of a closely held, family-owned corporation may wish to provide future employment for their children and grandchildren. In spite of some possible exceptions to the rule, and the arguments of some economists to the contrary, it does not appear to be unrealistic to assume that the principal goal of stockholders is monetary, be it over the short run or the long run.

This book, however, focuses on the goals of the managers of the firm rather than those of consumers, employees, the public, and stockholders. Obviously, decisions made by the firm's managers are not made in a vacuum and are by no means independent of the preferences of these groups.

In this book the problem of the firm will be defined in terms of a decision problem for the managers of the firm. We shall be interested in how managers should make decisions (*normative* economics) in order to achieve particular goals. To the extent that these normative models correspond to the real-world behavior of firms, we shall attempt to explain how managers of firms actually make decisions (*positive* economics).

Although we have reduced the scope of our discussion considerably by restricting ourselves to the goals of managers, we will find that managers themselves may have a multiplicity of complex goals. We shall classify the goals of managers as (1) profit, (2) functional, and (3) personal.

Although the goal of profit maximization could certainly be considered both a functional and a personal goal of managers, its long-standing position as by far the most popular goal of the firm in the eyes of economists at least partially justifies treating it separately. The goal of profit maximization rests primarily on the assumption that managers either voluntarily or of necessity behave in a manner consistent with the interests of the stockholders (assuming, of course, that the owners want to make a profit). To the extent that managers are motivated to relate their behavior to the goals of stockholders, profit maximization can be considered an operational goal of the firm.

This assumption has been criticized by economists, corporate managers, and social scientists. There are two basic criticisms of the goal of profit maximization. First, in large multibillion-dollar corporations run by professional managers who own very small percentages of the company's outstanding shares, there is strong evidence that the interests of corporate executives do not always coincide with those of the stockholders. Second, and a corollary to the first criticism, there is substantial empirical evidence to suggest that functional goals and personal goals of managers are more important than profit maximization. However, if the corporation is to survive in a market economy, at least someone, presumably the CEO, must be concerned with profitability.

Functional goals, on the other hand, deal with some subsystem of the firm rather than with the firm as a whole. They are, however, by no means independent of the goal of profit maximization or the personal goals of managers. Among many possible functional goals are (1) production, (2) sales and marketing, and (3) financial.

The goals of the production manager of a plant might include:

1 Complete all orders on time.
2 Minimize the sum of capital investment expenditures, operating costs, and in-process inventory costs.

**3** Achieve an even distribution of work loads among all production facilities and a growth production rate.

The sales and marketing manager may be motivated to maximize sales revenue, not profit. The philosophy of the sales manager is to sell everything in sight even if it means committing the firm to completely unrealistic production lead times on orders. The sales manager would opt for large inventories of finished goods to provide excellent service and short delivery times to the customers.

Finally, the chief financial officer has to worry about whether there is enough cash to support the company's production and marketing activities.

The job of balancing the conflicting goals of production, sales, and financial managers falls squarely on the shoulders of the CEO, who has to worry about the overall profitability of the firm.

A discussion of the goals of managers would be incomplete without at least some reference to personal goals. Although managers may very well pursue one of the previously mentioned functional goals, in a free society they will do so only if the pursuit of a given functional goal is consistent with their personal goals. A variety of personal goals has been suggested, ranging from salary, security, status, and power to prestige, social service, professional excellence, and personal satisfaction.

In spite of the importance of functional and personal goals for managers of firms, there is one inescapable fact: If the firm does not make a profit, it will not remain in business very long.

**Information**

The decision makers of the firm are assumed to have access to three different types of information: product-demand information, factor-supply information, and production-technology information.

Under the assumptions of microeconomics, product-demand information usually takes one of two possible forms. Either the firm knows the prices of each of its products or it knows the relationship between quantity demanded of each product and the price of that product. Demand theory, which is treated in Chapter 2, is concerned with the relationship between the quantity that will be bought and the price of a given product. But in the real world, the quantity demanded of a given product may depend not only on the price of the product but also on the price of competing products, consumer income, advertising expenditures, and population growth. Chapter 3 introduces empirical demand analysis and econometrics to deal with empirical demand relationships.

The firm is also assumed to have information about the availability and prices of its factor inputs: labor, capital, land, equipment, and raw materials.

Finally, the firm's decision makers are assumed to be familiar with the production technology available to the firm. The firm is assumed to possess one or more production transformation processes that enable it to convert factors of production (labor, capital, raw materials, etc.) into a number of different products (autos, trucks, computers, etc.). Alternative assumptions about factor-supply and production-technology information are presented in Chapters 4 and 5.

### Decisions

On the basis of a given set of goals and given product-demand, factor-supply, and production-technology information, the firm makes two types of decisions: input decisions and output decisions. The input decisions answer questions such as, "Which factors of production should the firm buy?" and "In what quantities should these factors be purchased?" The output decisions are concerned with questions such as, "Which products should the firm produce?" and "In what quantities should these products be produced?" A flowchart (Figure 1-1) provides a convenient graphical device for depicting the major decisions of the firm. The broken lines represent information flows, and the solid lines denote flows of factors of production and final products.

## MICROECONOMICS: THE LANGUAGE OF STRATEGIC PLANNING

This book contains three chapters on the application of microeconomics to strategic planning: Chapters 11, 12, and 13. To the best of our knowledge, this is virtually unprecedented in a textbook on microeconomics or managerial economics. This raises the obvious question of why so much emphasis should be placed on strategic planning in a book about applied microeconomics. The answer is rather straightforward. In our view, strategic planning is by far the

**FIGURE 1-1**
A flowchart of the decision process of a firm.

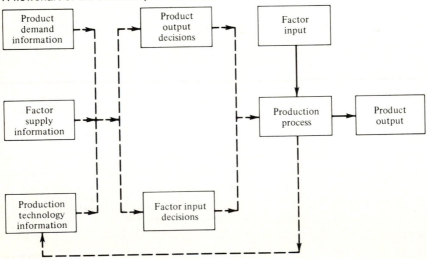

single most important application of microeconomics that the firm's decision makers will encounter. Strategic planning not only gets at the heart of the firm's long-term resource allocation problem, it represents the lifeblood of the firm's future.

In Chapter 11 we describe strategic planning in some detail and show its relationship to microeconomics. Chapter 12 describes two specific analytical tools for strategic planning: portfolio models and corporate simulation models. Special attention will be given in Chapters 11 through 13 to the problem of integrating corporate economics into the strategic planning process of the firm.

## THE POLITICS OF CORPORATE ECONOMICS

Since many corporate economists have gone directly from graduate school to work for corporations, they often have great difficulty making the transition from academic life to the corporate world. Since corporate economists are often situated close to the top of the company, they will obviously be noticed. It is not uncommon for corporate economists to find themselves embroiled in political conflicts with other corporate executives such as the vice president of planning, the vice president of finance, and the director of management science. The information gathered by corporate economists is potentially a source of power and may even be perceived as a threat by other senior executives. Unfortunately, there is little in the traditional training of corporate economists to prepare them for the highly political environment of large corporations. Chapter 13 will define some of the basic issues involved in the politics of corporate economics and propose some solutions as well.

## QUESTIONS AND PROBLEMS

**1-1** What is corporate economics, and why is it important as a decision-making tool?

**1-2** Define 10 specific decision-making problems for which corporate economics may prove to be a useful analytical tool.

**1-3** How can corporate economics be used to cope with the conflicting goals of marketing, production, and finance?

**1-4** Discuss the relevance of the economic theory of the firm to strategic planning.

**1-5** What are some of the limitations of corporate economics as a decision-making tool?

PART **TWO**

# MICROECONOMICS

# DEMAND THEORY

**CHAPTER OUTLINE**

**INTRODUCTION**

In the typical act of commerce a buyer hands over money, or the promise to
pay money, in exchange for a service or a quantity of goods. The fundamental
question for demand analysis is, "What factors determine the quantity of a

good that a purchaser seeks to buy?" The answers to that question with respect to a particular good make up a *demand function* for that good, which is to say a relationship between quantity demanded and the determinants of quantity demanded.

It is difficult to overstate the importance of knowledge of the demand function to a firm and how hard it is to acquire that knowledge. In comparison with an understanding of the costs and technology of production, knowledge about demand is usually more speculative. For example, consider a firm introducing a new product. How the unit cost of the new product will vary with the rate of production can usually be estimated reasonably well. However, of equal importance are the answers to questions such as, "If we charge $10 per unit, how many units will we sell?" and "If we advertise at the rate of $5,000 per week, by how much will this increase the quantity that can be sold?"

Demand functions may be applied to many different types of transactions. Households seek to buy goods from manufacturers. Manufacturers seek to buy productive inputs from households and from other manufacturers; so do governments. All parties seek credit from financial institutions. In this chapter we shall examine theoretical properties of demand functions. Chapter 3 will be concerned with the question of estimating actual demand functions.

### FEATURES OF DEMAND FUNCTIONS IN GENERAL

Consider for the sake of illustration a fictional grocery store chain in Omaha. Managers of the chain discover through market research that the quantity of carrots $(Q)$ which they can sell per week, measured in pounds, depends only on the price $(P)$, measured in dollars per pound, and on the amount of their advertising $(A)$, measured in dollars per week. Specifically, it is found that

$$Q = 12.9A - 1,000P \qquad (2\text{-}1)$$

This equation is a demand function. It says, for example, that customers of the chain will seek to buy 1,100 pounds per week when carrots are priced at $.19 per pound and the chain advertises at the rate of $100 per week. Thus,

$$Q = 12.9(100) - 1,000(.19) = 1,100$$

If the price is increased to $.29, holding advertising expenditures at $100, customers will wish to buy 1,000 pounds. That is,

$$Q = 12.9(100) - 1,000(.29) = 1,000$$

Assume for the moment that advertising is held at $A = \$100$. We can now write the demand function as

$$Q = 1,290 - 1,000P \qquad (2\text{-}2)$$

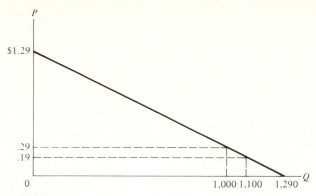

**FIGURE 2-1**
Demand curve for carrots.

where it is understood that the constant term reflects the impact of the unchanging level of advertising on quantity demanded. This permits us to present the relationship between $P$ and $Q$ graphically. Hence, Figure 2-1 shows the demand curve for carrots. As is conventional, $P$ is plotted on the vertical axis and $Q$ on the horizontal axis.

Solving equation (2-2) for $P$, we can write the demand function as

$$P = 1.29 - .001Q \tag{2-3}$$

This is the "slope-intercept" form which corresponds to the graphical representation, showing $P$ as the dependent variable. It is also often termed the inverse demand curve. The vertical axis intercept is 1.29, and the slope[1] is $-.001$.

More generally, of course, the vertical axis intercept represents the impact of all other variables influencing quantity demanded. In this example, we assume that there is only *one* other variable, *viz*, advertising. As we shall observe shortly, two additional determinants of demand predicted by theory are consumers' income and prices of close substitutes for carrots. Since, for this example, advertising is the only determinant of demand other than price, this can be made clear by writing the demand function as

$$P = .0129A - .001Q$$

Figure 2-2 shows what happens to the demand curve when $A$ changes. Initially, as before, $A = \$100$ fixes the demand curve with a vertical axis intercept

---

[1] The slope measures the change in the dependent variable $P$, $\Delta P$, which results from a small change in the independent variable $Q$, $\Delta Q$. In the case of a linear demand such as equation (2-3), the slope $\Delta P/\Delta Q$ is constant, or $-.001$. That is, for every 1-pound increase in $Q$, $P$ falls by $\$.001$. For nonlinear demands, the slope changes continuously along the curve.

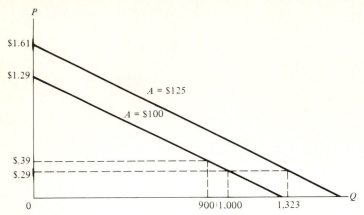

**FIGURE 2-2**
A shift in the demand for carrots as a result of increased advertising.

of 1.29. An increase in advertising to $A = \$125$ shifts the demand curve rightward. Since $.0129(125) = 1.61$, the new demand curve has a vertical axis intercept of 1.61. The slope, of course, is unchanged, and this implies that the two demand curves must be parallel.

To illustrate numerically, suppose price is set initially at $.39 and advertising at $100. The quantity demanded is shown in Figure 2-2 as 900 pounds. That is, according to equation (2-1),

$$Q = 12.9(100) - 1,000(.39) = 900$$

Now, let the chain cut its price from $.39 to $.29. The result is a movement along the original demand curve and an increase in quantity demanded from 900 to 1,000 pounds. In particular,

$$Q = 12.9(100) - 1,000(.29) = 1,000$$

Finally, suppose the chain decides to increase its advertising level from $100 per week to $125 but to keep the price at $.29. As noted above, this shifts the demand curve rightward and causes customers to demand 1,323 pounds. The calculation is

$$Q = 12.9(125) - 1,000(.29) = 1,323$$

We now consider some general features of demand functions.

1 The variable $Q$ in equation (2-1), of course, refers to the quantity demanded. With respect to a tangible product, quantity demanded is measured in real units of the product itself, such as pounds, crates, or gallons; it is not measured in dollars. With respect to a service, quantity demanded is frequently

measured in number of occurrences of service, such as number of items cleaned or number of patients treated.

**2** Measurement of quantity demanded requires specification of the time interval over which measurement is made. The quantity demanded of carrots at 39 cents per pound is plainly greater if we mean in the course of a year rather than in the course of a week. In addition to specifying the length of time spanned, it is necessary in the case of some goods (such as swimsuits, football tickets, or heating oil) to specify the season of the year in which the span falls. We know, for instance, that homeowners who heat by oil will seek to buy more oil per month in January than in July, even though the price of oil might be the same in both months.

A variable measured over elapsed time, such as pounds of carrots per week, is called a *flow* variable. One that is measured at a point in time, such as the number of autos owned on May 15, is called a *stock* variable. The dependent variable in a demand function can be of either type.

**3** Quantity demanded is the amount that purchasers would wish to buy, given the levels of the determinants of quantity demanded. It does not necessarily equal the quantity actually purchased. First, as a matter of fact, suppliers may not in the relevant time period have available for sale so large a quantity as the quantity demanded. Although customers of the Omaha grocery chain would wish to buy 1,100 pounds per week when carrots are priced at 19 cents per pound, the chain may have only 550 pounds to sell at that price so that just one-half of the quantity demanded is actually purchased. Second, as a matter of analytical design, quantity demanded may be a simulated result of having assigned hypothetical values to the determinants of quantity demanded in the demand function. Managers of the grocery chain might use demand function (2-1) to estimate how many pounds of carrots customers would attempt to buy if the price or amount of advertising were varied. Thus, managers could experiment with alternative pricing and advertising policies on paper before implementing the most profitable policy on the floors of their stores. This use of demand functions and other economic relationships is a very important one in both the study and the practice of corporate economics.

**4** There are always two parties to be identified in connection with a demand function: the party that seeks to buy and the party that seeks to sell. This point is no less significant for its obviousness. Demand function (2-1) would be quite different if it were meant to apply to the quantity demanded by a single customer of the grocery chain rather than to all customers, because a single customer wishes to buy fewer carrots per week than all the customers do. Likewise, demand function (2-1) would be quite different if it were meant to apply to the quantity demanded by customers of all grocery stores in Omaha rather than the customers of a single chain.

**5** A demand function is written in *explicit* form or in *analytic* form. The explicit form shows not only the determinants of quantity demanded but also the quantitative force of those determinants. Equation (2-1) is in explicit form, indicating, for example, that quantity demanded falls by 100 pounds per week for every 10-cent advance in the price per pound. In contrast, a demand function written in analytic form expresses the mere functional dependence of quantity demanded on its determinants and may additionally note the qualitative direction of that dependence if it is known or hypothesized. Thus equation (2-1) in analytic form would be $Q = f(A, P)$. This tells us that quantity demanded depends on price and advertising, but it does not tell us what quantity people seek to buy or by how much that quantity changes when the price or advertising level changes. Sometimes it is expedient to work with analytic forms, because an inquiry does not require the quantitative information afforded by the explicit forms. We shall work with each kind as the context requires.

## DEMAND FUNCTIONS OF A SINGLE CONSUMER

Arguably, there are no limits to the quantity of a good that one would wish to have in a given time period. Even if one's appetite for carrots vanished after 2 pounds per week, one might still wish to have 200 pounds more. The excess could be stored for later use, donated to friends or charities, or resold for money in order to buy other things.

While one may always wish to *have* more, one will not always wish to *buy* more. Purchase requires the surrender of purchasing power, of which there is a limited amount. The purchase of one thing precludes the purchase of other things, and one must choose. Therefore, quantity demanded of a good by a single consumer depends on (1) how much the consumer wants it, and its price, (2) how much the consumer wants other things, and their prices, and (3) the total amount of money that the consumer has to spend. If a customer is spending $I$ dollars on only two goods $X$ and $Y$ whose prices are $P_x$ and $P_y$, then on the foregoing reasoning we would write the consumer's demand functions in analytic form as

$$X = f(P_x, P_y, I) \qquad Y = g(P_x, P_y, I) \tag{2-4}$$

Economic theorists have greatly elaborated this line of reasoning. The theory has not yielded very many strong deductions about the properties of demand functions, but it has provided a coherent way of stating the empirical possibilities. This is a very useful function of theory. Because of the scope of this book, we cannot provide a complete summary of consumer behavior theory here. However, we include a brief mathematical treatment of this theory in Appendix B at the end of this chapter. There we show how the consumer demand functions (2-4) are derived and how consumer demand functions are aggregated to obtain market demand functions. We now turn to an examination of certain properties of market demand functions.

## PROPERTIES OF MARKET DEMAND FUNCTIONS

In this section we shall consider some important properties of demand functions. Perhaps the most important property is the *price elasticity of demand,*

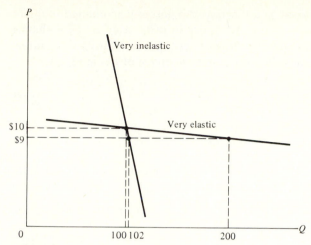

**FIGURE 2-3**
Very elastic and very inelastic demand curves.

that is, how much the quantity demanded will change as a result of a price change. It is also important to know by how much the quantity demanded will change as a result of a change in income or in the price of a substitute. Hence, we also consider the elasticities of those variables.

### Price Elasticity of Demand

In order to make clear what is meant by the elasticity, or responsiveness, of quantity demanded to price changes, consider Figure 2-3. Two hypothetical demand curves are shown. In each case, the initial price is $10, and 100 units are demanded at that price. In the case of the very elastic demand, a price reduction to $9 would increase quantity demanded by a large amount, from 100 units to 200 units. For the very inelastic demand curve, the $1 price reduction has a quite small effect; quantity demanded increases from 100 units to only 102 units. It is obvious that a business firm needs to know a lot about the elasticities of the demand functions for its products.

To emphasize this point further, suppose that the two curves in Figure 2-3 represented alternative hypotheses about the nature of demand held by a firm considering a reduction in price from $10 to $9. Assume that the average cost per unit is constant at $7. At the initial price and quantity, the firm makes a profit of ($10 − $7)(100) = $300. (That is, profit equals the profit per unit times the number of units.) If the demand is very elastic, the price reduction will increase profit by $100, since new profit will be ($9 − $7)(200) = $400. However, if the demand turns out to be very inelastic, the price reduction will be unprofitable. Profit will fall by $96, since new profit will be ($9 − $7)(102) = $204. We shall consider this example further later in this section.

The price elasticity of demand is defined as the percentage change in quantity demanded resulting from a 1 percent change in price. Let $\Delta P$ be a change in price of the good and $\Delta Q$ be the resulting change in the quantity demanded. If $\Delta P$ is very small, we can calculate the *point elasticity* of demand[2] as

$$
e = -\frac{\Delta Q}{Q} \div \frac{\Delta P}{P} \tag{2-5}
$$

$$
= -\frac{\Delta Q}{\Delta P} \cdot \frac{P}{Q}
$$

By convention, the negative sign is prefixed so that the elasticity will generally be a positive number. That is, for all negatively sloping demand curves, the ratio of $\frac{\Delta Q}{\Delta P}$ will be negative. The prefixed negative sign therefore makes the elasticity a positive number.

Note also that the elasticity is expressed in terms of *relative* changes in price and quantity rather than *absolute* changes. This makes it possible to compare the responsiveness of demand curves for different goods, since the elasticity measures are "units-free." Otherwise, the elasticity measures would depend on the units. A $1 price increase would make a big difference in the quantity of car washes demanded but none in the quantity of cars.

To illustrate the formula, suppose a firm knows but two points, $A$ and $B$, on its demand curve.

| Point | Price (P) | Quantity demanded (Q) |
|-------|-----------|------------------------|
| A     | 51        | 1,001                  |
| B     | 52        | 1,000                  |

To estimate the elasticity of demand, we use equation (2-5):

$$
e = -\frac{1,001 - 1,000}{1,000} \div \frac{51 - 52}{52} = .052
$$

Notice that we used point $B$, $Q = 1,000$ and $P = 52$, for the denominators. We could have used point $A$, and the estimate would have been quite close, or $e = .051$. The reason for the unimportance of which point was chosen is that the relative changes in price and quantity were small. On the other hand, if the relative changes are large, economists have adopted the formula for arc elasticity of demand:

$$
e = -\frac{\Delta Q}{(Q_a + Q_b)/2} \div \frac{\Delta P}{(P_a + P_b)/2} \tag{2-6}
$$

[2] In terms of calculus, the defintion of point elasticity is $-dQ/dP \cdot P/Q$.

$$= -\frac{\Delta Q(P_a + P_b)}{\Delta P(Q_a + Q_b)}$$

where the subscripts $a$ and $b$ refer to the two points on the demand curve. For example, let the two points be

| Point | Price (P) | Quantity demanded (Q) |
|-------|-----------|------------------------|
| A | 30 | 80 |
| B | 40 | 60 |

Then,

$$e = -\frac{(80 - 60)(30 + 40)}{(30 - 40)(80 + 60)} = 1$$

If, instead, equation (2-5) had been used, the values of $e$ would have been 1.33 or .75. The arc elasticity is therefore a compromise which uses an average of the $P$ and $Q$ values. Consequently, it is the best measure of the average price elasticity over the range in question.

An important point to stress is that the elasticity of demand is not the same as the slope of the demand curve. Recall from equation (2-5) that elasticity equals $-\frac{\Delta Q}{\Delta P} \cdot \frac{P}{Q}$. The demand for carrots, pictured in Figure 2-1, was given earlier by the equation

$$Q = 1,290 - 1,000P$$

This is a linear demand curve and has a constant slope $\frac{\Delta Q}{\Delta P} = -1,000$. Hence, its elasticity of demand is

$$e = 1,000\left(\frac{P}{Q}\right)$$

which clearly varies for every point on the demand curve. As the expression above shows, for points on the demand curve near the horizontal axis intercept, $P$ is very small relative to $Q$; hence, $e$ is very small. At the other extreme, near the vertical axis intercept, the reverse is true.

Table 2-1 presents elasticity estimates for selected points along the demand curve for carrots. The results are also shown graphically in Figure 2-4.

Notice that point $C$ corresponds to the midpoint along the demand curve; that is, the distance from the vertical axis intercept to point $C$ is equal to the distance from the horizontal axis to point $C$. The fact that the elasticity is unity

**TABLE 2-1**
ESTIMATES OF ELASTICITY OF DEMAND FOR SELECTED POINTS
ON DEMAND CURVE

| Point | Price (P) | Quantity demanded (Q) | Elasticity (e) |
|-------|-----------|-----------------------|----------------|
| A | 1.19 | 100 | 11.9 |
| B | .79 | 500 | 1.6 |
| C | .645 | 645 | 1.0 |
| D | .39 | 900 | .4 |
| E | .29 | 1,000 | .3 |

at this point is not a coincidence; it holds for all linear demand curves.[3] We shall make use of this result later in this chapter.

It is useful to introduce the conventional terminology regarding the values of elasticity before proceeding further.

| Value of elasticity | Demand curve said to be |
|---------------------|-------------------------|
| $e < 1$ | Inelastic |
| $e = 1$ | Unit-elastic |
| $e > 1$ | Elastic |

Hence, for points on the demand curve in Figure 2-4 above point $C$, the demand is "elastic"; at point $C$, it is "unit-elastic"; and for points below $C$, it is "inelastic."

### Price Elasticity and Money Expenditure

At the beginning of this section we gave an example showing why firms should be interested in the magnitude of the price elasticity. In the example, a price cut from $10 to $9 was unprofitable in the case of the very inelastic demand curve but profitable in the case of the very elastic demand curve. Let us explain this point more precisely.

Total money expenditure on a good is simply price times quantity, or $PQ$. If we think of the demand curve in question as pertaining to a single firm, $PQ$ also

---

[3] Let $Q = a - bP$. Then, by geometry, the midpoint on the demand curve lies vertically above the quantity $a/2$ (which is half the distance from the origin to the quantity demanded when price is zero). At this quantity, $P = a/2b$. Using equation (2-5),

$$e = b\left(\frac{a}{2b} \div \frac{a}{2}\right) = 1$$

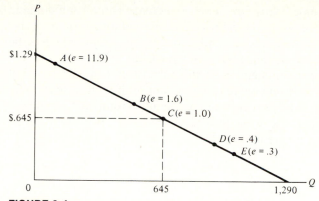

**FIGURE 2-4**
Elasticities at selected points along demand curve.

equals the firm's *total revenue*. The relationship between price changes and $PQ$ is given below.

| If demand is | A price decrease causes $PQ$ to | A price increase causes $PQ$ to |
| --- | --- | --- |
| Inelastic | Decrease | Increase |
| Unit-elastic | Not change | Not change |
| Elastic | Increase | Decrease |

   To understand these results, consider the case where demand is elastic. This means that a price decrease causes a greater percentage increase in $Q$ than the percentage reduction in $P$ (by definition of price elasticity). But this means that the product $PQ$ must rise, since the $Q$ increase exceeds the $P$ decrease. Similarly, if demand is unit-elastic, an increase in $P$ of, say, 10 percent is just offset by a 10 percent decrease in $Q$, and $PQ$ remains the same.[4]
   Returning to our example of the firm's pricing problem and interpreting $PQ$

---

[4] These results can be proved rigorously with calculus. Differentiate $PQ$ with respect to $P$:

$$\frac{d(PQ)}{dP} = Q + P \cdot \frac{dQ}{dP}$$

Dividing both sides by $Q$ gives

$$\frac{d(PQ)/dP}{Q} = 1 + \frac{dQ}{dP} \cdot \frac{P}{Q} = 1 - e$$

The sign of $d(PQ)/dP$ (since $Q$ is positive) depends on $e$. If $e$ is elastic, for example, this means $e > 1$, and therefore $d(PQ)/dP$ is negative. Hence, a price decrease will increase $PQ$.

as its total revenue, it becomes clear why a price decrease is foolish if demand is inelastic. A price decrease reduces total revenue, and yet total cost must rise since a greater quantity must be produced and sold. Clearly, profit (which is the difference between total revenue and total cost) must fall.

On the other hand, if demand is elastic, a price decrease can be, but is not necessarily, profitable. Total revenue will increase, but profit will increase only if the increment to total revenue exceeds the increment to total cost. In the example, the increment to revenue was ($9)(200) − ($10)(100) = $800 (recall that the lower price led to an increase in $Q$ from 100 to 200). The increment to

**FIGURE 2-5**
Total revenue, average revenue, and marginal revenue curves.

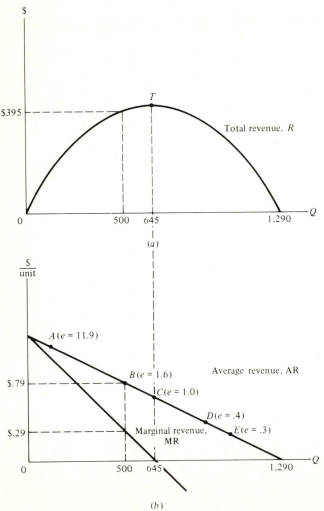

cost was only $(\$7)(200) - (\$7)(100) = \$700$ (average cost was assumed to be constant at \$7). Hence, profit increased by $\$800 - \$700 = \$100$. Had cost been rising with increased quantity, the price decrease could have been unprofitable.

### Total Revenue, Marginal Revenue, and Elasticity

We indicated above that total money expenditure $PQ$ can also be interpreted as total revenue $R$ if the demand curve is confronting a single firm. Here we focus on the revenue interpretation and regard the firm in question as the sole seller, or monopolist, of the good in question. We also explain more precisely the concept of incremental revenue, or *marginal revenue*, that was introduced above.

In Figure 2-5a and b we show the relationships among total revenue $R$, demand or *average revenue* AR, and marginal revenue MR. The demand curve is the demand for carrots curve shown in Figure 2-4 and is given by the equation

$$P = 1.29 - .001Q \qquad (2\text{-}7)$$

As noted above, the demand curve can be interpreted as the average revenue of the monopolist; i.e., price is simply the seller's average revenue. Hence, we shall use $P$ and AR interchangeably.

The equation for $R$ is obtained by multiplying equation (2-7) through by $Q$, since $R = PQ$.

$$R = PQ = 1.29Q - .001Q^2 \qquad (2\text{-}8)$$

Notice that point $T$, the top of the revenue "hill," corresponds to point $C$ on the AR curve where price elasticity $= 1$. Points to the left of $C$ correspond to price elasticities greater than unity and the rising portion of the revenue "hill." Points to the right of $C$ represent the inelastic portion of the AR curve and correspond to the falling portion of the $R$ function.

One value of Figure 2-5 is that it confirms visually the relationships discussed earlier between elasticities and changes in revenue (or $PQ$). For example, at point $B$ (where elasticity is 1.6, $P$ is \$.79, $Q$ is 500, and $R$ is \$395), consider a small price reduction which boosts $Q$ from 500 to 501. Figure 2-5a makes it clear that the value of $R$ will increase as quantity increases from $Q = 500$ to $Q = 501$. You should perform a similar exercise for a price decrease at, say, point $D$ to convince yourself that $R$ will fall when demand is inelastic.

We can now explain the marginal revenue, or MR, curve. In the example above, $Q$ changed from 500 to 501. Equation (2-8) can be used to show that $R$ changed from \$395 to \$395.29. That is, the increment to revenue from a 1-unit increase in $Q$, or MR, was \$.29. This is shown as the value of MR corresponding to $Q = 500$ in Figure 2-5b. In geometrical terms, of course, MR is the slope of the $R$ function. Hence, the MR curve shows at a glance how $R$ is affected. Notice that MR is positive in the price-elastic portion of the AR curve but negative in the inelastic portion; when elasticity is unity, MR is precisely zero.

Notice that the MR curve always lies beneath the AR curve. In fact, for a linear AR curve, the MR curve is always twice as steep as the AR curve. For example, the equation for the MR curve is[5]

$$\text{MR} = 1.29 - .002Q \tag{2-9}$$

To conclude this discussion we present below an expression that relates MR, $P$, and price elasticity $e$. The expression not only adds further insight into the relationships in Figure 2-5 but will also prove useful in later chapters. Hence,[6]

$$\text{MR} = P \left( 1 - \frac{1}{e} \right) \tag{2-10}$$

Observe, for example, that $e = 1$ implies $\text{MR} = 0$. Also, for $e < 1$, $\text{MR} < 0$. Finally, note that MR is less than $P$ for $0 < e < \infty$.

### Determinants of Price Elasticity

Consider Table 2-2, which provides estimates of the price elasticity of demand for selected goods and services. We shall not be concerned here with how the estimates were made; that is the subject of Chapter 3. Our interest here is the general issue of why some goods are price-elastic and others are price-inelastic. Several points can be made.

First, the price elasticity is likely to be higher the greater the number and closeness of substitutes. To a large degree, this depends on the definition of the good or service. For example we show food to be relatively inelastic. However, if we considered such commodities as beef, pork, and poultry, we would proba-bly find higher elasticities. Similarly, the demand for Budweiser would be more price-elastic than the demand for beer.

---

[5] $\text{MR} = \Delta R/\Delta Q$, or in calculus terms, $dR/dQ$. To obtain the MR equation, simply differentiate equation (2-8), the $R$ function:

$$\frac{dR}{dQ} = 1.29 - .002Q$$

[6] Since $R = PQ = P(Q)Q$, MR is

$$\frac{dR}{dQ} = \text{MR} = P + Q \cdot \frac{dP}{dQ} = P \left( 1 + \frac{Q}{P} \cdot \frac{dP}{dQ} \right)$$

The definition $e = -\dfrac{dQ}{dP} \cdot \dfrac{P}{Q}$ can be manipulated to yield $(Q/P)(dP/dQ) = -(1/e)$, which when substituted in the MR function gives equation (2-10).

**TABLE 2-2**
ESTIMATES OF PRICE ELASTICITIES

| Item | Price elasticity |
|---|---|
| Foreign travel | 4.1 |
| Automobiles | 1.2 |
| Beer | 1.1 |
| Electricity | 1.1 |
| Medical services | .5 |
| Gasoline | .5 |
| Food | .2 |

*Sources:* H. S. Houthakker and L. D. Taylor, *Consumption Demand in the United States: 1929–1970* (Cambridge, Mass.: Harvard University Press, 1966). Gregory C. Chow, *Demand for Automobiles in the United States* (Amsterdam: North-Holland Publishing Company, 1957). Herbert Klarman (ed.), *Empirical Studies in Health Economics* (Baltimore: Johns Hopkins Press, 1970). T. F. Hogarty and K. G. Elzinga, "The Demand for Beer," *Review of Economics and Statistics,* May 1972. Robert Halvorsen, "Residential Demand for Electric Energy," *Review of Economics and Statistics,* February 1975. H. Wold and L. Jureen, *Demand Analysis* (New York: John Wiley, 1953).

Second, the price elasticity is thought to be small for commodities that constitute only small fractions of customers' incomes or budgets. For example, the demand for pencils, salt, shoelaces, etc., would meet this criterion.

Third, necessities such as medicine or medical services tend to have relatively inelastic demands. At the other extreme, the demand for consumer durables, such as automobiles, television sets, and appliances, tends to be more elastic. Purchases of these items can usually be postponed, and because of the size of the purchase, it pays to shop around.

Finally, the time period over which the demand function is defined can be a determinant of elasticity. For example, in the short run the demand for gasoline is less elastic than it is in the long run. In the long run consumers can arrange for car pools, trade large cars for small ones, and even move closer to work.

An interesting example is the demand for crude oil. Beginning in 1973, the Organization of Petroleum Exporting Countries (OPEC)—consisting of such important oil-producing countries as Saudi Arabia, Iran, Iraq, Kuwait, and Venezuela—began increasing the world oil price extremely rapidly. For example, in mid-October 1973 the posted price of crude oil in the Persian Gulf was only $3 per barrel. By mid-1981 the price was about $35 per barrel. In his column in the *Washington Post* on July 16, 1981, Hobart Rowen offered these observations:

Oil consumption has dropped dramatically in response to staggering price increases.
OPEC, which in 1979 was producing about 31 million barrels a day of crude oil

out of a free world consumption of roughly 50 million barrels a day, is down to about 22 million barrels a day, out of a free world consumption of about 44 million barrels a day.

Part of the 6 million barrel-a-day contraction in usage can be traced to economic stagnation in many parts of the globe. But much of it is voluntary, a result of the incentive to switch from oil caused by the extraordinary boost in prices.

### Income Elasticity of Demand

Thus far we have been concerned primarily with price and its role in determining the quantity demanded. This should not be interpreted to mean that other variables are unimportant. Much of the technical discussion about price elasticity, for example, can be applied directly to such variables as income, prices of substitutes, advertising expenditures, etc. Hence, consider the income elasticity of demand.

$$e_I = \frac{\Delta Q}{Q} \div \frac{\Delta I}{I} \qquad (2\text{-}11)$$
$$= \frac{\Delta Q}{\Delta I} \cdot \frac{I}{Q}$$

where $Q$ is quantity demanded and $I$ is the aggregate income of all consumers.

Goods for which $e_I$ is positive are termed normal goods; that is, a 1 percent increase in income causes the quantity demanded to increase. There are some goods, however, that have negative income elasticities, and these are called inferior goods. Examples would include low-quality clothes and potatoes. In other words, as incomes rise, consumers buy less of these goods.

The magnitude of the income elasticity for a product is also of some concern to the seller. If it exceeds unity, this implies that the product's sales should grow more than proportionately with the growth of the economy. On the other hand, a low income elasticity implies that the product should not be affected greatly by shifts in economic activity and will not share proportionately in rising national income.

A number of agricultural products have been found to have low income elasticities: butter, cheese, eggs, flour, fruits, and meat. A commodity with an elasticity exceeding unity is restaurant consumption. As incomes rise, people can afford to eat out more frequently.

### Cross-Elasticities of Demand

We now turn to the prices of other products as a determinant of the quantity demanded. We begin by defining the cross-elasticity of demand.

$$e_{xy} = \frac{\Delta Q_x}{Q_x} \div \frac{\Delta P_y}{P_y} \qquad (2\text{-}12)$$
$$= \frac{\Delta Q_x}{\Delta P_y} \cdot \frac{P_y}{Q_x}$$

In words, $e_{xy}$ is the percentage change in quantity demanded of good $X$ as a result of a 1 percent change in the price of good $Y$. If $e_{xy}$ is positive, the two goods are *substitutes*. For example, if coffee prices increase, the demand for tea should increase. Hence, coffee and tea are substitutes.

If $e_{xy}$ is negative, the two goods are *complements*. Movie film and movie cameras are complements. As the price of movie cameras declines, the demand for movie film should rise.

We conclude this rather lengthy discussion of market demand functions by reporting a set of elasticities from a recent study of the residential demand for electricity in the United States. These results are contained in Table 2-3. The cross-elasticity of demand for electricity with respect to the price of natural gas is quite small, only .04. It does indicate, however, that electricity and gas are substitutes, as expected.

## MONOPOLY AND PERFECT COMPETITION DEMAND FUNCTIONS

It is important to make clear the distinction between market and firm demand functions. We do this by considering briefly the two extremes of market structures: monopoly and perfect competition. A more detailed treatment of market structures is contained in Chapter 6.

If there is just one seller in the market (a monopoly), the demand for the monopolist's product is the market demand function. In our discussion above of total and marginal revenue, we assumed the seller to be a monopolist.

The situation is much different when a great number of sellers are serving the market and each is capable of supplying only a tiny portion of it. To such a seller it may appear that the demand for his or her output is the horizontal line shown in Figure 2-6. Let $\bar{P}$ denote the prevailing price in the market. Since every seller is offering the same good and consumers have no reason other than price to buy from any particular seller, one seller could conclude that his or her sales would virtually disappear if he or she attempted a price higher than $\bar{P}$. Yet should the seller attempt a price lower than $\bar{P}$, consumers would demand a

**TABLE 2-3**
ESTIMATES OF ELASTICITIES OF
DEMAND FOR RESIDENTIAL
ELECTRIC ENERGY: 1961–1969

| Elasticity | With respect to |
|------------|-----------------|
| 1.15 | Price of electricity |
| .51 | Income per capita |
| .04 | Price of natural gas |

*Source:* Robert Halvorsen, "Residential Demand for Electric Energy," *Review of Economics and Statistics,* February 1975.

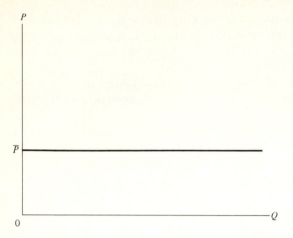

**FIGURE 2-6**
A horizontal demand curve facing a
perfectly competitive seller.

quantity far in excess of the seller's capacity. There would also be a needless sacrifice of revenue because sales which the seller would make at the lower price, he or she could make at $\bar{P}$. In summary, any one seller believes that he or she cannot affect the prevailing price and that consumers will demand any quantity which he or she is capable of producing and willing to sell at the prevailing price. This market structure is known as perfect competition.

That every seller in a perfectly competitive market might believe the demand for his or her product to be horizontal (as in Figure 2-6) does not contradict the fact that the market demand function is negatively sloping (as in Figure 2-1). The difference is entirely one of perspective. The market demand function presumes that all sellers move in unison to a different price level, whereas the demand function facing just one of the sellers presumes that the seller alone is moving to a different price level.

## IMPLICATIONS FOR SPECIFYING AN EMPIRICAL DEMAND FUNCTION

Theory, by suggesting to the corporate economist strong candidates for the significant determinants of quantity demanded, plays a useful role in the specification of empirical demand functions as well as in the evaluation of their plausibility. To review, theory suggests that the quantity demanded of a firm's product is likely to vary with:

1 *The ability of consumers to spend:* There are many ways to measure this variable. It can be measured by a household's gross income, after-tax income, after-tax income net of expenditures for necessities, or expenditures on the broad product grouping to which the firm's product belongs. If consumption of the good is concentrated in a known subset of the population (e.g., elderly peo-

ple), then the income measure preferably refers to that subset. Whatever the choice, it is advisable to deflate income measured in current dollars by a price index (such as the implicit price deflator for personal consumption expenditures) for all consumer goods. If all prices rise at the same rate as income, consumers' ability to spend will not change on that account. Failure to deflate could therefore lead to the false conclusion that quantity demanded is insensitive to variations in income, when in fact real income has not varied.

Ordinarily, an increase in income is expected to have a positive effect on quantity demanded.

**2** *Price:* One measures the price paid by the buyer rather than the price received by the firm when specifying a demand function. The former could exceed the latter because of shipping costs, selective excise and general sales taxes, and other charges paid by the consumer incident to purchase. In some cases the buyer's price is less than the seller's price because of subsidies paid by the government or other third parties on behalf of the buyer. It is also advisable to deflate the price by a comprehensive price index. The reason for deflating is to capture substitution in favor of or against the firm's product as a result of a change in the relative price of the product. If the price increases at a slower rate than prices do generally, the firm's product becomes a relatively cheaper source of utility, and quantity demanded will probably rise. Failure to deflate could lead to the false conclusion that the good has a demand curve with a positive slope.

Ordinarily, an increase in price is expected to have a negative effect on quantity demanded.

**3** *Price of closest substitute or complement:* The remarks concerning the measurement of price apply to the measurement of this variable, too, except that the expected effect depends on which type of relationship is being investigated.

**4** *Preference-modifying events:* There are many possibilities under this heading and many ways of attempting to take them into account. Seasonality or extraordinary publicity given the firm's product can be dealt with by the use of an econometric technique known as the dummy variable. Advertising by the firm is another candidate, although its measurement involves complexities that cannot be discussed here. (*Example:* how to account for countervailing advertising undertaken by rival firms, or whether to count advertising that merely promotes a company's name as advertising for one of its products.) Demographic variables may be significant determinants of quantity demanded when consumption of a good is associated with the age, location, or marital status of the population.

The unavailability of data may prevent the economist from testing all the determinants that he or she would like to include. Furthermore, it may prove to be true in a particular application that one or more of the potential determinants of quantity demanded is too weak to be detected. Nevertheless, it is a considerable advantage to know what to look for.

## QUESTIONS AND PROBLEMS

**2-1** When the price of a certain good is $P_1$, the quantity demanded is $Q_1$. When the price is cut to $P_2 = .75P_1$, the quantity demanded increases to $Q_2 = 1.3Q_1$.

  **a** What is the simplest way of calculating whether demand is relatively elastic or relatively inelastic between the two indicated points (without actually calculating the value of the elasticity)?

  **b** Using the best arithmetical definition, calculate the arc elasticity of demand between the two indicated points.

**2-2 a** Plot carefully on graph paper the demand curve whose equation is $Q = 9,600,000 - 400,000P$. Indicate below and also on your diagram the points where the following elasticity magnitudes occur:

| Elasticity | P | Q |
|---|---|---|
| 23 | | |
| 3 | | |
| 1 | | |
| 1/3 | | |

  **b** For the demand equation in part **a,** find the marginal revenue equation and find the elasticity when marginal revenue equals zero. Note the relation between the sign of marginal revenue and the value of the corresponding elasticity.

**2-3** After the price of gasoline rose from \$1.50 to \$1.80 per gallon, Lee reduced his purchases of gasoline from 30 to 26 gallons per month. Using the arc-elasticity formula, find the price elasticity of Lee's demand for gasoline.

**2-4** Which of the following pairs of goods are likely to be substitutes, and which are likely to be complements?

  **a** Tennis rackets and tennis balls

  **b** Tennis balls and golf balls

  **c** Apple pie and ice cream

  **d** Bowling and gasoline

  **e** Movies and television

**2-5** Would it ever make sense for a monopolist to choose a price on the demand curve where the price elasticity is less than unity? (A review of Figure 2-5 might help you answer this question.)

**2-6** What is the point elasticity of a horizontal demand curve? (*Hint:* In applying equation (2-5) note that the slope of a horizontal line is zero, but since price is on the vertical axis, the slope is $\Delta P/\Delta Q$, not $\Delta Q/\Delta P$. Hence, its reciprocal is needed for the formula.) Economists often refer to the elasticity of a horizontal demand curve as "perfectly elastic" and that of a vertical demand curve as "perfectly inelastic." Using equation (2-10), prove that $P = MR$ for a horizontal demand curve.

**2-7** Three families make up the population of a small New England town. Their respective demand functions for eggs are as follows:

| | |
|---|---|
| Family 1: | $q = 120 - 60p$ |
| Family 2: | $q = 72 - 36p$ |
| Family 3: | $q = 90 - 45p$ |

Quantity demanded $q$ is measured in dozens per year. Price $p$ is measured in dollars per dozen.

**a** Derive the group's demand function.

**b** How many eggs will the group and each family in the group attempt to buy if $p = \$1.30$?

**2-8** Suppose that $Q = 6,000 - 1,500p$ is the daily demand for milk by parents in a Texas town. Suppose that $Q = 1,500 - 750p$ is the daily demand for milk by adults other than parents in the same town. Quantity demanded $Q$ is measured in quarts per day and price $p$ is measured in dollars per quart.

**a** What is the combined daily demand for milk of all adults in town? (*Note:* Be careful that the demand function is defined so that no group demands a negative quantity.)

**b** Using the arc-elasticity formula, calculate the price elasticity of demand for each group separately and for all adults combined, given a change in $p$ from \$1.50 to \$1.70 per quart.

**2-9** Economists at Alpha Company believe that quantity demanded of their product ($Q$) depends on the after-tax income of Alpha's customers ($I$), the price of Alpha's product ($P$), and the price of Beta's competing product ($B$), according to

$$Q = 10IP^{-.4}B^{.2}$$

The economists forecast that the most likely trends over the coming year are for $I$ to fall by 1 percent, $P$ to increase by 12 percent, and $B$ to increase by 10 percent. If these things come about, what would be the predicted percentage change in quantity demanded? (*Hint:* It can be shown with calculus that the exponents of $I$, $P$, and $B$ in functions of this mathematical form are their respective elasticities. This function also has the property that these elasticities are constant and independent of the particular point on the demand function. To prove this for $B$, for example, find the partial derivative of $Q$ with respect to $B$ and multiply the result by $B/Q$.)

## BIBLIOGRAPHY

Dean, Joel: *Managerial Economics* (Englewood Cliffs, N. J.: Prentice-Hall, 1951), chap. 4.

Ferber, R.: "Consumer Economics, A Survey," *Journal of Economic Literature*, December 1973.

Hicks, John R.: *Value and Capital*, 2d ed. (New York: Oxford University Press, 1946).

Houthakker, H. J., and L. D. Taylor: *Consumer Demand in the United States*, 2d ed. (Cambridge, Mass.: Harvard University Press, 1970).

Knight, Frank H.: "Realism and Relevance in the Theory of Demand," *Journal of Political Economy*, 1944.

Mishan, E. J.: "Theories of Consumer's Behavior: A Cynical View," *Economica*, New Series, February 1961.

# CALCULUS AND OPTIMIZATION

**CHAPTER OUTLINE**

CALCULUS: RULES OF DIFFERENTIATION
  Background
  Rules for Finding the First Derivative
  Rules for Finding the Second Derivative
  Rules for Finding Partial Derivatives
OPTIMIZATION TECHNIQUES
  A Function of One Variable
  A Function of Two Variables with a Constraint

A recurrent question for teachers and students of economics is, "How much math?" Instructors are inclined to more mathematical presentations of economic material. They are accustomed to it, having been taught that way in graduate school and continuing to communicate that way in research publications; they are also aware of its potential to sharpen and deepen economic analysis. Students, who have not had these experiences and who as a group seem a bit intimidated by mathematics, often prefer less mathematical presentations of economic material. They complain, quite correctly in some instances, that economic substance is neglected or hidden by a preoccupation with graphs and equations. Too frequently there is frustration on both sides.

It is our opinion that (1) students should learn the quantitative techniques presented in the appendixes, and (2) we should indicate why. There are three reasons for students to make this effort.

### 1 To Quantify

Qualitative answers are usually insufficient. The typical inquiry is, "How much?" How much less gasoline would people burn if its price were raised by 25 percent? How much more investment would businesses undertake if the corporate income tax rate were cut to 30 percent? How many more people would enlist in military service if the basic pay were increased by 20 percent or if civilian unemployment were to rise another percentage point? Quantitative techniques are needed to address quantitative problems and to understand how others have addressed them.

## 2 To Analyze

In order to organize our thoughts about how something works, it helps to begin by writing down the various factors that may be involved as well as how they may be related. In some fields we would next turn to a physical system and inject mice, mix chemicals, or graft plants to test our ideas. But economists generally do not analyze through controlled experiments. Neither the national economy nor, on a smaller scale, a business enterprise is the economist's to experiment on, and in any case there are special difficulties when working with social systems in setting up two processes that are the same in all but one way.

Economists therefore make intangible models of economic processes. The model consists of equations, or relations between the factors that are thought to bear on the process being studied. By studying how the model functions, one attempts to learn how the real process works. This procedure is necessary and especially useful when an economic outcome is the result of factors too numerous and too interconnected to be held in the mind at once.

Mathematical modeling is a way of reasoning systematically. It is neither to be extolled nor rejected simply because it is mathematical. It should be tried today because it has proved useful in many previous applications.

## 3 To Communicate

Economics has its own language, and mathematics is a major contributor to that language. It has to be learned if you are to understand, weigh, and respond to an economist's line of reasoning.

The material in the appendixes has been selected for its relevance to economic quantification, analysis, and communication. The style of presentation is decidedly "how to."

## CALCULUS: RULES OF DIFFERENTIATION

Rates of change are a staple of economics: the change in quantity demanded per $1 change in price, the change in output per 1 worker-hour change in labor input, the change in total cost of production per 1-unit change in output level, and so on. Differential calculus is a technique for finding rates of change. Different rules apply to different situations. The most frequently used rules are presented below.

### Background

A function is a mathematical relationship between a dependent variable and one or more independent variables. Given the value of every independent variable, the function assigns a value to the dependent variable. Consider $y = 2x$. Variable $x$ is the independent variable; we do not know from this relationship why its value is whatever it is. Variable

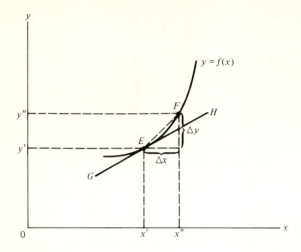

**FIGURE A-1**
Derivative as tangent to curve.

$y$ is the dependent variable; its value depends on the value of variable $x$ in a particular way. That particular way is the function which says that $y$ is twice as large as $x$. $y = 4x$ is a different function. Both functions are said to be explicit because they state how variable $y$ depends on variable $x$. If we wish merely to express the idea that $y$ is a function of $x$ but do not specify the explicit form of the relation, we write $y = f(x)$. This function is said to be in analytic form.

Consider a particular function $y = f(x)$. You may wish to think of $y$ as total cost and $x$ as output. If so, marginal cost MC is the change in cost resulting from a 1-unit change in output, or in symbols, $\Delta y/\Delta x$. (The symbol $\Delta$, the Greek capital delta, is used to represent a change in a variable.) In Figure A-1, we show the function and an estimate of $\Delta y/\Delta x$ at output level $x'$.

As $x$ is increased from $x'$ to $x''$, or by $\Delta x$, the variable $y$ is increased from $y'$ to $y''$, or by $\Delta y$. Geometrically, the ratio $\Delta y/\Delta x$ is the slope of the dashed line $EF$. As shown, the change in $x$ appears to be relatively large. Suppose $x' = 200$ and $x'' = 203$. Then $\Delta y$ is the "average" marginal cost for an increase of 3 units in output.

Now imagine what happens to $\Delta y/\Delta x$ as $\Delta x$ is reduced gradually. Point $F$ in Figure A-1 will slide down the curve toward point $E$. Consider the slope of $EF$ as $F$ approaches $E$. It will become flatter and flatter until we obtain (in the limit as $\Delta x$ approaches zero) the tangent line $GH$ to the curve at point $E$. The term for the slope of $GH$ is the "first derivative of $y$ with respect to $x$," or simply the "first derivative." It is denoted by $dy/dx$. We now consider rules for finding the first derivative in six different cases.

## Rules for Finding the First Derivative

### R1. Constant Function Rule: $y = k$

Let $k$ be a constant number. It can be an integer or a fraction, and it can be positive, negative, or zero. If $y = k$, then

$$\frac{dy}{dx} = 0$$

**Example If $y = 3$, then**

$$\frac{dy}{dx} = 0$$

In this case the value of $y$ does not depend at all on the value of $x$, and so of course a change in $x$ produces no change in $y$. We get the same information visually by looking at the graph of the function in Figure A-2. Values of $x$ are plotted horizontally, and values of $y$ are plotted vertically. The line $y = 3$ proceeds, from left to right, parallel to the $x$ axis. Wherever we choose to look along the line, its slope—that is, the ratio of the change in the value of $y$ to a 1-unit increase in the value of $x$—is zero. That is what we found when we used the constant function rule, and it is what we are saying in symbols when we write $dy/dx = 0$.

### R2. Power Function Rule: $y = x^n$

Let $n$ be a constant number. It can be an integer or a fraction, and it can be positive, negative, or zero. If $y = x^n$, then

$$\frac{dy}{dx} = nx^{n-1}$$

**Example If $y = x^1$, then**

$$\frac{dy}{dx} = 1x^{1-1} = 1x^0 = 1$$

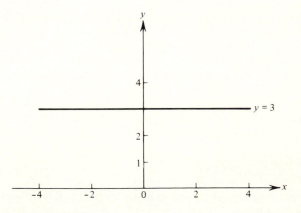

**FIGURE A-2**
Derivative of $y = 3$ is zero.

$y = 3$

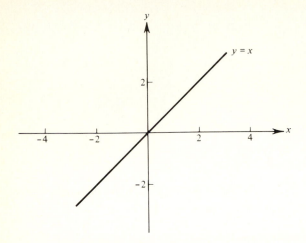

**FIGURE A-3**
Derivative of $y = x$ is unity.

According to this function the value of $y$ is the value of $x$. It follows that a 1-unit increase in $x$ is always matched by a 1-unit increase in $y$. We get the same information from the graph of this function in Figure A-3. Wherever we choose to look along the line, its slope is $+ 1$. (As a side issue, notice that we encountered the case of a variable which is raised to the zero power: $x^0$. The general rule is that any expression raised to the zero power equals 1.)

**Example If $y = x^2$, then**

$$\frac{dy}{dx} = 2x^{2-1} = 2x$$

The example is another illustration of the power function rule. It also introduces something new, for the first derivative of this function is not a constant number. Rather, the value of $dy/dx$ depends upon where the change in $x$ is taking place. Look at the labeled points on the graph of the function in Figure A-4. At point $A$, where $x = -3$, the line is headed downward, and its slope $dy/dx = 2(-3) = - 6$ is quite steep. At point $B$, where $x = - 1$, the line is still headed downward, but now more gently: $dy/dx = 2(-1) = -2$. At point $C$, where $x = 0$, the curve has reached its bottom and for just this instant has no slope: $dy/dx = 2(0) = 0$. Thereafter, the curve heads upward, and every unit increase in $x$ produces successively larger jumps in $y$: $dy/dx = 2$ at $x = 1$ (point $D$); $dy/dx = 4$ at $x = 2$ (point $E$); $dy/dx = 6$ at $x = 3$ (point $F$); etc. The general point is that the value of the first derivative of $y$ with respect to $x$ may depend on the level of $x$ at which that rate of change is being evaluated.

### R3. Sum Rule: $y = u(x) + v(x)$

Let $u = u(x)$ and $v = v(x)$ be two functions of the independent variable $x$. If their sum equals the dependent variable $y$ (that is, $y = u + v$), then

$$\frac{dy}{dx} = \frac{du}{dx} + \frac{dv}{dx}$$

Rule R3 is easy to remember because of the lyrical quality of the words: "The derivative of the sum is the sum of the derivatives."

**Example If $y = 3 + x$, then**

$$\frac{dy}{dx} = 0 + 1 = 1$$

Let $u(x) = 3$ and $v(x) = x$. By the constant function rule, $du/dx = 0$. By the power function rule, $dv/dx = 1$. Thus $dy/dx = 1$ by the sum rule.

**Example If $y = x^4 + x^2$, then**

$$\frac{dy}{dx} = 4x^3 + 2x$$

Let $u(x) = x^4$ and $v(x) = x^2$. Apply the power function rule to $u(x)$ and $v(x)$ separately and then apply the sum rule.

**R4. Difference Rule: $y = u(x) - v(x)$**

As in rule R3, let $u = u(x)$ and $v = v(x)$ be two functions of the independent variable $x$. If their difference equals the dependent variable $y$ (that is, $y = u - v$), then

$$\frac{dy}{dx} = \frac{du}{dx} - \frac{dv}{dx}$$

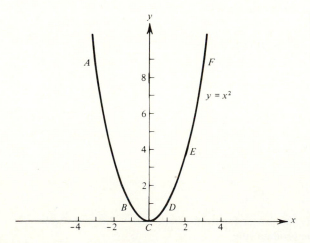

**FIGURE A-4**
Derivative of $y = x^2$ is 2x.

The words for stating rule R4 have the same lyrical sound as the words for R3: "The derivative of the difference equals the difference of the derivatives."

**Example If $y = x^3 - x$, then**

$$\frac{dy}{dx} = 3x^2 - 1$$

The result follows by letting $u(x) = x^3$ and $v(x) = x$, applying the power function rule to each, and then applying the difference rule.

### R5. Product Rule: $y = u(x) \cdot v(x)$

As in rules R3 and R4, let $u = u(x)$ and $v = v(x)$ be two functions of the independent variable $x$. If their product equals the dependent variable $y$ (that is, $y = uv$), then

$$\frac{dy}{dx} = u\frac{dv}{dx} + v\frac{du}{dx}$$

Note that rule R5 cannot be spoken in a catchy phrase. The derivative of the product is the not the product of the derivatives.

**Example If $y = 2x$, then**

$$\frac{dy}{dx} = 2$$

Even before thinking of the product rule, you know intuitively that $y$ will increase by 2 units whenever $x$ increases by 1 unit; in other words, the first derivative equals 2. Now verify your intuition. Let $u(x) = 2$ and $v(x) = x$. By the constant function rule, $du/dx = 0$, and by the power function rule, $dv/dx = 1$. Therefore,

$$\frac{dy}{dx} = 2(1) + x(0) = 2$$

(To generalize from the example, if $y = kx$, where $k$ is a constant number, then $dy/dx = k$.)

**Example If $y = (x^4)(x^2)$, then**

$$\frac{dy}{dx} = 6x^5$$

Let $u(x) = x^4$ and $v(x) = x^2$. By the power function rule, $dy/dx = 4x^3$ and $dv/dx = 2x$. Substituting these results in the product rule,

$$\frac{dy}{dx} = x^4(2x) + x^2(4x^3) = 2x^5 + 4x^5 = 6x^5$$

In this case we could have simplified the function at the outset to $y = x^6$ and, using only the power function rule, arrived at the same result:

$$\frac{dy}{dx} = 6x^{6-1} = 6x^5$$

**R6. Quotient Rule: $y = u(x)/v(x)$**

As in rules R3 through R5, let $u = u(x)$ and $v = v(x)$ be two functions of the independent variable $x$. If their quotient equals the dependent variable $y$ (that is, $y = u/v$), then

$$\frac{dy}{dx} = \frac{v(du/dx) - u(dv/dx)}{v^2}$$

As in rule R5, no catchy phrase will do for rule R6. The derivative of the quotient is not the quotient of the derivatives.

**Example If $y = (x + 10)/2x$, then**

$$\frac{dy}{dx} = -5/x^2$$

Let $u = x + 10$ and $v = 2x$. By the sum rule, $du/dx = 1$, and by the product rule, $dv/dx = 2$. Substituting these terms into the quotient rule gives

$$\frac{dy}{dx} = \frac{2x(1) - (x + 10)2}{(2x)^2} = \frac{-20}{4x^2} = \frac{-5}{x^2}$$

**Rules for Finding the Second Derivative**

The second derivative of a function is the amount by which the first derivative of that function changes when the independent variable $x$ increases by 1 unit. The second derivative is denoted $[d(dy/dx)]/dx$, or more commonly, $d^2y/dx^2$. Mechanically, the second derivative is found, using rules R1 through R6, by taking the first derivative two times in succession.

**Example If $y = x$, then**

$$\frac{dy}{dx} = 1 \qquad \text{(first derivative of } y = x\text{)}$$

and

$$\frac{d^2y}{dx^2} = 0 \qquad \text{(second derivative of } y = x \text{ and}$$

$$\text{first derivative of } \frac{dy}{dx} = 1\text{)}$$

In words, if $y$ equals $x$, then $y$ increases by 1 unit when $x$ does, and the increase in $y$ per unit increase in $x$ does not change when $x$ increases. In other words, if $y$ equals $x$, then the slope of the line $y = x$ equals unity, and the slope does not change as $x$ increases from $-1$ to $0$ to $+1$, etc. Return to Figure A-3 for visual verification of these statements.

**Example If $y = x^2$, then**

$$\frac{dy}{dx} = 2x \quad \text{and} \quad \frac{d^2y}{dx^2} = 2$$

As discussed in connection with Figure A-4, the slope of the line $y = x^2$ is different at points $A$, $B$, $C$, $D$, $E$, and $F$. The second derivative $d^2y/dx^2 = 2$ indicates that the slope increases as $x$ increases from $A$ (where the slope is very much negative) to $C$ (where it is zero) to $F$ (where it is very much positive).

**Example If $y = .25x^4 + .5x^2 - 10$, then**

$$\frac{dy}{dx} = x^3 + x \quad \text{and} \quad \frac{d^2y}{dx^2} = 3x^2 + 1$$

### Rules for Finding Partial Derivatives

We have to this point considered functions which have just one independent variable. Let us now consider functions which have two or more independent variables.

The function $A = LW$, which relates the area of a rectangle ($A$) to its length ($L$) and width ($W$), is a familiar example. Suppose we ask, "What is the first derivative of this function with respect to $W$?" or "By how much does $A$ change when $W$ increases by 1 unit?" The question, however, is incomplete because it is silent about independent variable $L$. $L$ might be increasing, decreasing, or not changing while $W$ is rising by 1 unit, and our answer about the change in area would differ accordingly. Therefore, we put the question precisely: "By how much does $A$ change when $W$ increases by 1 unit and $L$ remains constant?"

The answer to that question is called the first partial derivative of $A$ with respect to $W$. It is denoted $\partial A/\partial W$. The use of the symbol $\partial$ instead of $d$ indicates that all independent variables other than $W$ are being held constant. In the present case, $L$ is the only independent variable other than $W$.

The procedure for finding the first partial derivative of $A$ with respect to $W$ is quite easy. Apply rules R1 through R6 and treat $L$ as if it were a constant number rather than a variable. Thus, if $A = LW$, then

$$\frac{\partial A}{\partial W} = L(1) + W(0) = L$$

by using the product rule with $u(W) = L$ and $v(W) = W$. Notice by numerical substitution that the result is correct. Begin with a surface whose length is 10 feet, whose width is 20 feet, and whose area is therefore 200 square feet. If the width were stretched to 21 feet and the length held constant, area would rise by 10 square feet to 210 square feet: $\partial A/\partial W = L = 10$.

The second partial derivative with respect to $W$ is found taking the first partial derivative with respect to $W$ twice in succession. The second partial derivative is denoted $\partial^2 A / \partial W^2$. Thus, if $A = LW$, then

$$\frac{\partial A}{\partial W} = L$$

and

$$\frac{\partial^2 A}{\partial W^2} = 0$$

This result tells you what you probably already know. The increase in area per unit increase in width is the same for a rectangle of given length, whether the width increases from 20 to 21 feet or from 100 to 101 feet: $\partial A / \partial W$ does not depend on $W$, and so $\partial^2 A / \partial W^2 = 0$.

There is one more type of partial derivative. It is called the cross-partial derivative and in the present example is denoted $\partial^2 A / \partial L \partial W$. It is like the second partial derivative in that a first partial derivative is taken twice in succession. It differs in that the first partial derivative with respect to $W$ is taken in one round and the first partial derivative with respect to $L$ is taken in the other round. (Whether first $W$ and then $L$ or vice versa does not matter; the result is the same.) Thus, if $A = LW$, then

$$\frac{\partial A}{\partial W} = L$$

and

$$\frac{\partial^2 A}{\partial L \partial W} = 1$$

The result again makes sense, although the words for articulating the result are getting harder to follow. The increase in area per 1-foot increase in width (i.e., $\partial A / \partial W$) is $\partial^2 A / \partial L \partial W$ square feet greater when the length is 1 foot greater. Verify numerically by computing the change in area of a 10-foot-long rectangle whose width increases from 20 to 21 feet; then compute the change in area of an 11-foot-long rectangle whose width increases from 20 to 21 feet. The change in area in the first computation is 10 square feet; in the second, it is 11 square feet. The difference, 1 square foot, is $\partial^2 A / \partial L \partial W = 1$.

Two additional examples of the concepts in this subsection follow:

**Example If $y = 4x + 2xz^2$, then**

$$\frac{\partial y}{\partial x} = 4 + 2z^2$$

and

$$\frac{\partial^2 y}{\partial x^2} = 0$$

and

$$\frac{\partial y}{\partial z} = 4xz$$

and

$$\frac{\partial^2 y}{\partial z^2} = 4x$$

and

$$\frac{\partial^2 y}{\partial z \partial x} = 4z$$

**Example** If $y = 4x^{.75}z^{.25}$, then

$$\frac{\partial y}{\partial x} = 3x^{-.25}z^{.25}$$

and

$$\frac{\partial^2 y}{\partial x^2} = -.75x^{-1.25}z^{.25}$$

and

$$\frac{\partial y}{\partial z} = x^{.75}z^{-.75}$$

and

$$\frac{\partial^2 y}{\partial z^2} = -.75x^{.75}z^{-1.75}$$

and

$$\frac{\partial^2 y}{\partial z \partial x} = .75x^{-.25}z^{-.75}$$

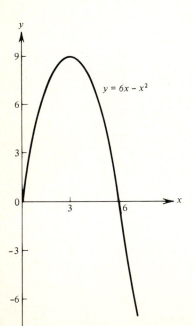

**FIGURE A-5**
Function with maximum at $x = 3$.

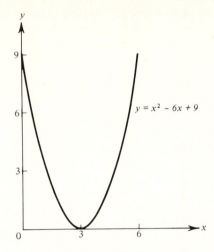

$y = x^2 - 6x + 9$

**FIGURE A-6**
Function with minimum at $x = 3$.

## OPTIMIZATION TECHNIQUES

Much economic reasoning is predicated on the behavioral assumption that people optimize. A consumer maximizes utility, a manager minimizes cost, and so on. There are techniques in the calculus for solving optimization problems. Here we show first how to optimize a function having just one independent variable and second how to optimize a function having two independent variables when allowable values of those variables are constrained by another relation. Coverage of these situations, plus the material in the other appendixes, is sufficient for topics raised in the body of this book.

### A Function of One Variable

Let the function $y = 6x - x^2$ describe the relationship between $y$ and nonnegative values of $x$. The function is plotted in Figure A-5. The appearance of the plot suggests first that $y$ attains its maximum at $x = 3$ and second that $y$ attains no minimum (because larger values of $x$ beyond $x = 3$ always result in smaller values of $y$).

Begin to the left of the maximum and let $x$ increase toward $x = 3$. Each increment in $x$ produces an increment in $y$: $dy/dx = 6 - 2x > 0$ for $0 \leq x < 3$. But the increment in $y$ gets successively smaller—i.e., $d^2y/dx^2 = -2 < 0$—until it vanishes altogether at precisely the maximal point: $dy/dx = 6 - 2x = 0$ at $x = 3$.

From these observations we infer two general statements which prove to be true:

**1** If the function $y = f(x)$ is maximized at $x = x^*$, then $dy/dx = 0$ when evaluated at $x^*$. This is called the first-order, or necessary, condition for the maximum.

**2** If $dy/dx = 0$ and $d^2y/dx^2 < 0$ when both are evaluated at $x^*$, then the function $y = f(x)$ is maximized at $x = x^*$. These are called the second-order, or sufficient, conditions for the maximum.

Parallel reasoning applies to finding the minimum of a function. Let us use $y = x^2 - 6x + 9$, plotted in Figure A-6 over nonnegative values of $x$, as an example. Apparently, it attains a minimum at $x = 3$ and has no maximum. Begin to the left of the minimum and let $x$ increase toward $x = 3$. Each increment in $x$ produces a decrement in

$y$: $dy/dx = 2x - 6 < 0$ for $0 \leq x < 3$. But the decrement in $y$ gets successively smaller in absolute value and hence larger in algebraic value—i.e., $d^2y/dx^2 = 2 > 0$—until it vanishes at precisely the minimal point: $dy/dx = 2x - 6 = 0$ at $x = 3$. To generalize from this example, the first- and second-order conditions for the minimum are as follows:

**1** If the function $y = f(x)$ is minimized at $x = x^*$, then $dy/dx = 0$ when evaluated at $x^*$.

**2** If $dy/dx = 0$ and $d^2y/dx^2 > 0$ when both are evaluated at $x^*$, then the function $y = f(x)$ is minimized at $x = x^*$.

Notice that we cannot tell from the information that $dy/dx = 0$ when $x = x^*$ whether the function has been maximized or minimized at $x^*$. One must check the second-order conditions to resolve the question.

Not all functions have a maximum or minimum. For example, if $x$ is allowed to take any value, then no maximum or minimum can be found for the function $y = 2x$. Increases in $x$ always lead to increases in $y$, and decreases in $x$ always lead to decreases in $y$. An attempt to discover a maximum or minimum by the method described above will signal the problem. Since $dy/dx = 2$, no value of $x$ satisfies the first-order condition $dy/dx = 0$.

On the other hand, a function may have both a maximum and a minimum. Consider $y = x^3/3 - x^2$, which is graphed in Figure A-7.

Setting the first derivative of this function equal to zero,

$$\frac{dy}{dx} = x^2 - 2x = 0$$

and solving yields two values: $x^* = 0$ and $x^* = 2$. The second derivative

$$\frac{d^2y}{dx^2} = 2x - 2$$

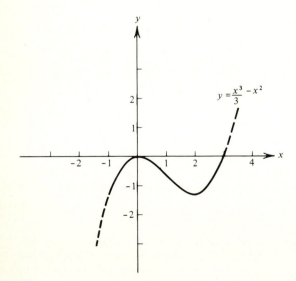

**FIGURE A-7**
Function with maximum and minimum.

equals $-2$ when $x^* = 0$ and equals 2 when $x^* = 2$. By the second-order conditions, $x^* = 0$ (at which $y = 0$) gives a maximum value of $y$, and $x^* = 2$ (at which $y = -4/3$) gives a minimum value of $y$. Notice, however, that these conclusions are valid only for values of $x$ that are greater than $-1$ and less than 3, within which range the function is drawn as a solid line in Figure A-7. When $x$ is outside this range, it takes on values that are greater than the "maximal" value or smaller than the "minimal" value. Thus, the technique described in this subsection and the next subsection may find only a local maximum or minimum, meaning that such a point is an extreme point relative to the points which are close to it but not necessarily relative to points which are farther from it.

## A Function of Two Variables with One Constraint

Suppose that we have 80 feet of fencing and wish to build a rectangular pen that encloses the maximum area. What should be the length $(L)$ and width $(W)$ of the pen? The problem is to choose values of two variables $(L, W)$ such that a function of the variables $(A = LW)$ is maximized, subject to a constraint on the choices $(2L + 2W = 80)$. Every backyard gardener or dog lover knows the answer to be a 20-foot square. To give a formal proof, we first rewrite the constraint as $L = 40 - W$; next we substitute for $L$ in the equation for area to obtain $A = 40W - W^2$, now a function of just one variable; and then, using the method described immediately above, we maximize $A$ by choosing $W$:

$$\frac{dA}{dW} = 40 - 2W = 0 \qquad \text{hence } W^* = 20$$

$$\frac{d^2A}{dW^2} = -2 < 0 \qquad \text{hence a maximum}$$

$L^*$ therefore equals 20, by substitution of $W^*$ into the constraining equation.

But when a problem of this sort is not so familiar, does not solve so neatly, or involves functions in analytic form, we use a different method called the Lagrangian method. Let us denote by $A = F(L, W)$ the function to be optimized and by $G(L, W) = 0$ the function that constrains. The steps in the Lagrangian method are as follows:

**1** Be sure that all terms in the constraining equation are moved to the left-hand side so that the right-hand side of the equation is zero.

**2** Multiply the constraining equation by the Lagrangian multiplier $\lambda$ and subtract the result from the function to be maximized. The entire expression is called the Lagrangian function:

$$Z(L, W, \lambda) = F(L, W) - \lambda[G(L, W)]$$

**3** Partially differentiate the Lagrangian function with respect to each of the choice variables and with respect to the Lagrangian multiplier. In each case equate the result to zero:

$$Z_L = F_L(L, W) - \lambda G_L(L, W) = 0$$
$$Z_W = F_W(L, W) - \lambda G_W(L, W) = 0$$
$$Z_\lambda = -G(L, W) = 0$$

($Z_L$ denotes the first partial derivative $\partial Z/\partial L$, $G_L$ denotes the first partial derivative $\partial G/\partial L$, etc.) If $F(L, W)$ is optimized and $G(L, W) = 0$ when both are evaluated at $L = L^*$, $W = W^*$, and $\lambda = \lambda^*$, then $L^*$, $W^*$, $\lambda^*$ is the solution to the preceding system of equations. These are the first-order conditions for the constrained optimum, but we do not know yet whether the optimum is a maximum or a minimum.

**4** Evaluate $H = 2Z_{LW}Z_{L\lambda}Z_{W\lambda} - Z_{LL}(Z_{W\lambda})^2 - Z_{WW}(Z_{L\lambda})^2$ at $L^*$, $W^*$, $\lambda^*$. ($Z_{LW}$ denotes the second partial derivative $\partial^2 Z/\partial L\,\partial W$, $Z_{L\lambda}$ denotes the second partial derivative $\partial^2 Z/\partial L\,\partial\lambda$, etc.) If $H > 0$, then the optimum is a maximum. If $H < 0$, the optimum is a minimum. These are the second-order conditions.

The results of these steps when applied to the problem of the rectangular pen are as follows:

**1** $2L + 2W - 80 = 0$

**2** $Z(L, W, \lambda) = LW - \lambda(2L + 2W - 80)$

**3** $Z_L = W - 2\lambda = 0$

$\left.\begin{array}{l} Z_W = L - 2\lambda = 0 \\ Z_\lambda = -(2L + 2W - 80) = 0 \end{array}\right\}$ from which $L^* = 20$, $W^* = 20$, $\lambda^* = 10$

**4** $Z_{LL} = 0 \qquad Z_{WW} = 0$

$Z_{LW} = 1 \qquad Z_{L\lambda} = -2$

$Z_{W\lambda} = -2 \qquad H = 8 > 0$, a maximum

In $\lambda^*$ the Lagrangian method yields output that we have not seen previously. The variable $\lambda$ is usually called the shadow price of the constraint. Its value tells us, to a very close approximation, how much $F(L, W)$ could be increased by if the constraining value were increased 1 unit. In our example, 80 feet of fencing will enclose a rectangular area of 400 square feet at most. If there were 81 feet of fencing, then at most 410.0625 square feet could be enclosed by building a 20.25-foot square. Therefore, the "cost" of being constrained to use 80 rather than 81 feet of fence is 10.0625 square feet. This is the information imparted by $\lambda^* = 10$.

For another example of constrained optimization, assume as facts the following:

**1** A retailer has a downtown store and a suburban store.

**2** The retailer wishes to sell 230 units of a particular good by the end of the month.

**3** The quantity $S$ that can be sold at the suburban store depends on the price per unit $P_S$ charged at that store according to the demand function $S = 600 - 20\,P_s$.

**4** The quantity $D$ that can be sold at the downtown store depends on the price per unit $P_D$ charged at that store according to the demand function $D = 400 - 10\,P_D$.

**5** The retailer wants to maximize sales revenue $R = P_DD + P_sS$.

The problems involve how much to sell at each store and at what price. Actually, the problems are not that numerous, because once we have chosen the prices, we will have chosen the quantities, and vice versa, because of the demand functions which relate price and quantity.

The results of the four-step procedure when applied to the retailer's maximization problem are as follows:

**1** $D + S - 230 = 0$

**2** $Z(D, S, \lambda) = (400 - D)\,D/10 + (600 - S)\,S/20 - \lambda(D + S - 230)$

For this step the revenue function, which is the function that is to be maximized, has been formed by rewriting the demand functions as

$$P_D = \frac{400 - D}{10}$$

$$P_S = \frac{600 - S}{20}$$

and multiplying by quantities $D$ and $S$ to obtain $R(D, S) = P_D D + P_S S$.

**3** $Z_D = 40 - .2D - \lambda = 0$
   $Z_S = 30 - .1S - \lambda = 0$
   $Z_\lambda = -(D + S - 230) = 0$

from which $D^* = 110$, $S^* = 120$, $\lambda^* = 18$.

These are the quantities to be sold at the two stores. Carrying $D = 110$ and $S = 120$ back to the demand functions implies prices of $P_D^* = \$29$ and $P_S^* = \$24$. Hence maximal revenues are $R^* = \$3,190 + \$2,880 = \$6,070$, an amount that could be increased by approximately $\$18$ (as $\lambda^* = 18$) if the retailer had had 231 objects to sell rather than 230.

**4** $Z_{DD} = -.2$    $Z_{SS} = -.1$
   $Z_{DS} = 0$      $Z_{S\lambda} = -1$
   $Z_{D\lambda} = -1$

Therefore $H = .3 > 0$, and the solution is a maximum rather than a minimum.

# CONSUMER BEHAVIOR
# THEORY

The derivation of the demand function for a consumer was described briefly in Chapter 2. Here, using the calculus tools developed in Appendix A, we present a mathematical treatment of the theory of consumer behavior.

In consumer theory, the demand functions of a single consumer are derived from the interaction of two concepts: the utility function and the budget constraint. The utility function is a formal way of expressing what a consumer prefers to have. The budget constraint expresses what a consumer can afford to buy. Assuming that a customer will select from all affordable combinations of goods (according to the budget constraint) the combination he or she most wants to have (according to the utility function), we derive the quantities that the consumer seeks to buy.

In order to understand the meaning of a consumer's utility function, suppose first that the consumer is shown many different bundles of goods. A bundle consists of specified amounts of various goods, measured in real units—for example, three French hens, two turtle doves, and a partridge in a pear tree. Then the consumer ranks the bundles according to his or her desire to have them, regardless of what it would cost to acquire them. Finally, the consumer gives to each bundle a number called a utility level. In the assignment of utility levels to bundles, the highest number is given to the bundle that the consumer has ranked first and most wishes to have, and the next highest number is given to the bundle that the consumer has ranked second. In general, in the comparison of any two bundles, the higher utility level is attached to the bundle which the consumer prefers to have. Where the consumer does not care whether he or she has any particular bundle from among two or more bundles, a tie occurs in the consumer's ranking of those bundles, the same utility level is given to each of them, and the consumer is said to be indifferent between them. The relationship which links a bundle with its utility level is the utility function.

Theory does not attempt to explain why a particular person has a particular utility function. That is, theory does not attempt to explain why a consumer ranks bundles and assigns utility levels as he or she does. Also, theory does not attempt to explain why different people rank the same bundles differently or assign them different utility levels, although it is taken for granted by economists that these differences are common. However, theory does posit two general properties of any consumer's ranking: *nonsatiation* and *transitivity*. Nonsatiation means that if two bundles consist of the same amounts of all but one good, with the first bundle having a greater amount of that good, any consumer will prefer to have the first bundle and will give a higher utility level to it than to the other bundle. Transitivity means that if a consumer ranks one bundle ahead of a second bundle and that second bundle ahead of a third bundle, he or she will rank the first bundle ahead of the third.

The assumed objective of the consumer is to maximize his or her utility level $U$. Utility level depends on the quantities of goods $x$ and $y$ which the consumer acquires. This relationship is represented by the consumer's utility function, $U = U(x, y)$. By the property of nonsatiation, the marginal utility of good $x$ is positive: $\partial U/\partial x > 0$. This is the increase in the consumer's utility level from having one more unit of good $x$ and an unchanged amount of good $y$. Similarly, $\partial U/\partial y > 0$. In choosing bundles, the consumer is limited by the size of his or her budget, which, because of nonsatiation, will be entirely spent: $p_x x + p_y y = I$.

In the Lagrangian format the problem is to maximize

$$L = U(x, y) - \lambda(p_x x + p_y y - I)$$

over the variables $x$, $y$, and $\lambda$. Assuming that some of each good is selected, the values of $x^*$ and $y^*$ (the quantities chosen) and $\lambda^*$ must be a solution to the following set of equations:

$$\frac{\partial L}{\partial x} = \frac{\partial U}{\partial x} - \lambda p_x = 0 \tag{B-1}$$

$$\frac{\partial L}{\partial y} = \frac{\partial U}{\partial y} - \lambda p_y = 0$$

$$\frac{\partial L}{\partial \lambda} = -(p_x x + p_y y - I) = 0$$

Equations (B-1) are the first-order conditions for a constrained maximization of utility level. In addition, the values of $x^*$ and $y^*$ must be such that

$$-p_x^2 \frac{\partial^2 U}{\partial x^2} - p_y^2 \frac{\partial^2 U}{\partial y^2} + 2p_x p_y \frac{\partial^2 U}{\partial x \partial y} > 0 \tag{B-2}$$

when the second partial derivatives are evaluated at $(x, y) = (x^*, y^*)$. Inequality (B-2) is the second-order condition for a maximum.

Let us rewrite the first two parts of equation (B-1) as

$$\lambda = \frac{\partial U/\partial x}{p_x} = \frac{\partial U/\partial y}{p_y} \tag{B-3}$$

When the consumer maximizes utility, he or she chooses the bundle $(x^*, y^*)$ which exhausts the budget and confers the same marginal utility for the last dollar of expenditure in every line of expenditure. The sense of equation (B-3) is that the consumer cannot increase his or her utility level above $U(x^*, y^*)$ by shifting dollars out of the purchase of good $x$ and into the purchase of good $y$, or vice versa. It may be that the last unit of good $x$ purchased raises his or her utility level more than the last unit of good $y$ purchased (i.e., $\partial U/\partial x > \partial U/\partial y$), but it must be the case that good $x$ comes at the higher price. It follows that the consumer's utility level rises by $\lambda^*$ as a result of his or her expenditure of the last dollar in the budget. For this reason, $\lambda^*$ is called the marginal utility of income. It is also called the shadow price of the budget constraint, because it indicates by how much the utility level would increase if the consumer's income could be raised above $I$ by \$1.

The values of $x^*$, $y^*$, and $\lambda^*$ depend on the values of some or all of the parameters in equation (B-1) and on the consumer's marginal utilities. Hence the consumer's demand functions are

$$x^* = f(p_x, p_y, I) \qquad y^* = g(p_x, p_y, I)$$

in which the particular manner (symbolized by letters $f$ and $g$) that $x^*$ or $y^*$ depends on prices and income is determined by the consumer's preferences for having different bundles.

## A Specific Illustration

Let Evelyn's utility function in explicit form be $U = xy + 4x$. For Evelyn, the marginal utility of good $x$ equals $\partial U/\partial x = y + 4$, a positive number whose magnitude depends on the amount of good $y$ that is chosen. The marginal utility of good $y$ is $\partial U/\partial y = x$, a positive number whose magnitude is the amount of good $x$ that is chosen. Substituting these expressions into equation (B-1) and solving yields Evelyn's demand functions

$$x^* = \frac{I + 4p_y}{2p_x} \qquad y^* = \frac{I - 4p_y}{2p_y} \tag{B-4}$$

and the shadow price of the budget constraint

$$\lambda^* = \frac{I + 4p_y}{2p_x p_y} \tag{B-5}$$

Evelyn seeks to buy some amount of good $x$, whatever her income and the prices of goods. However, she seeks to buy good $y$ only if her income is more than 4 times as large as $p_y$; accordingly, it is assumed that $I > 4p_y$. Note that the solution at equation (B-4) satisfies the second-order condition at inequality (B-2), as

$$\frac{\partial^2 U}{\partial x^2} = \frac{\partial^2 U}{\partial y^2} = 0 \qquad \frac{\partial^2 U}{\partial x \partial y} = 1$$

and hence 
$$-p_x^2 \frac{\partial^2 U}{\partial y^2} - p_y^2 \frac{\partial^2 U}{\partial x^2} + 2p_x p_y \frac{\partial^2 U}{\partial x \partial y} = 2p_x p_y > 0$$

When $I = \$20$, $p_x = \$1$, and $p_y = \$2$, then Evelyn, according to the demand function

(B-4) seeks to buy $x^* = 14$ and $y^* = 3$. The marginal utility from the last dollar of expenditure for $x^*$ and $y^*$ is 7, which is also the shadow price of Evelyn's budget constraint $\lambda^*$.

It is instructive to show this solution graphically. Figure B-1 shows a number of indifference curves in a graph in which the horizontal axis measures the quantity of $x$ and the vertical axis measures the quantity of $y$. Each point in the graph can be interpreted as a particular bundle of $x$ and $y$. An indifference curve is the locus of all bundles producing a given utility level. For example, the indifference curve labeled $U = 98$ is obtained by plotting the equation which results from setting Evelyn's utility function equal to 98. That is,

$$U = 98 = xy + 4x$$

or

$$y = \frac{98}{x} - 4 \tag{B-6}$$

Notice that indifference curves have higher utility levels the farther they lie from the origin. Also, we have shown only a small number of the infinite number of possible indifference curves.

The straight line represents Evelyn's budget constraint. Every point on the line represents a bundle that costs exactly \$20, her income level. It is simply the plot of $x + 2y = 20$. Hence, Evelyn is restricted to purchasing bundles on the line or below it.

The solution is now obvious. Evelyn seeks to reach the highest indifference curve possible without exceeding her budget constraint. This is point $E$, where the budget line is just tangent to the $U = 98$ indifference curve. Point $E$ represents the bundle $x = 14$, $y = 3$, as shown in Figure B-1 and calculated algebraically earlier.

One further observation should be made regarding the graphical solution. The tangency at point $E$ implies that the slope of the indifference curve is equal to the slope of the budget line. But this is just what equation (B-3), after rearranging, requires:

$$\frac{\partial U/\partial x}{\partial U/\partial y} = \frac{P_x}{P_y}$$

**FIGURE B-1**
Optimal choice of $x$ and $y$.

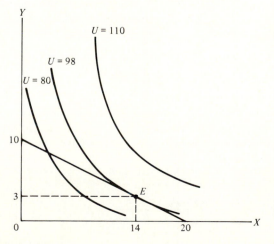

The term on the left (known as the marginal rate of substitution) is the absolute value of the slope of the indifference curve. This can be verified easily by comparing the derivative $dy/dx$, of equation (B-6) with the ratio of marginal utilities. Similarly, the term on the right is the absolute value of the slope of the budget line.

Let us now analyze the properties of Evelyn's demand functions.

First, we determine whether a good is normal or inferior for Evelyn. A normal good is one for which increases in income result in increases in consumption; an inferior good is one for which increases in income result in decreases in consumption. To determine this, we partially differentiate her demand function with respect to income and observe the sign of the result.

$$\frac{\partial x^*}{\partial I} = 1/2p_x > 0 \qquad \frac{\partial y^*}{\partial I} = 1/2p_y > 0$$

Therefore, both goods are normal. As a sidelight peculiar to this illustration, it follows that Evelyn spends exactly half the advance in income on good $x$ and half on good $y$: $\partial(p_x x^*)/\partial I = \partial(p_y y^*)/\partial I = 1/2$. Since $\partial x^*/x^*$ is the percentage change in quantity demanded and $\partial I/I$ is the percentage change in income, $(\partial x^*/x^*)/(\partial I/I) = (\partial x^*/\partial I)(I/x^*)$ is Evelyn's income elasticity of demand for good $x$ (denoted $e_{xI}$):

$$e_{xI} = \frac{\partial x^*}{\partial I}\frac{I}{x^*} = \frac{I}{(I + 4p_y)} < 1 \qquad e_{yI} = \frac{\partial y^*}{\partial I}\frac{I}{y^*} = \frac{I}{(I - 4p_y)} > 1$$

Thus, Evelyn's demand for good $x$ is income-inelastic, and her demand for good $y$ is income-elastic. However, both elasticities get closer and closer to 1 as her income gets larger. To show generally that a consumer spends a larger proportion of his or her budget on an income-elastic good after an increase in income, compute

$$\frac{\partial(p_y y^*/I)}{\partial I} = \frac{p_y[I(\partial y^*/\partial I) - y^*]}{I^2} = p_y y^* (e_{yI} - 1)/I^2$$

and observe that its sign is the same as the sign of $e_{yI} - 1$.

Second, we determine whether Evelyn's demand curves have negative slopes by partially differentiating her demand function (B-4) with respect to own-price and observing whether the sign of the result is negative:

$$\frac{\partial x^*}{\partial p_x} = -\frac{(I + 4p_y)}{2p_x^2} < 0 \qquad \frac{\partial y^*}{\partial p_y} = -\frac{I}{2p_y^2} < 0$$

Both of Evelyn's demand curves have the usual negative slope. We note that it is possible for inferior goods to have positively sloping demand curves, implying that higher prices increase the quantity demanded. These presumably rare goods are termed "Giffen goods."

To determine whether demand is price-elastic or otherwise, compute

$$e_{xp_x} = -\frac{\partial x^*}{\partial p_x}\frac{p_x}{x^*} = 1 \qquad e_{yp_y} = -\frac{\partial y^*}{\partial p_y}\frac{p_y}{y^*} = \frac{I}{I - 4p_y} > 1$$

Thus Evelyn's demand for good $x$ is unitarily elastic with respect to price, and her demand for good $y$ is price-elastic.

Third, we investigate substitutability and complementarity by partially differentiating the demand function for one good with respect to the price of the other good. As

$$\frac{\partial x^*}{\partial p_y} = \frac{2}{p_x} > 0 \quad \text{and} \quad \frac{\partial y^*}{\partial p_x} = 0$$

good $x$ is a substitute for good $y$, but good $y$ is neither a substitute for nor a complement to good $x$. In other words, Evelyn's demand for good $y$ does not depend on the price of good $x$. The cross-price elasticity of demand of good $x$ with respect to $p_y$ is

$$e_{xy} = \frac{\partial x^*}{\partial p_y} \frac{p_y}{x^*} = \frac{4p_y}{1 + 4p_y} < 1$$

Finally, to indicate that Evelyn's preferences are indeed a determinant of quantity demanded, let us rewrite her utility function as $U = xy + kx$. The parameter $k$, which to this point has been fixed at $k = 4$, could measure the quantity of advertising to which Evelyn is subjected in a period of time. As an alternative interpretation, $k$ could take a larger value in one season and a smaller value in a second season when there is a seasonal component to preferences. Using the same methodology we used to find demand function (B-4), we find that Evelyn's demand functions are now

$$x^* = \frac{I + kp_y}{2p_x} \qquad y^* = \frac{I - kp_y}{2p_y}$$

The level of advertising on good $x$ or the season of the year has become a determinant of quantity demanded. Increases in $k$, with other determinants of demand being held constant, increase $x^*$, decrease $y^*$, and affect the values of certain elasticities of demand.

The concept of a demand function for good $x$ can be applied just as well to a group of consumers as to a single consumer. There are likely to be significant differences between members of the group. People have different preferences and different amounts of money to spend. While they may be exposed to the same preference-modifying events, their preferences may be affected differently by those events. The common factors, by assumption, are that every consumer pays the same prices $p_x$ and $p_y$ and that the demand functions of every consumer result from the income-constrained maximization of utility.

The group's demand function for good $x$ tells us how many units the group wishes to purchase, given the determinants of quantity demanded that operate differentially on each of its members. Specifically, quantity demanded by the group (denoted $X^*$) equals the sum of quantities demanded by members of the group:

$$\sum_{i=1}^{n} x_i^* = X^* = F(p_x, p_y; I_1, \ldots, I_n; k) = \sum_{i=1}^{n} f_i(p_x, p_y, I_i, k) \tag{B-7}$$

$$\sum_{i=1}^{n} y_i^* = Y^* = G(p_x, p_y; I_1, \ldots, I_n; k) = \sum_{i=1}^{n} g_i(p_x, p_y, I_i, k)$$

The notation in equations (B-7) reminds us that quantity demanded by the group $(X^*)$ depends on the number of persons in the group (in this case, $n$), the preferences $(f_i)$ of each member of the group, the exposure of members to preference-modifying events $(k)$, the total income of the group and its distribution among members $(I_1, I_2, \ldots, I_n)$, and the prices of goods purchased by members $(p_x, p_y)$.

The properties of a group's demand function are characterized in the same way and by the same computational methods as the properties of a single consumer's demand function. Thus, for the group (though not necessarily for every member of the group), good $x$ might be normal, income-elastic, price-elastic, a substitute for good $y$, and so on.

# CHAPTER 3

# EMPIRICAL DEMAND ANALYSIS AND ECONOMETRICS

**CHAPTER OUTLINE**

## EMPIRICAL DEMAND ANALYSIS

In Chapter 2 we developed a conceptual framework for demand analysis that was based primarily on theoretical considerations. However, if demand analysis is to be useful to managerial decision makers, it must be possible to apply it to specific empirical situations. That is, managers would like to be able to predict the effects of alternative pricing policies and advertising expenditures on the quantity demanded of specific products. Basically, there are three analytical tools available for doing empirical demand analysis: (1) survey research, (2) controlled market experiments, and (3) econometric methods. By far the most important of the three approaches is econometrics. Therefore most of this chapter will be devoted to econometric modeling and its application to demand analysis.

### Survey Research

Survey research involves interviewing a company's customers or potential customers to ascertain their likely response to changes in price, advertising expenditures, prices of substitutes and complements, personal income, and other variables that influence consumer behavior. These interviews may be conducted face to face or by telephone or direct mail.

Unfortunately, survey research is severely limited by the respondents' ability to provide meaningful answers to the questions. For example, the interviewer might ask a consumer how he or she would respond to a 5, 10, or 25 percent increase in price, assuming no other changes in the market environment. Many people would not know how to answer this question before the fact. Alternatively, the interviewer might inquire about the effects of a price change in light of a major advertising campaign. How can consumers possibly respond if they have not experienced the advertising campaign?

Survey research is a very sophisticated art. To use it effectively as a tool of demand analysis requires an exceptional knowledge of psychology, statistical sampling procedures, and economics. To base product marketing policy decisions entirely on results obtained from survey research is risky business. We believe an optimal use of survey research is as a complement to econometric methods. *The New York Times* is an example of a firm that has successfully combined survey research with econometric methods to assist management in the design of strategies to increase circulation and advertising revenue.

### Controlled Market Experiments

At least in theory, it is possible for economists to perform controlled experiments either over time in a particular market or over a cross section of segmented markets. By varying pricing and marketing strategies over time or across different markets, economists can observe the response of consumers to alternative marketing strategies.

Controlled experiments in economics are difficult to implement and are often prohibitively expensive. First, it may be virtually impossible to control such factors as changes in consumers' tastes, changes in income, the availability of substitute products, and the marketing strategies of competitors. Second, it may also be difficult even to observe and collect data on such factors. Third, the company's customers may rebel if they discover they are the subjects of such an experiment. As is the case with survey research, controlled market experiments are seldom used by themselves as tools of demand analysis. However, in special situations they may be used to supplement the information obtained from econometric studies.

### Econometrics

Given the limitations of survey research and controlled experiments, it is not surprising to find that economists have turned to a somewhat more practical approach to quantifying demand relationships: econometrics. The objective of econometrics is to provide empirical content to economic theory.

There are at least three reasons why most of the Fortune 500 companies in the United States use econometric marketing models to conduct demand analysis studies. First, econometric models can be used to help economists and management improve their understanding of specific product markets. Second, they can be used to forecast the effects on sales volume of alternative pricing, advertising, and promotional policies. Third, they can also be used to evaluate the effects on sales revenues of changes in the national economy and in the marketing policies of competitors.

Although the examples chosen to illustrate econometrics in this chapter are based on demand analysis, econometrics can also be used in production and cost analysis, supply forecasting, and investment analysis as well as in forecasting inflation, interest rates, and other economic indicators of interest to corporate economists.

Econometric modeling involves four distinct activities:

1 Model specification
2 Parameter estimation
3 Validation
4 Policy simulation

Each of these activities will be described in some detail in this chapter. The reader is assumed to have been exposed to a basic course in statistics. Mathematics, proofs, and derivations will be kept to a minimum. Our approach to econometrics is pragmatic and makes considerable use of numerical examples.

### MODEL SPECIFICATION

The first step in the development of an econometric model involves the specification of the mathematical equation or equations for the model; that is, we must define the output or dependent variables and come up with explicit mathematical relationships linking these variables to a set of explanatory variables on the right-hand side of the equation. To illustrate how one goes about specifying an econometric model, consider the following structure for an econometric demand model.

$$\text{SALES} = f(D, \text{COMP}, E, \text{SALES}_{t-n}, \mu) \qquad (3\text{-}1)$$

If we are dealing with a multiproduct firm, then we need to specify at least one equation of the type given by equation (3-1) for every product produced by the firm. In equation (3-1) we use SALES to denote total sales volume for the given product. (SALES could also represent market share for that product.) On the right-hand side of the equation, the symbol $f$ represents a functional relationship. The explanatory variables on the right-hand side include $D$, which is used to represent a variety of managerial decision variables. In the case of a demand model, the relevant decision variables might include price, advertising, public relations, product quality, sales force, and distribution. Some of these variables may be expressed in dollar values; in other cases they may take the form of binary or dummy variables which simply indicate whether a particular policy is in effect. We utilize the symbol COMP in equation (3-1) to denote the influence of competitive variables on product sales. By competitive variables we mean variables which are determined by the behavior of competitors. These are variables over which a firm has little or no control. Although we may not be able to control the behavior of our competitors, we may be able to come up with reasonable hypotheses about how they behave. Among the competitive variables that we may want to include in a marketing model are the price and advertising strategy of competing firms in the industry. Next, we use the symbol $E$ to represent the effect of those variables which affect the sales of our firm but are not affected by the behavior of our firm. These would be national economic indicators for the countries in which our firm sells its product. Gross national product, total employment, unemployment, and the consumer price index might all be examples of external economic indicators which affect the sales of our firm. It is also possible to include such variables as wars and natural disasters in the same category.

Also included on the right-hand side of equation (3-1) is the variable $\text{SALES}_{t-n}$, which is a lagged dependent variable. In this case the subscript $n$ can take on the values 1, 2, 3, . . . . The reason for including $\text{SALES}_{t-n}$ is to allow for the possibility that sales in time period $t$ depend in part on explanatory variables in $t - 1, t - 2, t - 3, \ldots$ . A good example is the effect of past advertising outlays on current sales.[1] Although the inclusion of lagged variables in a

---

[1] To see how the lagged dependent variable gets on the right-hand side, consider the so-called Koyck distributed lag model:

$$\text{SALES}_t = a + \alpha A_t + \alpha\lambda A_{t-1} + \alpha\lambda^2 A_{t-2} + \ldots .$$

where $A_t$ is advertising outlay in period $t$, and $a$, $\alpha$, and $\lambda$ are parameters. The parameter $\lambda$ is assumed to be a fraction between 0 and 1, which implies that the impact of advertising declines geometrically with the length of the lag. Now, lag the equation above one period, multiply it by $\lambda$, and subtract the result from the equation above to get

$$\text{SALES}_t = (1 - \lambda)a + \alpha A_t + \lambda\,\text{SALES}_{t-1}$$

demand model may cause us some difficulties with parameter estimation, lagged dependent variables nevertheless represent an important form of structural specification and should at least be mentioned.

Finally, the last variable included on the right-hand side of equation (3-1) is $\mu$, which is used to denote a random error term. In a sense, $\mu$ represents a catchall variable that is included to account for that portion of the variation in SALES which has not been explained by the other four types of variables. We shall discuss the error term in detail later in this chapter.

## A Linear Demand Model

To further illustrate how one goes about specifying demand models, consider the simple linear example given by equation (3-2).

$$\text{SALES} = a + bP + c\,\text{ADV} + d\text{PR} + e\text{PC} + f\text{CADV} + g\text{GNP} + \mu \quad (3-2)$$

The coefficients $a, \upsilon, \ldots, g$ are parameters of the model which are to be estimated through the use of econometric techniques. Although equation (3-2) is a linear model, it contains many of the concepts required in building more complex, nonlinear models. Equation (3-2) contains three decision variables: price, advertising, and public relations. These variables are expressed, respectively, by the symbols $P$, ADV, and PR. Price will, of course, be measured in the appropriate monetary unit. Advertising may be measured either in monetary units or in some other form such as column inches for newspaper advertising, minutes or hours of television time, or number of billboards in place. Alternatively, advertising may also be expressed as a binary or dummy variable in such a way that ADV may take on a value of zero if a particular policy is not in effect or a value of 1 if a policy has been implemented. The PR variable may be expressed in a similar form. Our example model also includes two competitive variables PC and CADV, which are used to denote the pricing and advertising policy of our competitor. If we have more than one competitor in this industry, it may be necessary to include competitive variables for each of the more important competitors. The next variable included in equation (3-2) is GNP, which is simply the notation for gross national product. GNP is included in order to illustrate the possible effect which the national economy may be exerting on the sales of our product. GNP is only one of many possible national economic indicators that may be appropriate for our model. Unfortunately, there are no textbooks that prescribe the best among the leading national economic indicators for particular products. Selecting the best indicators is a matter of experience and judgment. The final variable included in equation (3-2) is a normally distributed random variable $\mu$, which is assumed to have a constant variance and a zero expected value. We shall discuss it thoroughly later.

The model described in equation (3-2) is admittedly simple, but it does include many of the important features of more complex marketing policy models. It should be emphasized that there is no point restricting ourselves to linear models for marketing policy. The estimation methodology we shall present is applicable to linear models, logarithmic models, polynomial models, and a variety of relationships beyond the simple model in equation (3-2).

In the case of a multiproduct firm, we would find it necessary to produce an entire set of equations of the type exemplified by equation (3-2). If some products were either complements or substitutes, then we would have an interdependent system of simultaneous equations.

The approach taken above assumes that it is possible to model the firm's sales or market-share directly; that is, we have assumed that we can formulate an equation explaining the behavior of sales for each product produced by the firm. Unfortunately, in many instances this may not be possible. We may find it necessary to build a model of the entire industry and then construct a separate model explaining our firm's share of the market.

### An Exponential Demand Model

An alternative specification of a demand function that is widely used by corporate economists is the exponential form

$$\text{SALES} = aP^b\text{ADV}^c\text{GNP}^d \tag{3-3}$$

Although we have deleted three of the variables contained in equation (3-2) to simplify the exposition of equation (3-3), the definitions of SALES, $P$, ADV, and GNP are identical to the definitions used in equation (3-2).

There are at least three reasons why some economists prefer the exponential specification of a demand relationship to the linear specification. First, in the exponential form the marginal effects of price $(P)$, advertising (ADV), and income (GNP) on the quantity demanded (SALES) are not constant but rather depend on the value of the particular independent variable as well as the other independent variables in the demand equation. For example, the partial derivative of SALES with respect to income

$$\frac{\partial\text{SALES}}{\partial\text{GNP}} = adP^b\text{ADV}^c\text{GNP}^{d-1} \tag{3-4}$$

contains all the variables that were included in equation (3-3). This means that the marginal effect of a change in GNP on the quantity demanded depends on the level of GNP as well as on price and advertising. This is in contrast to the linear model presented in equation (3-2), which assumes that all the marginal relationships are constant and independent of one another. Changing marginal relationships appear to be more realistic. For example, as income (measured by GNP) increases from a low level to a higher level, the demand for tenderloin of beef may increase continuously. It is unlikely that the increase in the quantity demanded of beef tenderloin will be linear. It is likely to be more rapid at lower income levels and gradually level off at higher income levels. Similar arguments can be made about the marginal effects of increases in advertising expenditures.

Second, the exponential demand function can easily be transformed into a linear relationship by taking the logarithms of both sides of equation (3-3):

$$\log\text{SALES} = \log a + b \cdot \log P + c \cdot \log\text{ADV} + d \cdot \log\text{GNP} \qquad (3\text{-}5)$$

where the parameters $a$, $b$, $c$, and $d$ are the same as those in equation (3-3), except that they can be estimated directly by using ordinary least squares.

Third, it is easy to show that demand functions of the form specified by equation (3-3) have constant elasticities given by the coefficients $b$, $c$, and $d$ which can be estimated by ordinary least-squares regression analysis. Consider, for example, the case of price elasticity of demand, which was defined in Chapter 2 to be

$$e = -\frac{\partial\text{SALES}}{\partial P} \cdot \frac{P}{\text{SALES}} \qquad (3\text{-}6)$$

If we differentiate equation (3-3) with respect to $P$, we get

$$\frac{\partial\text{SALES}}{\partial P} = abP^{b-1}\text{ADV}^c\text{GNP}^d \qquad (3\text{-}7)$$

Substituting the results of equation (3-7) into equation (3-6), we obtain

$$e = -abP^{b-1}\text{ADV}^c\text{GNP}^d \cdot \frac{P}{\text{SALES}} \qquad (3\text{-}8)$$

Substituting the value of SALES from equation (3-3) into equation (3-8) yields

$$e = -abP^{b-1}\text{ADV}^c\text{GNP}^d \cdot \frac{P}{aP^b\text{ADV}^c\text{GNP}^d} \qquad (3\text{-}9)$$

$$= -\frac{abP^b\text{ADV}^c\text{GNP}^d}{P} \cdot \frac{P}{aP^b\text{ADV}^c\text{GNP}^d}$$

$$= -b$$

Therefore, the price elasticity of demand is equal to $-b$, the negative of the exponent of price in equation (3-3). In a similar fashion it can be shown that $c$ and $d$ are the elasticities of demand with respect to advertising expenditures and income, respectively.

### Empirical Examples

**Dresser Industries**    One of the divisions of Dresser Industries has made extensive use of an econometric marketing model. The model contains 45 demand equations (15 products sold in three markets). Each of the 45 demand functions is of the following form:

$$\frac{S_i}{P_i} = f(M_1, \ldots, M_k, E_1, \ldots, E_n, Q_1, \ldots, Q_j, \ldots, Q_m) \qquad (3\text{-}10)$$

where $S_i$ = sales revenue of the $i$th product
$\quad\ P_i$ = relative price of the $i$th product
$\quad\ M$ = management decision variable
$\quad\ E$ = economic indicator of market activity
$\quad\ Q_j$ = quantity demanded of complementary products sold by Dresser
$\qquad\quad$ in the same market where $j \neq i$

Notice that quantity demanded is measured by an index of output, or revenue divided by price. This is often necessary in the real world because the product often consists of a variety of subproducts of different sizes and qualities. For example, consider the product paint. The firm would normally sell a variety of types and colors of paint in different sized containers. Hence, output might be approximated by dividing total revenues by the price of the most popular paint subproduct.

Equation (3-11) contains the specification for a demand equation for product 1 in market 2.

$$\frac{S_{12}}{P_{12}} = 30,442 \ \text{IV}^{.82} \text{UCC}^{-.82} \text{ORP}^{-1.02} \qquad (3\text{-}11)$$

where $S_{12}$ = sales revenue of product 1 in market 2
$\quad\ P_{12}$ = price of product 1 in market 2
$\qquad\ \text{IV}$ = investment
$\quad\ \text{UCC}$ = user cost of capital
$\quad\ \text{ORP}$ = output of rubber and miscellaneous plastic products

**CIBA-GEIGY**   The pharmaceutical industry in the United States is unique in terms of the richness of the marketing data available within the industry. CIBA-GEIGY, Ely Lilly, and Ross Labs have successfully implemented econometric demand models based on the following general specifications:

$$S_i = f(M_i, \text{PE}_i, \text{QPE}_i, \text{DE}_i, \text{QDE}_i, P_i) \qquad (3\text{-}12)$$

where $S_i$ = sales volume for product $i$
$\quad\ M_i$ = market sales volume for therapeutic market class of product $i$
$\quad\ \text{PE}_i$ = promotional expenditures for product $i$
$\ \text{QPE}_i$ = quality of promotional effort for product $i$
$\quad\ \text{DE}_i$ = detailing effort (sales calls on physicians) for product $i$
$\ \text{QDE}_i$ = quality of detailing message for product $i$
$\quad\ P_i$ = relative price of product $i$

The market sales volume for the therapeutic market class of each product $M_i$ is expressed as a separate regression equation for each product. Initial specifications of the market equations expressed $M_i$ as a function of time only. Empirical testing of the model suggested that a number of the drug markets were indeed influenced by the national economy. The $M_i$ equations were then respecified including national economic indicators as external variables. Products from the following therapeutic class markets have been modeled:

1 Anti-infectives
2 Analgesics and anti-inflammatory
3 Psychopharmaceuticals
4 Cough and cold preparations
5 Cardiovasculars
6 Nutritional sufficiency
7 Oral contraceptives
8 Diabetic therapy
9 Anticholinergics and antispasmodics
10 Antiobesity

**General Battery**  Finally, the General Battery Corporation, a division of Northwest Industries, has specified and estimated the following model to explain and predict industry sales for batteries:

$$S = f(\text{MV, PC, INV, TEMP}, Q_2, Q_3, Q_4) \qquad (3\text{-}13)$$

where $S$ = sales volume
  MV = population of motor vehicles two years old and older
  PC = personal consumption
  INV = change in business inventories
  TEMP = temperature variations from norm to first and fourth quarters
  $Q_2$ = second-quarter dummy variable
  $Q_3$ = third-quarter dummy variable
  $Q_4$ = fourth-quarter dummy variable

## PARAMETER ESTIMATION[2]

Once we have obtained a preliminary specification of our model, we must then collect the appropriate historical inputs as time series or cross-sectional data for estimating the parameters of the model. Generally speaking, we need a minimum of 7 to 10 observations to obtain the parameter estimates of relatively simple econometric equations. More complex models and equations involving more than, say, five or six right-hand variables may require substantially more historical observations for parameter estimation. Ideally, we would like to have in excess of 30 observations. Unfortunately, in the real world we frequently do not have the luxury of the number of observations we would like to have.

Once we have collected the necessary historical data and have specified the

---

[2] We are indebted to Professor Terry G. Seaks for a number of the ideas and diagrams included in this section.

theoretical model we intend to use, we must estimate the values of the parameters of the model. We begin by assuming that the model takes the form of a linear equation, although this assumption is later relaxed in favor of several alternative forms of nonlinearity.

The simplest form of linear model relating an output variable $Y$ to a right-hand-side external variable $X$ would be $Y = \beta_0 + \beta_1 X$. In such a model, $Y$ is represented as an exact linear function of $X$, and $\beta_0$ and $\beta_1$ are called the parameters of the model. As $X$ takes on different values, the model generates different values of $Y$ by multiplying $\beta_1$ times $X$ and adding $\beta_0$ to the result. If the value of $\beta_1$ is positive, then $Y$ and $X$ vary directly; if the value of $\beta_1$ is negative, then $Y$ and $X$ vary inversely. The value of $\beta_0$ is interpreted as the value that $Y$ takes on when $X$ takes on the value zero. However, it will be seen that it is often difficult to assign much confidence to estimated values of $\beta_0$ since very often the data values from which the model is estimated will not approach the value of $X = 0$. Thus, in practice it will be somewhat hazardous to put much weight on this estimate of $\beta_0$.

A graphical representation of the model $Y = \beta_0 + \beta_1 X$ is provided in Figure 3-1. The graph depicts a direct relationship between $X$ and $Y$, and the graph was generated by letting $\beta_0 = 3$ and $\beta_1 = .5$.

In developing a model that will be applicable to business and economic data, it is essential that the model incorporate some provision for randomness, inasmuch as economic relationships in the real world are never exact relationships such as the one pictured in Figure 3-1. Rather than assuming that $Y$ is an exact function of $X$, we can assume that $Y$ is a function of $X$ and a random error $\mu$. In this case the simplest linear model would be of the form

$$Y = \beta_0 + \beta_1 X + \mu \tag{3-14}$$

Data generated by a model of this form would not lie exactly along a straight line as in Figure 3-1, but the data would lie approximately along a line. The

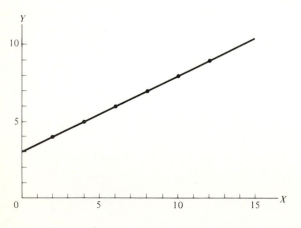

**FIGURE 3-1**
Simple linear function
$Y = 3 + .5X.$

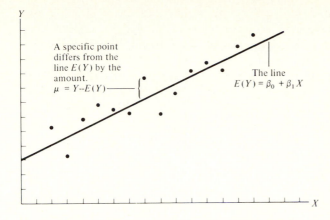

**FIGURE 3-2**
The line $E(Y) = \beta_0 + \beta_1 X$ and data points generated by the model $Y = \beta_0 + \beta_1 X + \mu$ ($\beta_0 = 3$, $\beta_1 = .5$).

deviations from the line $\beta_0 + \beta_1 X$ would of course depend on the size of the random error term $\mu$.

Now the specific $Y$ values do not coincide with the line, although the line shows where an average or typical $Y$ value would fall. The line $\beta_0 + \beta_1 X$ shows the average of expected values of $Y$, and this is usually denoted by

$$E(Y) = \beta_0 + \beta_1 X \tag{3-15}$$

An actual value of $Y$ will differ from its expected value by $\mu$ so that $Y = E(Y) + \mu$, which is the same as writing $Y = \beta_0 + \beta_1 X + \mu$. Equation (3-14) is the theoretical model describing $Y$, while equation (3-15) represents the expected or average relationship between $X$ and $Y$.

In Figure 3-2 we show a set of data points that are generated from the model $Y = 3 + .5X + \mu$, where $\mu$ is a random variable the exact probability distribution of which will be discussed below. For the moment the important idea to note about the figure is that the points (the $X$ and $Y$ pairs) lie roughly along a line but do not fall exactly on the line. The points that are plotted in Figure 3-2 are given in Table 3-1.

When we gather data on economic variables, we typically find ourselves in the position of having data like those shown in Table 3-1. Unfortunately, the exact parameters (intercept $= 3$, slope $= .5$) that underlie the relationship are unknown. The basic problem is to estimate the parameters of the relationship between the two variables. Once we have done this, we will then have to analyze how good our estimates are likely to be, since there is always a chance that we will misguess the true parameters by a large amount.

**Ordinary Least Squares**

The best-known method for estimating the unknown parameters of economic models is the method of least squares. In addition to being popular for its ease

**TABLE 3-1**
SAMPLE DATA
PLOTTED IN
FIGURE 3-2

| x | y |
| --- | --- |
| 1 | 3.05 |
| 2 | 5.65 |
| 3 | 2.70 |
| 4 | 6.05 |
| 5 | 7.15 |
| 6 | 6.15 |
| 7 | 5.90 |
| 8 | 8.65 |
| 9 | 4.95 |
| 10 | 7.10 |
| 11 | 8.80 |
| 12 | 9.60 |
| 13 | 8.60 |
| 14 | 10.60 |
| 15 | 11.55 |

of use, the method possesses many good statistical properties, which we shall discuss now.

The model that generated the data in Figure 3-2 was of the form $Y = \beta_0 + \beta_1 X + \mu$ so that each particular $Y$ value differed from the line $\beta_0 + \beta_1 X$ by the amount of the error term $\mu$. If we were to select some values $b_0$ and $b_1$ to be our estimates of the parameters $\beta_0$ and $\beta_1$, then these values would define an estimated line $b_0 + b_1 X$. Using these estimated parameters (also called estimated coefficients), we could then compute an expected or predicted value of $Y$ for each $X$. This computed value of $Y$ is

$$\hat{Y} = b_0 + b_1 X \tag{3-16}$$

which is the estimated form of equation (3-15).

It is important to understand the difference between the actual but usually unobserved line defined by $E(Y) = \beta_0 + \beta_1 X$ and the estimated line defined by $\hat{Y} = b_0 + b_1 X$. The difference is simply that the former is the line or average relationship that we seek to estimate, and the latter is a line that we use to estimate $E(Y)$. As we choose different values of $b_0$ and $b_1$, we have different estimating lines.

The method of least squares proceeds to estimate $b_0$ and $b_1$ such that the sum of the squared differences of the actual $Y$s from the estimated line is a minimum. That is, since any $b_0$ and $b_1$ will define a line $\hat{Y}$, we define the difference of actual $Y$ values from the $\hat{Y}$ line by $e = Y - \hat{Y}$. The goal of least squares is to choose $b_0$ and $b_1$ so that the sum of the squared errors $\Sigma e^2$ is a minimum, where the summation extends over the sample size $n$.

The calculation of the estimated coefficients $b_0$ and $b_1$ is a fairly easy and well-known process. If the sum of squared errors [(which may be expressed for $n$ observations on $X$ and $Y$ as $\Sigma(Y - b_0 - b_1X)^2$] is differentiated with respect to $b_0$ and $b_1$ and set equal to zero, two equations that describe $b_0$ and $b_1$ in terms of the observed values of $Y$ and $X$ result. Either a hand calculator or a digital computer can easily solve these two equations to obtain $b_0$ and $b_1$.[3] Equation (3-17) shows the estimated values of $b_0$ and $b_1$ that result from the use of that data in Table 3-1.

$$\hat{Y} = 3.1343 + .4957X \tag{3-17}$$

As can be seen from equation (3-17), $b_0 = 3.1343$ and $b_1 = .4957$. The least-squares estimates have managed to come fairly close to the true values $\beta_0 = 3$ and $\beta_1 = .5$.

### Test Statistics

Having observed that the least-squares line comes close to the true line, we now wish to investigate in some detail what we mean by "close." In the process of discussing how close the least-squares line is to the true line, we will be able to devise means for testing whether the observed relationship is due to some systematic factors. Also, the reason for distinguishing among the three separate equations (3-14), (3-15), and (3-16) should become clear.

In the discussion above we began from a hypothesized true relationship line that was assumed to be of the form $E(Y) = \beta_0 + \beta_1X$. Then, for some values of $X$, the actual values of $Y$ that we observed were generated by the process of adding a random error term $\mu$ to this equation so that $Y = \beta_0 + \beta_1X + \mu$. Obviously, the value of $Y$ will be influenced by the random error $\mu$. The distribution of $\mu$ will thus clearly play a crucial role in influencing the values of $b_0$ and

---

[3] Let $S$ represent the sum of squared errors. Then

$$\frac{\partial S}{\partial b_0} = 2\Sigma(Y - b_0 - b_1X)(-1) = 0$$

$$\frac{\partial S}{\partial b_1} = 2\Sigma(Y - b_0 - b_1X)(-X) = 0$$

After simplifying and rearranging, we get

$$(n)b_0 + (\Sigma X)b_1 = \Sigma Y$$
$$(\Sigma X)b_0 + (\Sigma X^2)b_1 = \Sigma XY$$

For the data in Table 3-1, the equations become

$$15b_0 + 120b_1 = 106.5$$
$$120b_0 + 1,240b_1 = 990.7$$

which yield the solution values for $b_0$ and $b_1$ given in equation (3-17).

$b_1$, since they were computed from observed $X$ and $Y$ values, and the latter values depend on $\mu$.

In order to make statements about the way the least-squares estimators $b_0$ and $b_1$ behave, it is necessary to know something about the distribution of $\mu$ or be willing to make some assumptions about the behavior of $\mu$. In practice one almost never has any reliable knowledge about the behavior of $\mu$, and so the practical solution is to make some reasonable assumptions. As will be seen later, the assumptions that are commonly made can frequently be tested to make sure that a model is not constructed on the basis of completely unrealistic assumptions about the error term.

In Figure 3-2 we presented a scatter of points that resulted from adding random error terms $\mu$ to the line $E(Y) = 3 + .5X$. The particular values of the random error terms were obtained by generating values with these properties:

**1** $E(\mu) = 0$. On average, the value of the error term is zero. Since each $Y$ value consists of $E(Y) + \mu$, this implies that the values of $Y$ center on the line given by $E(Y)$.

**2** $V(\mu) = \sigma^2$. All the different error terms have the same variance $\sigma^2$. In the example problem, a variance of 2.25 was used. This implies that the standard deviation of $\mu$ was the square root of 2.25, or 1.5.

**3** The error terms are independent of one another; that is, there is no correlation between the generated value of $\mu_1$ and $\mu_2$ or between any other pair of error terms. Each realized value of this random error is independent of the other values.

**4** The error terms follow a normal distribution. The distribution of $\mu$ is the familiar bell-shaped curve known as the normal curve.

**5** The error terms are statistically independent of the values of $X$; that is, the values of $\mu$ are completely unrelated to the values of $X$.

Although these are not the only assumptions that can be made (later in this chapter we shall deal with other assumptions that might be made), they are indeed quite simple. They are also very important assumptions for the following reason. Economists and statisticians have shown that if these assumptions hold regarding the true but usually unknown error $\mu$, then application of the least-squares method to the observed values of $Y$ and $X$ yields estimators of $\beta_0$ and $\beta_1$ that have very desirable statistical properties. In particular, the least-squares estimators $b_0$ and $b_1$ of the true parameters $\beta_0$ and $\beta_1$ can be shown to be unbiased and minimum-variance estimators. The fact that the estimators are unbiased guarantees that the values of $b$ are distributed evenly around the corresponding parameter $\beta$, or that $E(b_0) = \beta_0$ and $E(b_1) = \beta_1$. The minimum-variance property says simply that the spread of the distribution of $b$ is minimal for the class of all unbiased estimators.

*t* **Statistic** We are now in a position to consider the typical problem of an economist who tries to measure the relationship between $Y$ and $X$ from observed data and determine whether in fact there is any systematic relationship.

If the assumptions given above are met, statisticians have shown that a relationship between $Y$ and $X$ can be tested statistically, based on the use of a $t$ distribution. The test is based on the fact that $(b_0 - \beta_0)/s_{b_0}$ and $(b_1 - \beta_1)/s_{b_1}$ both follow the $t$ distribution, where $s_{b_0}$ and $s_{b_1}$ are the estimated standard errors of the least-squares coefficients. These standard errors are included in most standard computer program outputs for least squares. Table 3-2 contains a complete set of statistical data for the least-squares estimates for equation (3-17). Each of the terms in this table will be defined. It should be noted that the standard errors appear immediately to the right of the estimated coefficients.

The procedure for carrying out the $t$ test is as follows. An economist begins by formulating a null hypothesis. Since the case of no relationship between $Y$ and $X$ is captured by the case of $\beta_1 = 0$, this is very often the null hypothesis. A simple alternative hypothesis would be that $\beta_1 \neq 0$. Next, the economist must choose some probability level that will guide him or her in the selection of the null hypothesis or the alternative hypothesis; that is, based on the hypothesis that $\beta_1 = 0$, an economist can compute a $t$ statistic and from Table 1 (at end of book) can determine how likely it is to have observed the least-squares results obtained if in fact the true state of nature was $\beta_1 = 0$. If this likelihood is too small, the hypothesis that $\beta_1 = 0$ can be discarded in favor of the alternative hypothesis that $\beta_1 \neq 0$. Since this is the same as concluding that there is some systematic relationship between $Y$ and $X$, this procedure provides the economist with a method for systematically testing for a relationship between variables.

We now illustrate this procedure for the sample data shown in Table 3-1. Note that in this case we are dealing with a problem in which we know there is a relationship between $Y$ and $X$ because the values of $Y$ were generated by adding a random error to a linear function of the values of $X$. However, our example provides a convenient illustration, since we are in the fortunate position of omniscience here. We constructed data for which we know there is a relationship, and we wish to apply the methodology as if we were ignorant of the relationship to see whether we would in fact have discovered the relationship on the basis of the methodology alone rather than on the omniscience.

**TABLE 3-2**
ORDINARY LEAST-SQUARES ESTIMATES FOR $\hat{Y} = b_0 + b_1X$

| | $\hat{Y} = 3.1343 + .4957X$ | | |
|---|---|---|---|
| **Independent variables** | **Coefficient estimates** | **Standard errors** | **$t$ statistics** |
| Constant | 3.1343 | .7223 | 4.34 |
| $X$ | .4957 | .0794 | 6.24 |

$R^2 = .7497$                                 $F = 38.9325$
Std. error $= .7304$
Sum of squared errors $= 22.9748$

From Table 3-2, we see that the least-squares estimate of $b_1$ is .4957 with a standard error estimated to be .0794. For the null hypothesis that $\beta_1 = 0$, we can compute the following $t$ value:

$$t = \frac{.4957 - 0}{.0794} = 6.24 \tag{3-18}$$

Obviously, the $t$ value for testing that a coefficient is equal to zero is simply the ratio of the estimated coefficient to its estimated standard error. In Table 3-2 the $t$ values are displayed next to the estimated coefficients and the estimated standard errors. Thus, to test whether a coefficient is statistically different from zero, an economist need only consult the printout. As will be seen later, however, there are often circumstances in which the formula given above is useful. Such circumstances involve tests of hypotheses other than $\beta_1 = 0$.

To complete the test, an economist need only select a desired probability or test level and compare the computed $t$ value with the appropriate table value. This is most easily illustrated by the graph shown in Figure 3-3. The graph shows values of the $t$ distribution, a symmetric distribution that is centered on zero and has the property that the area under the curve is equal to 1. As indicated on the graph, only 5 percent of the area under the curve lies outside the limits indicated by $t = 2.160$ and $t = -2.160$. This area (shaded on the graph) is the area where a $t$ value will fall only 5 percent of the time. The values $\pm 2.160$ were obtained from Table 1. To find the appropriate value, one need know only the level of the test (5 percent here) and the degrees of freedom. The degrees of freedom are 13 in our example. The degrees of freedom can be found simply by subtracting from the sample size the number of coefficients estimated. Since the present sample size is 15, and two coefficients are estimated (a slope and an intercept), df $= 15 - 2 = 13$.

Since the computed $t$ value of 6.24 falls outside the region between $\pm 2.160$, we realize that there is less than a 5 percent chance of finding this computed $t$ value if in fact the hypothesis $\beta_1 = 0$ is correct. Thus, we would reject the hypothesis that $\beta_1 = 0$ on the basis of the sample evidence and instead accept

**FIGURE 3-3**
Performing a $t$ test on $\beta_1 = 0$, a 5 percent test with 13 degrees of freedom (df).

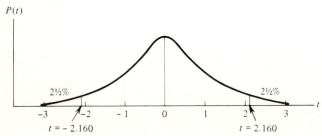

the alternative hypothesis that $\beta_1 \neq 0$. In so doing, we are concluding that there is statistical evidence of a relationship between the observed values of $Y$ and $X$.

How would the results have been interpreted if the computer $t$ value had fallen between the values $t = -2.160$ and $t = 2.160$? Would this have been evidence that there was not a relationship between $X$ and $Y$? The answer is no; this would not be a correct interpretation of the results. A $t$ value within the interval $\pm 2.160$ would mean that we could not reject $\beta_1 = 0$, but this is not the same thing as proving that $\beta_1$ is in fact zero. It would simply mean that for the data at hand, this hypothesis could not be rejected. Saying that something cannot be ruled out is not, however, the same thing as saying that it is demonstrated to be true. We shall return to this point when we discuss a least-squares model with several variables on the right-hand side.

Thus far we have assumed that we have no particular knowledge about the relationship of $Y$ and $X$ and that we merely want to test the null hypothesis of $\beta_1 = 0$ against an alternative hypothesis that $\beta_1 \neq 0$. This is called a two-tail test because, as the graph in Figure 3-3 illustrates, the rejection region includes areas in both the positive and negative extremes of the distribution. It will often be the case that we have enough a priori knowledge to frame a null hypothesis as $\beta_1 = 0$ and the alternative hypothesis as $\beta_1 > 0$; that is, we can effectively rule out a negative relationship based on theoretical considerations and test between the null hypothesis of no relationship and an alternative hypothesis of a positive relationship. It is intuitively reasonable that if one has this type of a priori knowledge about the possible sign of the relationship, it ought to require less evidence from the sample to establish that a relationship exists. This is indeed the case.

**R-Square**    A statistic that is often useful in interpreting a regression equation is the $R$-square ($R^2$) value. The $R^2$ is a number between 0 and 1 that measures the strength of the association between $Y$ and $X$. If all the $Y$ values lie exactly on the estimated line $\hat{Y} = b_0 + b_1 X$, then $R^2 = 1.0$; if all the $Y$ values are completely randomly scattered around the estimated line, then $R^2 = 0$.

The $R^2$ value can also be interpreted in several other ways that are often useful. One interpretation is that $R^2$ is the square of the simple correlation coefficient between $Y$ and $X$. The simple correlation coefficient is defined by the equation

$$r = \frac{\Sigma(Y - \bar{Y})(X - \bar{X})}{\sqrt{\Sigma(Y - \bar{Y})^2 \Sigma(X - \bar{X})^2}} \tag{3-19}$$

and has a value that varies between $-1$ and $+1$. Negative values indicate an inverse relationship between $X$ and $Y$, while positive values indicate a positive association. Values at the extremes of $-1$ and $+1$ occur only in the event of perfect inverse linear association and perfect positive linear association. In the event of no linear relationship between the $X$ and $Y$ values, the value $r$ is 0, as is the case with $R^2$.

In the regression example of Table 3-2, the $R^2$ was shown to be .7497. The square root of this value is .8658, which is the value that one obtains from equation (3-19).

In the simple regression model with $Y$ and $X$, there is a possible ambiguity as to the sign of $r$ if it is computed by taking the square root of $R^2$. The solution is very simply that $r$ will have the same sign as the slope coefficient $b_1$.

$R^2$ is often interpreted as a percentage; that is, the value of $R^2$ for the example of .7497 could be regarded as 74.97 percent.

$$R^2 = \frac{\Sigma(\hat{Y} - \bar{Y})^2}{\Sigma(Y - \bar{Y})^2} = \frac{\text{explained variation in } Y}{\text{total variation in } Y} \tag{3-20}$$

where the explained variation is the variation or movement in $Y$ that is explained by the right-hand-side variable $X$. The movement is said to be explained in the sense that $\hat{Y}$ differs from $Y$ because of the tendency of $\hat{Y}$ to rise or fall with different levels of $X$.

### Multiple Regression

Up to this point we have been discussing how to estimate models with a single right-hand-side variable. We now wish to broaden our investigation and look at the estimation of models with several right-hand-side variables. Fortunately, almost all the concepts presented thus far can be extended easily to the more general model with multiple right-hand-side variables.

In multiple regression we hypothesize a model of the form $Y = \beta_0 + \beta_1 X_1 + \beta_2 X_2 + \mu$ which is assumed to have generated the observed values of $Y$ in terms of several different right-hand-side $X$s. The method can accommodate any number of $X$s, but it will often be convenient to deal with two $X$s. If the equation $Y = \beta_0 + \beta_1 X_1 + \beta_2 X_2 + \mu$ is the model that generates the observed $Y$ values, it is analogous to the simple model for a single $X$ and a single $Y$ that was illustrated in Figure 3-2. In that diagram we noted that the regression line was the average or expected value of $Y$, $E(Y) = \beta_0 + \beta_1 X$, and the actual $Y$ values came from adding a random error term $\mu$ to this line to give the observed scatter of points shown in Figure 3-2. In the case of multiple regression, we have much the same situation, except that now the average or expected value of $Y$ is no longer a line but a plane. This plane is given by the equation $E(Y) = \beta_0 + \beta_1 X_1 + \beta_2 X_2$, and the observed values of $Y$ are assumed to differ from this plane by the additive error term $\mu$.

One of the most important points about multiple regression and one of the reasons for its popularity concerns the interpretation that is assigned to the values $\beta_1$ and $\beta_2$. These parameters obviously relate $E(Y)$ to $X_1$ and $X_2$. If we now ask the question, "What is the change in the average value of $Y$ if $X_1$ changes, given that the effects of $X_2$ are held constant?" the answer is the value of $\beta_1$. In the language of calculus, $\beta_1$ is the partial derivative of $E(Y)$ with respect to $X_1$. Similarly, $\beta_2$ shows the change that occurs in $E(Y)$ resulting from a small change in $X_2$, given that the effects of $X_1$ are held constant. This interpretation of the regression coefficients in multiple regression is one reason why the coefficients are sometimes referred to as partial regression coefficients.

It is important to stress that this concept of "holding constant" other variables is one of the crucial differences between multiple regression and the simple two-variable regression discussed earlier. If one wishes to measure the effect of $X_1$ on $Y$ while holding constant for $X_2$, the proper way to proceed is not to regress $Y$ on $X_1$ and simply ignore $X_2$. Rather, the correct procedure is to estimate the parameters of $Y = \beta_0 + \beta_1 X_1 + \beta_2 X_2 + \mu$ and then use the estimated value of $\beta_1$ to measure the effect of $X_1$ with $X_2$ held constant. To simply estimate $Y$ as a function of $X_1$ will generally yield incorrect estimates of the partial effects of $X_1$, since the estimated value of $\beta_1$ will reflect not only the influence of $X_1$ but also some of the influence of $X_2$ which could not be apportioned to $X_2$ since that variable was omitted from the estimated equation.

In order to obtain estimators of the $\beta$s in the multiple regression model, the procedure is identical to that in the simple model with an $X$ and a $Y$. The idea is to estimate the regression plane $E(Y) = \beta_0 + \beta_1 X_1 + \beta_2 X_2$ by $Y = b_0 + b_1 X_1 + b_2 X_2$ where the $b$s are chosen so that the sum of squared errors $\Sigma e^2$ (where $e = Y - b_0 - b_1 X_1 - b_2 X_2$ and there are as many $e$s as there are observations on the $Y$, $X_1$, and $X_2$ variables) is minimal. The exact calculations involved in obtaining the $b$s from the observed data are handled easily by the computer.

When we introduced the simple bivariate regression model, we did so by putting ourselves in the position of assuming that we knew the values of $\beta_0$ and $\beta_1$ and then generating $Y$ values by adding random error terms $\mu$ to a set of $X$s. Then we argued that if certain basic assumptions held concerning the error term $\mu$, the least-squares estimators $b_0$ and $b_1$ would possess desirable statistical properties. We then illustrated how the least-squares estimate did in fact come very close to reproducing the original values of $\beta_0$ and $\beta_1$ with which we started.

We could illustrate multiple regression in the same way, but instead we choose to start from the position of a given set of data for which we wish to estimate the $\beta$s. This will nearly always be the typical situation that the real world presents, since if the $\beta$s were known, we would never bother to estimate them in the first place. Just as the least-squares estimators have certain desirable properties in the case of simple regression, it can also be shown that they have the same properties in the case of multiple regression, provided that the same five assumptions about the error term $\mu$ continue to hold. In brief, these assumptions are that (1) the error terms have a mean of zero, (2) the error terms have the same variance, (3) different error terms are statistically independent, (4) the error terms are normally distributed, and (5) the right-hand-side variables are statistically independent of the error terms. Later in this chapter, we shall discuss some corrective procedures that can be applied if evidence indicates that these assumptions do not hold for a given set of data. We shall also discuss how one can check the validity of these assumptions.

**TABLE 3-3**
AN AUTOMOBILE DEMAND EQUATION

| $\hat{Q} = -.725 - .0488P + .0255I$ | | | |
|---|---|---|---|
| Independent variables | Coefficient estimates | Standard errors | *t* statistics |
| Constant | −.7247 | .7148 | − 1.01 |
| Price (*P*) | −.0488 | .0042 | −11.62 |
| Income (*I*) | .0255 | .0017 | 14.59 |

$R^2 = .8952$             $F = 106.7306$
Std. error = .6176
Sum of squared errors = 9.5352

**An Automobile Demand Model**   To illustrate the use of multiple regression, we present a simple model of the demand for automobiles. Conventional demand theory asserts that price and quantity will vary inversely if the effects of income (and possibly other prices) are held constant. In a classic study,[4] Gregory Chow gathered annual observations on price, quantity, and income to estimate a demand equation for automobiles in the United States. For price he used an average price of new cars, for quantity he utilized the stock of cars per capita (with old cars converted into an equivalent number of new cars units), and for income he employed a measure of permanent income. When Chow's demand equation was estimated with ordinary least squares, the results which appear in Table 3-3 were obtained. Abbreviating quantity, price, and income by their first letters, the estimated equation is

$$Q = -.725 - .0488P + .0255I \qquad (3\text{-}21)$$

Thus, the quantity demanded is seen to be a positive function of income $I$ and a negative function of price $P$, exactly as traditional demand theory would predict. Furthermore, this equation permits us to derive different predictions of $Q$ for various combinations of price and income that we might think would occur in the future.

When we discussed the simple regression model, the $t$ test was used to test the hypothesis that an individual slope coefficient was zero against the alternative hypothesis that the true value of the slope coefficient was not zero. The $t$ values shown in the last column of Table 3-3 can be used in exactly the same way in this equation. For a 1 percent one-tail $t$ test with 25 degrees of freedom, the appropriate $t$ value is 2.485. A one-tail test is logical since we would expect price to have either no effect or a negative effect, and we would expect income to have either no effect or a positive effect.

[4] Gregory Chow, *The Demand for Automobiles in the United States* (Amsterdam: North-Holland, 1957).

Since the $t$ value for income of 14.59 easily exceeds the table $t$ value of 2.485, we would reject the hypothesis that income has no effect and conclude that it is positively related to quantity. Similarly, since the $t$ value of $-11.62$ for price is far below the value of $-2.485$ that leaves 1 percent in the lower tail, we would reject the idea that price has no effect and accept the fact that it is negatively related to quantity. Thus, even though we do not know the true values of $\beta$s and must estimate them by least squares, our statistical estimates show us that if the correct theoretical specification is that quantity depends on price and income, then we can be very confident that the true values of the slope coefficients for price and income are not zero.

**$F$ Statistic**   The $R^2$ for the demand equation estimated by multiple regression can be interpreted in almost exactly the same way as the $R^2$ for the earlier equation that was estimated by simple regression. The value of .895 indicates that approximately 90 percent of the variation in the dependent variable is explained by the right-hand-side variables.

In judging the $R^2$ for a multiple regression, we now face a slightly different situation. In regression it is possible to test statistically whether the $R^2$ is different from zero. This amounts to a test of whether there is any explanatory power in the right-hand-side variables in the model. In the case of the simple model discussed earlier, it can be shown that the test of $R^2 = 0$ versus $R^2 > 0$ is identical to a two-tail test on the slope coefficient. Since we saw that a test on the slope coefficient could be carried out using the $t$ test, it follows that in the simple model a two-tail test on the slope coefficient is identical with a test on whether $R^2 = 0$. Asking whether there is any explanatory power in the model is identical with testing whether the slope coefficient differs from zero by means of a two-tail test.

In the case of multiple regression where there are several right-hand-side variables, clearly a test on $R^2 = 0$ cannot be equated with a $t$ test on a single coefficient for the simple reason that with several variables, one would not know which coefficient to look at. Would $R^2$ be insignificant if all the $t$ tests were insignificant? Would $R^2$ be significant if all the $t$ tests were significant?

It turns out that neither of these propositions is correct, but there is a simple way to test $R^2 = 0$ against $R^2 > 0$ in the multiple regression model. Such a test does not look at any individual right-hand-side variable but rather looks at all the independent variables together and asks whether they are significant as a group. To implement the test, one utilizes the $F$ distribution and the calculated $F$ value for a regression. In Table 3-3 the calculated $F$ statistic was found to be 106.73.

Unlike the $t$ test, which may be either a one- or a two-tail test, the $F$ distribution always is a one-tail test (the positive tail). Large values of the computed $F$ statistic lead one to reject that $R^2 = 0$ in favor of $R^2 > 0$. Another difference between the $t$ and the $F$ is that the $F$ distribution does not have a single number indicating degrees of freedom but rather two values. In our example illustrated in Table 3-3, the degrees of freedom are 2 and 25. The first number is simply the number of slope coefficients in the model (one for price and one for income), and the second is the sample size $n$ reduced by the total number of coefficients (counting slopes and the constant term). Thus, for the sample size of 28 with two right-hand-side variables plus a constant, the first value of df is 2 and the second value of df is 28 minus 3, or 25. Tables 2 and 3 (at end of book) contain 5 percent and 1 percent $F$ statistics, respectively. For degrees of freedom equal to 2 and 25 and a 1 percent test with 2 and 25 df, the $F$ statistic is 5.57 (Table 3).

Since the computed $F$ value of 106.73 far exceeds the table value, we would clearly reject that $R^2 = 0$ and conclude that in fact the true value is not zero. This is equivalent to concluding that the independent variables taken as a set are significant, although it does not guarantee that any individual variable is significant.

At this point it might be worthwhile to note a similarity between the $t$ statistic and the $F$ statistic. In multiple regression, the two statistics test different things, but in the case of simple regression, the two statistics are in fact almost interchangeable. In the simple case, the two-tail $t$ test will reveal a significant slope coefficient only if $X$ plays some role in explaining $Y$; and if X does explain Y, then we would expect to find a significant $R^2$. In the simple model, one will find that a significant $F$ statistic associated with $R^2$ will coincide exactly with a significant two-tail $t$ value on the slope coefficient. Thus, if one performs a $t$ test on the slope coefficient, it is unnecessary to test the $R^2$ since the results will be identical in the simple model. Hence, it would be unnecessary and useless to employ both the $t$ test and the $F$ test in the simple model, since they test for the same thing. (The only way in which they can differ is if a one-tail $t$ test is employed. Then the $t$ and the $F$ are not strictly related as described above.)

### Econometric Problems

The single-equation regression model described thus far in this chapter is based on a set of very specific assumptions, many of which are not valid in the real world. Attempts to force the single-equation least-squares model into situations in which the assumptions underlying the model do not hold true can lead to a host of econometric problems. We shall briefly summarize five of these problems.:

1 Multicollinearity
2 Autocorrelation
3 Simultaneous equations
4 Identification
5 Biased inconsistent estimates

**Multicollinearity**   One of the problems with econometric modeling is that in economics everything seems to be related to everything else. For example, consider a demand equation in which the right-hand-side variables include advertising expenditures, gross national product, and personal consumption expenditures for the economy as a whole. There is a very good chance that each of the three right-hand-side variables will be correlated with each of the other two. The problem of multicollinearity refers to the situation in which two or more of the right-hand-side variables in a regression model are highly correlated.

When multicollinearity is present in an econometric model, we may encounter great difficulty attempting to determine the contribution of the correlated independent variables to the variance of the dependent variable. In part, the problem of multicollinearity is one of attempting to extract too much information from limited data—more information than the single-equation regression model is capable of providing.

**Autocorrelation** One of the most prevalent econometric problems with time series data is the problem of autocorrelation, which involves the violation of the assumption that the error terms $\mu$ are independently distributed. Instead of being uncorrelated, values in different time periods are correlated. (The problem can occur with cross-sectional data, but it is far more often a problem with time series data.) Hence, if the value of $\mu_t$ is correlated with the value of $\mu_{t-1}$, the error terms are said to be autocorrelated. The problem with applying least squares to a set of data with autocorrelated errors is that we may tend to underestimate the standard errors of the individual coefficients, which may be unduly large. This may cause us to make incorrect inferences about the statistical significance of the right-hand-side variables taken either individually or as a whole. In short, we will have little or no confidence in the validity of either $t$ tests or $F$ tests when autocorrelation is present in the error terms.

A variety of empirical tests have been developed for objectively measuring the degree of autocorrelation in an econometric model; of these tests, the Durbin-Watson test[5] is probably the best known. Likewise, numerous techniques have been proposed for circumventing this problem. One of the easiest remedies to implement involves using the differences of historical observations over time rather than the actual observed values.

**Simultaneous Equations** In the discussion so far we have dealt with different types of models of the general form $Y = f(X_1, X_2)$, where there was a clear idea that the variables on the right influenced the variable on the left. We have not, however, dealt with the problem of two-way causation. The problem of simultaneous equations occurs when we have models of the form

$$Y_1 = f(Y_2, X_2) \tag{3-22}$$
$$Y_2 = f(Y_1, X_1)$$

---

[5] See J. Durbin and G. S. Watson, "Testing for Serial Correlation in Least Squares Regression," II *Biometrika* 38 (June 1951), pp. 159–178.

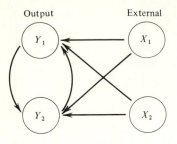

Output        External

**FIGURE 3-4**
Causal diagram for $Y_1 = f(Y_2, C_2)$ and $Y_2 = f(Y_1, X_1)$.

That is, in one equation $Y_1$ is a dependent variable, but in another equation $Y_1$ functions as an independent variable. The variable $Y_2$ functions in exactly the same way.

The variables $Y_1$ and $Y_2$ are output variables and can be solved simultaneously for their respective values. [This is a simple generalization of the idea that a model of the form $Y = f(X_1, X_2)$ can be used to forecast values of $Y$.] Output variables are simply identified by the fact that they (1) always appear on the left-hand side of at least one equation and (2) may appear on the right-hand side of one or more equations. External variables may also appear in simultaneous-equation models, and they are identified by the fact that they appear only on the right-hand side of equations. In equation (3-22), $X_1$ and $X_2$ were illustrative of external variables.

Figure 3-4 illustrates via a simple causal diagram the type of system interaction that is captured by the two-equation model $Y_1 = f(Y_2, X_2)$ and $Y_2 = f(Y_1, X_1)$. One important point to note from this diagram is that even though $X_2$ appears only on the right-hand side of the equation for $Y_1$, it affects both $Y_1$ and $Y_2$. The same argument applies to $X_1$. The reason that $X_2$ affects $Y_1$ and $Y_2$ is simply that $Y_1$ and $Y_2$ are simultaneously determined; even though $X_2$ appears to influence only $Y_1$, because $Y_1$ acts upon $Y_2$, so too does $X_2$ ultimately. This is the reason for the intersecting arrows going from $X_1$ to $Y_2$ and from $X_2$ to $Y_1$ in Figure 3-4.

As an example of a simultaneous-equation econometric model, consider the following three-equation model that has been estimated for Delta Air Lines from data over the period 1951–1971.[6]

$$\text{ALS} = -946.58 - \frac{468.32\text{CPIT}}{P} + 9.56C \tag{3-23}$$

$$\text{DLS} = -25.77 + .02\text{ALS} - .25\text{DLS}_{t-1} + 10.63\text{MKT} \tag{3-24}$$

$$\text{MKT} = .65 + 1.05\text{MKT}_{t-1} + .11\text{DY}_{t-1} \tag{3-25}$$

where ALS = airline industry sales
        $C$ = consumption of goods and services for the economy

[6] John M. McCann and David J. Reibstein, "Incorporating Marketing into Corporate Planning Models," Report No. 78-111, Marketing Science Institute, Cambridge, Mass, August 1978.

MKT = Delta marketing expenditures
DLS = Delta sales
DY = Delta net income
P = price deflator
CPIT = consumer price index for transportation

The interpretation of equation (3-23) is that airline industry sales (ALS) are inversely related to the relative price of transportation (CPIT/$P$) and positively related to aggregate consumption for the economy as a whole. From equation (3-24) we see that Delta Air Lines sales in the current year (DLS) are positively correlated with airline industry sales (ALS), negatively correlated with Delta sales in the previous year ($\text{DLS}_{t-1}$), and positively correlated with Delta's marketing expenditures (MKT). Finally, equation (3-25) shows that Delta's marketing expenditures in the current year (MKT) are positively related to its marketing expenditures in the previous year ($\text{MKT}_{t-1}$) and its net income in the previous year ($\text{DY}_{t-1}$).

Simultaneity can give rise to a number of different econometric problems including identification, simultaneous-equation bias, and the solution of systems of simultaneous linear or nonlinear equations.

**Identification**    In the foregoing discussion of two simultaneous equations, the reader may have wondered why we included $X_1$ and $X_2$ at all. Wouldn't it have been simpler to talk of the two simultaneous equations $Y_1 = f(Y_2)$ and $Y_2 = f(Y_1)$? It would indeed have been simpler in the sense of having fewer variables, but we would have run into a problem known as the identification problem. Briefly, the identification problem arises in a model where "everything depends on everything else." In such a model it is impossible to identify or isolate separate causal equations. The problem is basically a difficult mathematical problem, but it can be given a graphical treatment for a simple case.

To make our model realistic, consider the case where $Y_1$ and $Y_2$ represent price $P$ and quantity $Q$ in an economic model. Economic theory asserts that $P$ and $Q$ are simultaneously determined at the intersection of the supply curve and the demand curve, which provide the two equations of our model. Thus, two intersecting equations can in theory be used to solve for values of the two output variables of the model.

Consider now the problem of economists who gather data on $P$ and $Q$ and find that their data give them the scatter of points shown in Figure 3-5. From this collection of points, how can one proceed to estimate the demand equation and the supply equation; that is, how can one estimate $Y_1 = f(Y_2)$ and $Y_2 = f(Y_1)$? If we perform a least-squares regression, how do we know which is the demand equation and which is the supply equation? Or is either the correct equation? We have a problem in being able to logically identify or spot the two equations, and this problem precedes and makes impossible any meaningful estimation of the two equations. The situation in which everything depends on everything else leaves us stuck.

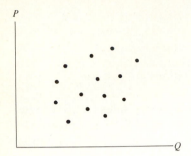

**FIGURE 3-5**
A collection of values for price ($P$) and quantity ($Q$): An identification problem.

Consider, however, a slight modification of the problem. Although demand theory asserts that the quantity demanded depends on price, that is not usually the only determinant of quantity. As was seen in the example in Table 3-3, a demand equation typically includes income on the right-hand side; that is, the demand equation is of the form $Y_1 = f(Y_2, X_2)$ in which quantity demanded $Y_1$ depends on price $Y_2$ and income $X_2$. We denote income by the variable $X_2$ to indicate that income is external and does not itself appear on the left-hand side of any equation. This is logical, for while income may influence quantity demanded, it is not reasonable that quantity demanded would influence income.

If we then consider the two equations $Y_1 = f(Y_2, X_2)$ (the demand curve) and $Y_2 = f(Y_1)$ (the supply curve), we could envision a situation such as that depicted in Figure 3-6. There we illustrate the supply curve along with several different demand curves, with the different demand curves resulting from different levels of income $X_2$. It will be noted that the intersection of the different demand curves with the single supply curve causes the supply curve to be traced out or identified by the intersection of the two curves.

If the state of nature is such that $Y_1 = f(Y_2, X_2)$ and $Y_2 = f(Y_1)$ and we observe the three dotted points in Figure 3-6, our knowledge about the variables in the model (the presence of income in the demand equation) lets us be sure that the three points in fact lie along a supply curve. The presence of the exter-

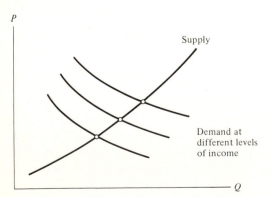

**FIGURE 3-6**
A supply and demand curve: Identifying the supply curve.

Supply

Demand at different levels of income

nal variable income $X_2$ in the demand equation has enabled us to identify the supply equation. How is this? The key lies not so much in the presence of $X_2$ in the demand equation as in its absence from the supply equation. The fact that $X_2$ did not occur in the supply equation means that the supply curve will not move in response to changes in $X_2$, while the demand curve will shift. And this shifting of the demand curve while supply holds still causes the demand curve to "cut" the supply curve at different points and thus identify the supply curve for us.

The fact that the absence of an external variable from the supply equation enabled us to identify it is an example of a proposition known as the order condition for identification. The name "order" is derived from the size or order of a certain matrix expression, but the basic idea of the order condition is easily grasped. To be able to identify and estimate an equation in a system of simultaneous equations, it is necessary that there be an absent external variable for each right-hand-side output variable. Thus, the supply equation which is of the form $Y_2 = f(Y_1)$ has one right-hand-side output variable. The system of which it is a part has one external variable ($X_2$ = income) which is absent from this equation. Thus we can identify and estimate this equation.

One can also apply this rule to the demand equation $Y_1 = f(Y_1, X_2)$. Here there is one right-hand-side output variable ($Y_2$ = price), but the only external variable associated with the system is not absent ($X_2$ = income appears on the right). Thus the demand equation is not identified and cannot be estimated if the system from which it comes is correctly described by the two equations $Y_1 = f(Y_2, X_2)$ and $Y_2 = f(Y_1)$.

Suppose that instead of these two equations, the supply and demand equations were $Y_1 = f(Y_2, X_2)$ and $Y_2 = f(Y_1, X_1)$, where $X_1$ is now some factor that influences the supply equation but does not influence the demand function directly. The variable $X_1$ might represent some cost factor or perhaps the availability of a raw material. In this case, both the supply and demand equations are now identified and can be estimated, since there is one external variable absent from each equation and there is one right-hand-side output variable in each equation.

In the case of the demand equation for automobiles presented earlier, the equation was identified in that the supply of automobiles was reasonably thought to be dependent on a number of external factors that were absent from the demand equation and thus permitted it to be identified.

Fortunately, most computer programs which are used to estimate the parameters for simultaneous-equation models contain a built-in check of the order condition for identification.

**Biased Inconsistent Estimates**   The method of ordinary least squares has good statistical properties in many circumstances, but unfortunately the method of least squares turns out to be particularly inappropriate for estimating an equation that is part of a simultaneous system of equations. The reason for this can be explained as follows. In our discussion of least squares, one of the five basic assumptions made about the behavior of the true regression line $Y = \beta_0 + \beta_1 X + \mu$ was that the right-hand-side variable $X$ and the error term $\mu$ were independent of each other. If one estimates a single equation out of a system of equations, this assumption of independence of the right-hand-side variables and the error term cannot possibly hold. To see why this is so, consider the equations to be estimated as $Y_1 = f(Y_2, X_2) + \mu_1$ and $Y_2 = f(Y_1, X_1) + \mu_2$.

Consider the first equation and note that the model will generate values of $Y_1$ and $Y_2$ given values of $X_1$, $X_2$, $\mu_1$, and $\mu_2$. We see that $\mu_1$ and $X_2$ along with $Y_2$ enter the right part of the first equation to determine $Y_1$. In the second equation we see that $Y_1$ is one of the factors influencing $Y_2$. Herein lies the problem. Since $\mu_1$ is related to $Y_1$ in the first equation, and $Y_1$ is related to $Y_2$ in the second equation, it must also be true that $Y_2$ and $\mu_1$ have some relationship to each other in the first equation. Thus, the assumption that the right-hand-side variables are independent of the error terms cannot possibly hold in a system of simultaneous equations. The very fact of simultaneity causes the output variables (right-hand-side $Y$s) to be correlated to some degree with the error terms in the equations.

If least squares is applied to estimate such equations, it can be shown that the resulting estimators will be biased. They will always be centered on the wrong target, and the direction of the bias will generally not be known. Clearly, application of least-squares estimation to a system of simultaneous equations poses some serious problems.

To get around the problem of bias, economists generally apply a method known as two-stage least squares, often abbreviated TSLS or 2SLS. As the name implies, the estimators turn out to have good statistical properties (better than the application of least squares), although the TSLS estimators do not have the property of being minimum-variance unbiased estimators. The most important property of the TSLS estimator is consistency. Consistency simply means that as we increase the number of observations in our sample, the expected values of the parameter estimates converge on the true expected values of the parameters of the equation. Thus, by increasing our sample size, we improve the quality of our parameter estimates. A detailed treatise on TSLS is beyond the scope of this book. The interested reader should refer to one of the econometrics textbooks listed at the end of the chapter.

## SOLUTION OF ECONOMETRIC MODELS[7]

To validate multiequation econometric models, to use them as forecasting tools, and to do simulation experiments with them requires solving the equations for the output variables over time in terms of given values of the external variables and policy variables as well as lagged values of the output variables generated in previous time periods.

Recursive models are trivial to solve and require no special attention. Simul-

---

[7] See Thomas H. Naylor, *Corporate Planning Models* (Reading, Mass.: Addison-Wesley, 1979), chap. 6.

taneous equation models, on the other hand, do necessitate the use of special computational techniques such as the Gauss-Seidel Method which are capable of solving systems of linear and/or nonlinear equations. Fortunately, most of the computer software packages currently available for doing econometric modeling, such as EPS, FCS, SIMPLAN, and XSIM, all have built-in subroutines which enable the user to automatically solve systems of simultaneous equations with simple one-word commands.

### A Model of the Textile Industry

To illustrate the results of solving a multiequation econometric model, consider the following four-equation model for estimating the demand and supply functions for the apparel and textile industries. The model is a monthly model estimated over the 10-year period 1953–1962.

**Apparel Demand**

$$D_A(t) = -552.71 + 300.81 \left[ \frac{DPI(t-1)}{CPI(t-1)} \right] + 96.94[A_D(t-1)] \quad (3\text{-}26)$$
$$+ 55.19[A_D(t-2)] + 94.38[A_D(t-3)] + 34.83M$$

**Apparel Supply**

$$O_A(t) = -4.38 + .01824[AD_A(t)] - 30.70[INV_A(t-1)] \quad (3\text{-}27)$$

**Textile Demand**

$$D_T(t) = .3029 + .0014[AO_A(t)] + .00064[IP_{DG}(t-1)] + .0083M$$
$$(3\text{-}28)$$

**Textile Supply**

$$O_T(t) = 58.99 + 41.20[D_T(t)] - 14.45 \left[ \frac{INV}{UO}(t-1) \right] \quad (3\text{-}29)$$
$$- .515M + .082t$$

The variables and identities included in the model are defined below.

#### Output Variables

$D_A$ = apparel retail sales in millions of dollars
$O_A$ = index of production of apparel products

$D_T$ = shipments of textile mill products in billions of dollars
$O_T$ = index of production of textile mill products

### External Variables

DPI = disposable personal income in billions of dollars
CPI = consumer price index
$A_D$ = magazine advertising for apparel and accessories in millions of dollars
$INV_A$ = inventories of apparel retail stores in millions of dollars
$IP_{DG}$ = index of production of durable goods
INV/UO = ratio of inventories of unfilled orders for textile mill products

### Status Variables

$M$ = monthly dummy variables, numbered 1 for January, 2 for February, ..., and 12 for December
$t$ = trend variable numbered 1 through 144
$AD_A$ = moving average of $D_A$
$AO_A$ = moving average of $O_A$
$AD_T$ = moving average of $D_T$

### Identities

$$AD_A(t) = \frac{1}{3} \sum_{r=1}^{3} D_A(t-r)$$

$$AO_T(t) = \frac{1}{6} \sum_{r=7}^{12} O_A(t-r)$$

$$AD_T(t) = \frac{1}{12} \sum_{r=1}^{12} D_T(t-r)$$

Our textile model is a recursive model in which apparel demand, equation (3-26), determines apparel supply, equation (3-27). Textile demand, equation (3-28), is determined by apparel supply. Finally, the textile supply function, equation (3-29), is determined by the textile demand function.

If we examine the individual equations in more detail, we see that apparel demand is a function of real disposable personal income lagged one month, a series of lagged moving averages of historical values of apparel demand, and a monthly dummy variable. Apparel supply depends on a moving average of apparel demand and inventories of apparel retail stores lagged one month. Textile demand is a function of a moving average of apparel output, the index of production of durable goods lagged one period, and the monthly dummy variable. Textile supply is a function of textile demand, the ratio of inventories to unfilled orders last month, and time.

Figures 3-7 through 3-10 contain the simulation results for our four-equation textile model. The model has been solved for the four dependent variables in terms of given external variables and values of the lagged output variables generated by the model in previous periods. The graphs compare the simulation results with the actual observed values of the dependent variables over the 10-year period 1953–1962.

## VALIDATION

The validation of econometric models includes three basic steps: rationalism, empiricism, and prediction. We shall summarize each of these steps briefly.

By *rationalism,* we mean that econometric models must be based on sound economic and market theory.

With regard to *empiricism,* we examine such test statistics as $R^2$, $t$ statistics, $F$ statistics, and Durbin-Watson statistics. Ideally, we would like to have econometric estimations characterized by high $R^2$'s (close to 1.00), statistical significance, and signs which make intuitive sense. Rarely are all these criteria satisfied by a single estimating equation. We tend to worry if the sign of a particular equation is contrary to our intuitive understanding of the system. For example, a positively sloped demand function makes us nervous. On the other

**FIGURE 3-7**
Apparel demand.

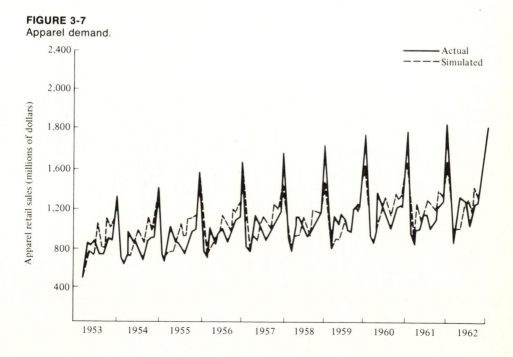

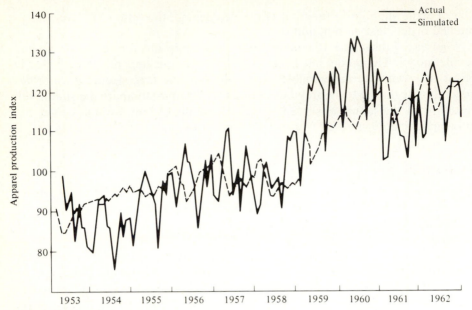

**FIGURE 3-8**
Apparel supply.

**FIGURE 3-9**
Textile demand.

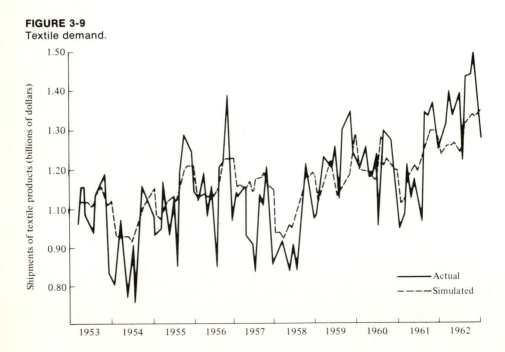

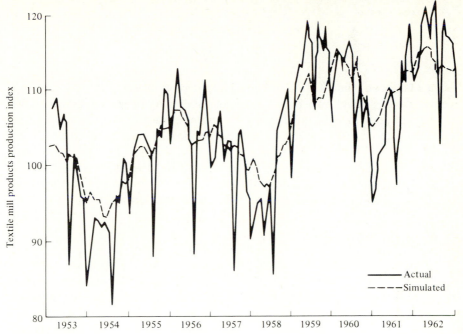

**FIGURE 3-10**
Textile supply.

hand, we may be willing to include the variable in the model if it has the right sign, even though it is barely statistically significant.

In the final analysis, *prediction* is probably the most powerful test of the validity of an econometric model; that is, if we are consistently able to forecast the behavior of sales, revenue, or market share with a high degree of accuracy through the use of a model, then our confidence in the validity of the model increases.

The two most common goodness of fit tests for validating the forecasting performance of econometric models are mean percent absolute errors and Theil's inequality coefficients.

The mean percent error statistic is calculated by the expression

$$\frac{1}{n} \Sigma \left| \frac{P_i - A_i}{A_i} \right|$$

where $P_i$ denotes the predicted value generated by the econometric model and $A_i$ denotes the corresponding actual observed value of the variable.

Theil's inequality coefficient $U$ provides another index which measures the degree to which an econometric model provides retrospective predictions $P_i$ of observed historical data $A_i$:

$$U = \frac{\sqrt{\frac{1}{n} \Sigma (P_i - A_i)^2}}{\sqrt{\frac{1}{n} \Sigma P_i^2} + \sqrt{\frac{1}{n} \Sigma A_i^2}}$$

$U$ varies between 0 and 1. If $U = 0$, we have perfect predictions. If $U = 1$, we have very bad predictions. It is somewhat analogous to a correlation coefficient, except that close fits are denoted by values close to zero. The correlation coefficient is of no use in validation since it would yield the same value for the series $P = 1, 2, 3, A = 10, 20, 30$ and $P = 1, 2, 3, A = 1, 2, 3$. The first values of $P$ and $A$ would represent horrible forecasts, and the latter values would represent perfect forecasts. For both series, $r = 1.0$, but only for the latter series does $U = 0$, indicating that the two series are identical.

## SIMULATION

Once we have come up with a model which has passed the aforementioned validity tests, we must turn our attention to the question of simulation experiments with the model. It should be noted that the procedures of specification, estimation, and validation described above are likely to be repeated many times before we develop an econometric model for which managers are willing to accept the results as a reasonable representation of the actual system. In other words, we are ready to consider policy simulation experiments only if management is willing to place confidence in the results of the policy simulation experiments run with the model. Typically, we will have to alter the specifications of our model, reestimating the parameters; change the computer program; and replicate the validity checks many times before we come up with a model which will be satisfactory to the management.

There are two important aspects of simulations conducted with an econometric model: experimental design and data analysis. The problem of experimental design refers to the selection of the specific values of the policy variables and external variables which are to be manipulated in the simulation experiments with the econometric model. The problem of data analysis refers to analysis and interpretation of the results generated by the simulation experiments. The book by Thomas H. Naylor entitled *Computer Simulation Experiments with Models of Economic Systems* (John Wiley, 1971) treats each of these two problems in considerable depth.

## LINKAGE TO NATIONAL MACROECONOMIC MODELS

### Rationale

Several of the econometric demand models described in this book contain exogenous economic indicators such as gross national product, consumption, investment, employment, etc. Specifically, the textile industry model and the

Delta Air Lines model contain numerous macroeconomic variables as input variables. This raises the obvious question of how one obtains accurate, timely historical data and forecasts for national economic indicators.

A recent survey of corporate users of econometric marketing models indicated that 90 percent of these companies subscribe to an econometric service bureau such as Chase Econometrics, DRI, Merrill Lynch Economics, or Wharton.[8] Each of these service bureaus provides its clients with forecasts for several hundred macroeconomic time series and literally thousands of historical time series.

### An Example Model

To illustrate what an actual macroeconomic econometric model looks like, we have included a simple expository model attributable to Professor Lawrence R. Klein.[9]

Suppose we are interested in testing the effects of one or more governmental fiscal policies on the behavior of the economy of the United States. To be more specific, suppose we are interested in the effects that (1) the governmental wage bill, (2) governmental demand, and (3) business taxes have on (1) consumption, (2) wages, (3) profits, (4) investment, (5) capital stock, and (6) national income. Given the objective mentioned above, it follows that we should formulate an econometric model that relates the six output variables defined above to the three policy variables. This model has two principal attributes. It is a relatively simple model, and it possesses many of the characteristics of more complex econometric models. The model consists of the following policy variables, output variables, and function relationships.

### Policy variables

$W2_t$ = governmental wage bill
$G_t$ = governmental demand
$T_t$ = business taxes

### Output Variables

$C_t$ = consumption
$W1_t$ = private wage bill
$P_t$ = nonwage income (profits)
$I_t$ = net investment
$K_t$ = capital stock at end of period $t$
$X_t$ = national income

[8] Thomas H. Naylor, "Experience with Corporate Econometric Models: A Survey," *Business Economics* (January 1981), pp. 79–83.

[9] This model is based on a model by Lawrence R. Klein as discussed in *Principles of Econometrics* by Henri Theil (New York: John Wiley, 1971).

### Behavioral Equations

Consumption Function:

$$C_t = a_1 + a_2 (W1_t + W2_t) + a_3P_t + a_4P_{t-1}$$

Investment Function:

$$I_t = b_1 + b_2P_t + b_3P_{t-1} + b_4K_{t-1}$$

Demand for Labor Function:

$$W1_t = c_2 + c_2X_t + c_3X_{t-1} + c_4t$$

### Identities

National Income Equation:

$$X_t = C_t + I_t + G_t$$

Profit Equation:

$$P_t = Y_t - W1_t - W2_t$$

Capital Stock Equation:

$$K_t = K_{t-1} + I_t$$

Some of the large-scale national econometric models contain more than 1,500 equations. Figure 3-11 contains a flowchart for the UCLA econometric model, which includes several hundred equations.

### Experience

In the survey of nearly 1,700 corporations conducted by Naylor,[10] 66.5 percent of the respondents indicated that they were using econometric models, 4.9 percent were developing an econometric model, 4.9 percent were planning to develop such a model, and 23.7 percent had no plans to develop a model. The two principal interests of those firms which subscribed to an econometric service bureau (90 percent of the respondents) were access to a national macroeconomic model and access to a historical data base. Easy access to historical data, frequent data base updates, and consistent forecasts were cited as the most important features of these econometric service bureaus. More timely informa-

---

[10] Naylor, op. cit., pp. 79–83.

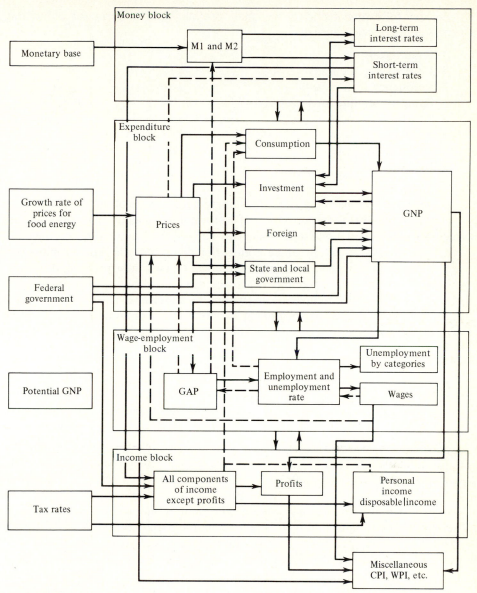

**FIGURE 3-11**
The UCLA econometric model.

tion, the ability to explore alternative economic scenarios, and greater understanding of the national economy were listed among the major benefits of the
service bureaus, according to corporate respondents to the survey. High computing costs and subscription costs as well as inaccurate forecasts were noted
as the principal shortcomings of the bureaus.

In the following sections, we shall outline eight criteria for evaluating econometric service bureaus:

1 Data bases
2 Forecasting accuracy
3 Relevance of forecasts
4 Number of equations
5 Short-term model
6 Long-term model
7 Industry forecasts
8 Industry models

**Data Bases**  Perhaps the single most important service offered by econometric service bureaus is the provision of historical macroeconomic data that are accurate, consistent, up to date, and easily accessible through timesharing computer terminals. Indeed, it can be argued that the prices charged by many service bureaus are justified primarily by the data bases they provide. Trying to keep track of changes in economic data generated by various government agencies is a job that few companies are willing to undertake on their own.

For those who are just beginning to work with econometric models, the NBER (National Bureau of Economic Research) data base may prove to be an attractive alternative. It contains over 5,000 economic time series, is available on numerous computer service bureaus, can be installed on the user's in-house computer, and is moderately priced. Alternatively, one service bureau has over 50,000 series available including state and regional data bases as well as macroeconomic data for Canada, Japan, and most countries of western Europe.

**Forecasting Accuracy**  We have repeatedly emphasized that econometric models should not be justified solely on the basis of forecasting accuracy. National econometric models are not exceptions to this rule. If one is interested in using a national econometric model primarily for forecasting the future, one should proceed with extreme caution. National econometric models forecast well during periods of relatively stable economic behavior, such as the period 1960–1968. They perform very badly during periods of uncertainty of the type experienced between late 1973 and early 1976. It is always interesting to watch econometric service bureau representatives squirm when confronted with the question, "How well did your model forecast the 1979–1980 recession?"

The fact that the forecasting track records of these models leaves something to be desired does not render them useless. They may still prove to be extremely powerful tools for answering "what if?" questions about the national economy.

Since 1973, Stephen K. McNees of the Federal Reserve Bank of Boston has published an annual report comparing the forecasting performance of the major econometric forecasting models in the United States. His reports appear in the

*New England Economic Review.* Although these reports are not easily read by lay people, they contain valuable information about the forecasting performance of the leading national econometric models.

**Relevance of Forecasts**   For many companies, the number of macroeconomic variables required to do successful econometric modeling may be relatively small. Some marketing models necessitate highly disaggregated industry data. The selection of an appropriate economic data base involves matching the user's particular data base requirements with the data bases that are currently available.

**Number of Equations**   The number of equations contained in national econometric models varies from fewer than 100 to nearly 1,500 equations. The real issue is not how many equations are in the model but whether the right series are included in order to meet the user's particular needs.

In general, large econometric models are difficult to manage, hard to understand when something goes wrong, and expensive to run. An obvious question is whether the increased power achieved with a 1,000-equation model is worth the extra computer charges and loss of user orientation caused by the greater complexity of the model. In general, larger models are not necessarily more useful or more accurate models.

**Short-Term Model**   Several of the econometric forecasting services offer two different types of national econometric forecasting models: short-term models and long-term models. Short-term forecasting models are usually quarterly models, the time horizon of which typically extends out for three years. The forecasting accuracy of the short-term models tends to be better than the forecasting accuracy of the long-term models.

Again, it is a matter of finding a short-term forecasting model tailored to meet the needs of a particular econometric modeling application.

**Long-Term Model**   For long-term strategic planning, a different type of national econometric model is required: a long-term econometric model. Long-term models are typically annual models capable of producing forecasts for periods of 10 to 15 years into the future.

For certain industries such as electric utilities, long-term forecasts are absolutely essential, given the long lead times required to develop additional generating capacity. Long-term econometric forecasting is, at best, a very tenuous business. Corporate economists should use long-term econometric models merely as a guide to the future, not as tools for forecasting the future.

**Industry Forecasts**   As part of their econometric services, some bureaus offer their clients forecasts by industry down to the two-digit SIC code level. In some cases, these forecasts are produced by an input-output model driven by the bureau's macroeconometric model. In other cases, individual econometric equations are specified for a limited number of variables for each industry. In general, the forecasting track record of these industry forecasts has not been impressive. This is not surprising, since it is unlikely that a given bureau could possess expertise on all categories of industry.

**Industry Models**   On the other hand, some bureaus have special expertise on a limited number of industries and have applied this expertise to develop highly sophisticated industry models for such industries as steel, agriculture, petrochemicals, and energy. Some of these models represent the state of the art of econometric modeling and may prove to be quite useful to companies in the appropriate industries.

### Other Econometric Models

Obviously, econometric modeling is by no means restricted to demand forecasting. Other corporate applications of econometrics include supply models, pricing models, production cost models, interest-rate forecasting models, and demographic models.

MARKET ANALYSIS QUESTIONNAIRE

1 Product name _____

2 Date _____

3 Name of product manager or analyst _____

_____

4 Number of firms in the market _____

5 Market share _____ %

6 The five largest firms in the market:

| Firm name | Market share |
|---|---|
| a _____ | _____ |
| b _____ | _____ |
| c _____ | _____ |
| d _____ | _____ |
| e _____ | _____ |

7 Description of product

_____

_____

_____

| 8 The major markets in which the product is sold | Percentage |
|---|---|
| a _____ | _____ % |
| b _____ | _____ % |
| c _____ | _____ % |
| d _____ | _____ % |
| e _____ | _____ % |

| 9 The major countries in which the product is sold | Percentage |
|---|---|
| a _____ | _____ % |
| b _____ | _____ % |
| c _____ | _____ % |
| d _____ | _____ % |
| e _____ | _____ % |

10 Six important leading indicators

**Indicator** **Lag**

a _____ _____

b _____ _____

c _____ _____

d _____ _____

e _____ _____

f _____ _____

11 Which of the following best describes the market?

a Perfect competition _____

b Monopoly _____

c Monopolistic competition _____

d Oligopoly _____

12 What is the basis for competition?

a Price _____

b Advertising _____

c Quality _____

d R&D _____

e Service _____

f Promotion _____

13 How does the quantity demanded respond to price changes?

_____

_____

_____

14 Are there a number of major customers? If so, please list them.

a _____

b _____

c _____

d _____

15 Is the demand for the product highly seasonal?

_____

_____

_____

16 Has this product been modeled using econometric or time series methods?

_____

17 List any special promotional programs and their dates. **Date**

a _____ _____

b _____ _____

c _____ _____

d _____ _____

e _____ _____

f _____ _____

g _____ _____

18 Describe the channels of distribution for the product.

_____

_____

_____

19 Are there any apparent nonlinear relationships in the model?

_____

20 What about the quality of the data? How far back do the time series go?

_____

_____

21 Are there any close substitutes for the product?

a _____

b _____

c _____

d _____

22 Are there any other products whose sales are closely related to the sales of this product (complementary goods)?

a _____

b _____

c _____

23 Can you think of any other unique features of the market for this product?

a _____

b _____

c _____

d _____

e _____

24 Are there any other variables which help explain the sales volume of this product?

a _____

b _____

c _____

d _____

25 Do you feel it is necessary to develop a model of the entire market for the product? What characteristics of the market should be modeled?

_____

_____

_____

26 What are the most important determinants of market share?

a _____

b _____

c _____

d _____

e _____

## QUESTIONS AND PROBLEMS

**3-1** Discuss the advantages and disadvantages of three alternative methods of doing empirical demand analysis.

**3-2** Is econometric modeling an art or a science?

**3-3** What is involved in specifying an econometric demand model?

**3-4** List the assumptions underlying the ordinary least-squares model.

**3-5** What constitutes a "good" econometric model?

**3-6** Is it more important for an econometric model to have good statistical properties or for the model to make sense?

**3-7** What are the consequences of the problems of multicollinearity and autocorrelation?

**3-8** How does one go about forecasting demand for a new product which does not currently exist and for which there are no historical data available?

**3-9** Discuss the forecasting limitations of econometric demand models.

**3-10** To what extent is the textile model described in this chapter consistent with the theories of demand presented in Chapter 2?

**3-11** How does one go about validating an econometric model?

**3-12** Discuss some of the possible trade-offs between large-scale national econometric models with over 1,000 equations and smaller models with fewer than 50 equations.

**3-13** Discuss the use of the market analysis questionnaire which appears at the end of the chapter.

## BIBLIOGRAPHY

Chow, Gregory: *The Demand for Automobiles in the United States* (Amsterdam: North-Holland, 1957).

Johnston, J.: *Econometric Methods* (New York: McGraw-Hill, 1972).

Kelejian, Harry H., and Wallace E. Oates.: *Introduction to Econometrics: Principles and Applications* (New York: Harper & Row, 1974).

Murphy, James L.: *Introductory Econometrics* (Homewood, Ill.: Richard D. Irwin, 1973).

Naylor, Thomas H. (ed.): *The Design of Computer Simulation Experiments* (Durham, N.C.: Duke University Press, 1969).

Naylor, Thomas H.: *Computer Simulation Experiments with Models of Economic Systems* (New York: John Wiley, 1971).

Naylor, Thomas H.: *Corporate Planning Models* (Reading, Mass.: Addison-Wesley, 1979).

Pindyck, Robert S., and Daniel L. Rubinfield: *Econometric Models and Economic Forecasts* (New York: McGraw-Hill, 1976).

Wonnacott, Ronald J., and Thomas H. Wonnacott: *Econometrics* (New York: John Wiley, 1970).

# PRODUCTION AND COST

As noted in Chapter 2, the fact that consumers wish to buy a certain quantity of a good at a given price does not guarantee that that quantity will be transacted. We must look at parties on the other side of the transaction and ask what quantities suppliers wish to sell at a given price. The answer depends very much on the suppliers' costs of production. Costs, in turn, depend on input prices, input levels, and the production capabilities of suppliers in converting inputs into outputs. We shall start at the end of this chain and deal with the production capabilities of a business first. Costs of production will be analyzed next. A discussion of the willingness of a business to supply various quantities of goods to buyers is deferred until Chapter 5.

## THE PRODUCTION FUNCTION

To illustrate the properties of the production function, we shall examine extensively a hypothetical business firm called the Bobcat Corporation. While the Bobcat Corporation provides the principal example, we shall refer several times to a more general case: Farmer Brown's production function.

### The Bobcat Corporation

The Bobcat Corporation uses two factors of production, or inputs, in order to make one type of product, or output. The inputs are labor and equipment. Both are flow variables, and both are measured in real units. The amount of labor employed $L$ is measured in worker-hours per time period. For example, if one worker puts in 35 hours per week and a second worker puts in 45 hours per week, then 80 worker-hours per week are employed. The amount of equipment (or capital) employed $K$ is measured in machine-hours per time period. Output is a flow variable that is measured in real units over the same time period as the inputs. Its quantity is denoted by $Q$.

We concede that a model in which there are just two kinds of inputs and one output does not describe the extent of the activities one sees in a business. Bobcat's labor and equipment need other kinds of inputs in order to function: at a minimum, land to rest on, a structure or structures for shelter, raw materials to work with, and energy for power and warmth. Even within the categories labor and equipment there are many different subcategories, each of which is correctly counted as a different factor of production. On the output side, it is evident that a firm typically produces more than one type of product. We start with a simple model because much that is fundamental in production analysis can be addressed adequately in this model and, indeed, can be seen more clearly because the situation has been simplified. However, once these fundamentals have been taken care of, the model is broadened in subsequent chapters to encompass firms that provide more than one product or employ more than two inputs.

The principal activity of the business firm is to transform inputs into salable outputs. The relationship which governs the transformation is called the production function:

$$Q = f(L, K)$$

For any given values of the input pair $(L, K)$, the production function gives the *maximum* amount of output that can be produced by the firm. "Maximum" is emphasized because managers can only lose by producing a lesser quantity. Suppose that the primary goal of managers at Bobcat is to maximize the profit of the enterprise. A level of output and a pricing policy are chosen, thus determining Bobcat's revenue. In order to maximize profit, managers would attempt to have that level of output produced at the least cost, and this means getting the most product it is possible to get out of the inputs that they are paying for.

The concept of a production function thus assumes that production is organized efficiently. The current state of technology in equipment and the skill levels of workers determine the maximal output to be gotten from the inputs employed, and managers should attempt to realize that maximal output. These are the fundamental determinants of the production function. If there should be a technological advance in equipment or an improvement in the skills of workers or managers such that a given number of worker-hours and machine-hours can yield more of the product than they previously could, the production function changes. In those cases, we would rewrite the production function with a different functional symbol, for instance, $Q = h(L, K)$, in order to express the improvements in production conditions. For any particular input pair $(L^0, K^0)$, $h(L^0, K^0) > f(L^0, K^0)$.

Before turning to the specifics of the Bobcat Corporation's production function, we analyze graphically a more general production function. Although this more general production function is characterized by only a single variable input, it illustrates several characteristics not possessed by the Bobcat production function. These properties, however, will be seen later to be relatively unimportant since profit-maximizing firms would avoid such properties (e.g., regions of the production function where increased inputs yield reductions in total output).

### Farmer Brown's Production Function

Consider Farmer Brown's production function for tobacco shown in Figure 4-1. Assume that Farmer Brown has a single acre of land with fixed quantities of labor (his family) and equipment. The one variable input is pounds of fertilizer $F$. Total product TP (or $Q$) is shown in 4-1$a$ as a function of $F$. Observe that TP increases at an increasing rate as fertilizer increases from zero to level $D$. As the amount of fertilizer is increased from $D$ to $G$, tobacco production continues to rise, but at a decreasing rate. Finally, as $F$ is added beyond level $G$, output actually falls.

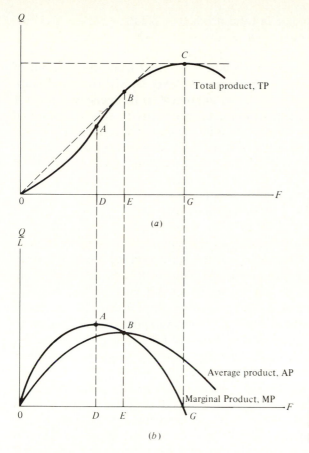

**FIGURE 4-1**
Farmer Brown's total product,
average product, and marginal
product curves.

This characterization of tobacco production seems to hold true for many productive activities. It is an empirical generalization, however, and need not describe all production functions. For example, the Bobcat Corporation's production function, as we shall see shortly, possesses only the curvature shown between points *A* and *C*.

The fact that output eventually begins to rise at a decreasing rate is sensible, however. The effect of more and more fertilizer, with all other inputs fixed, is bound to begin to diminish beyond some level. Tobacco plants can benefit from only so much fertilizer, and beyond some level (point *C*) fertilizer may actually be harmful.

The phenomenon is usually referred to as the law of diminishing marginal returns, and it can be made more precise by reference to Figure 4-1*b*. The two curves shown there are intimately related to the total production curve. The marginal product (MP) curve is the slope of TP. That is,

$$MP = \frac{\text{change in total product}}{\text{change in fertilizer}} = \frac{\Delta TP}{\Delta F}$$

and is defined as the addition to total product resulting from the last unit of input $F$. Notice that as $F$ increases from zero to level $D$, MP rises, but more and more slowly, until it attains a maximum at point $A$. It is precisely at point $A$ (with $F$ at level $D$) that diminishing marginal productivity sets in. Marginal product then declines continuously, eventually becoming negative. That is, for amounts of fertilizer greater than the level $G$, MP becomes negative.

The second curve in Figure 4-1$b$ is the average product (AP) curve. Since

$$AP = \frac{\text{total product}}{\text{fertilizer}} = \frac{TP}{F}$$

the AP curve can be derived geometrically by finding the slope of a ray from the origin to the TP curve. For example, a dashed line from the origin to point $B$ on the TP curve is shown in Figure 4-1$a$. The slope of this dashed line is simply BE (total product) divided by OE (fertilizer), or AP. Average product is at its maximum value here since all other rays to the TP curve have lower slopes. Notice that this particular dashed line also happens to be tangent to the TP curve and therefore has the same slope as TP (which is MP). Hence, AP and MP are equal at this level of fertilizer, as is shown in Figure 4-1$b$ at point $B$.[1]

Before returning to our discussion of the Bobcat Corporation, we should observe that Farmer Brown should use only amounts of fertilizer between levels $E$ and $G$.[2] As will become clear later in this chapter, using less than level $E$ implies that some other input (e.g., land) has a negative marginal product. Of course, using more than level $G$ makes fertilizer's MP negative. Clearly, profit can always be increased by reducing the quantity of an input experiencing negative marginal productivity.

## PROPERTIES OF BOBCAT'S PRODUCTION FUNCTION

Listed in Table 4-1 are several points which satisfy the particular production function of the Bobcat Corporation.[3] Each point consists of an input combina-

---

[1] This point can be made using calculus, noting that $MP = dQ/dF$ and $AP = Q/F$. When AP is at a maximum, its derivative with respect to $F$ equals zero, or

$$\frac{F \cdot MP - Q}{L^2} = 0$$

Hence, $F \cdot MP = Q$, or $MP = Q/F$.

[2] Many textbooks divide the production function into three "stages of production." Stage 1 is the range of $F$ between zero and level $E$ in Figure 4-1, stage 2 is the range between levels $E$ and $G$, and stage 3 is the range above level $G$. Hence, production should take place only in stage 2.

[3] The explicit form of the production function is $Q = 5\sqrt{LK}$.

**TABLE 4-1**
SELECTED POINTS FROM THE PRODUCTION FUNCTION OF BOBCAT
CORPORATION

| | Input levels | | |
|---|---|---|---|
| Point | Worker-hours (L) | Machine-hours (K) | Output level (Q) |
| A | 5 | 80 | 100 |
| B | 6.67 | 60 | 100 |
| C | 10 | 40 | 100 |
| D | 15 | 26.67 | 100 |
| E | 20 | 20 | 100 |
| F | 25 | 16 | 100 |
| G | 25 | 20 | 111.80 |
| H | 10 | 160 | 200 |
| I | 20 | 80 | 200 |
| J | 26.67 | 60 | 200 |
| K | 40 | 40 | 200 |
| L | 50 | 32 | 200 |
| M | 20 | 85 | 206.16 |
| N | 25 | 80 | 223.61 |
| O | 25 | 85 | 230.49 |
| P | 30 | 80 | 244.95 |
| Q | 15 | 240 | 300 |
| R | 30 | 120 | 300 |
| S | 45 | 80 | 300 |
| T | 60 | 60 | 300 |
| U | 75 | 48 | 300 |
| V | 20 | 320 | 400 |
| W | 40 | 160 | 400 |
| X | 60 | 106.67 | 400 |
| Y | 80 | 80 | 400 |
| Z | 106.67 | 60 | 400 |

tion and the maximum output to be gotten from the combination, given the state of technology and the skills of workers and managers. The listing is by no means complete, because for every input combination (including combinations not shown in Table 4-1) the production function gives a maximal value of output. Each point is designated by a capital italic letter for convenience of reference. Note that input or output levels do not have to be integers and that different combinations of inputs can yield the same maximum output.

The data in Table 4-1 are used to illustrate four basic properties of Bobcat's production function:

1 The marginal product of each input is positive.
2 The marginal product of each input decreases as more of the input is used.
3 Inputs are complementary in production.
4 Returns to scale are constant.

We now turn to a discussion of each property in detail.

**1** *Marginal products are positive:* Suppose Bobcat employs a greater quantity of one input while holding constant the level of employment of the second input (and all other inputs, if there are more than two). The assumption is that the marginal product of that input is positive.

Points *I, M, N, O,* and *P* have been extracted from Table 4-1 and put in Table 4-2 for the purpose of illustrating the concept and computation of a marginal product. Compare points *I* and *M.* Output rises by 6.16 when machine-hours are increased by 5 and worker-hours are unchanged, and so the marginal product of equipment between these points is 1.23 (6.16/5) units of output.[4] Similarly, comparison of points *I* and *N* indicates that output rises by 23.61 when worker-hours are increased by 5 and machine-hours are unchanged, and so the marginal product of labor between these points is 4.72 (23.61/5) units of output. Wherever we look in Table 4-1 or Table 4-2, we see that adding to one input and reducing no other input increases output.

**2** *Marginal products are decreasing:* Although increases in just one input yield increments in output, those increments of output become successively smaller. As noted earlier, this property is called the law of diminishing marginal returns to a factor of production.

Compare points *I, N,* and *P* in Table 4-2. In each case, 80 machine-hours are used. When worker-hours rise from 20 to 25, output rises by 23.61; but when yet another 5 worker-hours are added, output rises by 21.34 (244.95 − 223.61). It follows that the marginal product of labor is 4.72 between points *I* and *N* and 4.27 between points *N* and *P.* More generally, the marginal product of labor diminishes as more labor is used and all other inputs are held constant.[5] The same statement applies to equipment, but no calculations are shown because there are not enough data for them in Table 4-2.

The law of diminishing returns does not imply that the laborer who provides the thirtieth worker-hour is less capable or productive than the laborer who provides the first worker-hour. Rather, the key to understanding the law of diminishing returns is to remember that all other inputs are being held constant. As more and more laborers are put together with the same number of machines, each laborer has fewer machine-hours to work with, and therefore each laborer—whether the first or the last one hired—cannot produce as much.

---

[4] We should observe that this calculation is an "average" marginal product since machine-hours increased by 5. Marginal product is defined as the change in output from 1 additional machine-hour.

Since in note 3 we reported the production function to be $Q = 5\sqrt{LK}$, we can derive the marginal product of *K* precisely by finding the partial derivative of *Q* with respect to *K*. Or

$$\frac{\partial Q}{\partial K} = \frac{5}{2}\sqrt{L/K}$$

Hence, the marginal product is always positive. Substitution of the values of *L* and *K* for point *I* in the expression above gives the marginal product of *K* to be 1.25 units of output.

[5] This is easily seen by examining $\partial Q/\partial L = \frac{5}{2}\sqrt{K/L}$. Clearly, as *L* increases the marginal product of labor falls.

**TABLE 4-2**
MARGINAL PRODUCTS OF INPUTS BETWEEN SELECTED POINTS

| | Input levels | | | Marginal product of | |
|---|---|---|---|---|---|
| Point | Worker-hours (L) | Machine-hours (K) | Output level (Q) | Labor | Equipment |
| I | 20 | 80 | 200 | NA* | NA |
| M | 20 | 85 | 206.16 | NA | 1.23 (from I) |
| N | 25 | 80 | 223.61 | 4.72 (from I)† | NA |
| O | 25 | 85 | 230.49 | 4.87 (from M)† | 1.38 (from N) |
| P | 30 | 80 | 244.95 | 4.27 (from N) | NA |

*NA means "not applicable" because there are not enough data in the table to calculate the marginal product.
†(From I) means that the point is being compared with point I. (From M) means that the point is being compared with point M.

Like the assumption that marginal products are positive, the law of diminishing returns is not a statement that no other result is possible. It is a statement about what is likely to be true of the levels of factor employment from which managers are choosing. To see why a decreasing marginal product is the likely case, suppose that an additional worker-hour costs $6.50, that its marginal product is 4, and that a unit of output can be sold for $2.00. By hiring, the firm commits itself to pay $6.50 for a worker-hour the output of which will return $8.00 in revenue to the firm, for a profit of $1.50. Why should the firm stop hiring labor at this point if the marginal product of labor is still increasing? The next worker-hour employed would return to the company an increment in profit even greater that $1.50. It follows that a profit-seeking enterprise will push beyond the range, if any, over which marginal products are increasing and employ inputs at levels at which marginal products are positive but decreasing.

**3** *Factors are complementary:* We have seen that the fixedness of the amount of equipment is responsible for the diminishing marginal product of labor. Consequently, if the amount of equipment could be fixed at a higher level than before, then it would seem to follow that the marginal product of labor would be greater than before. More generally, the marginal productivity of one input may increase when a greater quantity of a second input is used. When that is true, the two inputs are said to be complementary in production. The property of complementarity, like the preceding assumptions, is to be understood as the empirical condition most likely to be observed.

The data in Table 4-2 indicate that labor and equipment are complementary at the Bobcat Corporation. First, compare points I and M with points N and O. In both instances, machine-hours are increased by 5 from 80 to 85. However, worker-hours are fixed at 20 in I and M and at 25 in N and O. The marginal product of equipment between points I and M is 1.23 [(206.16 − 200)/5], but between points N and O it is 1.38 [(230.49 − 223.61)/5]. Thus, the marginal productivity of equipment at Bobcat is greater when there are more laborers who can utilize the additional machine-hours. Now compare points $I$ and $N$ with points $M$ and $O$. In both instances, worker-hours are raised by 5 from 20 to 25, but the marginal productivity of labor is greater when the additional worker-hours are used in conjunction with more equipment.[6]

**4** *Returns to scale are constant:* What would happen to the level of output if managers increased all inputs by the same percentage? Output would rise because the marginal product of each input is positive, and every input is being increased. In addition, output would rise even more because of the interactive effect of higher input levels on the marginal product of any one type of input, because of complementarity. However, it is not clear whether output will rise more than, less than, or exactly in proportion to the increase in inputs. If output increases by a greater percentage than the percentage increase in inputs, the production function is said to exhibit *increasing* returns to scale. If by the same percentage *constant* returns to scale obtain, and if they obtain by a smaller percentage, then *decreasing* returns to scale exist.

Bobcat's production function is one of constant returns to scale. This can be verified by comparing points $A$, $H$, and $Q$ in Table 4-1. At point $H$, twice as much labor and equipment is used as at point $A$, and output at $H$ is twice that at $A$. At point $Q$, 3 times as much labor and equipment is used as is used at point $A$, and output at $Q$ is 3 times that at $A$.

The extent of returns to scale (or economies of scale) for a particular business firm is clearly of great importance. We shall return to this topic several times in this book. Later in this chapter we shall discuss the sources of economies of scale and some studies that have tried to measure their extent. Chapter 7 also reports some studies of this type in the context of so-called scale-economy barriers to entry. Finally, Chapter 12 considers a related issue—the "learning curve"—and how cumulative output can affect production and cost.

## ISOQUANT MAP

An alternative to tabulating certain points of the production function, as in Table 4-1, is to plot the points on an isoquant map, as in Figure 4-2. An isoquant is a line which connects all the input combinations $(L, K)$ that yield the same level of maximal output. Points $A$ through $F$ in Table 4-1 are just a few of the points that make up the isoquant $Q = 100$ in Figure 4-2,[7] points $H$ through $L$ are just a few of the points that make up the isoquant $Q = 200$, and so on. Only

---

[6] This point can be verified by showing that the cross-partial derivative of the production function with respect to the variables $L$ and $K$ is positive. Thus,

$$\frac{\partial^2 Q}{\partial K \, \partial L} = \frac{5}{4\sqrt{KL}} > 0$$

Or observe in note 5 that a higher $K$ will increase the marginal product of labor.

[7] The equation defining the $Q = 100$ isoquant can be found by setting the production function equal to 100. Hence $5\sqrt{LK} = 100$, or $K = 400/L$.

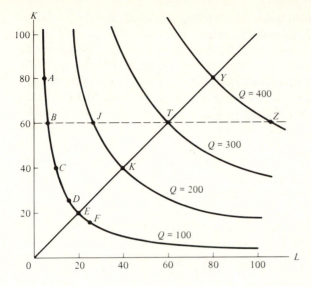

**FIGURE 4-2**
Selected isoquants from Bobcat's production function.

four isoquants are shown so that they may be distinguished. Since every point
in the $(L, K)$ quadrant is an input combination and is on an isoquant (for example, point $N$ is on the isoquant $Q = 223.61$), the depiction of all isoquants
would have resulted in a solid coloring of the quadrant.

Figure 4-2 reflects the properties of the production function that were discussed in the last section. Notice how frequently these properties are resorted
to as we explain the shape and position of isoquants.

First, every isoquant slopes downward because marginal products of labor
and equipment are positive. No other slope is consistent with that assumption.
An upward-sloping isoquant would incorrectly imply that no more output
results when both inputs are increased. A horizontal isoquant, or one with no
slope, would incorrectly imply that no more output results when only the
number of worker-hours is increased. A vertical isoquant would incorrectly
imply that no more output results when only the number of machine-hours is
increased. Although some portions of the isoquants drawn in Figure 4-2 come
close to appearing vertical or horizontal, they are not.

Second, two isoquants never touch or cross, because every point on an
isoquant map shows the maximum output which can be gotten from a given
input configuration. Suppose for the sake of argument that the isoquants
$Q = 100$ and $Q = 200$ touch or cross at the point $(L', K')$. In that event we
would have the contradiction that the maximum output producible with inputs
$(L', K')$ is both 100 and 200.

Third, because marginal products of labor and equipment are positive, one
passes over isoquants for successively higher levels of output as one travels
northeastward along any ray which begins at the origin. Line $EKTY$ is one such
ray. How rapidly one reaches higher levels of output while traveling along a ray
depends on the scale property of the production function. We have already

found that Bobcat's production function exhibits constant returns to scale. Thus, in moving from point $E$ to point $K$, both inputs are doubled and output doubles. In moving from point $K$ to point $Y$, both inputs are doubled again and output doubles again. Had Bobcat's production function been characterized by increasing returns to scale in this range, the isoquants for $Q = 200$, $300$, and $400$ would have been packed more closely together and would have been nearer to the isoquant for $Q = 100$. In the case of decreasing returns to scale, the isoquants would have been stretched apart more than is shown in Figure 4-2.

Fourth, the lateral spacing of isoquants is regulated by diminishing returns to labor. Lateral distance is measured along a horizontal line in Figure 4-2, which means that machine-hours are constant and worker-hours are changing. These are the conditions under which the marginal product of labor is defined. Because of diminishing returns to labor, successively larger additions of worker-hours are needed to raise output by a given amount. Thus, we expect the lateral distance between the $Q = 200$ and $Q = 300$ isoquants to be greater than the lateral distance between the $Q = 100$ and $Q = 200$ isoquants. The point is illustrated by following line $BJTZ$ in Figure 4-2, the data for which are given in Table 4-3. When machine-hours are fixed at 60, the additional worker-hours required to raise output by 100 units go from 20 ($26.67 - 6.67$) to 33.33 ($60 - 26.67$) to 46.67 ($106.67 - 60$) as the marginal productivity of labor declines. In a like manner, the vertical spacing of isoquants is regulated by diminishing returns to equipment.

Finally, an isoquant bends into the origin as it slopes downward (and so is said to be convex to the origin). In other words, the slope of the isoquant becomes more gradual as we slide down an isoquant from left to right. The alternative possibilities are that the slope stays the same or becomes steeper; however, our assumptions of diminishing returns to inputs and the complementarity of inputs are sufficient to rule out these alternatives. To see why that is so, it is first necessary to establish that the slope of an isoquant equals the ratio of the marginal product of labor to the marginal product of equipment.

We know that output rises by an amount equal to the marginal product of

**TABLE 4-3**
MARGINAL PRODUCTS OF INPUTS BETWEEN SELECTED POINTS

| Point | Input levels | | Output level ($Q$) | Marginal product of labor |
| | Worker-hours ($L$) | Machine-hours ($K$) | | |
|---|---|---|---|---|
| $B$ | 6.67 | 60 | 100 | NA* |
| $J$ | 26.67 | 60 | 200 | 5.00 |
| $T$ | 60.00 | 60 | 300 | 3.00 |
| $Z$ | 106.67 | 60 | 400 | 2.14 |

*NA means "not applicable" because there are not enough data in the table to calculate the marginal product.

labor ($MP_L$) when Bobcat employs an additional worker-hour. Therefore, output rises by the amount $MP_L \cdot \Delta L$ if Bobcat employs $\Delta L$ additional worker-hours, provided that $\Delta L$ is not too large. Similarly, we know that output falls by an amount equal to the negative of the marginal product of equipment ($-MP_K$) when Bobcat uses one fewer machine-hour. Therefore, output falls by the amount $-MP_K \cdot \Delta K$ if Bobcat uses $\Delta K$ fewer machine-hours. Suppose that the quantities $\Delta L$ and $\Delta K$ are deliberately chosen so that the gain in output from the employment of more labor equals the loss of output from the use of less equipment. In those circumstances, Bobcat's management has moved from one spot on an isoquant to another spot on the same isoquant and

$$MP_L \cdot \Delta L = -MP_K \cdot \Delta K$$

or, by rearranging terms,

$$\frac{MP_L}{MP_K} = -\frac{\Delta K}{\Delta L} \tag{4-1}$$

The right-hand side of equation (4-1) is the ratio of the change in vertical distance (machine-hours) to the change in horizontal distance (worker-hours) between two points on an isoquant—in short, the slope of the isoquant between those points (or more accurately, the negative of the slope).

If the slope of an isoquant becomes more gradual as more labor and less equipment are employed, then according to equation (4-1), $MP_L$ must be getting smaller relative to $MP_K$. As worker-hours are added, $MP_L$ falls as a result of diminishing returns to labor and $MP_K$ rises as a result of complementarity of inputs. As machine-hours are cut back, $MP_L$ falls because of the complementarity of inputs and $MP_K$ rises because of diminishing returns to equipment (working in the reverse direction). There are thus two forces which decrease $MP_L$ and two which increase $MP_K$, implying a decline in the $MP_L/MP_K$ ratio and a convex shape for an isoquant.

We have paid a lot of attention to the slope of an isoquant because it has an important economic interpretation. It shows how much more of one input can be substituted for how much less of a second input while maintaining production at a given level. This trade-off is called the rate of technical substitution (RTS) of labor for equipment. (The prepositions "of" and "for" should be distinguished. Labor is being added, and equipment is being replaced. Ordinarily, the rate of technical substitution of labor for equipment does not equal the rate of technical substitution of equipment for labor, since the latter is the reciprocal of the former.) Consider the $Q = 100$ isoquant in Figure 4-2, data for which are reproduced in Table 4-4 and begin at point $A$. By adding only 1.67 worker-hours, managers at Bobcat can release 20 machine-hours and still produce 100 units of output at point $B$. Put another way, 1 worker-hour substitutes for 12 (20/1.67) machine-hours between points $A$ and $B$. This is the rate of technical substitution. Similarly, 1 worker-hour substitutes for 6 (20/3.33) machine-hours

**TABLE 4-4**
RATE OF TECHNICAL SUBSTITUTION OF LABOR FOR EQUIPMENT

| | Input levels | | | Rate of technical |
| Point | Worker-hours (L) | Machine-hours (K) | Output level (Q) | substitution |
| --- | --- | --- | --- | --- |
| A | 5 | 80 | 100 | NA* |
| B | 6.67 | 60 | 100 | 12 |
| C | 10 | 40 | 100 | 6 |
| D | 15 | 26.67 | 100 | 2.67 |
| E | 20 | 20 | 100 | 1.33 |
| F | 25 | 16 | 100 | 0.80 |

*NA means "not applicable" because there are not enough data in the table to calculate the rate of technical substitution.

between points $B$ and $C$, for 2.67 (13.33/5) machine-hours between points $C$ and $D$, and so on.[8]

The production function, whether communicated by an equation, a table, or an isoquant map, represents the possibilities for production. It does not tell managers at Bobcat which point should be picked on the $Q = 100$ isoquant or, indeed, whether output should be 100 units.

### LONG-RUN AND SHORT-RUN PRODUCTION FUNCTIONS

We have to this point spoken of managers at the Bobcat Corporation as being able to choose to employ more or less labor and to use more or less equipment. However, these decisions take time to implement. Some additional worker-hours can be obtained at short notice by having the existing staff work overtime, but greater additions would require more time for finding and training new employees. Likewise, some additional machine-hours can be obtained by running equipment for longer periods before it is shut down for inspection, overhaul, and replacement of parts, although this practice increases the risk of a breakdown and a long delay for repairs. Greater additions of machine-hours would require more time for selecting new equipment, awaiting delivery, installing, and breaking in.

The production function $Q = f(K, L)$ that we have been discussing assumes that the quantity of any input can be changed. For this reason it is called a long-

---

[8] In notes 4 and 5 we have given expressions for $MP_L$ and $MP_K$. Their ratio is the rate of technical substitution of labor for equipment, or

$$\frac{MP_L}{MP_K} = \frac{(5/2)\sqrt{K/L}}{(5/2)\sqrt{L/K}} = \frac{K}{L}$$

Obviously, this ratio gets smaller when $L$ is increased and $K$ is decreased. Therefore, the isoquants are convex to the origin.

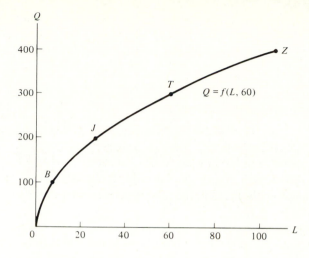

**FIGURE 4-3**
A short-run production function
for the Bobcat Corporation.

run production function. The long-run production function applies to situations in which it is realistic to believe that enough time will have elapsed for managers to have implemented all changes in inputs. For example, Bobcat may now be producing $Q = 200$ units per hour by using 26.67 worker-hours and 60 machine-hours per hour (point $J$ in Figure 4-2). Anticipating a great increase in demand, management wishes by this time next year to be able to produce $Q = 400$ units per hour by using 80 worker-hours and 80 machine-hours per hour (point $Y$). Although the skills required of a laborer at Bobcat are such that the work force can be changed rapidly, it will take a year for the additional equipment to be put in place and function normally. Therefore, Bobcat's long-run production function describes production possibilities when there is a year or more in which to make changes in input levels.

In the meanwhile, however, Bobcat's equipment is fixed at 60 machine-hours. Until the new equipment is ready, Bobcat can increase production only by hiring more labor. As the anticipated growth in demand materializes, Bobcat can respond by moving rightward along the horizontal line $BJTZ$ in Figure 4-2. Thus, in the short run—that is, the period in which it is possible to change only some of the inputs—Bobcat's production function is $Q = f(L, 60)$.[9]

This short-run production function is plotted in Figure 4-3 (points $B$, $J$, $T$, and $Z$ in Figure 4-3 match those in Figure 4-2). We already know a lot about the curve. It is a rising curve, because the marginal product of labor is positive. But the curve rises at a decreasing rate, because the marginal product of labor (which is the slope of the curve) falls as more labor is employed. Finally, the position of the entire curve, whether farther up or down, depends on the fixed number of machine-hours. Because of the complementarity of inputs, the short-

---

[9] The explicit form of this short-run production function is $Q = 5\sqrt{60L}$.

run production function with machine-hours fixed at 80 would lie above the short-run production function depicted in Figure 4-3.

We now return to the issue of returns to scale and consider this important property of the long-run production function more thoroughly.

## RETURNS TO SCALE: SOURCES AND MEASUREMENT

The extent of economies of scale is an important issue for any firm. If there are strong increasing returns to scale, the number of firms operating in an industry will tend to be small. The automobile industry, with some of the largest firms in the world, is an example. On the other hand, if there are no significant advantages to scale, there will tend to be many firms in the industry, as in the gasoline retailing industry.

A firm's competitive strategy is highly dependent upon the nature of returns to scale. In Chapter 7, for example, we describe Henry Ford's successful strategy of low-cost mass production which resulted in Ford Motor Company's winning 55 percent of the 1921 auto market.

### Sources of Returns to Scale

The specialization of labor and equipment that can be achieved as a result of larger size is an important source of increasing returns. The classic example is automobile assembly. As the rate of output increases, workers can specialize more narrowly and become highly efficient in a small number of tasks. Rather than installing a complete engine, a worker may be responsible for attaching one small part. Similarly, specialized automatic screw machines rather than general-purpose lathes might be used in producing ball bearings if the output is sufficiently large.

Another source of increasing returns to scale which is especially important in process industries (oil refineries, chemical plants, etc.) is the geometrical relationship between capacity and surface area. Consider a steel cylinder of length $L$ and radius $r$. The volume (or capacity) of the cylinder, which is proportional to output, is

$$\text{Output} \approx \pi r^2 L$$

The surface area of the cylinder, which is proportional to the steel input needed to construct the cylinder, is

$$\text{Steel input} \approx 2\pi r L$$

Now consider a doubling of $r$:

$$\text{Output} \approx \pi (2r)^2 L = 4(\pi r^2 L)$$
$$\text{Steel input} \approx 2\pi (2r) L = 2(2\pi r L)$$

Output has increased by a factor of 4, while input has increased by a factor of only 2. There is solid empirical support for this source of increasing returns.[10]

It is useful to distinguish between the rate of output and cumulative output (or volume) in some situations. Although our discussion has been restricted to the rate of output in the previous theoretical analysis, in some industries the total volume is more important. One reason is that intricate labor operations, such as in aircraft assembly and the manufacture of computer components, can be done much more efficiently as workers gain experience. This "learning curve" effect is considered in detail in Chapter 12.

All these sources of increasing returns to scale appear to have limits; that is, as the scale becomes larger, the advantages tend to diminish. Scaled-up process equipment eventually becomes unstable or requires special structural reinforcement. Specialization of labor can lead to dissatisfied workers and inefficiency as the tasks become more narrowly defined and therefore less interesting.

Turning to the sources of decreasing returns to scale, we find only one major explanation in the economics literature. The explanation is that as a firm increases in size, it becomes more and more difficult for the top management to exercise control over the entire organization. Thus, this "control loss" as the number of layers of management increases is a possible source of decreasing returns to scale.

However, according to some experts, this problem can be avoided by means of a decentralized multidivisional form of corporate organization. That is, by delegating authority and responsibility to operating divisions (such as General Motors did in creating Chevrolet, Buick, Oldsmobile, Pontiac, etc.), a company can largely offset control loss.

### Measurement of Returns to Scale

Evidence on the extent of returns to scale has been gathered by two basic methods. One method has been to obtain information from engineers who specialize in designing new plants and production units. The results of a major study of this type are reported in Chapter 7. The evidence generally indicates that increasing returns to scale prevail in many industries over initial output levels but soon become relatively constant.

Leslie Cookenboo has performed an interesting engineering analysis of returns to scale in crude oil pipelines.[11] Using a hydraulic formula for computing required horsepowers for various volumes of liquid flow in pipes of different sizes, he obtained an "engineering production function." The isoquant map shown in Figure 4-4 has been constructed using this production function.[12]

---

[10] See John Haldi and David Whitcomb, "Economies of Scale in Industrial Plants," *Journal of Political Economy*, August 1967.

[11] Leslie Cookenboo, Jr., *Crude Oil Pipe Lines and Competition in the Oil Industry* (Cambridge, Mass.: Harvard University Press, 1955).

[12] The explicit form of the production function is $Q^{2.735} = H \cdot D^{4.735} \div .01046$.

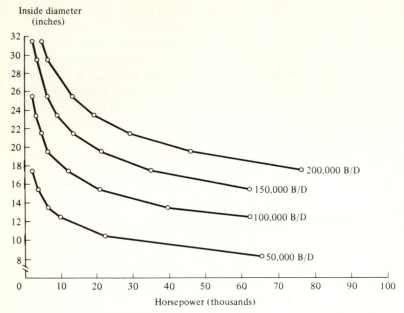

**FIGURE 4-4**
Isoquants for pipeline transportation of crude oil.

Output $Q$ is measured in thousands of barrels of crude oil per day that can be pumped over a 1,000-mile pipeline. The two inputs are represented by the pipe diameter $D$, measured in inches, and the horsepower $H$ of the pumping stations. Since the isoquants for equal increments of output become increasingly close together as one moves to progressively higher outputs, increasing returns to scale exist.

The second method for measuring returns to scale is econometric analysis. For example, one could collect data on the output rate and input quantities for an industry for each year over a certain period and then estimate the production function statistically. Or for a given year, data could be obtained for different firms, and the function could be estimated, where the observations are the data on individual firms.

A widely used specification for estimating production functions is the Cobb-Douglas specification. According to this specification, the explicit form of a firm's long-run production function is

$$Q = AL^\alpha K^\beta \tag{4-2}$$

The parameters ($A$, $\alpha$, and $\beta$) are constants whose values can be estimated by using the econometric techniques explained in Chapter 3.

Consider what these parameters can tell us about returns to scale. Begin with input levels ($L_0$, $K_0$) and output level $Q_0$. Increase inputs to ($L_1$, $K_1$), the

**TABLE 4-5**

ESTIMATES OF PRODUCTION FUNCTIONS
USING COBB-DOUGLAS SPECIFICATION

| Industry | $\alpha^*$ | $\beta\dagger$ | Sum of $\alpha$, $\beta$ |
|---|---|---|---|
| Textiles | .88 | .12 | 1.00 |
| Chemicals | .89 | .20 | 1.09 |
| Food | .51 | .56 | 1.07 |
| Paper | .56 | .42 | .98 |
| Primary metals | .59 | .37 | .96 |

$^*\alpha$ = coefficient of labor.
$\dagger\beta$ = coefficient of capital.
 *Source:* John R. Moroney, "Cobb-Douglas Production Functions and Returns to Scale in U.S. Manufacturing Industry," *Western Economic Journal,* December 1967.

new levels being a common multiple ($\lambda > 1$) of the former levels: $L_1 = \lambda L_0$ and $K_1 = \lambda K_0$. The new output level $Q_1$ is

$$Q_1 = A(\lambda L_0)^\alpha (\lambda K_0)^\beta \tag{4-3}$$
$$= \lambda^{\alpha+\beta}(AL_0^\alpha K_0^\beta)$$

or $\qquad\qquad Q_1 = \lambda^{\alpha+\beta}Q_0$

Therefore, output rises by the same multiple as the inputs rise by, and the production function exhibits constant returns to scale if $\alpha + \beta = 1$: $Q_1 = \lambda Q_0$. Increasing returns to scale are indicated when $\alpha + \beta > 1$, and decreasing returns to scale are indicated when $\alpha + \beta < 1$.[13]

We also observe that the Cobb-Douglas specification can be applied to a production process that uses three or more kinds of inputs. For example, if $M$ units of raw materials are a third input, the Cobb-Douglas long-run production function is

$$Q = AL^\alpha K^\beta M^\delta \tag{4-4}$$

The indicator for whether the production function exhibits constant, increasing, or decreasing returns to scale is now given by the relation of $\alpha + \beta + \delta$ to unity.

Table 4-5 provides some estimates of returns to scale for five industries. The last column reports the sum of the coefficients and therefore indicates the existence of increasing or decreasing returns. Apparently, production in these in-

---

[13] Observe that the explicit form of the Bobcat Corporation's production function $Q = 5\sqrt{LK}$ implies that $\alpha + \beta = 1$. This proves that Bobcat's production function is one of constant returns to scale.

dustries can be described as being quite close to attaining constant returns to scale.

## THE COST FUNCTION

The total cost of production which a business incurs over a given period of time can be computed by multiplying input quantities used during the period by their respective prices and then adding the results. When Bobcat Corporation pays $w$ dollars per worker-hour and $r$ dollars per machine-hour, the total cost $C$ of the input combination which consists of $L$ worker-hours and $K$ machine-hours is

$$C = w \cdot L + r \cdot K \qquad (4\text{-}5)$$

While this adding-up procedure is a correct way of finding total cost, it does not explain why this level of spending comes about. Specifically, why did Bobcat employ $L$ worker-hours and $K$ machine-hours? One answer is that it must have quantities of inputs which are sufficient to produce the level of output that managers wish to attain. We have not yet explained how the desired level of output is determined—that will come in Chapter 5, building on the results of this chapter—so let us stipulate that the output target is $Q = \overline{Q}$. But recall that there are numerous combinations of labor and equipment that make up the $Q = \overline{Q}$ isoquant. The question remains why, of all the input combinations along the isoquant, managers at Bobcat choose the particular combination $(L, K)$.

The assumption made in the theory of cost is that a company selects the input combination which minimizes the cost of achieving its output target. Finding the least-cost combination of inputs obviously involves consideration of the input prices $w$ and $r$. Thus we should find after further analysis that the amounts of labor and equipment employed depend on input prices and the output target:

$$L = L(\overline{Q}, w, r) \qquad K = K(\overline{Q}, w, r) \qquad (4\text{-}6)$$

Consequently, we should find that total cost ultimately depends on input prices and the output target:

$$C = C(\overline{Q}, w, r) \qquad (4\text{-}7)$$

Expression (4-7) is called a total cost function. It gives the minimum total cost of producing $\overline{Q}$ units of output when input prices equal $w$ and $r$. Cost function (4-7) is a more sophisticated concept than cost equation (4-5), because the cost function incorporates a mechanism for adjusting input quantities whenever there is a change in the price of labor, the price of equipment, or the output target. Hereafter, we will drop the special notation of $\overline{Q}$ for the output target and simply use $Q$.

## DISCUSSION OF INPUT PRICES

Before proceeding with an analysis which so much involves the prices of labor and equipment, it is worth a brief delay to discuss what these prices are. The discussion is necessarily general, for there is great variety in the ways businesses pay for the services of inputs.

The unit cost of labor measured in dollars per worker-hour $w$ is commonly called the wage rate. It consists of basic compensation plus certain other outlays. For a wage earner, basic compensation is, of course, the hourly wage. For a piecework employee, the basic hourly wage is derived from the ratio of the piece rate to the average number of hours spent in completing a piece. For a salaried employee, the basic hourly wage is derived from the ratio of the salary to the number of hours worked in the salary period. In addition to this basic compensation, employers make certain elective and nonelective outlays which should be included in the unit cost of labor. An example of an elective outlay is the contributions employers may make to employees' retirement or life insurance plans. Two examples of a nonelective outlay in the United States are the social security tax, revenues from which finance social security and Medicare benefits, and the unemployment insurance tax, revenues from which finance unemployment compensation benefits.

The unit cost of equipment measured in dollars per machine-hour $r$ covers charges for the maintenance and depreciation of equipment plus the net return that investors require. Depreciation is the decline in the value of the equipment from wear and technological obsolescence. Investors require a net return because they are deferring consumption to a future date; moreover, there is a risk that the investment will not pay off.

There are several ways to acquire the services of capital goods and as many ways to arrive at the price $r$. The various methods should lead to approximately the same figure, since the same charges and net return are being covered in any case. Bobcat could lease machine-hours on long-term contracts from a second firm, paying an explicit rental price sufficient both to meet the maintenance and depreciation expenses incurred by the lessor and to provide the minimal net return required by stockholders of the second firm. Alternatively, Bobcat could borrow funds and purchase equipment. Then it would have expenses for maintenance, depreciation, and interest which are expressible on a machine-hour basis. As yet another alternative, Bobcat could use its retained earnings and purchase equipment. Then it would have maintenance and depreciation expenses, but no explicit interest expense. However, interest earnings would be forgone by stockholders and should be included in price $r$ as an opportunity cost.[14]

An important conclusion to be drawn from this listing of possibilities is that

[14] The concept of opportunity cost is quite general in economics. If a firm invests $1,000 in project A, its opportunity cost is what it could have earned in its next best investment opportunity. Similarly, the opportunity cost of going to college is the income forgone by not working.

the production costs of a firm are, in economic theory, inclusive of a normal net return to funds invested in capital goods used by the firm. This is so whether the return appears in the firm's accounts (embedded in rental payments or as interest paid to creditors) or not (interest forgone by stockholders). A more detailed analysis of these concepts is given in Chapter 9.

## DERIVATION OF THE SHORT-RUN COST FUNCTION

In order for $C(Q, w, r)$ to be the minimum total cost of producing $Q$ units of output, a company must organize production efficiently. If the company does not get the maximum output from the inputs it uses, given the current state of technology in equipment and the skill levels of its managers and workers, then

**FIGURE 4-5**
Short-run cost functions for the Bobcat Corporation.

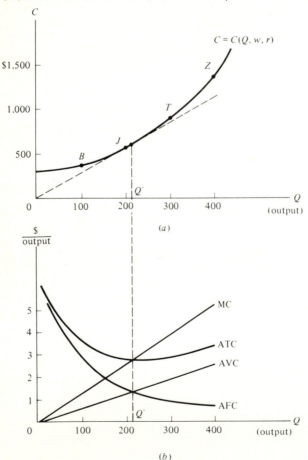

(a)

(b)

it is spending too much. Consequently, the input combination which minimizes the total cost of reaching the output target $Q$ is a combination $(L, K)$ which satisfies the company's production function $Q = f(L, K)$. This suggests that the cost function is linked to the production function, a connection that will be seen time and again.

The short-run cost function is derived in this section. A cost function refers to a period of time, the short run or the long run, in the same way that the production function does, because the minimum total cost in a period must be derived from an input combination which is feasible in that period. For example, the managers of Bobcat Corporation may know that the least costly way to hit the $Q = 200$ target is to hire 20 worker-hours and use 80 machine-hours. However, if Bobcat currently has only 60 machine-hours, then in the short run (the period of time which elapses until the additional equipment can be put in service) managers have to work with input combinations that include 60 machine-hours.

As discussed previously, $Q = f(L, K')$ is the short-run production function for the period in which a business is constrained to pay for $K'$ machine-hours, whether they have been leased, purchased with borrowed funds, or purchased with retained earnings. In these circumstances, the firm minimizes costs by hiring the minimum amount of labor which can, in combination with $K'$ machine-hours, produce the output target $Q$. This amount of labor $L_0$ is determined by the short-run production function $Q = f(L_0, K')$. Short-run total cost therefore equals $w \cdot L_0 + K'$. As the output target changes, the amount of labor and the total cost change. In this manner a correspondence is built up between the output target and the minimum short-run cost of attaining it. That correspondence is the short-run total cost function.

The short-run total cost function for Bobcat Corporation is graphed in Figure 4-5a. The data for the graph appear in Table 4-6. Points $B, J, T,$ and $Z$ satisfy Bobcat's short-run production with machine-hours fixed at 60. They can be tracked from Bobcat's isoquant map (Figure 4-2) to the short-run production function (Figure 4-3) to the short-run cost function (Figure 4-5a). Input prices are assumed to be $w = \$10$ and $r = \$5$.[15]

As shown in column 5 of the table, Bobcat pays $300 for the services of equipment whether it produces a lot of output or none at all. Such expenses are called fixed costs (FC) for that reason. Its payments for the services of labor, shown in column 6, range from zero to $1066.70 as more worker-hours are hired to hit higher output targets. Such expenses are called variable costs (VC) for that reason. Total cost $(C)$ is the sum of fixed cost and variable cost. It is listed

---

[15] Solving the short-run production function $Q = 5\sqrt{60L}$ for $L$ gives $L = Q^2/1,500$. Substituting this in the cost equation produces the short-run cost function

$$C = w\left(\frac{Q^2}{1,500}\right) + r60$$

Given the particular values for $w$ and $r$, we get $C = Q^2/150 + 300$.

**TABLE 4-6**
SHORT-RUN COST AND PRODUCTION DATA FOR THE BOBCAT CORPORATION

| (1) Point | (2) Output Q | (3) Labor L | (4) Eq't K' | (5) FC | (6) VC | (7) C | (8) ATC | (9) AFC | (10) AVC | (11) MC | (12) MPL |
|---|---|---|---|---|---|---|---|---|---|---|---|
| — | 0 | 0 | 60 | $300 | $ 0 | $ 300 | $ — | $ — | $ — | $ — | $ — |
| B | 100 | 6.67 | 60 | 300 | 66.7 | 366.7 | 3.67 | 3.00 | 0.67 | 0.67 | 15.00 |
| J | 200 | 26.67 | 60 | 300 | 266.7 | 566.7 | 2.83 | 1.50 | 1.33 | 2.00 | 5.00 |
| T | 300 | 60.00 | 60 | 300 | 600.0 | 900.0 | 3.00 | 1.00 | 2.00 | 3.33 | 3.00 |
| Z | 400 | 106.67 | 60 | 300 | 1066.7 | 1366.7 | 3.42 | .705 | 2.67 | 4.67 | 2.14 |

in column 7 of the table. The output and total cost pairs ($Q, C$) are points on the short-run cost function in Figure 4-5a.

Two properties of this function are apparent. First, it begins with cost equal to fixed cost when no output is produced. Second, it is a rising curve, because more worker-hours are required to increase output. What may be less apparent is the fact that the curve becomes steeper as it rises. Diminishing returns to labor (see column 12 of the table) are the reason for this property. Successively more labor must be added, hence successively greater increments to total cost must be experienced, in order to increase output by 1 unit. In the extreme, when so much labor has been hired that its marginal product is close to zero, total cost rises so rapidly that the line plotted in Figure 4-5a comes close to being vertical.

The amount by which total cost increases per unit increase in output is called the marginal cost. It is a very important concept in economics, for reasons that will be explained more fully in Chapter 5. Since it is the ratio of the change in cost to the change in output, marginal cost is the slope of the total cost curve. Bobcat's marginal cost of production is shown in column 11 of Table 4-6. When Bobcat produces a small quantity of output ($Q = 100$) rather than none at all, the marginal product of labor is high, and hence the marginal cost is just $0.67 [(366.7 − 300)/(100 − 0)]$ per additional unit of output. But when Bobcat boosts production from $Q = 300$ to $Q = 400$, the marginal cost is $4.67 [(1,366.7 − 900)/(400 − 300)]$ per additional unit of output.[16]

Bobcat's short-run marginal cost curve (MC) is plotted in Figure 4-5b. The other curves in the diagram are also derived from the data in the table. The short-run average total cost (ATC, column 8 in Table 4-6) is the ratio of short-run total cost to output: $C/Q$. The average total cost of producing $Q$ can be determined by running a ray from the origin in Figure 4-5a to a point on the total cost function. ATC is the slope of that ray. As output increases from $Q = 0$, the slope of the ray gets smaller until $Q = Q'$ (this particular ray is shown as the dashed line); for greater values of $Q$, the slope of the ray increases. Therefore, the ATC curve in Figure 4-5b falls until it reaches its smallest value at $Q = Q'$, and it rises thereafter.[17] The average fixed cost (AFC, column 9 in Table 4-6) is the ratio of fixed cost to output: $FC/Q$. Obviously, AFC is very large when output is very small, and it declines continuously as output increases. The short-run average variable cost (AVC, column 10 in the table) is the ratio of short-run variable cost to output: $VC/Q$.

---

[16] The more precise definition of marginal cost is $dC/dQ$; given the short-run cost function in note 15, $dC/dQ = Q/75$. This expression, of course, gives the slope of the total cost function at a particular value of $Q$. The calculations above, on the other hand, give the "average" marginal cost over a range of output.

[17] Since from note 15, $C = Q^2/150 + 300$, average total cost ATC $= Q/150 + 300/Q$. To find output where ATC is minimized, set the derivative of ATC with respect to $Q$ equal to zero and solve for output. Hence,

$$\frac{d(\text{ATC})}{dQ} = \frac{1}{150} - \frac{300}{Q^2} = 0 \qquad Q' \approx 212$$

The members of the "cost curve family" are related in two ways. First, when evaluated at any given $Q$, the height of the AFC curve equals the vertical distance between the ATC and AVC curves. This is true by definition, since ATC = AFC + AVC. Second, the MC curve lies below the ATC curve so long as the ATC curve is falling, lies above the ATC curve so long as the ATC curve is rising, and passes through the lowest point of the ATC curve at $Q = Q'$. (That MC = ATC at this point is indicated by the fact that the slope of the dashed ray in Figure 4-5$a$ represents both MC and ATC. No other ray can be tangent to the total cost curve and therefore have its slope represent MC.)

The relationship described above between marginal cost and average total cost is a matter of arithmetic, not economics. Whenever an average falls, it is because the quantity that has been added to the total after another trial is lower than the former average. You cannot have begun a bowling game with an average of 150, end the game with an average of 147, and have scored 150 or higher in that game. Similarly, whenever an average rises, it is because the quantity that has been added to the total after another trial is greater than the former average. If the average neither rises nor falls after another trial—as is true of ATC for a 1-unit change in output near $Q = Q'$—it is because the amount (MC) that is added to the total equals the average. Notice that the MC and AVC curves are related in the same way and for the same reason.

The set of cost curves that we have derived is only one of many sets. A different set results for different input prices or for machine-hours fixed at a different level in the short run. Suppose that $K' = 80$. Of course fixed cost is greater, and so the short-run total cost curve begins at a higher point on the vertical axis. However, we cannot infer that the entire total cost curve when $K' = 80$ lies above the entire total cost curve when $K' = 60$. The reason is that inputs are complementary. The greater amount of equipment enhances the marginal product of labor and hence reduces the marginal cost of production. This suggests that the two different total cost curves will eventually cross and that the short-run cost of producing a sufficiently high level of output will be less with $K' = 80$ than with $K' = 60$.[18]

In the particular case of the Bobcat Corporation, the short-run total cost function becomes steeper as it rises. This is true because diminishing returns to labor holds throughout the production function. In more general cases, in which there is an initial region of increasing returns before diminishing returns set in, the cost function will have the shape shown in Figure 4-6$a$. Such a total cost function would hold for the short-run production function of Farmer Brown shown in Figure 4-1$a$.

The cost curve family corresponding to this more general total cost function is shown in Figure 4-6$b$. The major difference between the cost curves in Figure 4-6$b$ and those in Figure 4-5$b$, of course, is that over an initial range of out-

---

[18] The short-run total cost function with $K' = 80$ is $C = Q^2/200 + 400$, following the method of note 15. It is easy to show that the two cost functions cross at about $Q = 245$. Hence, for $Q > 245$, total cost is lower for $K' = 80$ than for $K' = 60$.

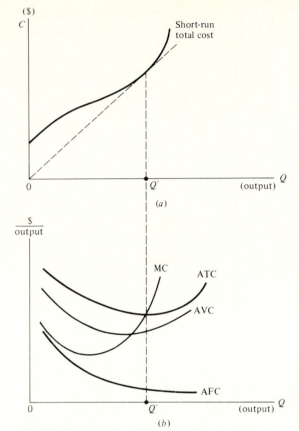

**FIGURE 4-6**
Short-run cost functions for the
general case.

put AVC and MC fall in the more general case. For the Bobcat Corporation
(Figure 4-5*b*), AVC and MC always slope upward.

## DERIVATION OF THE LONG-RUN COST FUNCTION

In the long run, managers are not constrained to employ any input at a constant
level and can search more freely for the input configuration that minimizes the
total cost of producing any target level of output. The long-run cost function is
derived in this section.

Let us arbitrarily pick an output target of $Q = 200$ in order to begin the
derivation. The questions are, Which of the input combinations along the
$Q = 200$ isoquant minimizes total cost? and What is the total cost? Consider a
tentative budget of $C_1$ dollars. Assuming that the company pays constant prices
for inputs, regardless of the quantities employed, $C_1$ could finance any input
combination $(L, K)$ for which $C_1 = wL + rK$. In Figure 4-7 the set of affordable
combinations consists of all combinations on or below the line marked $AB$. All

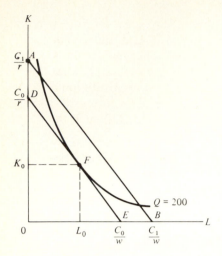

**FIGURE 4-7**
Least-cost production is at point $F$ for $Q = 200$.

input combinations on this line cost exactly $C_1$ dollars, and so it is called an isocost line. By rearrangement of the expression for $C_1$, we can write the equation of the isocost line for $C_1$ dollars of expenditure as

$$K = \frac{C_1}{r} - \frac{wL}{r} \tag{4.8}$$

The isocost line meets the vertical axis at a height of $C_1/r$, the greatest quantity of machine-hours that can be purchased if no worker-hours are hired. It meets the horizontal axis at $C_1/w$, the greatest quantity of worker-hours that can be purchased if no machine-hours are employed. The slope of the isoquant line, in absolute value, is the input price ratio $w/r$. The numerator of this ratio is measured in dollars per worker-hour and the denominator in dollars per machine-hour, and so the price ratio $w/r$ is actually a ratio of machine-hours to worker-hours. If its value were 2.0 because $w = \$10$ and $r = \$5$, then 2.0 machine-hours could be replaced by 1.0 worker-hour without changing total cost from $C_1$. Thus, the size of the budget affects the points where the isocost line strikes the vertical and horizontal axes, but it does not affect the slope of the isocost line.

Evidently the tentative budget is ample for financing production of the target level of output, for much of the $Q = 200$ isoquant is below the isocost line $AB$. Indeed, the tentative budget is too rich to be the least-cost budget. As smaller tentative budgets are considered, the isocost line shifts downward (because its intercepts are $C/w$ and $C/r$) in a parallel fashion (because its slope does not depend on $C$) until it becomes the isocost line $DE$. The total cost $C_0$ associated with isocost line $DE$ is the minimum budget. It enables production of $Q = 200$ but no greater amount, and only if the particular input combination $(L_0, K_0)$ is employed. Long-run total cost therefore equals $wL_0 + rK_0$.

The cost-minimizing input combination, point $F$ in Figure 4-7, is located at the point of tangency between the isocost line $DE$ and the isoquant for $Q = 200$. At the point of tangency, the slope of the isocost line and the slope of the isoquant are equal. The slope of the isocost line is the input price ratio $w/r$. The slope of the isoquant, of course, is the rate of technical substitution of labor for equipment (abbreviated as RTS). Thus, minimization of the total cost of producing $Q = 200$ implies the employment of inputs $(L_0, K_0)$ such that[19]

**1** $(L_0, K_0)$ is on the $Q = 200$ isoquant.
**2** RTS, evaluated at $(L_0, K_0)$, equals the ratio of the unit cost of labor to the unit cost of equipment: $\text{RTS} = w/r$.

These implications are sensible ones. The first implication says that production is carried out efficiently. The second implication can best be established and understood by supposing that it is incorrect and then showing that that supposition is inconsistent with cost minimization. Let $(L', K')$ be an input combination on the $Q = 200$ isoquant which is not at the point of tangency with the isocost line: $\text{RTS} \neq w/r$ at $(L', K')$. Suppose that $(L', K')$ is the least-cost combination. To be concrete, let $\text{RTS} = 3$ and $w/r = 2$. $\text{RTS} = 3$ means that the company can replace 3 machine-hours with 1 worker-hour without affecting output; but costs would be reduced in that event, because the expense of the additional worker-hour is completely offset by the savings from releasing just 2 machine-hours rather than 3 machine-hours. Therefore, $(L', K')$ is not the least-cost input combination, nor by the same logic is any other combination for which $\text{RTS} > w/r$. Now turn things around. Suppose that $(L', K')$ is an input combination on the $Q = 200$ isoquant for which $\text{RTS} = 1$ and $w/r = 2$. $\text{RTS} = 1$ means that the company can replace 1 worker-hour with 1 machine-hour without affecting output; yet costs would be reduced in that event, because the expense of the additional machine-hour is completely offset by the savings from releasing just $1/2$ worker-hour. Therefore, $(L', K')$ is not the least-cost combination, nor by the same logic is any other combination for which

---

[19] This result can be found by using the Lagrangian method explained in Appendix A to Chapter 2. The problem is to minimize cost subject to $Q = 200 = f(L, K)$. The Lagrangian expression is

$$Z = wL + rK - \lambda[f(L, K) - 200]$$

The first-order conditions for a constrained minimum are

$$\frac{\partial Z}{\partial L} = w - \lambda \frac{\partial f}{\partial L} = 0$$

$$\frac{\partial Z}{\partial K} = r - \lambda \frac{\partial f}{\partial K} = 0$$

$$\frac{\partial Z}{\partial \lambda} = f(L, K) - 200 = 0$$

Using the first two conditions, $(\partial f/\partial L)/(\partial f/\partial K) = \text{RTS} = w/r$. The third condition, of course, ensures that $(L_0, K_0)$ is on the $Q = 200$ isoquant.

RTS $< w/r$. Only when RTS $= w/r$ is it possible for the company to rearrange inputs, maintain production at the target level, and reduce total cost.

Another interpretation of RTS $= w/r$ is available when we recall that the rate of technical substitution of labor for equipment equals the marginal product of labor divided by the marginal product of equipment: RTS $= MP_L/MP_K$. If RTS $= w/r$, then $MP_L/MP_K = w/r$, and after rearrangement of terms, $MP_L/w = MP_K/r$. Since $MP_L$ is measured in units of output per worker-hour and $w$ is measured in dollars per worker-hour, the ratio $MP_L/w$ is measured in units of output per dollar. So is the ratio $MP_K/r$. Therefore, cost minimization implies that inputs are chosen so that the last dollar of expenditure on every type of input yields the same increase in output. There is no cost advantage to moving dollars from one type of input to another type.

To review, we chose a target level of output, constructed an isocost line having slope $w/r$, varied the tentative budget until the isocost line was tangent to the isoquant at some input combination $(L_0, K_0)$, and computed total cost as $wL_0 + rK_0$. Replication of this procedure, with each replication beginning with a different value of output, establishes a relation between total cost, output level, and input prices. That relation is the long-run total cost function $C = C(Q, w, r)$.

This derivation can be illustrated graphically in Figure 4-8 for the Bobcat Corporation. Four isoquants and isocost lines are shown. The four points of tangency ($A$, $B$, $C$, and $D$) shown define four points on the long-run total cost function. Connecting these points and all other points of tangency for isoquants and isocost lines not shown, we obtain the so-called long-run expansion path. Because Bobcat's production function is one of constant returns to scale, the expansion path is the straight line $0ABCD$. For more general cases, the expansion path can be nonlinear.

Total cost is predicted to rise when the price of one input goes up, other

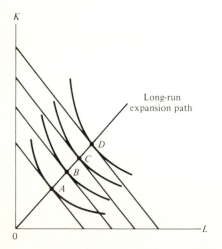

**FIGURE 4-8**
Long-run expansion path defines long-run total cost function.

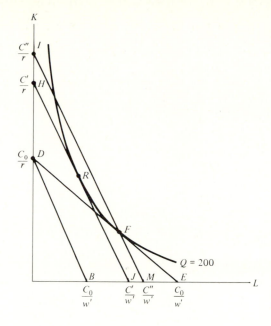

**FIGURE 4-9**
Impact of higher wage on total cost.

things being equal. Observe, for example, the effects of a higher wage rate $w'$ in Figure 4-9. The isocost line $DE$ for $C_0$ dollars of expenditure turns into line $DB$, which has a steeper slope ($w'/r$) and hits the horizontal axis closer to the origin (at $C_0/w'$). Budget $C_0$ is no longer sufficient to finance the production of $Q = 200$. A higher total cost of $C'$ is paid, for which budget the isocost line $HJ$ is tangent to the $Q = 200$ isoquant at point $R$. The new input combination has fewer worker-hours and more machine-hours than the former combination at point $F$. This substitution against the input which became relatively more expensive softens the impact upon total cost. Had the company kept its former input combination, it would have needed yet a larger budget $C''$ ($> C' > C_0$), corresponding to the isocost line $IM$, in order to produce $Q = 200$. The substitution against worker-hours illustrates again that total cost depends on input prices, not merely as multipliers of input quantities but also as determinants of input quantities: $L = L(Q, w, r)$ and $K = K(Q, w, r)$.

Long-run total cost (LRTC) for the Bobcat Corporation is simply a straight line from the origin, as shown in Figure 4-10a.[20] The explanation for this shape

---

[20] The derivation is straightforward. In note 8 we showed that RTS $= K/L$. Since RTS must equal $w/r$ for least cost, $K/L = w/r$. Using this equation and the cost equation $C = wL + rK$, we find by solving simultaneously that $L = C/2w$ and $K = C/2r$. Substituting these two expressions into the production function, $Q = 5\sqrt{KL}$ and rearranging gives the long-run total cost:

$$C = \frac{2\sqrt{rw}}{5} Q$$

Note that the equation $K/L = w/r$ is the equation of the expansion path shown in Figure 4-8.

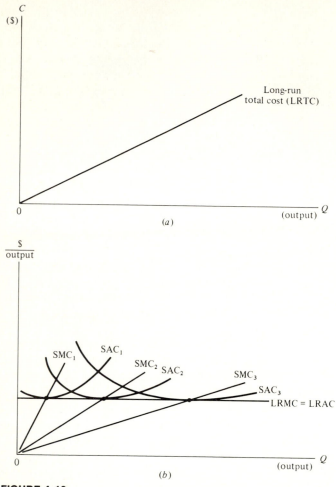

**FIGURE 4-10**
Long-run and short-run cost functions for the Bobcat Corporation.

follows directly from the fact that Bobcat's production function is one of constant returns to scale.

The long-run marginal cost (LRMC) and long-run average cost (LRAC)
curves are shown as the single horizontal line in Figure 4-10*b*. This result can
be explained geometrically since marginal cost is the slope of LRTC and
average cost is the slope of a ray from the origin to LRTC. A glance at Figure
4-10*a* reveals that these two slopes are constant and equal.

Of course, in the long run all costs are variable. Hence, in the long run there
is no distinction between fixed and variable costs. It is of interest, however, to
relate the short-run average total cost and marginal cost curves to the long-run
average cost curve.

Three short-run average total cost curves corresponding to three different fixed quantities of equipment are shown in Figure 4-10$b$. Notice that short-run average total cost is never less than long-run average total cost for any given rate of output. The reason is that managers have the latitude to choose from a greater number of input combinations in the long run. In our two-input model, Bobcat's managers can select any input combination along an isoquant in the long run, whereas in the short run they are restricted to just one combination on that isoquant. The ability to substitute for or against a fixed factor cannot increase total costs, and it typically reduces them. Employment of a fixed input may in the short run be fortuitously fixed at exactly the level which managers would have chosen in the long run for a given level of output. This possibility accounts for the tangencies of $SAC_1$, $SAC_2$, and $SAC_3$ with LRAC. The LRAC is said to be an "envelope" of the set of short-run average total cost curves.

In the more general case in which there is an initial region of increasing returns to scale followed by decreasing returns to scale, the long-run total cost function would have the shape shown in Figure 4-11$a$. The rationale is similar to that given earlier for the more general short-run total cost function (Figure 4-6$a$). Accordingly, this long-run total cost function yields the U-shaped long-run average cost (LRAC) and long-run marginal cost (LRMC) curves of Figure 4-11$b$.

In Figure 4-11$b$, three short-run average total cost and marginal cost curves are depicted, each corresponding to a different fixed quantity of equipment. Notice in particular $SAC_2$, which has the unique property that it is tangent to LRAC at the point where both curves attain minimum average cost. This short-run curve plays an important role in the theory of pure competition, which is analyzed in Chapter 6.

A final point of explanation about Figure 4-11$b$ is in order. At output $Q'$, for example, $SAC_1 = LRAC$ *and* $SMC_1 = LRMC$. This is not accidental. To understand this relationship, observe the dashed curve $ABC$ in Figure 4-11$a$, which represents the short-run total cost function corresponding to $SAC_1$ and $SMC_1$. This function lies everywhere above LRTC except at point $B$, where the two total cost curves are tangent. Since they are tangent, the slopes (and marginal costs) are equal; also, they share the same ray from the origin to point $B$, and this implies that the average costs are equal.

## EMPIRICAL EVIDENCE ON LONG-RUN COST FUNCTIONS

The shape of the long-run average cost curve provides an alternative approach to the study of economies of scale. We have discussed this issue earlier in the context of the long-run production function. Here we merely note that much econometric research has been directed at estimating the long-run function.[21]

[21] See, for example, A. A. Walters, "Production and Cost Functions," *Econometrica*, January 1963.

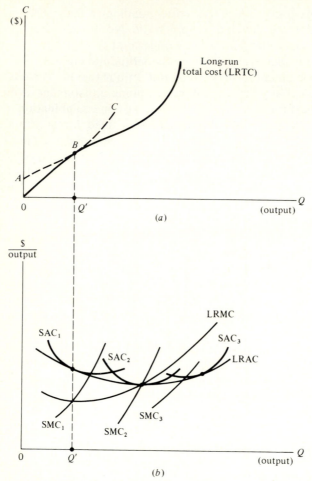

**FIGURE 4-11**
Long-run and short-run cost functions for the general case.

The typical finding has been that the LRAC curve generally declines over initial output levels but becomes horizontal thereafter (or rises only slightly). In other words, there is little empirical support for decreasing returns to scale (or diseconomies of scale) once minimum average cost is attained. Similar results have been found by engineering studies of cost functions; an important recent study is discussed in Chapter 7.

We conclude this lengthy analysis of cost by reporting an econometric cost function for electric power generation. The study by Christensen and Greene[22]

[22] L. R. Christensen and W. H. Greene, "Economies of Scale in U.S. Electric Power Generation," *Journal of Political Economy*, August 1976.

**TABLE 4-7**
COST AND OUTPUT DATA FOR SELECTED ELECTRIC POWER
COMPANIES IN 1970

| Company | Output, million kwh | Average cost, $/1,000 kwh |
|---|---|---|
| Newport Electric | 50 | 10.75 |
| Community Public Service | 183 | 7.03 |
| United Gas Improvement | 467 | 8.44 |
| St. Joseph Light & Power | 938 | 5.45 |
| Iowa Southern Utilities | 1,328 | 6.07 |
| Missouri Public Service | 1,886 | 5.47 |
| Rochester Gas & Electric | 2,020 | 8.89 |
| Iowa Electric Light & Power | 2,445 | 5.37 |
| Central La. Gas & Electric | 2,689 | 5.54 |
| Wisconsin Public Service | 3,571 | 6.02 |
| Atlantic City Electric | 4,187 | 7.00 |
| Central Illinois Public Service | 5,316 | 4.43 |
| Kansas Gas & Electric | 5,785 | 3.36 |
| Northern Indiana Public Service | 6,837 | 4.96 |
| Indianapolis Power and Light | 7,484 | 3.94 |
| Oklahoma Gas & Electric | 10,149 | 3.01 |
| Niagara Mohawk Power | 11,667 | 6.40 |
| Potomac Electric Power | 13,846 | 6.95 |
| Gulf States Utilities | 17,875 | 3.27 |
| Virginia Electric Power | 23,217 | 4.85 |
| Consolidated Edison | 29,613 | 8.43 |
| Detroit Edison | 30,958 | 6.05 |
| Duke Power | 34,212 | 4.84 |
| Commonwealth Edison | 46,871 | 5.43 |
| Southern | 53,918 | 4.30 |

*Source:* L. R. Christensen and W. H. Greene, "Economies of Scale in U.S. Electric Power Generation," *Journal of Political Economy,* August 1976.

used data for the year 1970 for 114 electric power companies in the United States. The data covered cost, output, and the average prices of capital, labor, and fuel for each firm. Table 4-7 lists some of these data for a selected number of firms.

A graph of their long-run average cost curve is reproduced as Figure 4-12. The curve shows an initial region of increasing returns (or falling average cost) and thereafter becomes relatively flat. We should note that a single large firm (the American Electric Power Company) was responsible for the slightly rising portion of the curve.

The authors also performed an interesting calculation concerning the efficiency of electric power production in the United States.

In 1970 if the combined output of all the firms in our sample had been produced at

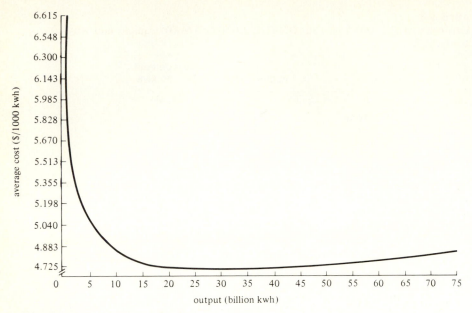

**FIGURE 4-12**
Long-run average cost curve for electric power production in 1970.

the minimum point on the average cost curve (0.473¢ per kilowatt hour), the total cost of production would have been $175.1 million less.[23]

That is, if all production had been by 33 hypothetical firms of optimal size, total cost would have been 3.2 percent lower that it actually was. A large number of electric power companies in the United States were apparently "too small" in 1970 and were operating in the region of output where average costs were falling rapidly.

## QUESTIONS AND PROBLEMS

**4-1** Explain the difference between the law of diminishing marginal returns and the concept of decreasing returns to scale.

**4-2** When Hampton and Son increased its employment of labor and equipment ($L$, $K$) from (65, 20) to (85, 20) to (100, 20), the company's output rose from 200 to 240 to 260 units. Is labor subject to diminishing returns at Hampton and Son?

**4-3** Managers at Scuppernong Company believe that 24 worker-hours per week could replace 3 machine-hours per week without affecting Scuppernong's output. The marginal product of labor is 2. What is the marginal product of equipment at Scuppernong?

**4-4** Given the information that (40, 25) and (20, 45) are two combinations of worker-

[23] Ibid., p. 675.

hours and machine-hours that are on the same isoquant of a particular company, which of the following combinations are not on that isoquant, and why?

| Bundle Label | Bundle (L, K) |
|---|---|
| A | (30, 35) |
| B | (25, 45) |
| C | (50, 20) |
| D | (40, 20) |
| E | (30, 30) |
| F | (50, 10) |

**4-5** By the word "productivity" some writers mean the ratio of output to worker-hours employed. In the short run, do diminishing returns to labor necessarily imply that productivity in a company will decline as more labor is hired?

**4-6** Can marginal cost be a negative number? Specifically, suppose that a manager asserts first that the minimum total cost of producing 49 units is $10,000 and second that the minimum cost of producing 50 units is $9,950. Assuming that a consistent definition of cost has been used in the two parts of the assertion, can you think of any plausible circumstances in which the two parts of the assertion could be consistent with each other?

**4-7** Assume that in the short-run a company's output $Q$ is related to its employment of worker-hours $L$ according to the production function $Q = 10L^{.5}$.

a How much labor must the company employ in order to reach the output target $Q = \overline{Q}$?

b In the short-run, machine-hours, the only other input utilized by the company, are fixed at 500. The price to the company of a worker-hour is $10, and the price of a machine-hour is $8. Derive the short-run total cost function for this company.

**4-8** The output $Q$ of Fast Company is produced with worker-hours $L$ and machine-hours $K$. Fast expects to pay $15 per worker-hour and $10 per machine-hour. What is the equation of the isocost line for $20,000 of expenditures on inputs by Fast?

**4-9** Mala Chi Company plans to produce at the rate of $Q = 1,000$. Managers at Mala Chi tentatively consider an input configuration for which the marginal product of labor is 16 and the marginal product of equipment is 8. They expect to pay $15 per worker-hour and $10 per machine-hour. Is the tentative input configuration a cost-minimizing configuration?

**4-10** A particular company spends $100,000 by employing 4,000 worker-hours and 4,000 machine-hours. With this input combination, the marginal product of labor is 32 and the marginal product of equipment is 8. How much does the company pay its workers? (You may assume the company minimizes cost.)

**4-11** This problem illustrates the so-called break-even chart, an important practical business tool. This application of cost functions assumes that average variable cost can be approximated as a constant for the relevant range of output. Another key assumption is that the price of the firm's product can be taken as fixed and unaffected by the amount the firm sells. These assumptions, of course, tend to restrict the usefulness of the break-even chart.

The Williams Wax Works is interested in determining how many gallons of wax it must sell to break even, or cover all costs. Its fixed cost (rent, overhead, etc.)

amounts to $50,000 per year. Average variable cost per gallon of wax is $1.50. If a gallon of wax can be sold for $2.50, how many gallons must be sold to break even? Plot the break-even chart. (The vertical axis of the chart should measure total cost and total revenue, and the horizontal axis should measure the quantity in gallons per year. Note that both total revenue and total cost will be straight lines and that they will intersect at the break-even output. Total cost, of course, has a vertical axis intercept of $50,000, while total revenue begins at the origin.)

**4-12** Suppose that the Williams Wax Works of problem 11 is considering an alternative, more automated technique for producing wax. The effect on cost would be to increase fixed cost to $75,000 per year but to lower average variable cost to $1.25 per gallon. Show this alternative cost function on the break-even chart of problem 11 and determine the new break-even output. Discuss which alternative Williams Wax Works should choose.

*Note:* Parts of the remaining problems require calculus.

**4-13** Marbles Technology has two adjacent plants. Output $F$ from the first and older plant depends on worker-hours $f$ employed in the plant according to the short-run production function $F = 18f^{.5}$. Output $S$ from the second and newer plant depends on worker-hours $s$ employed in the plant according to the short-run production function $S = 36s^{.5}$.

Managers at Marbles have hired $T$ total worker-hours and in the short run can allocate them to the two plants in any proportion. Assuming the goal to be maximization of total output $(F + S)$, given $T$, what proportion of the total worker-hours should be allocated to the older plant?

**4-14** Using the information and results of the previous problem, derive Marbles's short-run production function which relates total output $(F + S)$ to total worker-hours employed $(T)$.

**4-15** Assume that the long-run production function of a particular company is of the Cobb-Douglas type: $Q = L^{.75} K^{.25}$. If the company pays $w = \$12$ and $r = \$10$, how many machine-hours will it employ for every worker-hour that it employs, assuming that the company minimizes total cost?

**4-16** Consider $x = n + k$ as a possible specification of a production function. In what respects do the properties of this function conform or not conform to the properties of a production function as discussed in the text?

**a** Are marginal products positive?

**b** Are there diminishing returns to inputs?

**c** Are inputs complementary in production?

**4-17** Consider $x = nk - (12/n) - (16/k)$ as a possible specification of a production function. In what respects do the properties of this function conform or not conform to the properties of a production function as discussed in the text?

**a** Are marginal products positive?

**b** Are there diminishing returns to inputs?

**c** Are inputs complementary in production?

**4-18** The short-run total cost function at Heavy Tools, Inc., is estimated to be $C = 64 + 5Q + .25Q^2$, where $Q$ denotes the rate of output.

**a** Derive equations for Heavy Tool's average fixed cost (AFC), average variable cost (AVC), average total cost (ATC), and marginal cost (MC).

**b** Choose a few values of $Q$ between $Q = 12$ and $Q = 24$; plot the corresponding values of AFC, AVC, ATC, and MC; and verify that this short-run cost curve family has the general properties of the short-run cost curve family shown in Figure 4-6*b*.

**c** At what rate of output is the unit cost of production (ATC) minimized?

**4-19** Suppose that Heavy Tools, Inc., must pay a licensing fee of $36 regardless of how much it produces. Assume that its short-run total cost function, exclusive of the fee, is $C = 64 + 5Q + .25Q^2$.

**a** What is the short-run total cost function of Heavy Tools, inclusive of the fee?

**b** Repeat all steps of problem 4-18 using the short-run total cost function which is inclusive of the licensing fee. Which members of the cost curve family are not affected by the fee? Which members are affected and in what way? (*Example:* "The fee increases the AFC of producing $Q$ units by the amount $Q/36$ dollars.") Has the fee altered the rate of output which minimizes the unit cost?

**4-20** Suppose that Heavy Tools, Inc., must pay a $1 excise tax for every unit of output which it manufactures. Assume that its short-run total cost function, exclusive of the excise tax, is $C = 64 + 5Q + .25Q^2$.

**a** What is the short-run total cost function of Heavy Tools, inclusive of the excise tax?

**b** Repeat all steps of problem 4-18 using the short-run total cost function which is inclusive of the excise tax. Which members of the cost curve family are not affected by the fee? Which members are affected and in what way? Has the fee altered the rate of output which minimizes the unit cost?

## BIBLIOGRAPHY

Alchian, Armen A.: "Costs and Outputs," in Moses Abramovitz, et al., *The Allocation of Economic Resources* (Stanford, Calif.: Stanford University Press, 1959).

Anthony, R. N: "What Should Cost Mean?" *Harvard Business Review*, May–June 1970.

Clark, J. M.: *The Economics of Overhead Cost* (Chicago: University of Chicago Press, 1923).

Dean, Joel: *Managerial Economics* (Englewood Cliffs, N.J.: Prentice-Hall, 1951), chap. 5.

Hirshleifer, Jack: "The Firm's Cost Function: A Successful Reconstruction?" *Journal of Business*, July 1962.

Johnston, J.: *Statistical Cost Analysis* (New York: McGraw-Hill, 1960).

Stigler, G.: "The Economies of Scale," *Journal of Law and Economics*, October 1958.

Walters, A. A.: "Production and Cost Functions: An Econometric Survey," *Econometrica*, January–April 1963.

CHAPTER **5**

# OPTIMAL
# OUTPUT DECISIONS
# AND LINEAR
# PROGRAMMING

**CHAPTER OUTLINE**

**INTRODUCTION**

In this chapter we shall examine optimal output decision making, using two analytic techniques: marginal analysis and linear programming. First, cost and demand functions that were developed in previous chapters are brought together, and marginal analysis is applied to the problem of determining the level of output that maximizes profit. Both single-product and multiple-product output decisions by firms are examined.

Next, we shall introduce the mathematical technique known as linear programming and apply it to several problems of the firm, including choosing the optimal combination of processes[1] to produce a product, given fixed quantities of inputs. In effect, linear programming enables us to derive the production function which marginal analysis normally takes as given. A second problem that will be discussed and contrasted with marginal analysis is how linear programming can be used to determine the profit-maximizing level of outputs for a multiple-product firm.

While marginal analysis and linear programming are similar techniques in that both can be used to solve optimization problems, there are some important advantages which linear programming possesses in cases involving certain types of real-world problems. In fact, linear programming is one of the most practical and powerful managerial decision-making tools currently available. We shall explain these advantages in this chapter.

The chapter concludes with several illustrative, large-scale applications of linear programming to decisions of the firm. Later chapters also contain important applications to problems such as capital budgeting. Finally, Appendix C at the end of the chapter considers some of the more technical details of linear programming.

## MARGINAL ANALYSIS

### The Single-Product Firm

In Chapter 2 the concept of the demand curve confronting a firm was examined. For a firm in a competitive industry, we noted that the demand curve is a horizontal line at the existing market price (which is determined by the intersection of the industry demand and supply curves). Of course, the reason for this is that competition involves so many suppliers that a single firm's output cannot influence price. For simplicity, only "constant-price" demand curves are considered here. In Chapters 6 and 7, this assumption will be relaxed when we take up market structures such as oligopoly and monopoly.

In Chapter 4 we derived the various cost functions for the firm. Figure 5-1 brings together the demand curve and short-run cost curves for our hypothetical firm.

As shown, the price is fixed to the firm at $P_0$. The firm can sell all that it wishes at this price and, of course, none at a higher price. The firm consequently is concerned only with the choice of the level of output that will

---

[1] A process is a technique of production which combines inputs in fixed proportions. For example, one process might require 1 unit of capital and 2 units of labor to produce 1 unit of output.

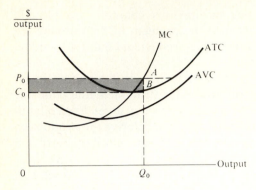

FIGURE 5-1
Short-run profit maximization.

yield maximum profit. Three short-run cost curves are also shown: MC, the marginal cost curve; ATC, the average total cost curve; and AVC, the average variable cost curve. Given this information, what level of output will produce a profit maximum?

To answer this question, we need a definition of profit $\pi$. In terms of our model here, profit is simply the difference between total revenue and total cost. Total revenue $R$ is simply price $P$ multiplied by quantity $Q$ or $PQ$. Total cost is denoted by $C$. Hence,

$$\pi = PQ - C(Q) \tag{5-1}$$

Since $C$ is a function of output, we indicate this by writing total cost as $C(Q)$.

The marginal analysis rule for profit maximization is that the firm should expand output until the rising marginal cost curve intersects the demand curve.[2] In short, the firm should equate MC and $P_0$. This is shown graphically in Figure 5-1 as determining the output $Q_0$.

The $P = MC$ rule can be explained easily. If output $Q_0$ is *not* the profit-max-

---

[2] The rule is easily derived with calculus. Given

$$\pi = PQ - C(Q)$$

where $P$ = price
$Q$ = output
$C(Q)$ = total cost
For $\pi$ to be a maximum, $d\pi/dQ$ must be equated to zero. Since, by assumption, $P$ is a constant, we obtain

$$P - \frac{dC}{dQ} = 0$$

or, since $dC/dQ$ is the definition of marginal cost MC, we can write

$$P = MC$$

The second-order condition for a maximum requires MC to be rising, as is indeed the case.

imizing output, then either increasing or decreasing output by 1 unit should increase $\pi$. If both directions of change in output reduce $\pi$, then profit is greatest at $Q_0$. Consider a 1-unit increase in output. For $\pi$ to increase, the marginal revenue from selling an additional unit of output is simply equal to $P_0$, the market price. The increase in cost is, by definition, marginal cost MC. Since MC lies above $P_0$ to the right of $Q_0$, the 1-unit increase in output leads to a *reduction* in $\pi$. Similarly, a 1-unit decrease in output reduces revenue more than it reduces cost (MC lies below $P_0$ to the left of $Q_0$). This again leads to a $\pi$ reduction, implying that $Q_0$ is indeed the profit-maximizing level of output.

Since $\pi$ is the difference between total revenue and total cost, we can show the amount of $\pi$ graphically as the area of the shaded rectangle in Figure 5-1. That is, total revenue is the rectangle $P_0 0 Q_0 A$, i.e., $P_0$ times $Q_0$, and total cost is the rectangle $C_0 0 Q_0 B$. (The value of ATC at output $Q_0$ is $C_0$, and so $C_0$ times $Q_0$ is total cost.) The difference between the two rectangles is equal to $\pi$, the shaded rectangle.

For the present case, profit is positive. This is, of course, simply a result of the assumed price $P_0$. In Figure 5-2 we turn to the optimal output decision for alternative assumptions about the level of market price.

Suppose market price is $P_1$. The profit-maximization output decision is again determined by the $P = MC$ rule. Hence, the firm should select output $Q_1$. Notice in this case that the firm is unable to cover all costs since price is less than average total cost (ATC). Thus, the best the firm can do in the short run is to operate at $Q_1$.

Since its revenues exceed its variable (or out-of-pocket) costs, the firm is at least contributing something toward its fixed (or overhead) costs, which it cannot avoid even by shutting down completely. Of course, in the long run, if the firm expects the price to continue at $P_1$ indefinitely, it should withdraw from the industry.

Next, consider the price $P_2$. At this price, the firm can just cover its variable costs since $P_2 = AVC$ at output $Q_2$. There is no contribution to overhead costs, and so the firm is indifferent between operating at $Q_2$ and simply stopping production completely. (We are abstracting from the case in which price is tem-

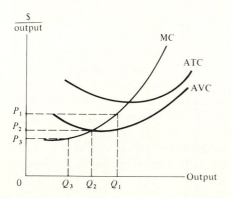

**FIGURE 5-2**
Alternate market prices and the firm's output decision.

porarily low and is expected to rise in the future. Such a case, when combined with shutting-down and starting-up costs, which are also ignored here, could make it profitable for the firm to continue production even when a price below $P_2$ prevails.)

Prices below AVC, such as $P_3$, make it definitely preferable to shut down rather than operate at $Q_3$, where $P = MC$. Prices below AVC, of course, imply that the firm cannot cover even its out-of-pocket costs.

To sum up, the single-product firm should produce the output level at which marginal cost equals price. However, if the market price falls below the firm's average variable costs, the firm should discontinue production altogether.

An interesting application of these ideas was described in an article in *Business Week* of April 20, 1963. The article dealt with the policy of Continental Airlines to run extra flights that were not expected "to do more than return their out-of-pocket costs—plus a little profit." According to *Business Week:*

> This philosophy leans heavily on marginal analysis. And the line leans heavily on Chris F. Whelan, vice-president in charge of economic planning, to translate marginalism into hard, dollars-and-cents decisions. . . .
>
> . . . Whelan's approach is this: He considers that the bulk of his scheduled flights have to return at least their fully allocated costs. Overhead, depreciation, insurance are very real expenses and must be covered. The out-of-pocket approach comes into play, says Whelan, only after the line's basic schedule has been set.
>
> "Then you go a step farther," he says, and see if adding more flights will contribute to the corporate net. Similarly, if he's thinking of dropping a flight with a disappointing record, he puts it under the marginal microscope: "If your revenues are going to be more than your out-of-pocket costs, you should keep the flight on."
>
> By "out-of-pocket costs" Whelan means just that: the actual dollars that Continental has to pay out to run a flight. He gets the figure not by applying hypothetical equations but by circulating a proposed schedule to every operating department concerned and finding out just what extra expenses it will entail. If a ground crew already on duty can service the plane, the flight isn't charged a penny of their salary expense. There may even be some costs eliminated in running the flight; they won't need men to roll the plane to a hangar, for instance, if it flies on to another stop.

### The Multiple-Product Firm

Although we have been concerned so far with firms that produce and sell only a single product, everyone would agree that few single-product firms exist in the real world. In fact, many of the large corporations in the United States produce and sell hundreds of products. In this section, we shall consider multiple-product firms. To keep things simple, a firm with two products is analyzed. Two products can be treated graphically quite effectively; more than two products requires one to resort to algebraic methods, with little change in the theoretical conclusions.

We shall assume that the firm has fixed quantities of inputs available to it and is a competitor in the two markets in which it sells. This is analogous to the discussion of the single-product firm earlier; i.e., prices are taken as given to the firm.

The technology for converting its fixed inputs into the two outputs $Q_1$ and $Q_2$ can be represented by a product transformation curve. Figure 5-3 shows the product transformation curve for our hypothetical firm.

The product transformation curve assumes that the firm is *efficient* in production. That is, it is assumed that if $0A$ units of $Q_1$ are being produced, then $0B$ units is the maximum amount of $Q_2$ that can be produced. Hence, points such as $T$ that lie on the curve itself imply efficiency in production. In contrast, points inside the curve, such as $R$, indicate inefficiency in production. This means that the firm could produce more of both products with its given inputs and with the given technology of production.

Product transformation curves are generally assumed to be concave to the origin, as shown in Figure 5-3. All product transformation curves necessarily have a negative slope, reflecting the fact that producing more of one product necessarily means reducing production of the other. The concave shape is not necessary. However, the underlying assumption—that for each additional unit of one product that is given up, the increase in output of the second product becomes progressively smaller—does appear to be a reasonable one.

Recall the assumption that all inputs are fixed to the firm. This means, for example, that machine capacity, assembly capacity, and finishing capacity are fixed in the short run. We ignore any variable inputs, or alternatively it can be assumed that other inputs, such as labor, have been purchased in advance on long-term contracts. The long-run decision could be handled by shifting outward the entire product transformation curve to reflect increases in inputs; however, for the present analysis, we choose to focus only on the short-run problem. As we shall see later in this chapter, linear programming is similarly concerned with optimization problems characterized by fixed input resources.

Having described the production side of the problem, consider next the demand side. Since all inputs are fixed, it follows that all costs are fixed as well.

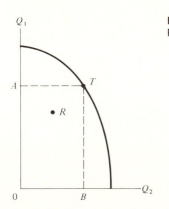

**FIGURE 5-3**
Product transformation curve.

Maximization of profit, therefore, is equivalent to maximization of revenue. That is, $\pi = R - C$ and $C$ is unaffected by the quantities of $Q_1$ and $Q_2$ produced. Letting $P_1$ and $P_2$ represent the market prices for $Q_1$ and $Q_2$, respectively, revenue can be written as

$$R = P_1Q_1 + P_2Q_2 \tag{5-2}$$

or

$$Q_1 = \frac{R}{P_1} - \frac{P_2}{P_1}Q_2 \tag{5-3}$$

Equation (5-3) is a useful rearrangement of equation (5-2) into its "slope-intercept" form. It clarifies how to graph the so-called isorevenue lines. If we assign $R$ a particular value, say $R_0$, then equation (5-3) becomes the simple linear relationship between $Q_1$ and $Q_2$ which is graphed in Figure 5-4. Notice that the vertical axis intercept is $R_0/P_1$ and the slope is $-(P_2/P_1)$. All points on the isorevenue line, i.e., all combinations of $Q_1$ and $Q_2$ satisfying the equation, will provide the same total revenue of $R_0$.

A family of isorevenue lines could be constructed. All the lines would be parallel since the slope depends only on the output price ratio. Since the intercept is given by $R_0/P_1$, lines farther from the origin would have higher intercept values and therefore would represent higher values of revenue.

In Figure 5-5 a family of isorevenue lines is superimposed on the product transformation curve. As observed above, profit maximization is equivalent to revenue maximization, since all costs are fixed. Hence, the firm should select the point on the product transformation curve that lies on the highest-valued isorevenue line. This point, $E$, is the point of tangency in Figure 5-5 and indicates that the optimal quantities of outputs are $Q_1'$ and $Q_2'$.

We can gain further insight by examining the tangency solution in more depth. Basically, the tangency means that the slope of the isorevenue curve equals the slope of the product transformation curve. We noted above that the

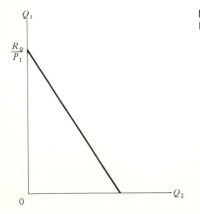

**FIGURE 5-4**
Isorevenue line.

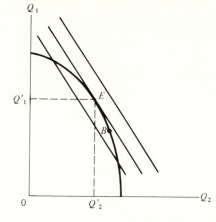

**FIGURE 5-5**
Optimal output levels.

(absolute value of the) slope of the isorevenue curve equals the ratio of the prices of the two products, or $P_2/P_1$. The absolute value of the slope of the product transformation curve is termed rate of product transformation, or RPT. It is simply the ratio $\Delta Q_1/\Delta Q_2$, and it can be interpreted as the number of units of $Q_1$ that can be obtained by sacrificing 1 unit of $Q_2$.

Suppose at some point on the curve, say $B$, RPT equals unity. This means that the firm can cut back on production of $Q_2$ by 1 unit and thereby release sufficient resources to produce an additional unit of $Q_1$. In short, it can transform 1 unit of $Q_2$ into 1 unit of $Q_1$.

Now assume that the product prices are $P_1 = \$2$ and $P_2 = \$1$ so that $P_2/P_1 = \frac{1}{2}$. Since the ratios are *not* equal, we know that this is not the profit-maximizing solution. The reason is simple. At production point $B$, sacrificing 1 unit of $Q_2$ implies a marginal opportunity cost of \$1, i.e., 1 unit of $Q_2$ multiplied by its price. The additional unit of $Q_1$, however, can be sold for \$2, thereby yielding a net increase in profit of \$1. Hence, the firm should reduce $Q_2$ production and increase production of $Q_1$. Only when the two ratios are equal, at point $E$ in Figure 5-5, will it be true that profit cannot be increased.

## LINEAR PROGRAMMING

In the remaining sections of this chapter we shall introduce the mathematical optimization technique known as linear programming. Although mathematical techniques closely related to linear programming can be traced back much further, linear programming was not developed until 1947. In that year, George B. Dantzig, a Stanford mathematician, published the complete description of that technique as we know it today. Dantzig developed linear programming as a tool for solving planning problems of the United States Air Force.

Although linear "programming" and computer "programming" are completely unrelated as such, computer development has been extremely important for the success of linear programming. Linear programming is a technique for solving a problem by iteration. That is, the linear programming technique requires that a system of linear equations be solved over and over, with one variable being changed each time until the final solution is obtained. An industrial example might involve 300 variables and 200 equations. To reach the final solution might require solving the system simultaneously 100 times. Clearly, without a high-speed computer to perform the calculations, a linear programming solution might be unattainable at a reasonable cost.

Since marginal analysis is an alternative technique for solving optimization problems, a key objective is to compare the two techniques to make clear the advantages and disadvantages of each. To oversimplify somewhat, marginal analysis is primarily valuable as a tool for elucidating general economic principles, while linear programming is best suited for solving actual managerial problems. As we have seen in the preceding sections of this chapter, marginal analysis uses such concepts as marginal product, marginal cost, and marginal revenue. While these concepts are necessarily implicit in good decision making, it is not inaccurate to observe that corporate decision makers often find these concepts difficult to relate to their specific problems. The underlying concepts of linear programming, by contrast, are more familiar to managers and are consequently easier to apply.

At this point it should be helpful to present the mathematical formulation of a linear programming problem. The typical problem is one of optimizing (maximizing or minimizing) an objective function:

$$Z = \sum_{j=1}^{n} C_j X_j$$

subject to constraints of the form

$$\sum_{j=1}^{n} a_{ij} X_j \lesseqgtr b_i \qquad (i = 1, 2, \ldots, m)$$

and the nonnegativity conditions

$$X_j \geq 0 \qquad (j = 1, 2, \ldots, n)$$

where $X_j$ = quantity of $j$th variable of interest to decision maker, where there are $n$ variables being considered

$C_j$ = per unit contribution to objective function (profit or cost) of $j$th variable, where there are $n$ variables

$Z$ = objective function to be maximized or minimized

$a_{ij}$ = coefficient of $j$th variable in the $i$th constraint, where there are $m$ constraints and $n$ variables

$b_i$ = $i$th requirement, where there are $m$ requirements in all; for example, $b_i$ might represent quantity of a certain raw material available to decision maker

An important advantage of linear programming is its capability for handling inequality constraints. For example, a firm may wish to maximize profit subject to the constraint that no more than 800 hours of machine capacity (its present capacity) be used. Linear programming does not require that all 800 hours be used; it may be optimal to leave the machines idle part of the time. Marginal analysis, by contrast, is not well suited for handling such cases.

Since linear programming assumes linear relationships, it is more restrictive than marginal analysis. Notice in the equations above that both the objective function and the constraints are linear. This means, for example, that as output increases, costs and revenues must increase linearly. This is sometimes a disadvantage and in certain situations could lead to quite erroneous decisions. We should add that nonlinear programming techniques do exist, although they involve advanced mathematics beyond the scope of this book.

Hence, both techniques belong in the tool kit of the corporate economist. The appropriate function of each will become more clear as linear programming is explained in the following sections.

In the next section we shall examine the linear programming production function for a single-product firm. A linear programming isoquant is derived and compared with the marginal analysis isoquant. The linear programming isoquant will be shown to consist of a series of connected straight-line segments, although with the same general shape as the smooth and continuous marginal analysis isoquant. The following section uses the graphical method of linear programming to solve for the profit-maximizing level of outputs for a multiple-product firm. An algebraic technique (the simplex method) suitable for solving large-scale problems is explained intuitively, but a complete description is reserved for Appendix C. The final section presents a large-scale application of linear programming.

## The Linear Programming Production Function

Before turning to the assumptions underlying the linear programming model of production, we shall review briefly the marginal analysis model developed in Chapter 4. The most general production function can be represented by an isoquant which shows all the various combinations of the two inputs (or factors of production) that can be used to produce a given level of output. An example is shown in Figure 5-6.

Points $A$, $B$, and $C$, in Figure 5-6 show three of the possible combinations of the two inputs that can be selected to produce the given level of output $\overline{Q}$. For certain marginal analysis problems, this may be a perfectly acceptable way of representing the firm's production function. However, for a particular real-world firm, it is more likely to be the case that the firm can combine its inputs only in several well-defined ways, or processes.

Suppose, for example, that a single-product firm has two processes available to it, both of which require two inputs: labor and machine capacity. Process 1 requires 5 worker-hours and 1 machine-hour to produce 1 unit of output $Q$, and

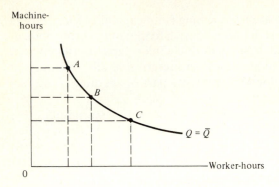

Machine-hours

$Q = \bar{Q}$

Worker-hours

0

**FIGURE 5-6**
Marginal analysis isoquant.

process 2 requires 1 worker-hour and 2 machine-hours to produce 1 unit of $Q$. Thus, a process is simply a particular technique of production involving a fixed proportion of the inputs. In contrast to the infinite number of processes that the marginal analysis isoquant in Figure 5-6 simply assumes, the linear programming isoquant must be derived from knowledge of a finite number of processes.

For our example here, the linear programming isoquant is easily derived. In Figure 5-7 we show the first step in the derivation of the isoquant map for our firm.

As before, the inputs are shown on the axes. Furthermore, each process is represented by a ray from the origin. Observe that the slope of a ray represents the ratio of the inputs which define that process.

The coordinates of points $A$, $B$, and $C$ and the corresponding value of $Q_1$

**FIGURE 5-7**
Linear programming processes.

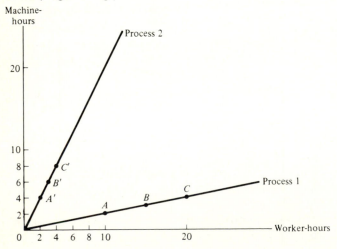

Machine-hours

Process 2

Process 1

Worker-hours

(the subscript indicates the process used to produce $Q$) in Figure 5-7 are given below.

| Point | Worker-hours | Machine-hours | $Q_1$ |
|-------|--------------|---------------|-------|
| A | 10 | 2 | 2 |
| B | 15 | 3 | 3 |
| C | 20 | 4 | 4 |

Since process 1 is defined by the requirement that 5 worker-hours must be combined with 1 machine-hour to produce 1 unit of $Q$, it is clear that all three points lie on the ray. Also, one may easily calculate that $A$ corresponds to production by process 1 of 2 units of $Q$. Similarly, $B$ corresponds to a level of 3 units of $Q$, and $C$ corresponds to 4 units of $Q$. Thus one restriction on the applicability of linear programming models is suggested: The production process must have the property of constant returns to scale (e.g., doubling the inputs results in a doubling of output).

Points $A'$, $B'$, and $C'$ in the figure lie on the ray representing process 2. The coordinates and associated values of $Q_2$ are given below.

| Point | Worker-hours | Machine-hours | $Q_2$ |
|-------|--------------|---------------|-------|
| A' | 2 | 4 | 2 |
| B' | 3 | 6 | 3 |
| C' | 4 | 8 | 4 |

We now have two points on each of three isoquants. That is to say, $A$ and $A'$ lie on the isoquant representing an output of 2 units of $Q$, $B$ and $B'$ lie on the $Q = 3$ isoquant, and $C$ and $C'$ lie on the $Q = 4$ isoquant.

Point $A$ is one production plan for producing a total output of 2 units, *viz,* process 1 operates at a level of 2 units, and process 2 operates at the zero level. Similarly, $A'$ is another production plan for producing a total output of 2 units; here process 2 is at the level $Q_2 = 2$, and process 1 is shut down. The next question concerns the possibility of using processes 1 and 2 simultaneously to produce a total output of 2 units.

It can be shown that the straight-line segment connecting points $A$ and $A'$ is the locus of all combinations of processes 1 and 2 which produce a combined output of 2 units. To see this, refer to Figure 5-8.

Point $M$, which is located on $A'A$ such that $A'M/A'A = .3$ represents a combination of processes 1 and 2 such that 0.6 units of $Q$ are produced by process 1 and 1.4 units of $Q$ are produced by process 2. The rule is quite general: If $A'M/A'A = k$, then $k$ times 2 units of $Q$ are produced by process 1, and $(1 - k)$ times 2 units of $Q$ are produced by process 2.

Two units of $Q$ can be produced by the production plan specified by $M$. This plan requires $OD$ units of labor and $OE$ units of machine capacity. And 1.4

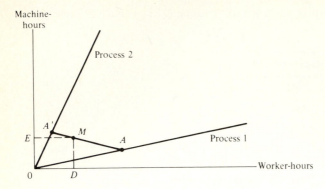

**FIGURE 5-8**
Locus of combinations of
processes 1 and 2 to produce
2 units of output.

units of $Q$ are produced by process 2 and 0.6 units by process 1. Furthermore, it is a simple matter to determine the input quantities required by each process.

### Process 1

(5 worker-hours per unit of $Q$)0.6 units = 3 worker-hours
(1 machine-hour per unit of $Q$)0.6 units = 0.6 machine-hours

### Process 2

(1 worker-hour per unit of $Q$)1.4 units = 1.4 worker-hours
(2 machine-hours per unit of $Q$)1.4 units = 2.8 machine-hours
In summary, the input requirements of $M$ are:

|  | Worker-hours | Machine-hours |
|---|---|---|
| Process 1 | 3.0 | 0.6 |
| Process 2 | 1.4 | 2.8 |
| Total | 4.4(= 0D) | 3.4(= 0E) |

If point $M$ should represent the optimal production plan, we then could report the following information: (1) total output, (2) the levels of each of the two processes, (3) the inputs required by each process, and (4) the aggregate inputs (4.4 worker-hours and 3.4 machine-hours). Hence, the linear programming approach provides more information than marginal analysis provides. The marginal analysis model would provide only information of types 1 and 4 above.

The linear programming isoquant can now be shown in Figure 5-9 for comparison with the marginal analysis isoquant shown in Figure 5-6.

We shall call attention to one final point in regard to Figure 5-9. The isoquant shown includes segments parallel to the axes which have not been explained. These parallel segments simply show that further additions of an input are redundant and cannot increase output when the other input is fixed.

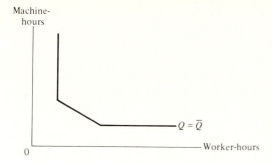

Machine-
hours

$Q = \bar{Q}$

Worker-hours

0

**FIGURE 5-9**
Linear programming isoquant.

We should emphasize that both models of production (marginal analysis and linear programming) have their place. The appropriate model depends on the objective of the analyst. For an analyst interested in problems of market price determination, marginal analysis may be appropriate; if a problem within the firm is the subject, linear programming may be better. It might be added that marginal analysis, which envisages the production function as an infinite number of processes, might be better suited for long-run analysis in which all types of productive processes are, in principle, conceivable. Linear programming, which views the firm as possessing only a finite number of alternative processes, might be more suitable for short-run analysis.

Having completed our comparison of the isoquants implied by linear programming and marginal analysis models of production, we turn to the multiple-product firm's problem of output determination. Since we shall use graphical analysis, we must restrict the firm to two products. More than two products would reduce the clarity of the exposition considerably. This restriction of the graphical method also requires us to limit the number of processes to one for each product. However, an algebraic technique which can handle any number of outputs and processes (the simplex method) for solving linear programming problems will be explained later.

For our example, we shall use a manufacturer of television receivers who seeks the profit-maximizing output levels for its two major products: black-and-white and color television sets.

### Profit Maximization for a Multiple-Product Firm: Television Assembly

A medium-scale manufacturer of television receivers has production facilities for assembling two types of television sets: black-and-white and color sets. At the present time the firm is producing only one model of each type of set. The black-and-white set retails for $198 and contributes $15 to profit and overhead, whereas the color set sells for $499.95 at the retail level and contributes $45 to profit and overhead. Both the black-and-white sets and the color sets are 21-inch table models.

The television manufacturer is concerned with the problem of deciding how to best utilize its production facilities to maximize profits. Since labor skills and plant equipment are completely interchangeable with regard to the production of the two types, varying quantities of both black-and-white and color sets can be produced on the same day. The present demand for television sets is such that the company can sell as many sets as it can produce. In fact, some thought has been given to the possibility of either expanding the capacity of the present production facilities or adding a second production shift.

**Objective Function**   The objective of the television manufacturer is to produce that quantity of black-and-white and color television sets which will maximize total contribution to profit and overhead[3] subject to the constraints imposed by the capacity of the existing assembly plant. This profit objective may be expressed algebraically by letting $Q_b$ denote the quantity of black-and-white sets produced in one day and letting $Q_c$ denote the quantity of color sets produced in one day. Since the unit contributions to profit and overhead for $Q_b$ and $Q_c$ are \$15 and \$45, respectively, the profit function is given by $\pi$:

$$\pi = 15Q_b + 45Q_c$$

We must now determine the values of $Q_b$ and $Q_c$ that will maximize $\pi$ and still satisfy the restrictions imposed by the present production facilities of the assembly plant.

The manufacture of television receiving sets involves the assembly of approximately 1,000 components to a metal chassis base and the insertion of the chassis and the speaker into a cabinet. The process consists of three essential steps: (1) the fabrication of major components, (2) chassis and set assembly, i.e., the wiring and assembly of components to a metal chassis and the insertion of the chassis and speaker into a cabinet, and (3) final inspection and testing.

**Fabrication Constraint**   Most of the major components of television sets are prepared on separate subassembly lines before movement to the main assembly line. However, speakers, cabinets, and transformers are purchased from outside suppliers. With the exception of color cathode-ray picture tubes, the manufacturer always carries an inventory consisting of a sufficient number of components to satisfy the daily production requirements for both black-and-white and color television sets. The plant has a daily production capacity of only 50 color cathode-ray picture tubes, and technical constraints prevent the purchase of color tubes from outside suppliers. This constraint on the production of color television sets may be expressed by the following algebraic relationship, if we

---

[3] Throughout the discussion of this problem the term "profit" will be used as an abbreviation for the expression "contribution to profit and overhead."

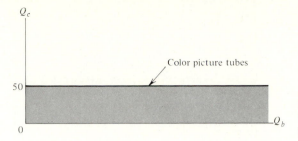

**FIGURE 5-10**
Production constraint for color
picture tubes.

again let $Q_c$ denote the number of color television sets manufactured in one
day.

$$Q_c \leq 50 \qquad (5\text{-}4)$$

This inequality indicates that the number of units of $Q_c$ must be less than or
equal to 50, where 50 is the daily supply of color picture tubes.

The significance of this relation is shown graphically in Figure 5-10. The
area bounded by the equation ($Q_c = 50$), the $Q_b$ axis, and the $Q_c$ axis is the area
of technical feasibility with regard to the constraint imposed by the limitation
on the supply of color picture tubes. (We restrict this area to positive values of
$Q_b$ and $Q_c$ because negative values are not meaningful in an economic sense.)
Any combination of values of $Q_b$ and $Q_c$ that lies either within or on the boundary of the shaded area of Figure 5-10 is a feasible solution to the problem in the
sense that it satisfies the color picture tube constraint. It will be noted that although $Q_c$ may not exceed 50 units, there is no upper limit imposed on $Q_b$.
However, we must now consider several additional constraints that will tend to
reduce the area of technical feasibility, or feasible region, and place an upper
limit on $Q_b$.

**Assembly Constraint** A black-and-white set must spend 1 worker-hour on
the assembly line, whereas a color set must spend 1.6 worker-hours on this
line. As there are 30 employees working on the assembly line, the daily capacity of the line is ($8 \times 30$) or 240 worker-hours of production. Algebraically, the
assembly-line constraint is given by

$$1.00_b + 1.6Q_c \leq 240 \qquad (5\text{-}5)$$

This relation indicates that the number of units of $Q_b$ multiplied by the 1.0
worker-hours that each unit requires on the assembly line plus the number of
units of $Q_c$ multiplied by the 1.6 worker-hours that each unit of $Q_c$ requires on
the assembly line must be less than or equal to 240, where 240 is the amount of
labor capacity, measured in worker-hours per day, available for assembly
operations.

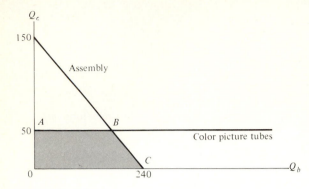

**FIGURE 5-11**
Color picture tubes and assembly constraints.

The effect of this second constraint is shown graphically in Figure 5-11. The feasible region has now been reduced considerably and takes the form of a convex polygon (or set) with corner points 0, $A$, $B$, and $C$.[4]

We should note that the assembly constraint line shown in Figure 5-11 was obtained by plotting constraint (5-5) as if it were an equation rather than an inequality. Hence, all points on the line satisfy the assembly constraint exactly; points below and to the left of the line represent combinations of $Q_b$ and $Q_c$ that do not require all 240 worker-hours of assembly capacity.

**Final Inspection Constraint** Black-and-white sets each require 0.5 worker-hours of testing and final inspection, whereas color sets require 2.0 worker-hours. The plant employs 20 full-time inspectors and one part-time inspector. The part-time inspector spends only 2 hours per day inspecting television sets. Hence, the inspection capacity of the plant is $(8 \times 20.25)$ or 162 worker-hours. Mathematically, the inspection constraint may be expressed as

$$0.5Q_b + 2.0Q_c \leq 162 \qquad (5-6)$$

The final set of feasible solutions can now be shown in Figure 5-12. This is obtained by incorporating the effect of inspection constraint (5-6) with the previously described constraints. The result is to reduce the feasible region to the convex set $0ABCD$ in Figure 5-12.

At this point we digress briefly to compare the marginal analysis and linear programming analyses of the two-product firm. The reader should refer back to

---

[4] A convex polygon is a polygon of the form represented by $(A)$ as opposed to that represented by $(B)$. A corner point of a convex polygon is simply the intersection of two sides of a convex polygon. A convex polygon (or set) has the property that a straight-line segment connecting any two points in the polygon (or set) lies entirely within the polygon (or set).

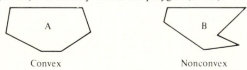

Convex         Nonconvex

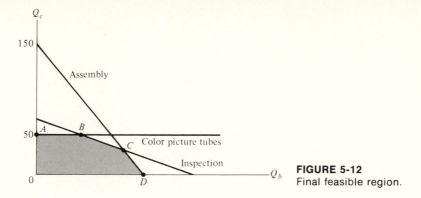

**FIGURE 5-12**
Final feasible region.

Figure 5-3, which shows the marginal analysis product transformation curve. The linear programming version of the product transformation curve is $ABCD$ in Figure 5-12. Hence, both curves are concave to the origin, although the marginal analysis curve is smooth and continuous while the linear programming curve consists of a series of connected straight-line segments.

Recall also that in our comparison of isoquants, the marginal analysis isoquant (Figure 5-6) was smooth and continuous while the linear programming isoquant (Figure 5-9) consisted of a series of connected straight-line segments. Hence, one might view linear programming as a special case of the general marginal analysis model.

**Optimal Output Decision**   Up to this point our efforts have been devoted to defining those combinations of black-and-white and color television sets which could be produced within the limits imposed by the production capacity of the plant. Having accomplished this objective, we can now return to our overall objective: to determine the combination of black-and-white and color television sets that will maximize total profits.

The profit function, previously defined as

$$\pi = 15Q_b + 45Q_c$$

can be graphed as a family of parallel straight lines such that the value of $\pi$ increases as the line becomes farther removed from the origin. By rearranging the profit function

$$Q_c = \frac{\pi}{45} - \frac{1}{3}Q_b$$

we see that the slope of each line in this family of lines is equal to $-1/3$ and that the intercept is $\pi/45$. Each line represents the locus of a set of combinations of $Q_b$ and $Q_c$ that yields the same profit. Hence, these lines are called isoprofit lines; three particular isoprofit lines are shown in Figure 5-13.

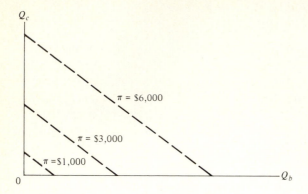

**FIGURE 5-13**
Iso-profit lines for black-and-white and color sets.

The problem thus becomes one of determining that isoprofit line which is farthest away from the origin but still contains at least one point that is technically feasible. If we superimpose the isoprofit lines of Figure 5-13 on the feasible region shown in Figure 5-12, it can be seen in Figure 5-14 that none of these three isoprofit lines yields an optimum solution. The lines representing total profits of $1,000 and $3,000 are not as far from the origin as is technically possible, whereas the $6,000 profit line does not intersect the technically feasible area at any point and is therefore unobtainable. However, there is an additional line that is farthest away from the origin and still includes a point (point $C$) of the feasible region $0ABCD$. This is the line of maximum profit, and it is shown to be $4,335. (The reader should compare the solution here with that given in Figure 5-5 for the marginal analysis case.)

Point $C$, the optimal solution, is a corner point of the feasible region and corresponds to a production of 184 black-and-white sets and 35 color television sets. Before we explain how the values of $Q_b$ and $Q_c$ were found, it should be observed that a very important theorem of linear programming states that the

**FIGURE 5-14**
Graphical solution indicating optimum combination of black-and-white and color sets.

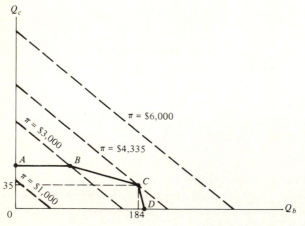

optimal solution will always be at a corner point.[5] Although we shall not prove this theorem here, readers should be able to convince themselves of its validity by imagining isoprofit lines with various slopes in the context of Figure 5-14.

The fact that the optimal solution always corresponds to a corner point is very important. It implies that the corner-point solution can always be found algebraically by solving simultaneously the equations for the intersecting constraint lines. In Figure 5-14, the two intersecting constraint equations that determine point $C$ are

$$1.0Q_b + 1.6Q_c = 240 \qquad \text{assembly constraint}$$
$$0.5Q_b + 2.0Q_c = 162 \qquad \text{inspection constraint}$$

Solving the assembly constraint equation for $Q_b$ and substituting the result into the inspection constraint equation yields

$$0.5(240 - 1.6Q_c) + 2.0Q_c = 162$$

or $$Q_c = 35$$

Since $Q_b = 240 - 1.6Q_c$, we also have $Q_b = 184$. Substituting these values into $\pi = 15Q_b + 45Q_c$, we obtain the maximum value of $4,335.

Knowing that the optimal solution will be at a corner point of the feasible region suggests a completely algebraic procedure for solving this problem. Solve for the $Q_b$, $Q_c$ values for each corner point and compute the corresponding value of profit. The optimal solution is then obtained by simply choosing the corner point with the highest profit. This information for all of the corner points in Figure 5-14 is tabulated below:

| Corner point | $Q_b$ | Profit at $15 per unit | $Q_c$ | Profit at $45 per unit | Total profit |
|---|---|---|---|---|---|
| 0 | 0 | 0 | 0 | 0 | 0 |
| A | 0 | 0 | 50 | $2,250 | $2,250 |
| B | 124 | $1,860 | 50 | $2,250 | $4,100 |
| C | 184 | $2,760 | 35 | $1,575 | $4,335 |
| D | 240 | $3,600 | 0 | 0 | $3,600 |

Hence, the problem of solving linear programming problems with many variables and many constraints can be handled algebraically by the above procedure. It would, however, be very inefficient in a computational sense because each corner point represents the simultaneous solution to a set of linear equations. Fortunately, the simplex method described in Appendix C can be employed to reduce the number of solutions (or corner points) needed.

[5] In the special case where the slope of the isoprofit lines is equal to the slope of one of the constraints, there will not be a unique optimal solution. Nevertheless, even in this case a corner point is at least as good as any other feasible point. Hence, it is correct to assert that the optimal point can always be taken to be a corner point.

Basically, the simplex method is an algorithm (computational procedure) for moving from one corner point to another in such a way that many corner points are ignored but the optimal corner point is reached eventually. The idea is that one begins, for example, at corner point 0 in Figure 5-14. At point 0, of course, $\pi = 0$. Then the simplex method determines whether moving to point $A$ or point $D$ would increase $\pi$ at the greatest rate. As is shown in Appendix C, the answer is point $A$. Hence, corner point $A$ is the second solution. Next, the simplex method calls for movement to point $B$ and finally to point $C$. Each new corner point (or solution) results in a higher level of $\pi$ than the previous one. At point $C$, no further moves are possible that will increase $\pi$; hence $C$ is the optimal solution.

**Shadow Prices**   An important set of values that the simplex method solution also provides is the set of so-called shadow prices, or opportunity profits, of the constraints. In our television-assembly example, each of the three constraints has a shadow price associated with it. The shadow price of the assembly constraint, for example, is $6.25. This means that if the firm had an additional worker-hour of assembly capacity (i.e., 241 rather than 240), maximum profit would increase by $6.25.

A graphical explanation is given in Figure 5-15. An increase in assembly capacity from 240 to 241 simply shifts that constraint outward, enlarging the feasible region from $0ABCD$ to $0ABC'D'$. The shaded area represents the actual amount by which the feasible region is enlarged (although our drawing is not to scale). Profit at $C'$ exceeds profit at $C$ by $6.25, which is the shadow price of assembly capacity.

It is quite possible that the most important benefit to be derived from the solution of a linear programming problem is not the optimal solution itself but rather the shadow prices of the resources (color picture tubes, assembly-line capacity, and final testing capacity) that are in limited supply and impose constraints on the variables of the problem. Although we are interested in finding an optimal solution to problems that have been formulated under a set of clearly defined conditions, we are also interested in finding the value of altering

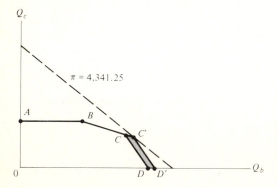

**FIGURE 5-15**
Effect of increasing assembly capacity by 1 unit.

these conditions. How would our profits be affected by an increase in the capacity of the assembly line? Should we produce 50 color picture tubes each day? Should we make any changes in our final testing capacity? These are questions of real economic significance that can be answered by examining the shadow prices of the optimal solution to a linear programming problem.

Before turning to some further applications of linear programming, we should observe briefly that each linear programming problem has a so-called dual problem associated with it. If the initial formulation of the linear programming problem (the primal problem) is a maximization problem, the dual problem is a minimization problem. There are a number of further close relationships between the two problems, including the fact that the values of the objective functions in the optimal solutions are the same. Furthermore, the values of the variables that determine the optimal solution of the dual problem are the shadow prices of the constraints of the primal problem. One advantage of the dual problem is that the dual is sometimes easier to solve computationally, and it provides all the results of the primal. The dual problem is explained in detail in Appendix C.

## A Cost-Minimization Problem: Soap Blending

To illustrate a minimization problem, we consider a firm that manufactures soap products. The firm finds that it cannot satisfy the demand for one of its powdered laundry soap products during a particular week. The firm is confronted with a loss of sales amounting to approximately 1,000 pounds simply because its production capacity is inadequate. Although this situation is only temporary, the firm does have a way to satisfy the excess demand.

Specifically, the firm is considering buying powdered soap from two other manufacturers and blending them into soap that would at least meet the specifications of the soap currently being marketed by the company. That this is possible has been established through previous experience. There are two questions of economics associated with this possibility. First, what would be the optimum quantities of soap 1 and soap 2, the soaps produced by the two manufacturers, to purchase in order to satisfy demand and to provide a product identical with the present product? Second, would this be a profitable venture?

The company can purchase as much soap 1 and soap 2 as it needs for $.10 and $.08 per pound, respectively. It can sell the additional 1,000 pounds of soap for $200. However, it will incur additional costs of $25 for blending, packaging, handling, and shipping the extra 1,000 pounds of soap.

To the consumer the three most important characteristics of powdered laundry soap are washing power, sudsiness, and hardness. By analyzing certain chemical and physical characteristics of soap it is possible to actually measure the respective characteristics of a particular soap product. Extensive research has indicated that the particular soap product in question must have a washing power factor of at least 6.5, a sudsiness factor of at least 3.0, and a hardness factor no greater than 4.0

The two soaps that are being considered for blending purposes have the following characteristics:

|                | Soap 1 | Soap 2 |
|----------------|--------|--------|
| Washing power  | 6      | 9      |
| Sudsiness      | 2      | 6      |
| Hardness       | 1      | 5      |

The company's research department has determined that the characteristics of the two soaps being considered for blending combine linearly by weight when blended. In other words, if equal weights of soap 1 and soap 2 are combined, the resulting blend will have the following characteristics: washing power, 7.5; sudsiness, 4.0; and hardness, 3.0.

As can be seen, this particular blend has the required characteristics for the company's product. However, it may not be the ratio of soap 1 and to soap 2 that yields the lowest possible cost.

In order to determine the minimum-cost blend of soap 1 and soap 2 that will satisfy demand (1,000 pounds) and meet the required product specifications, we must first define the objective function.

If we let $X_1$ denote the quantity of soap 1 (in pounds) and $X_2$ denote the quantity of soap 2 (in pounds) used in the blend, the objective of the firm is to minimize the cost function

$$Z = 0.10X_1 + 0.08X_2$$

The next part of the problem is to define the constraints imposed by the required product characteristics and the demand situation.

The washing power factor constraint may be expressed algebraically by the inequality

$$\frac{6X_1}{1,000} + \frac{9X_2}{1,000} \geq 6.5$$

The expression $X_1/1,000$ denotes that proportion of the blend having a washing power factor of 6.0, whereas $X_2/1,000$ denotes that proportion of the blend having a washing power of 9.0. Thus, the inequality states that the proportions of soap 1 and soap 2 must be such that a blend will be produced whose washing power factor is at least 6.5.

The sudsiness and hardness constraints may be expressed in a similar manner:

Sudsiness:    $\dfrac{2X_1}{1,000} + \dfrac{6X_2}{1,000} \geq 3$

Hardness:    $\dfrac{1X_1}{1,000} + \dfrac{5X_2}{1,000} \leq 4$

A fourth constraint, which recognizes the demand situation, must be added. The total weight of the blend must be equal to the total weight demanded:

$$X_1 + X_2 = 1,000$$

When both sides of the washing power, sudsiness, and hardness constraints are multiplied by 1,000, the four constraints become

$$6X_1 + 9X_2 \geq 6,500$$
$$2X_1 + 6X_2 \geq 3,000$$
$$1X_1 + 5X_2 \leq 4,000$$
$$X_1 + X_2 = 1,000$$

Of course, to complete the definition of this linear programming problem, we add the nonnegativity conditions:

$$X_1 \geq 0$$
$$X_2 \geq 0$$

The graphical solution to this problem is very simple. Because of the equality constraint, the feasible region is the straight-line segment $AB$ in Figure 5-16. We leave it as an exercise for the reader to actually derive the feasible region. Three isocost lines are also shown in Figure 5-16. Since the present problem is a minimization problem, the solution is that point in the feasible region which lies on the lowest attainable cost line. Clearly, this is point $B$.

The final solution calls for a blend consisting of 250 pounds of soap 1 and 750 pounds of soap 2. The total cost of the raw materials required to produce 1,000 pounds of soap of the desired quality is $85. The cost of blending, packaging, and handling the 1,000 pounds of soap is $25. Hence, the total cost of producing 1,000 additional pounds of soap with the required attributes is $25 plus $85, or $110. Since the company can sell this soap for $200, it would appear that the purchase of 250 pounds of soap 1 and 750 pounds of soap 2 would

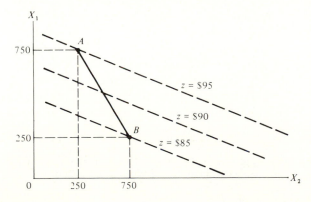

**FIGURE 5-16**
Cost-minimization solution.

be a favorable alternative. Naturally, the profitability of this alternative would have to be compared with the profitability of other alternatives before a final decision could be made. Other alternatives might include expanding the capacity of the soap plant, buying soap from other suppliers, or turning the account over to a competitor.

We should emphasize that the problems explained above have been quite simple and that both could be solved almost by inspection. The reason for this was to make it possible to explain graphically the principles of linear programming. Although we have provided only an intuitive explanation for the simplex method here (Appendix C contains a complete exposition), we conclude the chapter with a real-world problem in order to illustrate a large-scale application of linear programming that must be solved with the simplex method and a computer.

## THE EVANGELINE COFFEE COMPANY[6]

The Evangeline Coffee Company of New Orleans, Louisiana, imports, blends, and roasts green coffees for distribution in a six-state area along the Gulf Coast. The company markets three different blends of coffee under the following brand names: Cafe d'Elite, Plantation, and Creole. Cafe d'Elite is a luxury item served exclusively by leading hotels, fine restaurants, and espresso coffeehouses. Plantation is the company's leading product in terms of volume. It has widespread distribution throughout the company's six-state marketing area. The Creole blend is a dark-roast, low-quality coffee with chicory that is sold in southern Louisiana.

### Coffee Blending

Coffee is by no means a homogeneous commodity. A beverage may be made from any coffee, but the product sold commercially to the ultimate consumer is usually a blend. Blending is necessary to harmonize the widely varying characteristics of different coffees in order to produce a desired flavor. Coffees differ in inherent characteristics and are further differentiated on a quality basis by the prominence of such characteristics. Thus, the problem of the trade is to translate consumer taste distinctions into the kinds and proportions of coffees forming a blend necessary to produce a given result in the cup.

The seven most important characteristics of coffees and blends of coffees have been found to be strength, acidity, caffeine content, liquoring value, hardness, aroma sweetness, and body. All these characteristics are described by a trade jargon that helps to identify any particular lot as to its commercial utility and therefore more or less establishes a value for it in relation to all other kinds, types, and grades of coffees.

---

[6] This section is based on a case contained in Thomas H. Naylor, Eugene T. Byrne, and John M. Vernon, *Introduction to Linear Programming* (Belmont, Calif.: Wadsworth, 1971).

The composition of any given blend of coffee is usually a closely guarded trade secret. Standard good brands of coffee in the United States are a blend of 15 to 40 percent of mild Colombian or Central American coffees with good Brazilian coffees. High-quality brands are blends of milds and may contain no Brazilian coffee, whereas the cheapest coffees may consist entirely of Brazils.

Coffee merchants have considerable latitude in varying their blend formulas as conditions dictate. Changing price differentials between coffee types may require changes in formulas from month to month. Generally, such changes will be undertaken for the purpose of adjusting cost factors without creating any noticeable change in cup quality. Cup testing, performed by expert coffee tasters, is essential to arriving at the right combination.

## Recent Developments

As a result of a recent operations research study, Evangeline has achieved considerable success in attempting to quantify the seven major taste characteristics of coffee. This was accomplished by the development of a rating scale for five of the taste attributes of coffee. For example, every type of green coffee that is available in any significant quantity has been assigned an index number between 0 and 10 according to its relative strength. Those coffees which have a "very strong" taste are assigned numbers close to 10. Those which are relatively mild are assigned numbers near 5. Weak coffees are assigned numbers near 0. Similar indexes have been developed to express relative differences in liquoring value, hardness, aroma, and body. It was not necessary to develop such an index to measure acidity or caffeine content, since acidity can be determined by measuring the pH factor, and caffeine content is measured as a percentage of weight. It has also been found that the taste characteristics of different types of coffees combine linearly when blended.

## Evangeline's Blends

The Evangeline Coffee Company has developed a rigid set of requirements for each of its three blends. A failure to satisfy these requirements may result in a significant decline in sales. Hence, every possible step must be taken to ensure blends of constant quality within the limits stipulated below.

|  | Cafe d'Elite (high quality) | Plantation (medium quality) | Creole (low quality) |
|---|---|---|---|
| Strength | $\leq 8.0$ | $\leq 7.0$ | $\geq 9.0$ |
| Acidity | $\leq 3.5$ | $\leq 4.0$ | $\leq 5.0$ |
| Caffeine | $\leq 2.8$ | $\leq 2.2$ | $\leq 2.4$ |
| Liquoring value | $\geq 7.0$ | $\geq 6.0$ | $\geq 5.0$ |
| Hardness | $\leq 2.5$ | $\leq 3.0$ | $\leq 7.8$ |
| Aroma | $\geq 7.0$ | $\geq 5.0$ | $\geq 4.0$ |
| Body | $\geq 7.0$ | $\geq 6.0$ | $\geq 7.0$ |

TABLE 5-1 SUPPLY OF GREEN COFFEES

| Green coffees available | Price per pound | Available supply, lb | Strength index | Acidity, pH | Percent caffeine content | Liquoring value | Hardness index | Aroma sweetness index | Body index |
|---|---|---|---|---|---|---|---|---|---|
| 1. *Brazils* | | | | | | | | | |
| Santos 4s Bourbon | $0.35 | 25,000 | 6 | 4.0 | 1.8 | 6 | 2 | 8 | 8 |
| Santos | 0.36 | 10,000 | 6 | 3.9 | 1.6 | 6 | 3 | 9 | 8 |
| Rios | 0.20 | 75,000 | 10 | 4.5 | 1.0 | 5 | 7 | 4 | 6 |
| Victorias | 0.17 | 50,000 | 10 | 5.0 | 0.9 | 3 | 8 | 2 | 6 |
| 2. *Colombians* | | | | | | | | | |
| Medellins | $0.44 | 5,000 | 8 | 3.0 | 3.0 | 8 | 2 | 7 | 9 |
| Bogotas | 0.43 | 5,000 | 9 | 3.0 | 2.5 | 7 | 2 | 6 | 8 |
| Manizales | 0.45 | 4,000 | 8 | 3.0 | 3.0 | 9 | 1 | 7 | 10 |
| Bucara-Mangas | 0.41 | 20,000 | 7 | 4.0 | 2.0 | 6 | 2 | 7 | 7 |
| 3. *Mexicans* | $0.36 | 5,000 | 5 | 3.5 | 1.5 | 6 | 3 | 9 | 8 |
| 4. *Guatemalans* | $0.34 | 4,000 | 6 | 3.6 | 1.1 | 6 | 4 | 7 | 7 |
| 5. *El Salvadors* | $0.36 | 5,000 | 6 | 3.2 | 1.4 | 6 | 3 | 8 | 8 |
| 6. *Africans* | | | | | | | | | |
| Robustas | $0.19 | 100,000 | 10 | 5.1 | 1.7 | 5 | 9 | 1 | 5 |

On the first day of each month the company forecasts its green coffee requirements for the period of time beginning one month from that day. (The company operates on the basis of a monthly planning period.) Since green coffees are imported from Latin America and Africa, it may take as long as one month from the time an order is placed before it arrives at the Port of New Orleans. Hence, one month of lead time is required for all orders. For example, green coffees to be roasted in February must be ordered on the first day of January.

On the first day of a particular month, the company found that its available supply of green coffees was limited to 12 different types, as indicated in Table 5-1. These 12 coffees could be delivered to New Orleans before the first day of the following month. According to Table 5-1, these coffees vary according to price, quantity available, and taste characteristics.

Forecasts indicate that the demand for the company's three blends during the coming month will be as follows.

| Blend | Forecast demand, lb |
|---|---|
| Cafe d'Elite | 10,000 |
| Plantation | 60,000 |
| Creole | 30,000 |

The company is confronted with the problem of determining an optimum combination of available green coffees for next month's roasting operation. It must determine a combination that will satisfy both the demand requirements and the quality requirements for each of its 3 blends as well as minimize the total cost of purchases of green coffee.

## Problem Formulation

Clearly, this problem is too complex to solve by inspection. Since it involves the simultaneous solution of 36 equations, the need for a computer is obvious. We indicate below only a concise mathematical formulation of the problem with examples of the different types of constraints involved.

Let $X_{ij}$ = the quantity of the $i$th green coffee used in the $j$th blend, where ($i = 1, 2, \ldots, 12$) and ($j = 1, 2, 3$).

Let $C_i$ = the cost per pound of the $i$th coffee ($i = 1, \ldots, 12$). Then the objective of the coffee company is to minimize

$$\sum_{i=1}^{12} \sum_{j=1}^{3} C_i X_{ij}$$

This is equivalent to saying that the company wants to minimize the function

$$Z = \quad 35X_{11} + 36X_{21} + 20X_{31} + 17X_{41} + 44X_{51} + 43X_{61}$$
$$+ 45X_{71} + 41X_{81} + 36X_{91} + 34X_{10,1} + 36X_{11,1} + 19X_{12,1}$$
$$+ 35X_{12} + 36X_{22} + 20X_{32} + 17X_{42} + 44X_{52} + 43X_{62}$$
$$+ 45X_{72} + 41X_{82} + 36X_{92} + 34X_{10,2} + 36X_{11,2} + 19X_{12,2}$$
$$+ 35X_{13} + 36X_{23} + 20X_{33} + 17X_{43} + 44X_{53} + 43X_{63}$$
$$+ 45X_{73} + 41X_{83} + 36X_{93} + 34X_{10,3} + 36X_{11,3} + 19X_{12,3}$$

There are three different types of linear constraints imposed on the variables ($X_{ij}$'s) in this problem: demand, supply, and quality. There are three demand constraints, one for each of the company's products. These may be represented by the mathematical expression

$$\sum_{i=1}^{12} X_{ij} = D_j \qquad j = 1, 2, 3$$

where $D_j$ is the demand for the $j$th blend ($j = 1, 2, 3$). For example, the demand constraint for Cafe d'Elite (where $j = 1$) would be

$$X_{11} + X_{21} + X_{31} + X_{41} + X_{51} + X_{61} + X_{71}$$
$$+ X_{81} + X_{91} + X_{10,1} + X_{11,1} + X_{12,1} = 10,000$$

The demand constraints for the Plantation and Creole blends would be of a similar nature.

There are 12 supply constraints, one for each of the 12 available green coffees. These may be represented by the expression

$$\sum_{j=1}^{3} X_{ij} \leq S_i \qquad i = 1, 2, \ldots, 12$$

where $S_i$ is the available supply of the $i$th green coffee. For example, the supply constraint for Santos 4s (where $i = 1$) would be expressed as

$$X_{11} + X_{12} + X_{13} \leq 25,000$$

The supply constraints for the other green coffees would be of a similar form.

There are 21 quality constraints, 7 for each of the company's three blends. These may be expressed as

$$\sum_{i=1}^{12} a_{ik} X_{ij} \lesseqgtr D_j b_{jk} \qquad j = 1, 2, 3,$$
$$k = 1, 2, \ldots, 7$$

where $a_{ik}$ = $k$th quality characteristic of the $i$th green coffee
$\quad\quad D_j$ = demand for the $j$th blend
$\quad\quad b_{jk}$ = $k$th characteristic of the $j$th blend

For example, the "strength" restriction for Cafe d'Elite (where $j = 1$ and $k = 1$) may be expressed as

$$6X_{11} + 6X_{21} + 10X_{31} + 10X_{41} + 8X_{51} + 9X_{61} + 8X_{71} + 7X_{81}$$
$$+ 5X_{91} + 6X_{10,1} + 6X_{11,1} + 10X_{12,1} \le (10,000)|(8)$$

Similar constraints must be included for each of the seven quality characteristics of the three blends.

### Solution

The final solution, obtained by computer algorithm, is given below. To emphasize further the need for a computer, the simplex method required the simultaneous solution of 36 equations 72 times. The optimal solution resulted in a total expenditure of \$33,558 for green coffees.

FINAL SOLUTION

|  | Blend | | |
|---|---|---|---|
| Green coffee | Cafe d'Elite | Plantation | Creole |
| Santos 4s |  | 20,000 | 5,000 |
| Bourbon Santos |  | 10,000 |  |
| Rios |  |  | 5,000 |
| Victorias |  |  | 12,000 |
| Medellins | 2,750 | 2,250 |  |
| Bogotas |  |  | 5,000 |
| Manizales | 1,500 |  | 2,500 |
| Bucara-Mangas |  | 15,000 |  |
| Mexicans |  | 5,000 |  |
| Guatemalans | 750 | 3,250 |  |
| El Salvadors | 5,000 |  |  |
| Robustas |  | 4,500 |  |

## QUESTIONS AND PROBLEMS

**5-1** Suppose the Acme Corporation can produce widgets according to the total cost function below:

$$C = 43.2 + 2X + .3X^2$$

   **a** Find Acme's MC, ATC, and AVC functions.
   **b** At a fixed price of 14, what output level will maximize Acme's profit?
   **c** If the fixed price falls to 8, what is the profit-maximizing output level? What is the amount of profit? Should Acme continue to operate? Why or why not?
**5-2** Explain the major similarities and differences between linear programming and marginal analysis. Are both tools equally useful to management? Why or why not?
**5-3** A manufacturer can produce two different products $X$ and $Y$ during a given time period. Each of these products requires four different manufacturing operations:

grinding, turning, assembly, and testing. The manufacturing requirements in hours per unit of product are given below for $X$ and $Y$.

|           | X | Y |
|-----------|---|---|
| Grinding  | 1 | 2 |
| Turning   | 3 | 1 |
| Assembly  | 6 | 3 |
| Testing   | 5 | 4 |

The available capacities of these operations in hours for the given time period are: grinding, 30; turning, 60; assembly, 200; testing, 200. The contribution to overhead and profit is $2 for each unit of $X$ and $3 for each unit of $Y$. The firm can sell all that it produces at the prevailing market price. Determine the optimum amount of $X$ and $Y$ to produce during the given time period.

**5-4** A scrap-metal dealer has received an order from a customer for at least 2,000 pounds of scrap metal. The customer requires that at least 1,000 pounds of the shipment of metal be high-quality copper that can be melted down and used to produce copper tubing. Furthermore, the customer will not accept delivery of the order if it contains more than 175 pounds of metal that she deems unfit for commercial use, that is, metal that contains an excessive amount of impurities and cannot be melted down and refined profitably.

The dealer can purchase scrap metal from two different suppliers in unlimited quantities with the following percentages (by weight) of high-quality copper and unfit scrap.

|                | Supplier A | Supplier B |
|----------------|------------|------------|
| Copper         | 25%        | 75%        |
| Unfit (scrap)  | 5%         | 10%        |

The costs per pound of metal purchased from supplier A and supplier B are 10 cents and 40 cents, respectively. Determine the optimum quantities of metal for the dealer to purchase from each of the two suppliers.

**5-5** The Baxter Manufacturing Company has two processes for producing trash cans. It can produce a can by combining 5 units of labor with 1 machine unit or by combining 1 unit of labor with 2 units of machine capacity. Each can contributes 1 unit toward profit and overhead, and the Baxter Company has 90 units of machine capacity and 200 units of labor available. Determine the production plan that maximizes profit.

**5-6** The Allen Advertising Agency has estimated an "effective exposure" measure for each of two advertising media on behalf of its client, the Boyles Bat Company. Interestingly, Allen estimates that each full-page color advertisement in *Ball* magazine has the same effective exposure of 10,000 units as the sponsorship of a half-hour television show. The Boyles Bat Company has a $100,000 advertising budget for the next six months and stipulates that its advertising program must include full-page ads in at least two issues of *Ball*. (No more than one full page per issue is worthwhile, and *Ball* is a monthly magazine.) If it costs $20,000 per television show and $10,000 for a page in *Ball*, how should Boyles allocate its budget for the next six months in order to maximize total effective exposure?

**5-7** Suppose the Boyles Bat Company of problem 5-6 should also advise Allen that it wished to sponsor at least three television shows in addition to the two pages in *Ball*. How does this new stipulation affect the advertising program determined in problem 5-6? How should Allen advise Boyles concerning this new requirement?

**5-8** Mr. Forrest Smith is the owner and manager of a small manufacturing company. His company produces and sells two products: mops and brooms.

The demand for brooms has been very stable, and Smith feels certain that he can sell all the brooms he wishes at a net contribution to profit of $1 per unit. The mop market, however, is unstable. Smith estimates that the net unit contribution of mops is likely to be somewhere in the range of $.50 to $1.50. To plan production, Smith has decided to investigate two cases. Case 1 corresponds to a net unit contribution of mops of $.50, and case 2 corresponds to $1.50.

The production processes for mops and brooms can be described as follows. Mops require 1 worker-hour of labor and two runs on Smith's mop-and-broom machine; brooms require 1 worker-hour of labor and one run on Smith's mop-and-broom machine. The company has 20 worker-hours of labor and a capacity of 20 runs on the mop-and-broom machine.

Mr. Smith must produce at least 10 brooms regardless of profit considerations, because he has a long-standing order with a very important customer for 10 brooms per period. Because of a limitation on raw materials for mops, no more than five mops can be produced.

**a** For case 1, what is the optimum production schedule and maximum contribution to profit?

**b** For case 1, if Smith could rent five more runs on a mop-and-broom machine for 25 cents per run, should he? What about further increases in runs at the same price of 25 cents per run?

**c** For case 2, answer the questions in part **a**.

**d** For case 2, answer the questions in **b**.

**5-9** What are shadow prices and how are they useful to management?

## BIBLIOGRAPHY

Baumol, William J.: "Activity Analysis in One Lesson," *American Economic Review,* December 1958.

Dantzig, George B.: *Linear Programming and Extensions* (Princeton, N.J.: Princeton University Press, 1963).

Dorfman, Robert, Paul Samuelson, and Robert Solow: *Linear Programming and Economic Analysis* (New York: McGraw-Hill, 1958).

Gass, S. I.: *Linear Programming: Methods and Applications,* 3d ed. (New York: McGraw-Hill, 1969).

Zionts, S.: *Linear and Integer Programming* (Englewood Cliffs, N.J.: Prentice-Hall, 1974).

APPENDIX **C**

# THE SIMPLEX METHOD AND DUALITY

## LINEAR PROGRAMMING: INTRODUCTION[1]

In Chapter 5 linear programming was introduced, and several example problems were solved graphically. This appendix is a continuation of that introductory material and has the objective of providing a detailed exposition of the algebraic method of solution known as the simplex method.

---

[1] This appendix is based on the exposition of linear programming contained in Thomas H. Naylor, Eugene T. Byrne, and John M. Vernon, *Introduction to Linear Programming* (Belmont, Calif.: Wadsworth, 1971).

We shall begin by providing some fundamentals of simultaneous systems of linear equations. As noted in Chapter 5, the simplex method is an algorithm for solving a simultaneous system of linear equations iteratively, each time adding one new variable and removing one old variable. Hence, the need to review some basics of simultaneous linear equations should be evident.

First, we shall discuss the conditions under which linear equations have (1) a unique solution, (2) an infinite number of solutions, and (3) no solutions. Then the Gauss-Jordan elimination method for solving linear equations will be explained. The concept of a basic solution and its importance in linear programming is the next topic. The final sections deal with the derivation of a set of rules for generating basic solutions and the simplex method itself.

## CONSISTENCY AND INDEPENDENCE

Consider the linear equation

$$4X_1 + 8X_2 = 10 \qquad \text{(C-1)}$$

Now we add a second equation and require that it be satisfied simultaneously with equation (C-1):

$$1X_1 - 0.5X_2 = 1 \qquad \text{(C-2)}$$

Graphing the equations together in Figure C-1, we obtain two intersecting straight lines.

By the simultaneous solution of the two equations we refer to the pairs of values of $X_1$ and $X_2$ which satisfy both equations simultaneously. It is obvious from Figure C-1 that only one pair of values of $X_1$ and $X_2$ can satisfy both equations: the values of $X_1$ and $X_2$ which correspond to the intersection point. The solution is said to be unique.

Notice that we have two equations in two variables. Does it always hold true that two equations in two variables (or $n$ equations in $n$ variables) will yield a unique solution? To answer this question, suppose that equation (C-2) had been

$$2X_1 + 4X_2 = 5 \qquad \text{(C-2')}$$

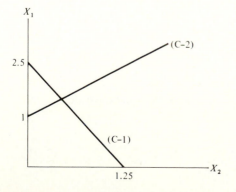

**FIGURE C-1**
A unique solution.

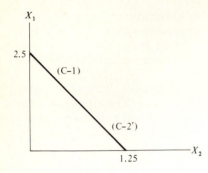

**FIGURE C-2**
An infinite number of solutions.

Graphing equations (C-1) and (C-2'), we obtain the results shown in Figure C-2. The two equations coincide and appear as a single straight line. But what is the solution? Each and every pair of values of $X_1$ and $X_2$ on the line is a solution. That is, there is an infinite number of solutions in this case, even though we still have two equations and two variables. What distinguishes this case from the first case, in which the solution was unique? The answer is that equations (C-1) and (C-2') are not independent. Equation (C-2') "adds no new information"; it can be obtained simply by multiplying both sides of equation (C-1) by 0.5.

One final case is possible. Let equation (C-2) now become

$$2X_1 + 4X_2 = 6 \tag{C-2''}$$

As depicted graphically in Figure C-3, we get two parallel lines. In this third case there is no solution. No pair of values of $X_1$ and $X_2$ can possibly satisfy both equations. The equations are said to be inconsistent.

In summary, even given an equal number of variables and equations, a unique solution is not guaranteed. There will be an infinite number of solutions if the equations are not independent, and there can be no solution if the equations are inconsistent. Only if the equations are both independent and consistent are we assured a unique solution.

## GAUSS-JORDAN ELIMINATION

We shall now consider a method for solving a system of linear equations. However, before illustrating the method, we need to recall two mathematical properties which will be used.

**1** Division of each term of an equation by a constant does not alter the solution to the equation system.

**2** Multiplication of each term of one equation by a constant and then addition of the result to a second equation does not alter the solution to the equation system.

Let us return to our earlier example.

$$4X_1 + 8X_2 = 10 \tag{C-1}$$
$$1X_1 - 0.5X_2 = 1 \tag{C-2}$$

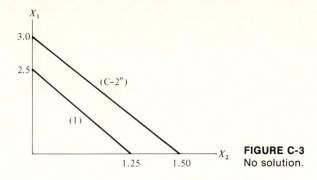

**FIGURE C-3**
No solution.

The object is to use the two properties to transform equations (C-1) and (C-2) so that the solution is obvious. The solution will be obvious if the coefficients of the variables can be transformed into an identity matrix. An identity matrix is simply a square array of the numbers 0 and 1 in the form[2]

$$\begin{bmatrix} 1 & 0 \\ 0 & 1 \end{bmatrix}$$

The first row of the matrix should be viewed as the coefficients of $X_1$ and $X_2$ in equation (C-1), and the second row should be similarly associated with equation (C-2). The solution will be obvious once the original system is transformed into the identity matrix form. The value of $X_1$ will be the constant on the right-hand side of the first equation, and $X_2$ will equal the constant of the second equation.

Since the coefficient of $X_1$ in the first equation must be 1, we apply property 1 to equation (C-1) by dividing through by 4. The result is

$$1X_1 + 2X_2 = 2.5 \tag{C-1a}$$

The coefficient of $X_1$ in equation (C-2) must become 0. If we apply property 2 by multiplying equation (C-1a) by $-1$ and adding the result to equation (C-2), we get

$$0X_1 - 2.5X_2 = -1.5 \tag{C-2a}$$

The coefficients of equations (C-1a) and (C-2a) (the coefficient matrix) at this stage are

$$\begin{bmatrix} 1 & 2 \\ 0 & -2.5 \end{bmatrix}$$

To complete the transformation to an identity matrix, we divide equation (C-2a) through by $-2.5$, obtaining

$$0X_1 + 1X_2 = 0.6 \tag{C-2b}$$

---

[2] This is a second-order identity matrix having two rows and two columns. We will need a third-order identity matrix later in this appendix.

Next, multiply equation (C-2b) by $-2$ and add the result to equation (C-1a). The resulting equation is

$$1X_1 + 0X_2 = 1.3 \tag{C-1b}$$

The coefficients of equations (C-1b) and (C-2b) now form the desired identity matrix:

$$1X_1 + 0X_2 = 1.3$$
$$0X_1 + 1X_2 = 0.6$$

The unique solution is $X_1 = 1.3$, $X_2 = 0.6$. This, of course, corresponds to the point of intersection in Figure C-1.

We can now make a general statement about the solution of a system of $n$ linear equations in $n$ variables. Such a system will have a unique solution if and only if the system can be transformed into the identity matrix form. To verify this point, the reader is urged to apply the Gauss-Jordan method to the cases given above, in which the equations were not independent and in which they were inconsistent.

## LINEAR PROGRAMMING EQUATION SYSTEM

The system of equations in linear programming is always characterized by the fact that the number of variables exceeds the number of equations. This is sometimes called a system of underdetermined equations. Although we have not explicitly discussed systems in which the number of equations is less than the number of variables, we have done so in effect. The case discussed earlier, in which an infinite number of solutions is possible, is actually an underdetermined system. To understand why this is so, recall that the second equation in our example was simply a multiple of the first. It therefore added nothing new and could have been dropped from the system. If dropped, the first equation should be viewed as a system of one equation in two variables, or an underdetermined system.

Consider the equations

$$4X_1 + 8X_2 + 2X_3 = 10 \tag{C-3}$$

and
$$2X_1 + X_2 + 3X_3 = 2 \tag{C-4}$$

There are an infinite number of solutions to the equations above. To see why, arbitrarily set $X_3$ equal to 1. The equations then become

$$4X_1 + 8X_2 = 10 - 2(1) = 8$$
$$2X_1 + X_2 = 2 - 3(1) = -1$$

We are now back to two equations in two variables. Since the equations are independent and consistent, a unique solution can be found. But our choice of $X_3 = 1$ was arbitrary. We could set $X_3$ equal to any number and then solve the two equations in two variables for $X_1$ and $X_2$. Hence, an infinite number of solutions is possible. Of course, we could just as easily have set either $X_1$ or $X_2$ equal to some value and solved for the other two variables.

An important subset of the set of all possible solutions is the set of basic solutions.[3] A basic solution for our example, equations (C-3) and (C-4), is obtained by setting one variable equal to zero and solving for the other two. Thus, three basic solutions to equations (C-3) and (C-4) could be obtained by setting $X_1$, $X_2$, and $X_3$, in turn, equal to zero and solving for the other two variables. The basic solutions are given below:

Set $X_1 = 0$; then: $\qquad$ $X_2 = 1.18$ $\qquad$ $X_3 = 0.27$
Set $X_2 = 0$; then: $\qquad$ $X_1 = 3.25$ $\qquad$ $X_3 = -1.5$
Set $X_3 = 0$; then: $\qquad$ $X_1 = 0.5$ $\qquad$ $X_2 = 1$

To generalize, let $m$ be the number of equations and $n$ be the number of variables. The typical linear programming problem is characterized by $n > m$. A basic solution is obtained by setting $n - m$ variables equal to zero and solving the resulting system of $m$ equations in $m$ variables for the values of the $m$ variables. Of course, we shall find a basic solution only if the resulting $m$ equations in $m$ variables are independent and consistent.

## BASIC SOLUTIONS IN LINEAR PROGRAMMING

As an example, we shall select a three-equation, five-variable problem. One reason for using the larger system is to provide a slightly more complex illustration of the Gauss-Jordan method; another reason is to examine the mathematics of the television-assembly linear programming problem described in Chapter 5. The discussion should also provide insight into the simplex method, which will be used to solve the same problem in the last section.

Recalling the three inequality constraints in Chapter 5, we had

$$Q_C \leq 50$$
$$1.0Q_B + 1.6Q_C \leq 240$$
$$0.5Q_B + 2.0Q_C \leq 162$$

It was also pointed out that $Q_C$ and $Q_B$ must be nonnegative, since it is not meaningful to speak of producing negative quantities of television sets.

The set of feasible solutions to the problem was shown by the shaded region in Figure 5-12 in Chapter 5. It is possible to convert the three inequalities into a system of three equations which will have the identical set of solutions. The reason for the conversion is simply that the algebraic method for solving equations is easier than the one for solving inequalities. The trick is to add slack variables to the inequalities. For example, adding a slack variable $S_1$ to the color tube constraint gives

$$Q_C + S_1 = 50$$

In order to preserve the inequality, $S_1$ must be restricted to nonnegative values. For

---

[3] A set is simply any well-defined collection of distinct objects. The players on a particular baseball team, for example, would be a set, and the set of pitchers on that team would be a subset of the set.

example, $S_1 = -5$ would imply $Q_C = 55$, which is impossible. $S_1$ can be interpreted as the number of color tubes *not* used in production, or the excess capacity in the supply of color tubes.

Adding slack variables to the three inequalities yields the following system of equations:

$$0Q_B + 1Q_C + 1S_1 + 0S_2 + 0S_3 = 50 \tag{C-5}$$
$$1Q_B + 1.6Q_C + 0S_1 + 1S_2 + 0S_3 = 240 \tag{C-6}$$
$$0.5Q_B + 2.0Q_C + 0S_1 + 0S_2 + 1S_3 = 162 \tag{C-7}$$

We must also add the restriction that the five variables be nonnegative:

$$Q_B, Q_C, S_1, S_2, S_3 \geq 0$$

As a result, we have three equations in five variables, or an underdetermined system of equations. The set of feasible (nonnegative) solutions is infinite and can be shown graphically as the shaded region in Figure C-4. Since $Q_C$ and $Q_B$ are on the axes, it is easy to understand the geometrical interpretation of their values. However, what is the interpretation of $S_1$, $S_2$, and $S_3$ in Figure C-4? The three equations were graphed by setting their respective slack variables equal to zero. Hence, any point on the horizontal line, the graph of equation (C-5), implies that $S_1 = 0$. Similarly, points on the other lines imply that $S_2$ and $S_3$ equal zero. Each line in the figure is identified by the slack variable associated with its equation.

Which of the infinite solutions in the figure are basic solutions? There are nine basic solutions, and they are numbered 1 through 9. Notice that each basic solution corresponds to an intersection point. If one studies the figure carefully, it is apparent that each intersection point has the property that two of the five variables are equal to zero. But of course, this is the definition of a basic solution. That is, in the five-variable, three-equation case, set two variables equal to zero and solve the three-variable, three-equation system for the values of the other three variables.

**FIGURE C-4**
Set of feasible solutions and basic solutions.

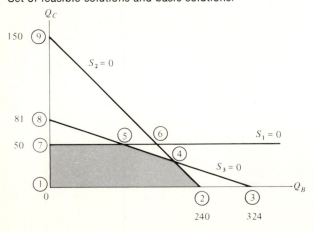

Observe also that not all nine basic solutions are feasible. In fact, there are only five basic feasible solutions: numbers 1, 2, 4, 5, and 7. Graphically, the basic feasible solutions correspond to the corner points of the feasible region. As we pointed out in Chapter 5, the optimum is always at a corner point. We can now say that the optimum solution will be a basic feasible solution.

This last statement is of profound importance and is normally referred to as the fundamental theorem of linear programming. It is valuable for solving linear programming problems because it is not necessary to examine each of the infinite feasible solutions but only the basic feasible solutions.

The simplex method is a search procedure that compares the value of the objective function for various basic feasible solutions. Clearly, solving a linear programming problem would be much more difficult if *all* feasible solutions had to be examined. In fact, the logic of the simplex method makes it unnecessary even to examine all the basic feasible solutions, and this reduces the computational problem even more.

We now turn to the algebraic process for determining the basic feasible solutions.

Table C-1 shows nine basic solutions obtained by setting two variables out of the five equal to zero. To fill in the blanks requires in each case a simultaneous solution of three equations in three variables. To find the first basic solution, $Q_C$ and $Q_B$ are both set equal to zero in equations (C-5) through (C-7). Since $Q_C$ and $Q_B$ are equal to zero, we can eliminate them from the equations. This yields

$$1S_1 + 0S_2 + 0S_3 = 50$$
$$0S_1 + 1S_2 + 0S_3 = 240$$
$$0S_1 + 0S_2 + 1S_3 = 162$$

The Gauss-Jordan method of solution requires a transformation of the coefficient matrix above into the identity matrix. Since it is already in that form, we merely read the solutions as $S_1 = 50$, $S_2 = 240$, and $S_3 = 162$. These values, together with $Q_B = Q_C = 0$, constitute the first basic solution.

Table C-1 gives the complete list of basic solutions and indicates those which are feasible (that is, nonnegative). You should relate these algebraic results to their graphical counterparts in Figure C-4.

Consider how solution 4, for example, is obtained. First, we set $S_2 = S_3 = 0$ in equations (C-5) through (C-7) and obtain three equations in three variables. Although we

**TABLE C-1**
BASIC SOLUTIONS

| Solution number | $Q_C$ | $Q_B$ | $S_1$ | $S_2$ | $S_3$ | |
|---|---|---|---|---|---|---|
| 1 | 0 | 0 | 50 | 240 | 162 | Feasible |
| 2 | 0 | 240 | 50 | 0 | 42 | Feasible |
| 3 | 0 | 324 | 50 | −84 | 0 | |
| 4 | 35 | 184 | 15 | 0 | 0 | Feasible |
| 5 | 50 | 124 | 0 | 36 | 0 | Feasible |
| 6 | 50 | 160 | 0 | 0 | −18 | |
| 7 | 50 | 0 | 0 | 160 | 62 | Feasible |
| 8 | 81 | 0 | −31 | 110.4 | 0 | |
| 9 | 150 | 0 | −100 | 0 | −138 | |

could drop $S_2$ and $S_3$ from the equations, we will not do so. It is necessary to carry them along in the simplex method, and it seems appropriate to begin the practice here.

$$0Q_B + 1Q_C + 1S_1 + 0S_2 + 0S_3 = 50 \qquad \text{(C-8)}$$
$$1Q_B + 1.6Q_C + 0S_1 + 1S_2 + 0S_3 = 240 \qquad \text{(C-9)}$$
$$0.5Q_B + 2.0Q_C + 0S_1 + 0S_2 + 1S_3 = 162 \qquad \text{(C-10)}$$

The coefficients of $Q_B$, $Q_C$, and $S_1$ are not in identity matrix form. First, we interchange equations (C-8) and (C-9) in order to get the necessary 1 for the coefficient of $Q_B$.

After interchanging equations (C-8) and (C-9) and adding $-0.5$ times equation (C-9) to equation (C-10), we have

$$1Q_B + 1.6Q_C + 0S_1 + 1S_2 + 0S_3 = 240 \qquad \text{(C-9)}$$
$$0Q_B + 1Q_C + 1S_1 + 0S_2 + 0S_3 = 50 \qquad \text{(C-8)}$$
$$0Q_B + 1.2Q_C + 0S_1 - 0.5S_2 + 1S_3 = 42 \qquad \text{(C-10)}$$

To get zeros as the $Q_C$ coefficients in equations (C-9) and (C-10), add $-1.6$ times equation (C-8) to equation (C-9) and add $-1.2$ times equation (C-8) to equation (C-10).

$$1Q_B + 0Q_C - 1.6S_1 + 1S_2 + 0S_3 = 160 \qquad \text{(C-9)}$$
$$0Q_B + 1Q_C + 1S_1 + 0S_2 + 0S_3 = 50 \qquad \text{(C-8)}$$
$$0Q_B + 0Q_C - 1.2S_1 - 0.5S_2 + 1S_3 = -18 \qquad \text{(C-10)}$$

Then divide equation (C-10) by $-1.2$ to get

$$0Q_B + 0Q_C + 1S_1 + \frac{5}{12}S_2 - \frac{5}{6}S_3 = 15 \qquad \text{(C-11)}$$

Next, add 1.6 times equation (C-11) to equation (C-9) and $-1$ times equation (C-11) to equation (C-8) to get zeros as coefficients of $S_1$ in equations (C-9) and (C-8), respectively. In identity matrix form we now have

$$1Q_B + 0Q_C + 0S_1 + \frac{20}{12}S_2 - \frac{16}{12}S_3 = 184 \qquad \text{(C-9)}$$

$$0Q + 1Q_C + 0S_1 - \frac{5}{12}S_2 + \frac{10}{12}S_3 = 35 \qquad \text{(C-8)}$$

$$0Q_B + 0Q_C + 1S_1 + \frac{5}{12}S_2 - \frac{10}{12}S_3 = 15 \qquad \text{(C-11)}$$

The basic solution is now easily seen to be

$$Q_B = 184$$
$$Q_C = 35$$
$$S_1 = 15$$
$$S_2 = 0$$
$$S_3 = 0$$

To review our results thus far, we shall rewrite the original equations in tabular form. Rather than placing the variables after the coefficients, we shall simply place the appropriate variable as a column heading and omit the equalities. The right-hand-side constants are shown in the column headed by $P_0$. The simplex method makes use of this tabular form, which is the reason for introducing it here.

SOLUTION 1

| Solution | $Q_B = Q_C = 0$ | | | | | |
|---|---|---|---|---|---|---|
| | $Q_B$ | $Q_C$ | $S_1$ | $S_2$ | $S_3$ | $P_0$ |
| $S_1$ | 0 | 1 | 1 | 0 | 0 | 50 |
| $S_2$ | 1 | 1.6 | 0 | 1 | 0 | 240 |
| $S_3$ | 0.5 | 2 | 0 | 0 | 1 | 162 |

We began by interpreting the equation above as a basic solution in which $Q_B = Q_C = 0$. Recall that the coefficients of the other variables are in the proper identity matrix form for us to read off the solution. Each row (or equation) is given the variable name according to the solution it specifies. Thus, the first row indicates the solution of $S_1$ to be 50, the second row shows $S_2 = 240$, and third row yields $S_3 = 162$.

The next result described was the basic solution in which $S_2 = S_3 = 0$. We used the Gauss-Jordan method to transform the coefficients of $Q_B$, $Q_C$, and $S_1$ into identity matrix form, yielding the solution below.

SOLUTION 4

| Solution | $S_2 = S_3 = 0$ | | | | | |
|---|---|---|---|---|---|---|
| | $Q_B$ | $Q_C$ | $S_1$ | $S_2$ | $S_3$ | $P_0$ |
| $Q_B$ | 1 | 0 | 0 | 20/12 | −16/12 | 184 |
| $Q_C$ | 0 | 1 | 0 | −5/12 | 10/12 | 35 |
| $S_1$ | 0 | 0 | 1 | $\boxed{5/12}$ | −10/12 | 15 |

## GENERATING NEW BASIC SOLUTIONS

Now we shall illustrate the algebraic process which is the essence of the simplex method. Given, say, basic solution 4, how can we generate a new basic solution in which one of the zero variables in solution 4 is permitted to become nonzero? We want to make either $S_2$ or $S_3$ nonzero and simultaneously make either $Q_B$ or $Q_C$ or $S_1$ zero. Of course, we must maintain *two* zero variables in order for the new solution to be basic. That is why we must make one of the nonzero variables zero when we make a zero variable nonzero. Henceforth, we shall refer to a zero variable as a nonbasic variable and a nonzero variable as a basic variable. (Sometimes we shall refer to the basic variables as the solution variables, since they appear in the solution column.)

In the next section we shall discuss how one chooses the particular nonbasic variable that enters the solution and how one chooses the particular basic variable that leaves.[4]

---

[4] There are two major considerations involved in this decision. One is to select as the entering variable that variable which will increase the value of the objective function at the greatest rate. The other consideration is to make the selection so that the resulting basic solution will also be feasible.

For the present, assume that we have selected $S_2$ to enter the solution and $S_1$ to leave. That is, we want to find the basic solution in which $S_1 = S_3 = 0$. The graphical representation is that we are moving from solution (or corner point) 4 to solution 5 in Figure C-4.

The new solution must have an identity matrix associated with its basic variables $Q_B$, $Q_C$, and $S_2$. Referring back to solution 4, we need to transform the equations to get a 1 for the coefficient of $S_2$ in the third equation (where the coefficient is now 5/12). We have circled this coefficient and shall refer to it as the pivot element. Notice that the pivot element lies in the entering variable column and the leaving variable row. We must also obtain zeros for the coefficients of $S_2$ in the first and second rows.

The first step in deriving solution 5 is to get a 1 in the place of the pivot element. The Gauss-Jordan method calls for division of the row by the pivot element, or by 5/12. The result is shown below, where we have also replaced $S_1$ by $S_2$ in the solution column.

| Solution | $Q_B$ | $Q_C$ | $S_1$ | $S_2$ | $S_3$ | $P_0$ |
|---|---|---|---|---|---|---|
| $Q_B$ | 1 | 0 | 0 | 20/12 | −16/12 | 184 |
| $Q_C$ | 0 | 1 | 0 | −5/12 | 10/12 | 35 |
| $S_2$ | 0 | 0 | 2.4 | 1 | −2 | 36 |

Bear in mind that the object is to obtain an identity matrix as the coefficient matrix of the new basic variables $Q_B$, $Q_C$, and $S_2$. To complete this transformation we must get zeros in column $S_2$, rows $Q_B$ and $Q_C$.

Multiply the $S_2$ row in the table above by −20/12 and add the result to the $Q_B$ row. Then multiply the $S_2$ row by 5/12 and add the result to the $Q_C$ row. You should be familiar with these Gauss-Jordan procedures by now. The result is given below.

SOLUTION 5

| Solution | $Q_B$ | $Q_C$ | $S_1$ | $S_2$ | $S_3$ | $P_0$ |
|---|---|---|---|---|---|---|
| | | | $S_1 = S_3 = 0$ | | | |
| $Q_B$ | 1 | 0 | −4 | 0 | ②  | 124 |
| $Q_C$ | 0 | 1 | 1 | 0 | 0 | 50 |
| $S_2$ | 0 | 0 | 2.4 | 1 | −2 | 36 |

The solution is $Q_B = 124$, $Q_C = 50$, $S_2 = 36$, $S_1 = 0$, and $S_3 = 0$.

Finally, to summarize how one basic solution can be generated from another, we list the following rules.

Let $E$ be the nonbasic variable which is to enter the solution (become basic) and let $L$ be the basic variable which is to leave (become nonbasic).

**1** The pivot element lies in the $L$ row and the $E$ column of the old solution table.

**2** Divide each number in the $L$ row of the old table by the pivot element. The result is the $E$ row in the new table.

**3** For all other rows, say row $K$, take the negative of the number in row $K$ of the old table and in the pivot element column. Multiply this by the $E$ row of the new table and add the result to the $K$ row to obtain the $K$ row for the new table.

To illustrate the rules, we take one last example. We want to derive solution 7 from solution 5. That is, we select $S_3$ as the entering variable and $Q_B$ as the leaving variable.

**Rule 1**

The pivot element is the 2 in row $Q_B$, column $S_3$ of solution 5.

**Rule 2**

Division of row $Q_B$ by 2 yields the new row $S_3$:

| Solution | $Q_B$ | $Q_C$ | $S_1$ | $S_2$ | $S_3$ | $P_0$ |
|---|---|---|---|---|---|---|
| $S_3$ | 1/2 | 0 | −2 | 0 | 1 | 62 |

**Rule 3**

Multiply row $S_3$ by 0 and 2, respectively, and add the results to rows $Q_C$ and $S_2$, respectively, to obtain new rows $Q_C$ and $S_2$:

| Row $Q_C$ | $Q_B$ | $Q_C$ | $S_1$ | $S_2$ | $S_3$ | $P_0$ |
|---|---|---|---|---|---|---|
| 0 times $S_3$ row | 0 | 0 | 0 | 0 | 0 | 0 |
| + old $Q_C$ row | 0 | 1 | 1 | 0 | 0 | 50 |
| New $Q_C$ row | 0 | 1 | 1 | 0 | 0 | 50 |

| Row $S_2$ | $Q_B$ | $Q_C$ | $S_1$ | $S_2$ | $S_3$ | $P_0$ |
|---|---|---|---|---|---|---|
| 2 times $S_3$ row | 1 | 0 | −4 | 0 | 2 | 124 |
| + old $S_2$ row | 0 | 0 | 2.4 | 1 | −2 | 36 |
| New $S_2$ row | 1 | 0 | −1.6 | 1 | 0 | 160 |

Place the new rows in the solution 7 table:

SOLUTION 7

| Solution | $Q_B$ | $Q_C$ | $S_1$ | $S_2$ | $S_3$ | $P_0$ |
|---|---|---|---|---|---|---|
| | | | $S_1 = Q_B = 0$ | | | |
| $S_3$ | 1/2 | 0 | −2 | 0 | 1 | 62 |
| $Q_C$ | 0 | 1 | 1 | 0 | 0 | 50 |
| $S_2$ | 1 | 0 | −1.6 | 1 | 0 | 160 |

## THE SIMPLEX METHOD

The simplex method[5] is an algebraic procedure that through an iterative process progressively approaches and ultimately reaches an optimum solution. The simplex

[5] The simplex method described here is not a particularly efficient procedure for electronic computers. Hence, a streamlined version known as the revised simplex method has been developed for that purpose. Since a discussion of the revised simplex method requires a knowledge of matrix algebra, we omit it here.

method may be summarized briefly as follows:

**1** Define the problem in terms of a linear objective function subject to a set of linear constraints.

**2** Introduce slack variables to convert inequalities into equalities and provide a basic feasible solution to the problem.

**3** Construct the initial simplex table for a basic feasible solution.

**4** Determine which variable should be entered into the solution (become basic) if the solution is not optimum.

**5** Determine which variable should leave the solution (become nonbasic).

**6** Construct a new simplex table reflecting the changes that have been made in the solution.

**7** Repeat steps 4 through 6 until an optimum solution is reached, i.e., until the solution cannot be further improved.

To explain the simplex method we shall continue with our example problem of television assembly that was set forth in Chapter 5. To review briefly, the problem is to determine the quantities of black-and-white and color television sets $Q_B$ and $Q_C$ which maximize the profit function

$$Z = 15Q_B + 45Q_C$$

subject to the following constraints imposed by the present production facilities:

Color picture tube supply:     $Q_C \leq 50$
Set assembly capacity:     $1.0Q_B + 1.6Q_C \leq 240$
Final inspection capacity:   $0.5Q_B + 2.0Q_C \leq 162$

The key steps which we must focus on here are steps 4 and 5, to which we now turn. Solution 1, given in tabular form on page 187, will now be referred to as our initial simplex table. The additional columns and rows, as shown in Table C-2, will be explained below.

The production requirements for producing one black-and-white set and one color set are found in columns 1 and 2, respectively. Column 1 indicates that the production of one black-and-white set requires 1.0 worker-hours of set assembly-line capacity and 0.5 worker-hours of final testing capacity. Column 2 shows that the production of one color

**TABLE C-2**

| | | Column | 1 | 2 | 3 | 4 | 5 | |
| | | $C_j$ | 15 | 45 | 0 | 0 | 0 | |
| Row | $C_i$ | Solution | $Q_B$ | $Q_C$ | $S_1$ | $S_2$ | $S_3$ | $P_0$ |
| 1 | 0 | $S_1$ | 0 | (1.0) | 1 | 0 | 0 | 50 |
| 2 | 0 | $S_2$ | 1.0 | 1.6 | 0 | 1 | 0 | 240 |
| 3 | 0 | $S_3$ | 0.5 | 2.0 | 0 | 0 | 1 | 162 |
| | | $Z_j$ | 0 | 0 | 0 | 0 | 0 | 0 |
| | | $C_j - Z_j$ | 15 | 45 | 0 | 0 | 0 | |

set requires 1.0 color picture tubes, 1.6 worker-hours of set assembly-line capacity, and 2.0 worker-hours of testing capacity. Although columns 3, 4, and 5 may be interpreted in a manner similar to that of columns 1 and 2, very little is gained by such an interpretation. For example, column 3 indicates that the production of 1 unit of color picture tube excess capacity requires 1.0 color picture tubes. (Recall that $S_1$, $S_2$, and $S_3$ are the so-called slack variables, which measure the amount of unused capacities of color picture tubes, set assembly, and final inspection.)

The elements in the $C_j$ row (where the $j$ subscript refers to the column number) are the coefficients of the variables in the objective function, that is, the gross contributions to profit and overhead per unit for each variable $Q_B$, $Q_C$, $S_1$, $S_2$, and $S_3$. The elements in the $C_i$ column (where the $i$ subscript refers to the row number) are the contributions to profit and overhead per unit for each of the three basic variables $S_1$, $S_2$, and $S_3$ in the initial basic feasible solution. The fact that the $C_i$'s are all equal to zero in the initial solution indicates that it is not profitable to have the plant lie completely idle. That is, total profit is

$$Z = 0(50) + 0(240) + 0(162) = 0$$

Under each column is a $Z_j$ total. Notice that total profit, as calculated above, is $Z_0$ (the value of $Z_j$ in column $P_0$ of Table C-2). The $Z_j$ total of the other columns is the amount of gross profit that is forfeited by introducing 1 unit of the variable in the $j$ column into the solution.

For example, suppose that we want to produce one color set $Q_C$. The production requirements for one color set are given in column 2:

1.0 color picture tube
1.6 worker-hours of assembly capacity
2.0 worker-hours of testing capacity.

Thus, the basic variables in the solution ($S_1$, $S_2$, and $S_3$) would each be reduced by the amounts above. The value of $S_1$ would be reduced from 50 to 49, $S_2$ would be reduced from 240 to 238.4, and $S_3$ would be reduced from 162 to 160. Altogether, the value of profit would be reduced by

$$C_1(1) + C_2(1.6) + C_3(2.0)$$

where the $C_i$'s are the profit function coefficients of $S_1$, $S_2$, and $S_3$. In this example, the $C_i$'s are all equal to zero so that

$$Z_2 = 0(1.0) + 0(1.6) + 0(2.0) = 0$$

We find that the production of 1 unit of $Q_C$ has the opportunity cost of using resources that were previously used in the production of $S_1$, $S_2$, and $S_3$. The opportunity cost in this case is zero, because reducing production of $S_1$, $S_2$, and $S_3$ has no effect on profit. However, this is not the complete story. The color set directly contributes \$45 to profit (as shown in the $C_j$ row) so that the *net effect* on profit is $C_2 - Z_2$, or \$45 − 0 = \$45. Thus, the $C_j - Z_j$ row shows the net effect on profit of producing an additional unit of the $j$th variable.

If we let $a_{ij}$ denote the element in the $i$th row and $j$th column of the table, the $Z_j$'s (including $Z_0$) are defined by

$$Z_j = \sum_{i=1}^{3} C_i a_{ij} \qquad (j = 0, 1, 2, 3, 4, 5)$$

$$Z_1 = 0(0) \quad + 0(1.0) + 0(0.5) = 0$$
$$Z_2 = 0(1.0) + 0(1.6) + 0(2.0) = 0$$
$$Z_3 = 0(1) \quad + 0(0) \quad + 0(0) \quad = 0$$
$$Z_4 = 0(0) \quad + 0(1) \quad + 0(0) \quad = 0$$
$$Z_5 = 0(0) \quad + 0(0) \quad + 0(1) \quad = 0$$
$$Z_0 = 0(50) \quad + 0(240) + 0(162) = 0$$

and the $C_j - Z_j$ row of Table C-2 is

$$C_1 - Z_1 = 15 - 0 = 15$$
$$C_2 - Z_2 = 45 - 0 = 45$$
$$C_3 - Z_3 = 0 \quad - 0 = 0$$
$$C_4 - Z_4 = 0 \quad - 0 = 0$$
$$C_5 - Z_5 = 0 \quad - 0 = 0$$
$$C_0 - Z_0 = 0 \quad - 0 = 0$$

### Determine Which Variable to Enter

Having completely defined the initial simplex table, we must now determine whether an optimum solution has been achieved. Stated differently, we want to find out whether the value of the profit function will be increased by introducing some quantity of $Q_B$ or $Q_C$ (the two nonbasic variables) into the solution. The answer to this question may be found in the $C_j - Z_j$ row, for it indicates that there would be a gain of $15 for each black-and-white set produced and $45 for each color set produced. It further indicates that nothing would be gained at this point by increasing the excess capacity of the plant, that is, by increasing the quantities of $S_1$, $S_2$, and $S_3$ that are presently in the solution. As long as there is at least one $C_j - Z_j$ that is positive (greater than zero), an optimum solution has not been reached. The solution can be improved by introducing into the solution some quantity of that variable which has the highest positive value in the $C_j - Z_j$ row: the variable with the greatest net unit profit. Although profit can be increased by introducing some positive quantity of any variable with a positive value in the $C_j - Z_j$ row, the simplex criterion for selecting which variable to introduce into the solution is to select the variable with the highest unit contribution to profit and overhead.

Referring to the $C_j - Z_j$ row, we find that $45 represents the largest net unit profit in the row. Since total profits will be increased by $45 for each color set produced, we shall introduce as many units of $Q_C$ into the solution as is technically feasible.

### Determine Which Variable to Remove

In the initial solution the variable $Q_C$ was assumed to be equal to zero and thus was not one of the three basic variables contained in the solution. However, we decided above to enter $Q_C$ into the solution. Since there are three constraint equations, there must be exactly three variables with nonnegative values in the solution. Hence, one variable must leave the solution to permit the entrance of $Q_C$; that is, one variable must be set equal to zero (must become nonbasic).

This is equivalent to saying that we shall introduce the maximum amount of $Q_C$ that is technically feasible. But this feasibility is determined by the number of units of excess capacity, that is, the values of $S_1$, $S_2$, and $S_3$. In other words, units of $Q_C$ will be produced up to and including the point where either (1) all the available color picture tubes have been used ($S_1 = 0$), (2) there is no longer any set assembly-line capacity available ($S_2 = 0$), or (3) there is no final testing capacity available ($S_3 = 0$). When the maximum amount of $Q_C$ has been entered into the solution, either $S_1$, $S_2$, or $S_3$ will be equal to zero, depending on which constraint is most limiting. Thus, we shall still have three equations with exactly three solution variables.

For each unit of $Q_C$ brought into the solution, 1.0 units of $S_1$ (color picture tubes), 1.6 units of $S_2$ (set assembly-line capacity), and 2.0 units of $S_3$ (testing capacity) must be removed (subtracted) from the solution. These numbers are called coefficients of exchange, for in effect we are exchanging 1.0 units of $S_1$, 1.6 units of $S_2$, and 2.0 units of $S_3$ for 1 unit of $Q_C$.

In this problem no more than 50 units of $S_1$, 240 units of $S_2$, or 162 units of $S_3$ may be removed from the solution. This is equivalent to saying that no negative production is possible. Dividing these capacity limits by the appropriate exchange coefficients will yield the following three limits to the number of units of $Q_C$ that can be brought into the solution:

$$\frac{50}{1.0} = 50$$

$$\frac{240}{1.6} = 150$$

$$\frac{162}{2.0} = 81$$

It can be seen that 50 is the smallest capacity constraint and therefore the largest number of units of $Q_C$ that can be brought into the solution. The production of 50 color television sets removes all the $S_1$ (color picture tubes) from the solution, since there were only 50 color picture tubes available in the first place. In the graphical solution this is equivalent to going out along the $Q_C$ axis from the origin until the first capacity constraint is reached. This corresponds to solution 7 in Figure C-4. It is clear in the figure that the other two possibilities, solutions 8 and 9, are not feasible solutions.

## Construct a New Simplex Table

A new simplex table must now be constructed that will reflect the changes caused by introducing 50 units of $Q_C$ into the solution and removing 50 units of $S_1$. This is equivalent to saying that we must now generate a new basic feasible solution in which $Q_C$ is the entering variable and $S_1$ is the leaving variable.

The new solution will induce changes in the exchange coefficients, the $P_0$ column, the $C_i$ column, and the $Z_j$ and $C_j - Z_j$ rows. The values of these new coefficients must be computed in order to test for an optimum solution. If the new solution is not optimum, the procedure must be repeated until an optimum solution is found.

**TABLE C-3a**

|       |       | Column  | 1     | 2     | 3     | 4     | 5     |       |
|-------|-------|---------|-------|-------|-------|-------|-------|-------|
|       |       | $C_j$   | 15    | 45    | 0     | 0     | 0     |       |
| Row   | $C_i$ | Solution | $Q_B$ | $Q_C$ | $S_1$ | $S_2$ | $S_3$ | $P_0$ |
| 1     | 45    | $Q_C$   | 0     | 1.0   | 1     | 0     | 0     | 50    |
| 2     | 0     | $S_2$   |       |       |       |       |       |       |
| 3     | 0     | $S_3$   |       |       |       |       |       |       |

Since variable $Q_C$ is being introduced into the solution and variable $S_1$ is being removed from the solution, $Q_C$ will be substituted for $S_1$ in the solution column of the simplex table (Table C-3a). The new variable contributes \$45 per unit to profit, and hence the $C_i$ value for the first row becomes \$45.

In order to calculate the exchange coefficients for rows 1, 2, and 3, we apply the rules for generating new basic solutions which were derived at the end of the last section.

**Rule 1**

The pivot element is the circled 1.0 in row 1, column 2 of Table C-2. (It is located in the entering variable column and the leaving variable row.)

**Rule 2**

Division of row 1 of Table C-2 by 1.0 yields the new row 1 shown in Table C-3a.

**Rule 3**

Multiply row 1 in Table C-3a by $-1.6$ and $-2.0$ (negatives of numbers in the pivot element column, rows 2 and 3 of Table C-2) and add the results to rows 2 and 3, respectively, of Table C-2. This gives the two new rows 2 and 3 which appear in Table C-3b:

| Row 2 | $Q_B$ | $Q_C$ | $S_1$ | $S_2$ | $S_3$ | $P_0$ |
|-------|-------|-------|-------|-------|-------|-------|
| $-1.6$ times row 1 (Table C-3a) | 0 | $-1.6$ | $-1.6$ | 0 | 0 | $-80$ |
| + old row 2 (Table C-2) | 1.0 | 1.6 | 0 | 1 | 0 | 240 |
| New row 2 (Table C-3b) | 1.0 | 0 | $-1.6$ | 1 | 0 | 160 |

| Row 3 | $Q_B$ | $Q_C$ | $S_1$ | $S_2$ | $S_3$ | $P_0$ |
|-------|-------|-------|-------|-------|-------|-------|
| $-2.0$ times row 1 (Table C-3a) | 0 | $-2.0$ | $-2.0$ | 0 | 0 | $-100$ |
| +old row 3 (Table C-2) | 0.5 | 2.0 | 0 | 0 | 1 | 162 |
| New row 3 (Table C-3b) | 0.5 | 0 | $-2.0$ | 0 | 1 | 62 |

We can now enter the new coefficients in Table C-3b.

One additional comment on the coefficients in Table C-3b is necessary. Two negative exchange coefficients appear in column 3. These may cause some confusion if the significance of a negative coefficient is not understood. As we have already seen, a positive exchange coefficient in a simplex table indicates that quantity of a variable which must be removed from the solution in order to introduce a unit of some variable that is not currently in the solution. Referring to column 1 in Table C-3b, we can see that in order to introduce 1 unit of $Q_B$ (that is, produce one black-and white television set) it is necessary to remove 0 units of $Q_C$—since, obviously, color picture tubes are not used in the production of black-and-white sets—1 unit of $S_2$, and 1/2 unit of $S_3$. This, too, is obvious, since each unit of $Q_B$ requires 1 worker-hour of set assembly capacity and 1/2 worker-hour of final inspection capacity.

On the basis of the logic presented above, we are now led to the conclusion that a negative exchange coefficient requires not that something be removed from the solution but rather that something be brought into the solution. Let us see why this is so. Column 3 of Table C-3b shows a negative 1.6 and a negative 2.0. Thus, if the $C_j - Z_j$ row indicated that some slack color picture tube capacity would be created, what exactly would be involved? Clearly, for each unit of $S_1$ brought into the solution, one color set is removed, as indicated by the positive exchange coefficient (1.0 in row 1, column 3). Since one color set is now removed from the solution, 1.6 worker-hours of $S_2$ (set assembly capacity) and 2.0 worker-hours of $S_3$ (final inspection capacity) are automatically created, that is, brought into the solution. We therefore conclude that although the magnitude of a positive exchange coefficient is a limiting factor on the number of units of a new variable that can be introduced into the solution, the existence of a negative exchange coefficient is not a limiting factor.

The $C_i$'s in Table C-3b are 45, 0, and 0 for rows 1, 2, and 3, respectively. The $Z_j$ row includes

$$
\begin{aligned}
Z_1 &= 45(0) & + 0(1.0) & + 0(5) & = & \quad 0 \\
Z_2 &= 45(1) & + 0(0) & + 0(0) & = & \quad 45 \\
Z_3 &= 45(1) & + 0(-1.6) & + 0(-2) & = & \quad 45 \\
Z_4 &= 45(0) & + 0(1) & + 0(0) & = & \quad 0 \\
Z_5 &= 45(0) & + 0(0) & + 0(1) & = & \quad 0 \\
Z_0 &= 45(50) & + 0(160) & + 0(62) & = & \,2{,}250
\end{aligned}
$$

**TABLE C-3b**

| | | Column | 1 | 2 | 3 | 4 | 5 | |
| | | $C_j$ | 15 | 45 | 0 | 0 | 0 | |
| Row | $C_i$ | Solution | $Q_B$ | $Q_C$ | $S_1$ | $S_2$ | $S_3$ | $P_0$ |
| 1 | 45 | $Q_C$ | 0 | 1 | 1.0 | 0 | 0 | 50 |
| 2 | 0 | $S_2$ | 1.0 | 0 | −1.6 | 1 | 0 | 160 |
| 3 | 0 | $S_3$ | (0.5) | 0 | −2.0 | 0 | 1 | 62 |
| | | $Z_j$ | 0 | 45 | 45 | 0 | 0 | 2,250 |
| | | $C_j - Z_j$ | 15 | 0 | −45 | 0 | 0 | |

The value of $Z_0$ is actually the value of the profit function when

$$Q_C = 50 \qquad Q_B = 0$$
$$S_2 = 160 \qquad S_1 = 0$$
$$S_3 = 62$$

The $C_j - Z_j$ row is computed in the same manner as before.

### Repeat Steps 4 through 6 Until Optimum Is Obtained

Upon completion of the second simplex table we must again ask whether an optimum solution has been obtained. A quick glance at the $C_j - Z_j$ row of Table C-3b shows that each unit of $Q_B$ introduced into the solution at this point will increase profits by $15. Since there is a positive quantity in the $C_j - Z_j$ row, an optimum solution has not been found.

In order to determine the maximum amount of $Q_B$ that can be introduced into the solution, it is necessary to divide the exchange coefficients given for $Q_B$ (black-and-white sets) into the production quantities in the $P_0$ column. This calculation appears below.

$$\frac{50}{0} = \infty$$

$$\frac{160}{1.0} = 160$$

$$\frac{62}{0.5} = 124$$

From these figures it is evident that it is physically impossible to introduce more than 124 units of $Q_B$ into the solution and produce more than 124 black-and-white sets. This is due to the fact that there are only 62 worker-hours of $S_3$ (final testing capacity) available, and each black-and-white set requires 0.5 worker-hours of final testing.

Hence, a third simplex table must be formulated, reflecting the effects of introducing 124 units of $Q_B$ into the solution and removing 62 units of $S_3$. The pivot element in Table C-3b now becomes the circled 0.5. Applying rules 1 through 3 for generating new basic solutions, we obtain the coefficients in rows 1, 2, and 3 of Table C-4.

The computational procedures for developing the elements in the $Z_j$ and $C_j - Z_j$ rows are identical to those of the previous two simplex tables.

In Table C-4 the values of the solution variables are

$$Q_C = 50$$
$$S_2 = 36$$
$$Q_B = 124$$

This solution corresponds to solution 5 in Figure C-4. We began at the origin, moved up the $Q_C$ axis to solution 7, and have now moved horizontally to solution 5. Each time, the value of the profit function increased. Thus, the current value of profit is $4,110.

**TABLE C-4**

| Row | $C_i$ | Column<br>$C_j$<br>Solution | 1<br>15<br>$Q_B$ | 2<br>45<br>$Q_C$ | 3<br>0<br>$S_1$ | 4<br>0<br>$S_2$ | 5<br>0<br>$S_3$ | $P_0$ |
|-----|-------|-----------|-----|-----|-----|-----|-----|-----|
| 1 | 45 | $Q_C$ | 0 | 1 | 1 | 0 | 0 | 50 |
| 2 | 0 | $S_2$ | 0 | 0 | (2.4) | 1 | −2 | 36 |
| 3 | 15 | $Q_B$ | 1 | 0 | −4 | 0 | 2 | 124 |
| | | $Z_j$ | 15 | 45 | −15 | 0 | 30 | 4,110 |
| | | $C_j - Z_j$ | 0 | 0 | 15 | 0 | −30 | |

$$Z_0 = 15(124) + 45(50) = \$4,110$$

However, Table C-4 also fails to yield an optimum solution, since it is possible even now to improve the solution by introducing the maximum amount of $S_1$ that is technically feasible. As can be seen below, the maximum amount of $S_1$ that can be brought into the solution is 15 units because of the limited supply of $S_2$.

$$\frac{50}{1} = 50$$

$$\frac{36}{2.4} = 15$$

$$\frac{124}{-4} = -31$$

All 36 worker-hours of $S_2$ (set-assembly capacity) are thereby removed from the solution and replaced by 15 idle color picture tubes $S_1$.

Once again, applying the rules for generating new basic solutions, a fourth simplex table can be derived in which the pivot element in Table C-4 is the circled 2.4.

Table C-5 indicates that there are no longer any positive elements in the $C_j - Z_j$ row. Since all these elements are either equal to zero or negative, the value of the objective function cannot be increased by introducing a new variable into the solution. Hence, an optimum solution has been achieved. From Table C-5 the optimum solution is found to be

$$Q_C = 35$$
$$S_1 = 15$$
$$Q_B = 184$$

which corresponds to solution 4 in Figure C-4.

The value of the profit function is

$$Z_0 = \$15(184) + \$45(35) + 0(15) + 0(0) + 0(0) = \$4,335$$

**TABLE C-5**

| Row | $C_i$ | Solution | Column $C_j$ | 1 15 $Q_B$ | 2 45 $Q_C$ | 3 0 $S_1$ | 4 0 $S_2$ | 5 0 $S_3$ | $P_0$ |
|-----|-------|----------|--------------|------------|------------|-----------|-----------|-----------|-------|
| 1 | 45 | $Q_C$ | | 0 | 1 | 0 | −5/12 | 10/12 | 35 |
| 2 | 0 | $S_1$ | | 0 | 0 | 1 | 5/12 | −10/12 | 15 |
| 3 | 15 | $Q_B$ | | 1 | 0 | 0 | 20/12 | −16/12 | 184 |
| | | $Z_j$ | | 15 | 45 | 0 | 6.25 | 17.50 | 4,335 |
| | | $C_j - Z_j$ | | 0 | 0 | 0 | −6.25 | −17.50 | |

However, the value of the optimum solution should come as no surprise to us, since it is identical with the results achieved in Figure 5-14 in Chapter 5 by the graphical method. As in the graphical solution, the optimum solution provided by the simplex method calls for the production of 184 black-and-white sets and 35 color sets, yielding a total contribution to profit and overhead of $4,335.

## SHADOW PRICES

The variable $S_2$ has a $C_j - Z_j$ value, or net-contribution-to-profit value, of −$6.25. This means that a unit of this variable (slack worker-hours of set assembly-line capacity) introduced into the solution at this point would reduce the value of the profit function by $6.25. Since the capacity of this line is fully utilized, introducing one hour of slack time corresponds to reducing the capacity of this line by 1 unit, which would reduce the optimum solution by $6.25. If in fact the original set assembly-line capacity had been 1 worker-hour less than 240, the optimum solution would have a value of $6.25 less. Likewise, if the original set assembly-line capacity were 1 worker-hour more than the 240, the optimum solution would be increased by $6.25. In other words, the net contribution to profit per unit at this stage represents the value of a marginal unit of set assembly-line capacity implied by the solution. These marginal profits are usually referred to as shadow prices.

For the corporate decision maker, the shadow price is defined as the profit of forgone opportunities, or in other words a comparison between the alternative that was accepted and the alternative that was rejected. A decision rule in which opportunity profits are involved hinges on a comparison between what the firm is doing and what it could be doing; it is the difference between those alternatives that constitutes the relevant profit consideration. The value of −$6.25 is the difference between the alternative of not increasing set assembly-line capacity by 1 worker-hour and the alternative of increasing set assembly-line capacity by 1 worker-hour.

## THE DUAL PROBLEM

Every linear programming problem has a dual problem associated with it. For example, in the television-assembly problem the method of solution chosen determines the production of that quantity of black-and-white and color sets which maximizes the re-

**TABLE C-6**

|   | + |  | ≤ |
|---|---|---|---|
|   | $Q_B$ | $Q_C$ |   |
|   | 0 | 1.0 | 50 |
|   | 1.0 | 1.6 | 240 |
|   | 0.5 | 2.0 | 162 |
| Max | 15 | 45 |   |

turns from the sets and, at the same time, does not violate the production-capacity constraints. The dual to this problem determines that value or price assigned to each unit of capacity which minimizes the value of the total input or processes used while not violating, as a lower limit, the contribution to profit and overhead per unit for each type of set. The solution of one of these problems also solves the other.

The primal problem of the television manufacturer is one of determining $Q_B$, $Q_C \geq 0$, which will maximize $Z = 15Q_B + 45Q_C$ subject to

| Color tubes: | $1.0Q_C \leq 50$ | (C-12) |
|---|---|---|
| Set assembly: | $1.0Q_B + 1.6Q_C \leq 240$ | (C-13) |
| Final inspection: | $0.5Q_B + 2.0Q_C \leq 162$ | (C-14) |

This problem is described in tabular form in Table C-6. The constraints may be read from this table by interpreting a single vertical line as + and the double vertical line as ≤. The function to be maximized is given in the bottom row, namely, $15Q_B + 45Q_C$.

To obtain the dual problem, we must extend Table C-6 to the form of Table C-7. Reading down each column of Table C-7, the constraints may be derived by interpreting a single horizontal line as + and the double horizontal line as ≥. The function to be minimized is given by the column to the right of the vertical double line, namely, $50N_1 + 240N_2 + 162N_3$.

**TABLE C-7**

|   |   | + |  | ≤ |
|---|---|---|---|---|
|   |   | $Q_B$ | $Q_C$ | Min |
| + | $N_1$ | 0 | 1.0 | 50 |
| + | $N_2$ | 1.0 | 1.6 | 240 |
| ≥ | $N_3$ | 0.5 | 2.0 | 162 |
|   | Max' | 15 | 45 |   |

The dual problem of the television manufacturer is one of determining $N_1$, $N_2$, $N_3 \geq 0$ which will minimize $g = 50N_1 + 240N_2 + 162N_3$ subject to

| | | |
|---|---|---|
| Unit profit of black-and-white sets: | $1.0N_2 + 0.5N_3 \geq 15$ | (C-15) |
| Unit profit of color sets: | $1.0N_1 + 1.6N_2 + 2.0N_3 \geq 45$ | (C-16) |

In this case $N_1$, $N_2$, and $N_3$ are the values, or prices, assigned respectively to each color picture tube, each worker-hour of set assembly-line capacity, and each worker-hour of final testing capacity.

At this point, it may help you to refer back to the previous section, "Shadow Prices." There we referred to the variables $N_1$, $N_2$, and $N_3$ as shadow prices and interpreted them as opportunity profits of the resource constraints.

The objective of the dual problem is to minimize $g$, the value of the total input or processes used (color picture tubes, set assembly-line capacity, and final testing capacity), without violating the contribution to profit and overhead per unit for black-and-white and color sets as a lower limit. The profit constraint for black-and-white sets means that 1 worker-hour of assembly time multiplied by its value per worker-hour plus 0.5 worker-hours of final testing time multiplied by its value per worker-hour must exceed the unit profit contribution of black-and-white sets. The color set profit constraint means that 1.0 color picture tube multiplied by its value per picture tube plus 1.6 worker-hours of set assembly time multiplied by its value per worker-hour plus 2.0 worker-hours of final testing time multiplied by its value per worker-hour must be greater than or equal to the per unit contribution to profit of color sets.

Before solving the dual problem we shall state, without proof, duality theorem 1. This remarkable theorem should give you some insight into the reason for our interest in the dual problem. So far, we have merely pointed out that by reversing everything in the primal problem we obtain something called the dual problem.

### Duality Theorem 1

If either the primal or the dual problem has a finite optimum solution, then the other problem has a finite optimum solution, and the values of the two objective functions are equal.

Thus, we discover that maximizing $Z$ subject to constraints (C-12) through (C-14) yields the same value as minimizing $g$ subject to dual problem constraints (C-15) and (C-16). In other words, since the maximum value of $Z$ earlier was found to be $4,335, the minimum value of $g$ must also equal $4,335.

Using the simplex method, we now solve the dual problem. Before doing so, however, we need to explain artificial variables, which are necessary in cases of "greater than" inequalities. Consider constraint (C-15) and introduce a slack variable $T_1$:

$$1.0N_2 + 0.5N_3 - T_1 = 15$$

That is, the sum of $1.0N_2 + 0.5N_3$ may be equal to 15 if there is no slack, or it may exceed 15, requiring some positive value for $T_1$.

Of course, for the basic feasible solution in the simplex method, the slack variable used for each equation must be nonnegative. If we set $N_2$ and $N_3$ equal to zero and solve for $T_1$, we find that $T_1 = -15$. This negative solution violates our previous assumption concerning simplex solutions—that the simplex method considers only nonnegative solutions. A second extra variable, known as an artificial variable, must therefore be inserted into the equation to provide a nonnegative basic feasible solution. We will call the new variable $A_1$. If $A_1$, which provides a basic feasible solution, were to appear in the final solution, it would mean that constraint (C-15) could be violated. Hence, we must ensure that $A_1$ does *not* appear in the final solution. This is accomplished by assigning to $A_1$, and to any other artificial variable we may be using, a very high coefficient in the objective function. This coefficient $M$ ensures that $A_1$ will be driven out of the solution.

We now return to the problem of solving the dual problem. By introducing slack ($T$) and artificial ($A$) variables, we obtain the initial basic feasible solution. Table C-8 is the initial simplex table.

To save space we shall show the final simplex table only. Table C-9 represents the optimum solution. Note that we have also dropped the artificial variables, since their only function was to provide an initial solution.

The minimum value of $g$ in the dual problem is indeed \$4,335. There are other aspects of the optimum solution to the dual that should be related to the optimum solution to the primal problem (Table C-5). For example, the optimum values of $Q_B$ and $Q_C$ appear as the $C_j - Z_j$ values in columns 4 and 5 of the dual table, and the optimum values of $N_1$, $N_2$, and $N_3$ appear in the $C_j - Z_j$ row of the primal table, columns 3, 4, and 5.

The economic interpretation of the primal-dual relationship can best be explained by introducing a second duality theorem. First, however, recall that the primal variables of our television problem are $Q_B$ and $Q_C$, the quantities of the two types of sets which are produced. The dual slack variables $T_1$ and $T_2$ can be viewed as related to $Q_B$ and $Q_C$, respectively, via the dual constraints. That is, $T_1$ measures the excess of value imputed to the resources producing $Q_B$ above the unit profit contribution of $Q_B$. Rearranging constraint (C-15) after adding the slack variable gives

$$T_1 = 1.0N_2 + 0.5N_3 - 15 \qquad \text{(C-17)}$$

Furthermore, the dual variables $N_1$, $N_2$, and $N_3$ are related to the primal slack variables $S_1$, $S_2$, and $S_3$ via the primal constraints. For example, the primal slack variable $S_1$ measures the quantity of color picture tubes not used in the production of television sets. The variable $N_1$ is, of course, the imputed value, or price, of color picture tubes. Rearranging constraint (C-12) after adding the slack variable gives

$$S_1 = 50 - 1.0Q_C \qquad \text{(C-18)}$$

**Duality Theorem 2**

**a** If a dual variable ($N$) is optimally nonzero, then its related primal slack variable ($S$) must optimally be zero.

**b** If a dual slack variable ($T$) is optimally nonzero, then its related primal variable $Q$ must optimally be zero.

The proof can be sketched as follows: Add slack variables to equations (C-12) through (C-16). Multiply equation (C-12) through by $N_1$, equation (C-13) by $N_2$, and equation (C-14) by $N_3$. Add these three equations. The right-hand side is

**TABLE C-8**

| Row | $C_i$ | Column | 1 $C_j$ 50 | 2 240 | 3 162 | 4 0 | 5 M | 6 0 | 7 M | |
|-----|-------|--------|------------|-------|-------|-----|-----|-----|-----|---|
| | | Solution | $N_1$ | $N_2$ | $N_3$ | $T_1$ | $A_1$ | $T_2$ | $A_2$ | $P_0$ |
| 1 | M | $A_1$ | 0 | 1.0 | 0.5 | −1 | 1 | 0 | 0 | 15 |
| 2 | M | $A_2$ | 1.0 | 1.6 | 2.0 | 0 | 0 | −1 | 1 | 45 |
| | | $Z_j$ | M | 2.6M | 2.5M | −M | M | −M | M | 60M |
| | | $C_j - Z_j$ | 50 − M | 240 − 2.6M | 162 − 2.5M | M | 0 | M | 0 | 0 |

202

**TABLE C-9**

| Row | $C_i$ | Solution | 1<br>50<br>$N_1$ | 2<br>240<br>$N_2$ | 3<br>162<br>$N_3$ | 4<br>0<br>$T_1$ | 5<br>0<br>$T_2$ | $P_0$ |
|-----|-------|----------|------|------|------|------|------|------|
| | | Column<br>$C_j$ | | | | | | |
| 1 | 240 | $N_2$ | 5/12 | 1 | 0 | −5/3 | 5/12 | 6.25 |
| 2 | 162 | $N_3$ | 5/6 | 0 | 1 | 4/3 | −5/6 | 17.50 |
| | | $Z_j$ | 35 | 240 | 162 | −184 | −35 | 4,335 |
| | | $C_j - Z_j$ | 15 | 0 | 0 | 184 | 35 | |

$50N_1 + 240N_2 + 162N_3$, or $g$. Hence, the left-hand side is equal to $g$. Thus

$$g = 1.0Q_cN_1 + S_1N_1 + 1.0Q_BN_2 + 1.6Q_cN_2 + S_2N_2 + 0.5Q_BN_3 + 2.0Q_cN_3 + S_3N_3$$

Now multiply equation (C-15) by $Q_B$ and equation (C-16) by $Q_C$. Add these two equations. The right-hand side is $15Q_B + 45Q_C$, or $Z$. Thus

$$Z = 1.0N_2Q_B + 0.5N_3Q_B - T_1Q_B + 1.0N_1Q_C + 1.6N_2Q_C + 2.0N_3Q_C - T_2Q_C$$

Duality theorem 1 states that the optimal values of $g$ and $Z$ must be equal. Hence, equating the right-hand sides of $g$ and $Z$ and dropping terms appearing on both sides, we obtain

$$S_1N_1 + S_2N_2 + S_3N_3 = -T_1Q_B - T_2Q_C$$

or

$$T_1Q_B + T_2Q_C + S_1N_1 + S_2N_2 + S_3N_3 = 0$$

At least one variable in each term must be zero to satisfy the equation, which is what duality theorem 2 states.

Since the selection of the maximizing problem as the primal problem was arbitrary (the minimizing problem could just as well have been called the primal problem), the theorem will also hold true if we reverse the names. That is, let the minimizing problem be the dual. Then, for example, the first part of the theorem states that if $Q$ is optimally nonzero, its related $T$ must optimally be zero.

In short, duality theorem 2 can be stated as the following "either-or" conditions:

$$Q_BT_1 = 0 \tag{C-19}$$
$$Q_CT_2 = 0 \tag{C-20}$$
$$N_1S_1 = 0 \tag{C-21}$$
$$N_2S_2 = 0 \tag{C-22}$$
$$N_3S_3 = 0 \tag{C-23}$$

where the conditions hold true only for the values of the variables in the optimum solution. Thus, in equation (C-19), *either* $Q_B$ is zero *or* $T_1$ is zero.

We can demonstrate the validity of the either-or conditions for the television problem, where the solutions were

| Primal solution | Dual solution |
|---|---|
| $Q_B = 184$ | $T_1 = 0$ |
| $Q_C = 35$ | $T_2 = 0$ |
| $S_1 = 15$ | $N_1 = 0$ |
| $S_2 = 0$ | $N_2 = 6.25$ |
| $S_3 = 0$ | $N_3 = 17.50$ |

Hence

$$Q_B T_1 = (184)(0) = 0 \qquad\qquad \text{(C-24)}$$
$$Q_C T_2 = (35)(0) = 0 \qquad\qquad \text{(C-25)}$$
$$N_1 S_1 = (0)(15) = 0 \qquad\qquad \text{(C-26)}$$
$$N_2 S_2 = (6.25)(0) = 0 \qquad\qquad \text{(C-27)}$$
$$N_3 S_3 = (17.50)(0) = 0 \qquad\qquad \text{(C-28)}$$

Now we shall examine the economic sense of these conditions. If $Q_B$, the optimal number of black-and-white sets, is nonzero, then $T_1 = 0$ means that the imputed value of resources used in producing a black-and-white set exactly equals the unit profit contribution of black-and-white sets. This is also true of color sets, and it means that we have selected the correct prices to exactly apportion profits to the resources. But what is the meaning of the requirement that $Q_B$ must equal zero if $T_1$ is positive? If $T_1$ is positive, the value of the resources used in producing a black-and-white set exceeds the unit profit contribution of a black-and-white set. It is clear that $Q_B$ should be zero in this case. To illustrate, we refer to dual constraint (C-15), which, after adding the slack variable, becomes

$$1.0N_2 + 0.5N_3 - T_1 = 15 \qquad\qquad \text{(C-29)}$$

The sum of the first two terms on the left is the value of the resources used in producing a black-and-white set. The constant 15 is the unit contribution to profit of the set. A positive $T_1$ means that

$$1.0N_2 + 0.5N_3 > 15$$

which is the signal that $Q_B$ should, therefore, be zero. An analogous argument can be made for condition (C-20).

Either-or conditions (C-21), (C-22), and (C-23) are similar; hence, we shall limit our discussion to the rationale for conditions (C-26) and (C-27). In condition (C-26), since $S_1 = 15$, then $N_1$ must be zero. But what is $S_1$? This is a slack variable which indicates that in the optimum solution there are 15 unused color television tubes. If there are surplus color tubes, it is only common sense to expect that the imputed value (opportunity profit) of a color tube must be zero. An additional color tube would not be of any value, since it is the other resources that are binding, and the extra color tube could only increase the existing surplus of tubes.

The other side of the condition is illustrated by equation (C-27). Here, since $N_2 = 6.25$, then $S_2$ must be zero. There could be no surplus set assembly worker-hours ($S_2$ could not be positive) or the value of those worker-hours would necessarily be zero. Since $S_2$ is zero, this means that all set assembly worker-hours are being used and that this constraint is binding. Since an additional assembly worker-hour would permit an increase in profit of 6.25, its imputed value is positive.

Thus, duality theorem 2 specifies a set of either-or conditions which relate the primal and dual variables in the optimum solution. The conditions have very plausible economic interpretations.

To conclude the discussion of duality, we should point out that sometimes a computational advantage can be gained by solving the dual problem rather than the primal one. This will be true if the dual problem has fewer constraints than the primal, since the number of simplex tables depends more on the number of constraints than on the number of variables.

# THREE

## COMPETITIVE STRATEGY AND ANALYSIS

# THEORY OF
# MARKET STRUCTURES

## INTRODUCTION

The pricing policy of a corporation is constrained not only by cost and overall market demand factors but also by the nature and degree of competition in its various markets. In this chapter, we shall examine three theoretical market structures; the fourth principal market structure, oligopoly, will be treated in Chapter 7. For comparative purposes, we describe these four market structures briefly below.

   **1** *Perfect competition:* This market structure exists when there is such a large number of buyers and sellers that none can influence price individually. Hence, all market participants are so-called price takers. It must also be the case that the products of all sellers are viewed as being identical (or "homogeneous") by all buyers. Furthermore, sellers must be able to enter or leave the industry freely, and cost and price information must be known to all.

**2** *Monopoly:* A monopolist is the sole supplier of a commodity for which there are no close substitutes. Entry by potential competitors is restricted.

**3** *Monopolistic competition:* This market structure is somewhat of a hybrid of perfect competition and monopoly. While there are many firms, each is assumed to have a slightly differentiated product. That is, buyers are willing to pay slightly higher prices for the products of their preferred sellers; furthermore, these preferences may be due to any number of reasons: physical differences in the product, service or location differences, or image differences created by advertising.

**4** *Oligopoly:* An oligopolistic industry is one with a small number of sellers. The key requirement is that the number of sellers be small enough to induce each seller to consider possible reactions by rivals.

Oligopoly is the market structure prevailing in many important industries, e.g., automobiles, steel, aluminum, copper, petroleum refining, tires, electrical motors and generators, synthetic fibers, farm machinery, aircraft engines, and computing equipment. Because of the variety of ways in which sellers can be assumed to react to their interdependence, no single theory of oligopoly is widely accepted by economists. In our view, the most satisfactory approach to oligopoly theory requires the use of some concepts emphasized in the literature of industrial organization analysis. Since that topic will be introduced in Chapter 7, we defer our treatment of oligopoly.

Two additional market structures that we will not discuss are monopsony and bilateral monopoly. Both are variants of the monopoly model. Monopsony is the case of a single buyer, and bilateral monopoly is the case of a single buyer confronting a single seller.

Before turning to detailed analyses, we should comment briefly on the determinants of market structures. Why are some industries competitive and others monopolistic or oligopolistic? Although we shall consider this topic again in Chapter 7, a few key reasons can be set forth here. Perhaps the most important determinant of market structure is the extent of economies of scale in relation to the size of the market. For example, if minimum unit cost is attainable only at an output equal to one-third of the total market demand, we would expect an oligopolistic market structure to emerge. The automobile industry is a case in point. Other determinants include mergers and government policies.

## PERFECT COMPETITION

The four key assumptions are (1) many buyers and sellers, (2) homogeneous products, (3) easy entry and exit, and (4) complete information. Few real-world industries can satisfy all these assumptions, although some agricultural markets are believed to come close.

### Short-Run Equilibrium

Our first task is to develop the short-run supply curve of a competitive industry. Recall that by short-run we mean that period of time in which some of the firm's inputs are fixed. For example, the short-run can be thought of as that period during which the firm's plant and equipment are essentially fixed but during which the firm can vary other inputs such as labor and raw materials. Once the short-run supply curve is derived, it can be combined with the market demand curve to show how market price and output are determined.

It should be helpful at this point for the reader to review briefly the discussion of short-run profit maximization at the beginning of Chapter 5. Figure 5-2 on page 149 demonstrates that the firm in a perfectly competitive industry will supply output as determined by the intersection of the given price and its marginal cost (MC) curve. However, if price falls below average variable cost (AVC), the firm will shut down and supply zero output. Hence, the *firm's* short-run supply curve can be shown in Figure 6-1 as the curve $AB$.

Point $A$ corresponds to the intersection of AVC and MC in Figure 5-2. For prices below $P_2$, the firm's supply curve coincides with the price axis (where output is zero). The curve $AB$ is simply the firm's MC curve above minimum AVC.

The next step is to aggregate the short-run supply curves for all firms to obtain the industry supply curve. In principle, this is simply a matter of adding the outputs of all firms for a given price. Figure 6-2 indicates the technique for three typical firms. Of course, more firms than three are needed to qualify as perfect competition, but the technique of addition of firms' supply curves is the point of interest here.

The curve $SS'$ is the result of adding the three firms' curves $BB'$, $CC'$, and $DD'$. For example, at the given price $A$, add the firms' outputs horizontally;

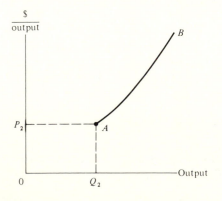

**FIGURE 6-1**
Short-run supply curve of firm.

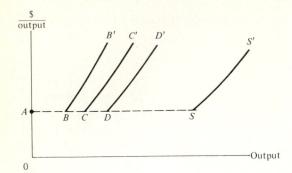

**FIGURE 6-2**
Addition of short-run supply curves
of three firms.

that is, $AB + AC + AD = AS$. All other points on $SS'$ can be obtained similarly by adding the firms' outputs at higher prices.[1]

Hence, the short-run supply curve for a competitive industry is fundamentally the aggregation of the MC curves of the member firms. It should be interpreted as the schedule of total outputs supplied at alternative prices. Combining the supply curve with the market demand curve for the commodity (as shown in Chapter 2), we can determine the short-run price and output equilibrium. Such an equilibrium is shown in Figure 6-3.

The intersection of market demand[2] $DD'$ and short-run supply $SS'$ is at price $P_0$ and output $Q_0$. This is the short-run market equilibrium. The reason for the term "equilibrium" can be understood best by considering prices above and below $P_0$. At price $P_1$, for example, firms wish to supply output $Q_1'$, but consumers will buy only the smaller output $Q_1$. This "excess supply" at price $P_1$ will lead to price cuts by suppliers unable to find desired buyers. This downward pressure on price will continue until price $P_0$ is attained. We leave it to the reader to investigate how a price below $P_0$ will create "excess demand," thereby creating pressure for a price increase. Only at the equilibrium price is there no further pressure for a price change.

Before we turn to the long-run equilibrium, consider how the equilibrium is affected by shifts in demand. Suppose as the result of opening up trade with foreign countries, demand increases, or shifts rightward, from $D_0D_0'$ to $D_1D_1'$ in Figure 6-4.

The result of this shift in demand is to increase the equilibrium price and output to $P_1$ and $Q_1$, where the new demand curve $D_1D_1'$ intersects the supply curve $S_0S_0'$. If firms in the original equilibrium are not making profits, it will probably be the case that the higher price will yield positive profits. If so, these

---

[1] To be rigorous, we should make the assumption that all input prices are constant and are not bid up by the expanding industry output. Hence, firms' supply curves do not shift upward as industry output increases.

[2] Observe that the *market* demand curve in a competitive market has a negative slope; a typical *firm*, however, supplies such a small fraction of total output that its demand curve is horizontal (i.e., price is perceived as fixed) at the equilibrium price $P_0$.

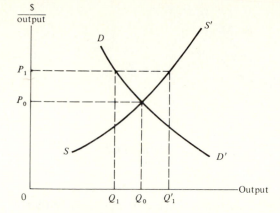

**FIGURE 6-3**
Short-run market equilibrium.

positive profits[3] will act as a signal to attract new firms into the industry. We turn to the effects of entry on the equilibrium in the next section.

### Long-Run Equilibrium

In the long run, it is assumed that firms can adjust scales of plant and equipment and that new firms can enter. To analyze this case, consider Figure 6-5, which shows a typical firm's long-run average cost (LRAC) and long-run marginal cost (LRMC) curves.

The minimum point on the LRAC curve is at unit cost $C_0$ and output $Q_0$, where LRMC intersects LRAC from below. Recall also that the LRAC curve

---

[3] Recall that profits are defined as revenues minus *all* costs, including an average return to investors or stockholders. Hence, positive profit implies an above-average return on investment.

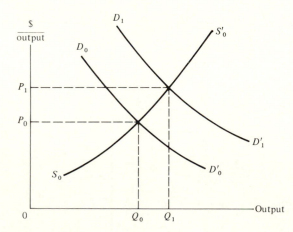

**FIGURE 6-4**
Demand shift and new equilibrium.

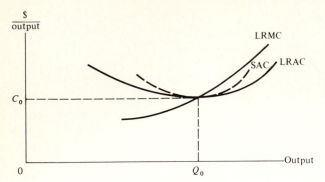

**FIGURE 6-5**
Long-run cost curves.

is the envelope curve to all possible short-run average cost curves, and there exists one such average cost curve that is tangent to the LRAC at its minimum point. This short-run curve is shown by the dashed curve SAC in Figure 6-5.

Since the long run is, by definition, that period of time sufficient for firms to make all desired adjustments, it follows that the typical firm will be in long-run equilibrium only when it is producing output $Q_0$ at a unit cost of $C_0$ (with the plant corresponding to SAC). The reason is that with all firms alike and with free entry, price must continue to fall until it equals minimum unit cost $C_0$. Prices above $C_0$ permit positive profits, and this will attract further entry as well as scale adjustments by existing firms until all profits are eliminated by the declining price.

Figure 6-6 should provide further insight into the long-run adjustment process. Figure 6-6a shows a typical firm, and Figure 6-6b shows the industry. Initially, demand $D_0D_0'$ and short-run supply $S_0S_0'$ intersect at price $P_0$ and output $Q_0$, as shown in Figure 6-6b.

**FIGURE 6-6**
Short-run and long-run adjustment process.

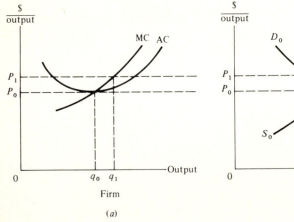

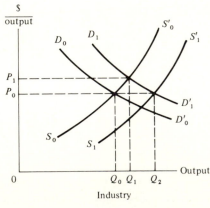

(a) Firm

(b) Industry

By assumption, the industry is in short-run and long-run equilibrium, as is each firm. (The AC curve is the same as the dashed SAC curve shown in Figure 6-5, and MC is its associated marginal cost curve.)

Now, suppose market demand increases to $D_1D_1'$ as a result of an increased demand for exports. The short-run equilibrium of the industry is determined by the intersection of the new demand curve and the old short-run supply curve, $S_0S_0'$. The new price becomes $P_1$. Each firm increases its output by moving up the MC curve until its increased marginal cost equals the new price $P_1$. Recall again that the short-run supply curve implies a period of time too short for entry by new firms or for existing firms to adjust their plant scales.

In the long run, what will happen? The industry is no longer in long-run equilibrium; firms are now earning positive profits. That is, at output $q_1$, the typical firm's price $P_1$ exceeds its average cost AC. Since AC includes *all* costs, including a normal rate of return on capital, new firms will be attracted to enter the industry by the prospect of earning above-normal returns. (Note that in the initial long-run equilibrium at output $q_0$ and price $P_0$, zero profits were being made since price was equal to AC.)

The entry of new firms eventually shifts the supply curve to $S_1S_1'$. The market price falls back to $P_0$, and output increases to $Q_2$. With the greater number of firms in the industry, each firm moves back to its initial equilibrium at price $P_0$ and output $q_0$, and profits are back to zero. Hence, long-run equilibrium is reattained.

Hence, as long as new firms can enter and produce with the same costs shown in Figure 6-6a, the long-run supply curve is a horizontal line at price $P_0$. Such an industry is referred to as a constant-cost industry. If as the industry expands with the entry of new firms, the cost curves shift upward, the long-run supply curve rises with increasing output. Such upward shifts in costs could be due to increasing input prices. A rising long-run supply curve indicates an increasing-cost industry. Similarly, a decreasing-cost industry possesses a falling long-run supply curve.

## A Case Study: Oil and Natural Gas

The petroleum industry is often viewed in the popular press as a clear example of monopoly. One is constantly bombarded with facts about the huge profits of Exxon, Texaco, Gulf, Mobil, Shell, and other large international oil companies.

One also hears about the international oil cartel known as the Organization of Petroleum Exporting Countries (OPEC) and such events as the famous Arab oil embargo of October 1973. For example, in mid-October 1973 the posted price of crude oil in the Persian Gulf was $3.01 per barrel. By January 1974, OPEC members had used the embargo to raise the price to $11.65 per barrel. By mid-1981, the price had risen to about $35 per barrel. Hence, it might seem odd for us to use oil and natural gas as an example of competition.

The explanation is that the oil industry is made up of many sectors, some of which are in fact highly competitive. There is no question about the monopoly power of OPEC (as led by Saudi Arabia) is setting the world price of crude oil. However, most specialists in petroleum industry economics consider the supply of oil and natural gas within the United States to be reasonably competitive.

Consider, for example, the description given below by two experts, James Griffin and Henry Steele of the University of Houston:

> In the onshore exploration for oil and natural gas, there have been virtually no entry barriers, as evidenced by the fact that in 1971 there were 3350 producers of crude oil and natural gas. The existence of a competitive group of service industries makes the necessary technology, manpower, and equipment readily available to independent oil operators.
>
> Exploration firms generally have equal access to promising properties. Promising oil formations can be leased from the numerous private land owners or, in the case of government-owned mineral rights, tracts can be leased from the government in competitive lease sales. Another potential constraint, the capital to conduct a given exploration activity, seldom exceeds $5 million. Such funds could be raised through banks and the sale of working interests to private investors. Finally, state laws typically assure all producers of a market for their oil. So-called "rateable" take laws require that if a refiner purchases oil in a given oil field, it cannot discriminate against any producer in the field by refusing to purchase its oil. For example, any crude oil purchaser buying in a given field must be willing to purchase the same percentage of production, irrespective of who produced the oil. Thus if Texaco elects to purchase all of its own crude oil in a given field, they must also be willing to take crude oil at the same rate from other producers in the field.[4]

It is logical to ask next about the market-shares of Exxon and other large companies. Even if there are 3,350 producers, it is conceivable that 95 percent of sales might be accounted for by a few large firms. The answer is that the market is not dominated by a few large producers. The four largest producers have a combined market-share of only about one-quarter of the total market. As we shall see in Chapter 7, this is relatively low when compared with other major industries.

The energy policy of the United States in the mid-1970s was to control the maximum prices of oil and natural gas directly. The origin of these controls was quite different for oil than for gas, but for our example that is unimportant. The important point is that in the late 1970s, the policy changed to one of price decontrol for both oil and gas.

In terms of Figure 6-6$b$, the basic idea is that controls kept the price at $P_0$, even though the short-run equilibrium required a price of $P_1$. The higher price would have attracted entry, resulting in increased output in the long run.

Of course, we do not claim that Figure 6-6 is an exact description of the complex oil and natural gas industry. Prices were not held constant by the controls, but they were kept from rising as rapidly as they would have been in the absence of controls. In the case of crude oil, imports are important, but they are ignored in Figure 6-6. Also, the long-run supply curves for oil and gas probably

---

[4] James M. Griffin and Henry B. Steele, *Energy Economics and Policy* (New York: Academic Press, 1980), p. 256.

rise with output rather than being flat. However, despite these inadequacies, the general mechanism which describes the response of a competitive industry to a price increase is applicable.

An editorial in *Business Week* of June 29, 1981, characterized the oil and gas situation as follows:

> According to classical economic theory, a free market will respond to a rise in prices by bringing in new sources of supply as well as by reducing demand. Bureaucrats often think that they know better. It is worth noting, therefore, that the performance of domestic oil and gas exploration has been exactly what Adam Smith or Alfred Marshall would have predicted when the Arabs started pushing up prices.
>
> Economist Richard Greene, writing in *Monthly Labor Review,* points out that from the end of 1973 to the end of 1980, jobs in U.S. oil-and-gas and coal mining industries jumped by 90%, about six times as fast as employment in the nonfarm private economy. Significantly, 37%—more than one-third of the total increase —occurred in two years, 1979 and 1980. This upsurge followed an announcement on April 4, 1979, of phased decontrol of prices on newly discovered domestic oil. Since that announcement, oil and natural-gas job rolls have been growing at the rate of 6,600 workers a month, with no end in sight.
>
> From 1973 to 1979, a parade of academic and consumerist witnesses solemnly assured Congress that lifting controls on domestic oil would enrich the oil companies at the expense of the poor without having any effect on supply and employment. The record at this point unmistakably shows that higher oil prices have done exactly what they were supposed to do: They have touched off a storm of activity, attracted ample new investment, created new jobs that the economy badly needs, and added substantially to domestic supply. Score: Classicists 1, Revisionists 0.

## MONOPOLY

A monopolist is the sole seller of a product with no close substitutes. The demand side consists of many buyers, and entry is barred. Entry may be barred for several reasons. For example, the monopolist may control the entire supply of a basic input. Alcoa is often used as an example since it once controlled almost the entire supply of bauxite in the United States. Another reason why entry may be barred is patent ownership or some other legal right to be the sole producer.

Real-world monopolies are rare, though there are examples, such as IBM, of firms with quite large shares of their markets. Of course, there are the so-called natural monopolies, which are regulated by government commissions (electric, gas, and telephone public utilities), but we shall defer their treatment until Chapter 8. The OPEC cartel, even though it consists of a large number of oil-producing nations, acts like a monopolist in the world crude oil market.

### Monopoly Equilibrium

The monopolist shows the same profit-maximizing behavior as the pure competitor. However, the monopolist's demand curve is the same as the *market* demand curve; it slopes downward and to the right. This means that the monopo-

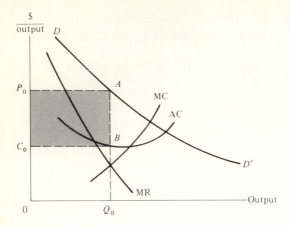

**FIGURE 6-7**
Monopoly equilibrium.

list's output will affect the price. Whereas marginal revenue[5] to the competitor is simply existing price, marginal revenue to the monopolist is always *less* than price. The explanation is that an extra unit of output results in a lowering of price not only for the marginal unit but for all earlier units as well. This is indicated graphically in Figure 6-7 by the placement of the marginal revenue schedule MR below the demand curve.

The profit-maximizing output for the monopolist is determined by the equality of marginal revenue and marginal cost.[6] The logic of this rule is the same as that given in Chapter 5 for the perfect competitor's $P = MC$ rule. (Price and marginal revenue are identical for perfect competitors.) The equilibrium output is $Q_0$ in Figure 6-7. At this output, price must be $P_0$, as given by the demand curve $DD'$.

The monopolist's average cost AC at output $Q_0$ is $C_0$. Hence, profit is equal to the shaded area (total revenue $P_0 0 Q_0 A$ minus total cost $C_0 0 Q_0 B$). Of

---

[5] The term "marginal revenue" means the change in total revenue resulting from a change in output. For a perfect competitor, price $P$ is a parameter, and so total revenue $R$ is $PQ$ (i.e., price times output), and marginal revenue MR is just

$$\text{MR} = \frac{dR}{dQ} = P$$

A monopolist, however, perceives that price will fall as output increases (according to the demand curve). Hence, $R = P(Q)Q$, and

$$\text{MR} = \frac{dR}{dQ} = P + Q\frac{dP}{dQ}$$

Since $dP/dQ$ is negative (the demand curve has a negative slope), the second term is negative, and MR is necessarily less than $P$.

[6] Since $\pi = R - C$, $d\pi/dQ = dR/dQ - dC/dQ = 0$. Hence, MR = MC is the general rule for profit maximization for firms in any market structure. Of course, in perfect competition MR = $P$, and so $P = MC$ is an alternative statement of the rule for profit maximization. But in monopoly, $P > MR$, and so the rule $P = MC$ does not hold.

course, it is possible for a monopolist to earn zero profit if price happens to equal average cost. Such a case would imply that the average cost curve would be just tangent to the demand curve.

We have not emphasized the short-run versus long-run distinction in discussing monopoly equilibrium because it makes little difference to the analysis. Of course, in the long run the monopolist will adjust its scale to the lowest cost available, and profits will persist indefinitely.

The fact that the monopolist can earn positive profits in long-run equilibrium is, of course, a result of the assumption that entry is barred. When the barrier to entry is not absolute, the monopolist may find it unprofitable (because of entry) to set price at the level determined by the intersection of MR and MC. The price set in these cases would be somewhere below $P_0$ but above the price determined by the intersection of MC and the demand curve. The precise level would depend on the height of the entry barriers and other dynamic factors. These important considerations will be explored further in Chapter 7.

### Inefficiency of Monopoly

The inefficiency of resource allocation brought about by monopoly is important to understand because it is the primary economic basis for antitrust policy and much government regulation. Consider an economy in which there are only two industries. Industry A is perfectly competitive, and industry B is a monopoly. To make the simplest possible assumptions, let both industries be characterized by constant-cost production. Figure 6-8a shows the equilibrium of industry A, and Figure 6-8b shows the equilibrium of monopolist B.

The first observation we shall make is that in industry A price equals marginal cost, but in industry B price exceeds marginal cost. Since price repre-

**FIGURE 6-8**
Equilibria of competitive industry and monopolist.

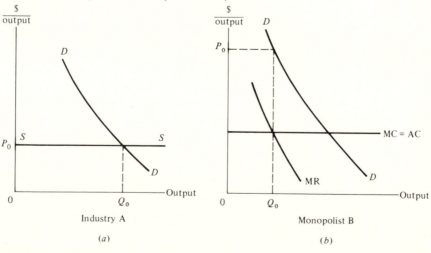

Industry A

(a)

Monopolist B

(b)

sents a measure of the value consumers attach to the last unit bought and marginal cost is the cost to society of the same unit, it is easy to demonstrate that the allocation of resources is inefficient.

Simply imagine the following hypothetical experiment. Suppose a dollar's worth of resources was somehow taken from industry A, and monopolist B was induced to use these resources to expand production. What would happen to the value of output of the economy?

Since price equals marginal cost in industry A, the removal of a dollar's worth of resources results in a fall in the value of its output by $1. In the monopoly, since price is greater than marginal cost, the dollar's worth of resources produces an output that consumers value at some amount greater than $1. The net effect is that the value of output is down by $1 in industry A, but this is more than offset by the increased value of output in the monopoly. Hence, total value of output rises as a result of the reallocation.

The next logical question is, "How much does the *total* misallocation cost society?" It is clear that at the margin, improvements can be made; but how long can these improvements go on? In general, such a reallocation would continue to benefit society until the monopoly was completely eliminated, at which point price would equal marginal cost in both industry A and monopoly B.

### Deadweight Loss from Monopoly

Economists often compute the so-called deadweight loss as a measure of the social cost of monopoly. This deadweight loss can be explained as follows.

We show the loss in Figure 6-9 as the area of the shaded triangle $BEC$. To make the exposition simple, we assume the marginal cost MC and average cost AC are constant. A monopolist will set output at $Q_m$ (or price at $P_m$). If the industry is competitive, equilibrium output and price will be $Q_c$ and $P_c$. (This assumes that costs are unaffected by the type of market structure.)

The essential idea is that social benefits are measured by the area beneath the demand curve.[7] This area represents the total amount of money that consumers are willing to pay for the output. Recall that the demand curve indicates that some people would be willing to pay as high as $0A$ for a unit of output, additional people would pay slightly less than $0A$, and so forth. If the actual market price is $P_c$ for everyone, there is a net "savings," or consumers' surplus, which is given by the triangular area $AP_cC$. That is, consumers' surplus is equal to the total area beneath the demand curve minus the amount actually paid (the amount actually paid, of course, equals the price $P_c$ times the quantity $Q_c$, or rectangle $P_c0Q_cC$).

---

[7] To be perfectly correct, we must assume that the marginal utility of income is constant for all consumers. If it is not, the area under the demand curve is an incorrect measure of social benefit. However, most economists agree that the area under the demand curve is almost always a usable approximation. The exceptions would be those goods which account for very large fractions of consumers' expenditures. For a clear discussion, see Walter Nicholson, *Microeconomic Theory* (Hinsdale, Ill.: Dryden Press, 1978), p. 355.

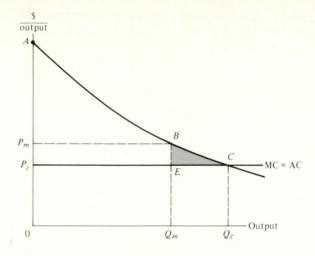

**FIGURE 6-9**
Deadweight loss from monopoly.

Under monopoly, the consumers' surplus is triangle $AP_mB$; under competition, the corresponding area is triangle $AP_cC$. The net difference, or deadweight loss in consumers' surplus as a result of monopoly, is measured by the small shaded triangle. The rectangular area $P_mP_cEB$ is not considered a deadweight loss. The consumers' loss of that area upon monopolization is exactly offset by the gain to the monopolist in the form of profits. Of course, this transfer from consumers to the owners of the monopoly may well be of great concern to policymakers. However, economists generally take the position that they are in no better position to make judgments as to who the most deserving individuals are than anyone else. It is also argued that these equity considerations are best dealt with by means of fiscal policies, e.g., tax policies.

Griffin and Steele[8] have reported that the deadweight loss triangle *BEC* resulting from the OPEC monopoly price for crude oil was $19.8 billion for the year 1980 alone. Also, the transfer from consuming nations to OPEC member nations (rectangle $P_mP_cEB$) amounted to $127.3 billion in 1980. These dramatically large estimates, however, are unique to the world oil market. Many studies of deadweight losses in American industries have been made, and the results have generally shown that such losses are quite small, on the order of 2 percent or less of gross national product.

**Price Discrimination**

So far we have assumed that the monopolist can charge only a single price to all customers. This is clearly unrealistic. Price discrimination, i.e., charging different prices to different customers, that is not justified by cost differences is a common practice.

One example would be the pricing policy of the American Economic Associ-

[8] Griffin and Steele, op. cit., p. 92

ation. Membership for full professors costs $40.25 per year, while assistant professors must pay $28.25 and students only $14.25. Other examples include the rates charged by electric utilities and telephone companies. Residential customers, commercial customers, and industrial customers are all charged separate rates.

The rationale for price discrimination is simple. Often the monopolist can make higher profits through discrimination. Two conditions are necessary for successful price discrimination. First, the monopolist must be able to separate its customers into submarkets and prevent resales among these submarkets. Clearly, if the group charged the lowest price could resell the monopolist's product to the other groups, the discriminatory prices could not be sustained. Surgeons are quite successful at this since it is impossible for a poor patient who receives a low-price operation to resell it to a rich patient who would be charged a higher price.

The second condition necessary for successful price discrimination is that the price elasticities of demand must differ across the submarkets. As we shall see, if the elasticities are the same for all groups, nothing can be gained by segregating the market. The profit-maximizing prices for all submarkets will be identical.

Consider a monopolist who can segregate the market into two groups, with the demand curve $D_1 D_1'$ and $D_2 D_2'$, as shown in Figure 6-10. The associated marginal revenue curves are $R_1 R_1'$ and $R_2 R_2'$, and the marginal cost curve is MC. The profit-maximizing solution is obtained by first adding horizontally $R_1 R_1'$ and $R_2 R_2'$ to yield $RR'$. This schedule shows, for each level of marginal revenue, the total output necessary to keep marginal revenue in each submarket at this level. The intersection of $RR'$ and MC therefore determines total output $Q$ and the associated marginal cost $C$.

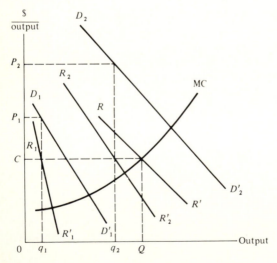

**FIGURE 6-10**
Price discrimination equilibrium for two submarkets.

To determine the prices and outputs in each submarket, marginal revenue in each submarket must be equated with marginal cost $C$. Thus, the outputs $q_1$ and $q_2$ are found from the intersections of $R_1R_1'$ and $R_2R_2'$ and the horizontal dashed line of height $C$. The prices $P_1$ and $P_2$ are determined from the demand curves $D_1D_1'$ and $D_2D_2'$ at these outputs.

The logic of this rather complicated geometrical procedure is quite simple. The key principle is that profit maximization requires that marginal revenue in each submarket be equal to the common marginal cost. If this were *not* the case, a change in the allocation of output among submarkets would yield higher total profit. For example, suppose $MR_1 = \$12$ and $MR_2 = \$10$. The firm could increase total revenue, holding total output (and cost) constant, by allocating one less unit of output to the second submarket and one more unit to the first submarket. This reallocation would continue until the two submarkets produced equal marginal revenues.

The principle that $MR_1$ must equal $MR_2$ can be used to make an important point about elasticities of demand. Since, as shown in Chapter 2, equation (2-10),

$$MR_1 = P_1\left(1 - \frac{1}{e_1}\right)$$

and

$$MR_2 = P_2\left(1 - \frac{1}{e_2}\right)$$

where $e_1 =$ elasticity of demand at $P_1$
$\quad\quad e_2 =$ elasticity of demand at $P_2$

and $MR_1 = MR_2$, it follows that

$$\frac{P_1}{P_2} = \frac{1 - 1/e_2}{1 - 1/e_1}$$

Hence, the profit-maximizing prices will be related to the elasticities. If $e_1$ is larger (more elastic) than $e_2$, then $P_1$ will be lower than $P_2$. In short, the price-discriminating monopolist should charge a relatively low price in the submarket with the more elastic demand. Finally, as noted earlier, if $e_1 = e_2$, then $P_1 = P_2$, and there is no point in discrimination.

This type of price discrimination is customarily referred to as "third-degree" price discrimination. "Second-degree" discrimination refers to the case in which a particular customer is charged different prices for different blocks of output. For example, an electricity consumer might pay 5 cents per kilowatt hour (kwh) for the first 300 kwh consumed per month, 4 cents kwh for the next 700 kwh, etc. "First-degree," or perfect, price discrimination refers to the limiting case in which the monopolist extracts from each customer the full value of consumers' surplus.

## MONOPOLISTIC COMPETITION

The theory of monopolistic competition is commonly attributed to Professor E. H. Chamberlin of Harvard University. During the 1920s economists had become somewhat disenchanted with the two polar extremes of perfect competition and monopoly. It was thought that real-world markets seldom matched the underlying assumptions of either model. Chamberlin published his theory in a 1933 book[9] as one attempt to rectify the situation.

Monopolistic competition is characterized by a market structure in which there are many firms selling differentiated products that are close substitutes for each other. An important contribution of the theory was that it introduced the concept of product differentiation into the economics literature in a serious way. According to Chamberlin,

> A general class of product is differentiated if any significant basis exists for distinguishing the goods (or services) of one seller from those of another. Such a basis may be real or fancied, so long as it is of any importance whatever to buyers and leads to a preference for one variety of product over another.[10]

When we begin to think about goods and services that we buy ourselves, it is clear that differentiated products are the rule rather than the exception. For example, soap, automobiles, food, gasoline, and housing are all differentiated. Even if we really believe that all brands of gasoline are the same, the retail service stations provide different levels of service, have different locations, and differentiate themselves in other ways.

Producers' goods (goods sold to other firms rather than to the final consumers) are perhaps more often undifferentiated. General Motors, for example, can specify that it needs a certain gauge of cold rolled carbon steel sheet. It then bases its decision largely on the prices offered by the various steel manufacturers. Similarly, in agricultural markets it is difficult to imagine a food processor paying more for a certain grade of wheat because of advertising claims by farmers.

Hence, we can describe the degree of differentiation by the slope of the demand curve confronting the seller. In Figure 6-11, three demand curves are shown. The undifferentiated demand curve is perfectly horizontal, indicating that the seller has no ability to raise price without losing all sales. This is, of course, the type of demand curve that the purely competitive firm faces. The two other curves show that the seller does possess some ability to raise price without losing all sales. Because the firm in a monopolistically competitive market competes with rivals whose products are good substitutes for its own, the "slightly differentiated" demand curve is applicable. These curves assume, of course, that rivals' prices are held fixed.

Chamberlin stressed that firms in monopolistic competition compete through advertising and variation in product quality in addition to price. Either

---

[9] E. H. Chamberlin, *The Theory of Monopolistic Competition* (Cambridge, Mass.: Harvard University Press, 1933).
[10] Ibid, p. 56.

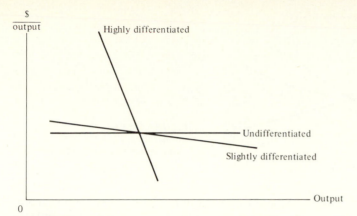

**FIGURE 6-11**
Demand curves facing sellers of differentiated and undifferentiated goods.

of these strategies, for example, could be expected to increase the slope of the firm's demand curve, i.e., increase the degree of product differentiation. Of course, the demand curve might also be expected to shift upward as a result of advertising or improved product quality.

Hence, the firms in a monopolistically competitive market maximize profit by choosing output (or price), the amount of advertising, and product quality. It simplifies matters to assume that the firms have already selected the amount of advertising and the product quality that are most profitable, thereby enabling us to focus on the traditional price and output variables. (For readers interested in a mathematical analysis of a firm's profit-maximizing choice of both price and advertising outlay, we have included Appendix D at the end of this chapter.)

The short-run equilibrium of a representative firm is shown in Figure 6-12. Since price $P_0$ exceeds average cost $C_0$, the firm makes a positive profit.

**FIGURE 6-12**
Short-run equilibrium of firm in monopolistic competition.

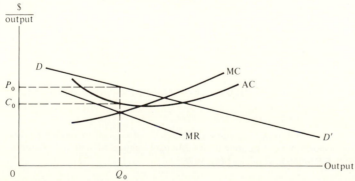

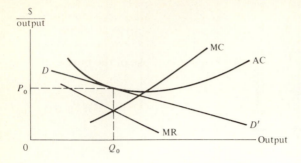

FIGURE 6-13
Long-run equilibrium of firm in
monopolistic competition.

When we turn to the long-run equilibrium, the model becomes more analogous to the model of perfect competition. Given the positive level of profit, new
firms can be expected to enter the monopolistically competitive product group.

Gasoline service stations, a common example of monopolistic competition,
may be used to illustrate the adjustment process. New stations, attracted by the
high returns, would enter the market, causing the total demand for gasoline to
be divided among more service stations. This would cause the demand curve
facing a single station to shift leftward. This shifting would continue until profit
was eliminated, and the long-run equilibrium would be as shown in Figure 6-13.
The equilibrium is characterized by a tangency between the demand curve and
the average cost curve, implying that price equals average cost. Notice also
that the firm does not produce at the minimum point on its long-run average
cost curve.

The evaluation of the efficiency of resource allocation of this model is subject to some controversy. Even though profit is zero, price exceeds marginal
cost, and this causes many economists to conclude that monopolistic competition results in an inefficient allocation of resources. However, Chamberlin
argued that this inefficiency is the cost of what consumers really want in terms
of product differentiation.

> The fact that equilibrium of the firm when products are heterogeneous normally takes
> place under conditions of falling average costs of production has generally been
> regarded as a departure from ideal conditions.... However, if heterogeneity is part
> of the welfare ideal, there is no prima facie case for doing anything at all. It is true
> that the same total resources may be made to yield more units of product by being
> concentrated on fewer firms.... But unless it can be shown that the loss of satisfac-
> tion from a more standardized product is less than the gain through producing more
> units, there is no "waste" at all, even though every firm is producing to the left of its
> minimum point.[11]

Chamberlin's theory has been criticized. For example, it has been argued

---

[11] E. H. Chamberlin, "Product Heterogeneity and Public Policy," *American Economic Review*,
vol. 40, 1950, p. 289. For a more modern treatment, see Michael Spence, "Product Differentiation and Welfare," *American Economic Review*, May 1976.

that the theory is almost "empty" since there are few, if any, testable predictions that can be derived from it.[12] Also, if the demand curve is only slightly downward-sloping, some economists see little difference in the predictions of the monopolistic competition model as compared with those of the pure competition model. In any event, Chamberlin made a significant contribution by calling attention to the need for studying advertising and variation in product quality—and not solely price—as decision variables of the firm. His theory has also had a fundamental impact on industrial organization analysis, the subject of Chapter 7.

## QUESTIONS AND PROBLEMS

**6-1** Explain the distinction between short-run and long-run equilibrium in perfect competition.

**6-2** In a perfectly competitive industry there is an indefinitely large number of potential producing firms, each of which could produce 80 units of output at a minimum long-run average cost of $90 per unit (other outputs involve a somewhat higher cost per unit). The industry demand is $Q = 5{,}800 - 20p$.

**a** State the equation that describes the industry's long-run supply schedule.

**b** What is the long-run equilibrium price $(p_0)$, industry output $(Q_0)$, output of each firm $(q_0)$, number of active firms $(n_0)$, and total profit of each firm $(\pi)$?

**c** When each active firm is in long-run equilibrium, it has the short-run total cost function $C = 1{,}600 + 50q + .25q^2$. Calculate the implied average cost (AC), average variable cost (AVC), and marginal cost (MC) functions.

**d** Calculate the short-run supply schedule of the individual firm

$$q = q(p) =$$

**e** When the industry is in the above long-run equilibrium, what is its short-run supply schedule?

$$Q = Q(p) =$$

**f** Suppose now that the industry demand suddenly shifts so that consumers wish to buy 2,400 units more than before at any given price. What is the equation for the new industry demand schedule?

**g** In the short run, when the existing firms can change their outputs but no firm can change its plant and equipment, what will be the effects of the increase in demand?

$P =$          $n =$

$Q =$          $\pi =$

$q =$

---

[12] See, for example, G. C. Archibald, "Chamberlin versus Chicago," *Review of Economic Studies*, October, 1961.

**h** Finally, what will be the long-run effect of the increase in demand?

$P =$                        $n =$

$Q =$                       $\pi =$

$q =$

**6-3** Consider a monopolist who faces a demand of $P = 100 - 4Q$ and has a total cost of $C = 50 + 20Q$.
Find the profit-maximizing values of

$P =$                    Profit $=$

$Q =$

**6-4** Consider a monopolist whose demand and total cost functions are

$P_1 = 80 - 5Q_1$

$P_2 = 180 - 20Q_2$

$C = 50 + 20(Q_1 + Q_2)$

The monopolist here is the same as in problem 6-3, except that here we assume that the monopolist can separate the market into two submarkets, and resales between the markets are not possible.
**a** Show that the sum of the two demand curves here equals the demand curve in problem 6-3.
**b** Find the equilibrium values of

$Q_1 =$                    $P_1 =$                        Profit $=$

$Q_2 =$                    $P_2 =$

for the discriminating monopolist. Compare the profit made in problems 6-3 and 6-4.
**c** Compute the elasticity of demand in each submarket and note the correlation between price and elasticity.
**6-5** Return to problem 6-3 and assume that the government imposes a tax of $8 per unit on the monopolist's output.
**a** Find

$P =$                    Profit $=$

$Q =$

Tax revenue $=$

**b** Suppose instead the government imposed a lump sum tax of $72 on the monopolist. Find

$P =$                    Profit $=$

$Q =$

Tax revenue $=$

**c** Compare the two situations carefully.

**6-6 a** Given a demand curve for industry output $Q = 50 - 5P$, assume constant costs of $6 per unit. Calculate the size of the social loss if the industry were operated as a monopoly. What is the loss as a percentage of the value of output under competitive conditions?

**b** "Monopoly is a bad thing for consumers but a good thing for producers. So on balance, we can't be sure that monopoly is responsible for any loss in economic efficiency." Do you agree or disagree? Why?

**6-7** What distinguishes the monopolistic competition market structure from perfect competition? From monopoly?

## BIBLIOGRAPHY

American Economic Association: *Readings in Price Theory,* George J. Stigler and Kenneth Boulding (eds.), (Homewood, Ill.: Irwin, 1952).

Chamberlin, E. H.: *The Theory of Monopolistic Competition,* 6th ed. (Cambridge, Mass.: Harvard University Press, 1950).

Harberger, Arnold C.: "Monopoly and Resource Allocation," *American Economic Review,* May 1954.

Smith, V.: "An Experimental Study of Competitive Market Behavior," *Journal of Political Economy,* April 1962.

Stigler, George J.: "Perfect Competition, Historically Contemplated," *Journal of Political Economy,* February 1957.

---

# SPECIAL PRICING MODELS

---

**APPENDIX OUTLINE**

DORFMAN-STEINER MODEL

A NUMERICAL APPLICATION

SEQUENTIAL MONOPOLY AND TRANSFER PRICING

In this appendix we shall present first a model of the joint determination of price and advertising outlay that maximizes profit. This model is usually referred to as the Dorfman-Steiner model. We shall then consider the sequential monopoly model, i.e., the case of a monopolist supplier selling to a price taker who is also a monopolist. Then we shall relate this model to the problem of transfer pricing. Transfer pricing is concerned with determining what price one division of a multidivisional firm should charge another division of the same firm.

**DORFMAN-STEINER MODEL**

Let the demand and cost functions of the firm be given as

Demand: $\qquad\qquad\qquad\quad Q = Q(A, P)$ $\qquad\qquad\qquad\qquad\qquad$ (D-1)

Total production cost: $\qquad\quad C = C(Q)$ $\qquad\qquad\qquad\qquad\qquad$ (D-2)

where $P$ = price
$\qquad Q$ = quantity
$\qquad A$ = advertising outlay
$\qquad C$ = total production cost
$\qquad \pi$ = total profit

The profit function is, by definition,

$$\pi = PQ - C - A \tag{D-3}$$

The firm seeks to maximize $\pi$ by selecting appropriate values of $P$ and $A$. Mathematically, this requires a simultaneous solution to the two equations which are obtained by taking the partial derivatives of $\pi$ with respect to $P$ and $A$ and equating them to zero. The resulting two equations are

$$\frac{\partial \pi}{\partial A} = P \frac{\partial Q}{\partial A} - \frac{\partial C}{\partial Q} \frac{\partial Q}{\partial A} - 1 = 0 \tag{D-4}$$

$$\frac{\partial \pi}{\partial P} = P \frac{\partial Q}{\partial P} + Q - \frac{\partial C}{\partial Q} \frac{\partial Q}{\partial P} = 0 \tag{D-5}$$

First, consider equation (D-4). If we multiply both sides through by $A/PQ$ and define $(\partial Q/\partial A)(A/Q)$ as the elasticity of $Q$ with respect to advertising, or $E_a$, then it can be written as

$$E_a \frac{P - MC}{P} = \frac{A}{PQ} \tag{D-4'}$$

where we denote $\partial C/\partial Q$ as marginal cost MC.

Next, consider equation (D-5). If we multiply both sides through by $P/Q$ and define $-(\partial Q/\partial P)(P/Q)$ as the elasticity of $Q$ with respect to price, or $E_p$, then it can be written as

$$\frac{1}{E_p} = \frac{P - MC}{P} \tag{D-5'}$$

Finally, substitute equation (D-5') into equation (D-4'), and an interesting result is obtained.

$$\frac{A}{PQ} = \frac{E_a}{E_p} \tag{D-6}$$

The left-hand side of equation (D-6) is the ratio of advertising to sales, and the right-hand side is the ratio of the advertising elasticity to the price elasticity. Hence, the ratio of advertising to sales that will maximize the firm's profit will be higher the higher is the advertising elasticity $E_a$ and the lower is the price elasticity $E_p$. This result was first published by Robert Dorfman and Peter Steiner in the December 1954 issue of the *American Economic Review*.

To illustrate the formula, various econometric estimates of $E_p$ and $E_a$ for the cigarette industry have been reported. One study reported $E_p$ of .51 and $E_a$ of .03 to .05. These numbers would imply a ratio of advertising to sales of .06 to .10 if the cigarette industry were viewed as a monopoly. The actual ratio during this period was about .05.

## A NUMERICAL APPLICATION

The Bullet Corporation has estimated that its profit function, equation (D-3), in explicit form is

$$\pi = 800 - 4Q - 2Q^2 + 100A + 4QA - 8A^2 \tag{D-7}$$

where $\pi$ = profit
  $Q$ = quantity
  $A$ = advertising outlay

To find the profit-maximizing levels of $Q$ and $A$, set the partial derivatives of $\pi$ with respect to $Q$ and $A$ equal to zero and solve the resulting equations simultaneously. Hence,

$$\frac{\partial \pi}{\partial Q} = -4 - 4Q + 4A = 0$$

$$\frac{\partial \pi}{\partial A} = 100 + 4Q - 16A = 0$$

The simultaneous solution is $Q = 7$ and $A = 8$.

To make sure that profit is maximized (rather than minimized) for these values of $Q$ and $A$, the second-order conditions for a maximum must be satisfied. These are that

$$\frac{\partial^2 \pi}{\partial Q^2} < 0$$

$$\frac{\partial^2 \pi}{\partial A^2} < 0$$

$$\frac{\partial^2 \pi}{\partial Q^2} \frac{\partial^2 \pi}{\partial A^2} > \left( \frac{\partial^2 \pi}{\partial Q \partial A} \right)^2$$

Evaluating these partial derivatives at $Q = 7$ and $A = 8$ gives

$$\frac{\partial^2 \pi}{\partial Q^2} = -4 < 0$$

$$\frac{\partial^2 \pi}{\partial A^2} = -16 < 0$$

$$\frac{\partial^2 \pi}{\partial Q \partial A} = 4 > 0$$

Clearly, the second-order conditions are satisfied, and profit is therefore at a maximum.

## SEQUENTIAL MONOPOLY AND TRANSFER PRICING

First we consider the case of sequential monopoly. Assume that firm S (the supplier) sells an input $X$ to firm B (the buyer). Firm B converts input $X$ into a final product at a conversion cost of $c$ per unit. For example, suppose the final product is a lawn mower and input $X$ is the engine for the lawn mower. Hence, fixed-proportions production is assumed to hold for firm B. Each lawn mower requires exactly one engine and $c$ dollars worth of other inputs. For this reason we can use the symbol $X$ to refer to either the number of engines or the number of lawn mowers.

As the term "sequential monopoly" implies, we assume that both firm S, the supplier, and firm B, the buyer, are monopolists. While various assumptions are possible, we assume that firm B is a price taker. That is, it ignores the fact that it is the sole buyer of $X$ and therefore forgoes any potential monopsony power that it might exert. In other words, by assumption, firm B treats any price announced by firm S as a fixed parameter.

Let the demand for lawn mowers be

$$X = 100 - P_L \tag{D-8}$$

where $X$ = number of lawn mowers (and engines)
$P_L$ = price charged by firm B for lawn mowers

Since it costs $c$ per unit to convert an engine into a lawn mower, firm B's profit function is

$$\pi_B = P_L X - cX - P_x X \tag{D-9}$$

where $P_x$ is the price charged by firm S for an engine. Substituting equation (D-8) into equation (D-9) gives

$$\pi_B = (100 - X) X - cX - P_x X \tag{D-10}$$

To maximize $\pi_B$, set the derivative of $\pi_B$ with respect to $X$ equal to zero and obtain

$$\frac{d\pi_B}{dX} = 100 - 2X - c - P_x = 0 \tag{D-11}$$

or

$$X = \frac{1}{2}(100 - c - P_x) \tag{D-12}$$

Equation (D-12) is the derived demand for engines. That is, it is the demand curve for engines derived from the final consumer demand for lawn mowers. We now consider firm S's profit-maximizing decision. The profit function $\pi_s$ is

$$\pi_s = P_x X - TC \tag{D-13}$$

where $TC$ = total production cost of $X$
$= 10 + 5X + X^2$

Hence, using equation (D-12) to eliminate $P_x$, we obtain

$$\pi_s = (100 - 2X - c)X - (10 + 5X + X^2)$$

and

$$\frac{d\pi_s}{dX} = 100 - 4X - c - 5 - 2X = 0 \tag{D-14}$$

Solving equation (D-14) for $X$ yields

$$X = \frac{1}{6}(95 - c)$$

Suppose we take the cost of conversion $c$ to be 5, then $X = 15$, and so $P_x = 65$ [from equation (D-12)]. Thus, firm S will charge 65 for an engine. According to equation (D-12), firm B will then buy 15 engines and will sell 15 lawn mowers at a price of 85 [according to its demand curve (D-8)].

We can summarize the results as follows:

| Firm B | Firm S |
|---|---|
| $\pi_B = 225$ | $\pi_S = 665$ |
| $P_L = 85$ | $P_x = 65$ |
| $X = 15$ | $X = 15$ |

These results can also be shown graphically in Figure D-1. The curve $P_L$ is the demand for lawn mowers, $P_x$ is the derived demand for engines, and $MR_x$ is the marginal revenue curve[1] associated with the demand curve $P_x$. The $MC_x$ curve[2] is the marginal cost of producing engines.

Firm S maximizes profit by equating $MR_x$ and $MC_x$ at output $X = 15$ and charging $P_x = 65$. Notice that $P_x = 100 - 2X - c$ is not only firm S's derived demand but is also what we might term firm B's *net* marginal revenue (NMR) curve; i.e., it is firm B's marginal revenue[3] *minus c*, the conversion cost per unit. Hence, firm B equates net marginal revenue with its marginal cost of engines (the horizontal line[4] at $P_x = 65$). This intersection also occurs at $X = 15$ and yields the price of lawn mowers of $P_L = 85$. This, then, is the sequential monopoly equilibrium.

Now consider the same basic situation, except assume that the two firms are divisions of a single multidivisional firm. The issue is now, What price should division S charge division B? In other words, what should the so-called transfer price of engines be? In terms of Figure D-1, the answer should be evident. Equate the NMR curve and the $MC_x$ curve at output $X = 22.5$ and charge a transfer price equal to marginal cost (or 50). The price of lawn mowers will then be 77.5, and total profit of the integrated firm is 1,002.5. Notice that total profit exceeds the combined profit in the sequential monopoly case of 890 ($\pi_B = 225$ plus $\pi_S = 665$).

---

[1] The $MR_x$ function is obtained by differentiating the total revenue function. Total revenue $R$ is $P_x X$ and, using equation (D-12), is

$$R = 100X - 2X^2 - cX$$

Hence, $MR_x = 100 - 4X - c$.

[2] The $MC_x$ function is obtained by differentiating the total cost function $TC = 10 + 5X + X^2$. Hence, $MC_x = 5 + 2X$.

[3] Firm B's marginal revenue is the derivative of its total revenue function. Firm B's total revenue function is $P_L X$, or $100X - X^2$. Hence, marginal revenue is $100 - 2X$.

[4] Recall the assumption that firm B takes the price of engines announced by firm S as a fixed parameter.

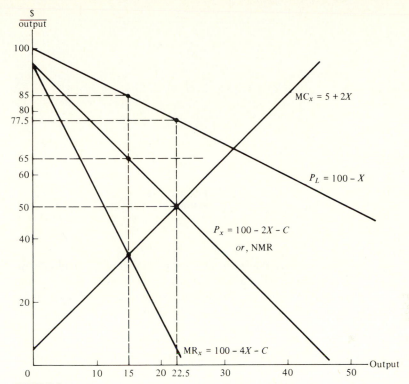

**FIGURE D-1**
Sequential monopoly and vertically integrated firm equilibria.

These results can be verified by writing the profit function for the vertically in-tegrated firm as

$$\pi = P_L X - cX - (10 + 5X + X^2) \qquad \text{(D-15)}$$

Substituting $P_L = 100 - X$ and equating the derivative of $\pi$ with respect to $X$ to zero gives

$$\frac{d\pi}{dX} = 100 - 2X - c - 5 - 2X = 0$$

or

$$100 - 2X - c = 5 + 2X \qquad \text{(D-16)}$$

Notice that the left-hand side of condition (D-16) is NMR and the right-hand side is $MC_x$ (of course, $c$ could be moved to the right-hand side to produce the traditional marginal revenue = marginal cost equality, where marginal cost would include produc-tion *and* conversion). For $c = 5$, the solution is $X = 22.5$. Substituting $X = 22.5$ in equa-tion (D-15) gives $\pi = 1,002.5$.

In summary, the correct transfer price that the supplying division should charge is

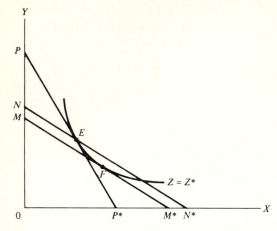

**FIGURE D-2**
Inefficiency in input choice due to
transfer price set above marginal cost.

marginal cost.[5] We might also observe that everyone would benefit by vertical integration as compared to sequential monopoly. The price of lawn mowers is lower (77.5 compared to 85) and output is higher (22.5 compared to 15), which is a favorable result for consumers. And combined profit is higher (1,002.5 compared to 890), which is favorable for the multidivisional firm.

To conclude this analysis, let us consider a somewhat more subtle inefficiency that can be created if division S fails to charge division B a transfer price equal to marginal cost. This inefficiency arises when the production function of division B is characterized by variable proportions.[6] In the example above, engines and "other inputs" were combined in fixed proportions to produce lawn mowers.

Assume that division B produces output $Z$ with two inputs: input $X$, which it buys from division S at $P_x$, and input $Y$, which it buys from a perfectly competitive industry at a price equal to its constant marginal cost $MC_y$. To produce a given quantity of $Z$, say $Z^*$, division B must decide on the combination of $X$ and $Y$ to employ. In short, its problem is to pick a point on the isoquant $Z = Z^*$ shown in Figure D-2.

As was explained in Chapter 4, the least-cost combination of $X$ and $Y$ is determined by the tangency of the isocost line and the isoquant. The slope of the isocost line for division B equals the ratio of the two input prices $P_x/MC_y$. Assume for the present that $P_x = MC_x$ and that $MC_x$ is constant. Isocost line $MM^*$ in Figure D-2 is constructed to have the slope $MC_x/MC_y$. Hence, point $F$ is the least-cost input mix.

Now assume that division S sets its transfer price $P_x$ to be greater than $MC_x$. Division B will now confront an isocost line $PP^*$ with a steeper slope $P_x/MC_y$ than $MM^*$. That is, the slope of $MM^*$ equals the ratio of the marginal costs $MC_x/MC_y$, while the slope of $PP^*$ equals $P_x/MC_y$. The result of charging a price for $X$ above its marginal cost is to induce division B to substitute away from the relatively expensive input $X$ and to choose input mix $E$.

The key point, of course, is that input mix $E$ does not minimize total cost. The isocost

---

[5] We have presented one simple case of transfer pricing here. Many alternative situations arise in practice. For further analysis of this issue, see Jack Hirshleifer, "On the Economics of Transfer Pricing," *Journal of Business,* July 1956.

[6] This analysis is based on John M. Vernon and Daniel A. Graham, "Profitability of Monopolization by Vertical Integration," *Journal of Political Economy,* July–August 1971.

line with the "correct" slope (reflecting the true cost conditions) is $MM^*$. By passing another isocost line $NN^*$ through point $E$ with the same slope as $MM^*$, it becomes clear that $E$ lies on a higher than necessary isocost line. The slope of $PP^*$ sends an incorrect signal to division B, inducing division B to use too little $X$ and too much $Y$.

A numerical example should be instructive. Suppose division B's production function is $Z = 5XY$, where $Z$ is its output, $X$ is the amount of the input it buys from division S, and $Y$ is the amount of the second input that it buys from a competitive industry. Let $P_x = \text{MC}_x$ initially, where $\text{MC}_x = 1$, and $P_y = \text{MC}_y = 2$. Suppose that division B wishes to produce 20 units of $Z$. What is the least-cost method of producing these 20 units?

As shown in Figure D-2, cost minimization requires a tangency between the isoquant and the isocost line. Recall from Chapter 4 that the slope of the isoquant equals the ratio of the marginal products, and the slope of the isocost line equals the ratio of the input prices. Hence, by equating these two slopes we obtain

$$\frac{5Y}{5X} = \frac{1}{2} \tag{D-17}$$

The production function for $Z = 20$

$$20 = 5XY \tag{D-18}$$

provides the second equation necessary to solve for the least-cost combination of $X$ and $Y$. Solving equations (D-17) and (D-18) simultaneously gives

$$X = 2.83 \qquad Y = 1.42$$

The total cost of production is then obtained by multiplying each input by its price, or

$$\text{Total cost} = (1)(2.83) + (2)(1.42) = 5.7$$

Now suppose division S charges a price $P_x$ greater than $MC_x$, say $P_x = 2$. Division B now sees the "incorrect" slope for the isocost line, i.e., isocost line $PP^*$ in Figure D-2. Hence, division B now uses a revised equation (D-17), or

$$\frac{5Y}{5X} = \frac{2}{2}$$

Solving the above equation simultaneously with equation (D-18) yields the solution

$$X = 2 \qquad Y = 2$$

Hence, the excessive price for $P_x$ induces division B to use less $X$ and more $Y$. The true total cost, however, is

$$\text{Total cost} = (1)(2) + (2)(2) = 6.0$$

which is greater than in the previous case. It is important to note that the true total cost must be computed by using the correct input prices, equal to marginal costs. In terms of Figure D-2, the isocost line $MM^*$ corresponds to a total cost of 5.7, and the isocost line $NN^*$ corresponds to a total cost of 6.0.

# CHAPTER 7

# INDUSTRIAL ORGANIZATION AND COMPETITIVE ANALYSIS

**CHAPTER OUTLINE**

**INTRODUCTION**

In Chapter 6 we described the theoretical market structures of perfect competition, monopoly, and monopolistic competition. Because these theoretical models are so abstract, they have been found to be of limited value to economists interested in understanding real-world markets.

Economists specializing in the field known as industrial organization have extended the theory of market structures in several directions in order to make it a more useful tool for analyzing actual industrial markets. Important methods of extension have included the development of concepts more amenable to empirical measurement and the incorporation of a richer set of variables.

The origin of industrial organization is generally attributed to the work of Professor Edward S. Mason of Harvard University in the 1930s.[1] While Mason's interest was motivated largely by a public policy concern for evaluating industrial performance, the tools of industrial organization are equally important for the corporate economist interested in the competitive performance and strategy of the firm.

Industrial organization economists use a general methodological approach to the economic analysis of markets that is based on three key concepts: (1) structure, (2) conduct (or behavior), and (3) performance. The linkage among these three concepts is that the structure (number of sellers, height of entry barriers, etc.) of a market explains or determines to a large degree the conduct (pricing policy, advertising, etc.) of the participants in the market, and the performance (efficiency and progressiveness) of the market is simply an evaluation of the results of the conduct.

Although the direction of causation is usually assumed to flow from structure to conduct, this does not preclude the possibility that conduct can change structure. The belief that the primary direction of causation is from structure to conduct is exemplified by a statement of Edward S. Mason:

> Under similar market conditions may not firms be expected to pursue similar policies and practices? A careful study of the empirically determinable differences in market structure may go far in explaining observable differences in policy and practice. . . .
>
> Consideration of the structure of the tire market appears to indicate that [it] exerts a decisive influence on price policies. . . . While the personality of Firestone, plus the fact that his firm is admittedly a low-cost producer, has no doubt been an important factor, it seems probable that if Firestone, like God in another context, had not existed the structure of the tire market would have created him.[2]

Thus far we have been rather careless in our use of terms such as "market," "industry," and "market structure." At this stage, however, we shall be more careful and set forth in more detail the definition of these important concepts.

It is easy to fall into the habit of using the terms "market" and "industry" interchangeably, and generally no harm results. In fact, a market refers to a group of closely related sellers and buyers, while an industry refers to the sellers only. In practice, the problem of delimiting an industry is difficult.

Stigler has suggested the following economic criteria:

> An industry should embrace the maximum geographical area and the maximum variety of productive activities in which there is a strong long-run substitution. If buyers

---

[1] See, for example, Edward S. Mason, "Price and Production Policies of Large-Scale Enterprise," *American Economic Review,* March 1939.

[2] Ibid p. 70.

can shift on a large scale from product or area B to A, then the two should be combined. If producers can shift on a large scale from B to A, again they should be combined.

Economists usually state this in an alternative form: All products or enterprises with large long-run cross-elasticities of either supply or demand should be combined into a single industry.[3]

Of course, the adjectives "strong" and "large" necessarily require that judgment be used in setting industry and market boundaries. As we shall see in Chapter 8, the outcome in many antitrust cases turns on the question of industry definition. For example, DuPont was found not guilty of monopolization because cellophane was not the "correct" market; rather, the correct market included all flexible packaging materials (Saran, Glassine, polyethylene, etc., *and* cellophane).

Once we have in mind what a market is, we can turn to the important concept of market structure. Joe Bain, an important pioneer in the field, states that

market structure for practical purposes means those characteristics of the organization of a market that seem to exercise a strategic influence on the nature of competition and pricing within the market.[4]

The most important elements of market structure are the concentration of sellers (e.g., the combined market-share of the four leading sellers), the concentration of buyers, the conditions of entry to the market, and the degree of product differentiation. Other important elements of market structure include the rate of growth of market demand, the price elasticity of market demand, and the structure of costs (extent of economies of scale and the proportion of total costs which are fixed).

Conduct refers to the behavior of sellers in competing with one another in the market. Thus, conduct includes policies of sellers toward pricing, product design, sales promotion, research and innovation, and legal tactics.

Society as well as management is ultimately concerned with performance. That is, how well do firms in an industry perform in terms of efficiency and progressiveness? More specifically, Bain has listed five measures that are useful in assessing the efficiency and progressiveness dimensions of performance:

1 The height of price relative to the average cost of production.

2 The relative efficiency of production so far as this is influenced by the scale or size of plants and firms (relative to the most efficient) and by the extent of excess capacity.

3 The size of sales promotion costs relative to the costs of production.

4 The character of the product, including choice of design, level of quality, and variety of product within any market.

5 The rate of progressiveness of the firm and industry in developing both

---

[3] George J. Stigler, "Introduction," in National Bureau of Economic Research, *Business Concentration and Price Policy* (Princeton, N.J.: Princeton University Press, 1955), p. 4.

[4] Joe Bain, *Industrial Organization*, 2d ed. (New York: John Wiley, 1968), p. 7.

**FIGURE 7-1**
The structure-conduct-performance analysis of industrial organization.

products and techniques of production, relative to evidently attainable rates and relative to the costs of progress.[5]

Market performance should therefore be a key variable in constructing rational public policy toward business. Supposedly, antitrust laws, direct regulation, and other governmental restrictions on competition are designed to improve market performance by affecting market structure and conduct. Clearly, it is essential to know how structure affects performance. For example, would a policy of reducing concentration in the automobile industry lead to increased efficiency in that industry? Also, it is necessary to know how the actual performance of an industry compares with its potential performance. For example, is the progressiveness of the steel industry as great as it could be?

The industrial organization approach can be summarized with a simple diagram, as shown in Figure 7-1.

The arrows indicate that the direction of causality is from structure to conduct to performance. Of course, over long-run periods there can be feedback from conduct to structure. For example, innovation or price warfare can increase concentration through the removal of former rivals.

In the next two sections we shall discuss in detail two key elements of market structure: concentration and barriers to entry. The following section will examine oligopolistic pricing behavior. Next we shall discuss some statistical tests that have sought to relate the price and profit performance of industries to their respective market structures. While our treatment of industrial organization analysis is necessarily selective, ignoring such important topics as innovation and advertising, we hope that the value of the approach will be made clear. Readers desiring a comprehensive treatment of the field should consult the excellent text by F. M. Scherer.[6]

To conclude the chapter, we shall discuss how industrial organization can be used in the analysis of competition and the formulation of strategy.

## CONCENTRATION

The theoretical market structures (perfect competition, monopoly, etc.) are defined almost completely according to the numbers of sellers and buyers. The

[5] Ibid., p. 12.
[6] F. M. Scherer, *Industrial Market Structure and Economic Performance,* 2d ed. (Chicago: Rand McNally, 1980).

empirical analog stresses not only numbers but also relative sizes of sellers and buyers and is termed the "concentration" of the market. Here we shall consider seller concentration.

While economists have devised many indexes to measure concentration, the most widely used measure is the concentration ratio. The concentration ratio is simply the share of total industry sales accounted for by the $x$ largest sellers.

A fundamental problem with concentration ratios is that they describe only one point on the entire size distribution of sellers. Consider the size distributions of the two hypothetical industries shown in Table 7-1. Clearly, industries A and B have the same four-firm concentration ratio, *viz*, 80 percent. However, noting the other information in Table 7-1, most observers would regard the two industries as likely to exhibit quite different patterns of competitive behavior. Suppose now that we compute the three-firm ratios. Industry B is now seen to be "more concentrated" (75 percent versus only 60 percent for industry A). The basic problem is that this type of measure wastes relevant data.

To pursue this point, consider the size of distributions of the two industries shown as concentration curves in Figure 7-2. The height of a concentration curve above any integer $x$ on the horizontal axis measures the percentage of the industry's total sales accounted for by the $x$ largest firms. In general, the curves will rise from left to right and at a continuously diminishing rate. In the limiting case of identical shares, such as in industry A, the curve becomes a straight line. The curves reach their maximum height of 100 percent where $x$ equals the total number of firms in the industry. If the curve of industry B is everywhere above the curve of industry A, then industry B is more concentrated than industry A. However, when the curves intersect, as they do in Figure 7-2, it is impossible to state which is the more concentrated industry, unless we devise a new definition.

The most widely available concentration ratios are those compiled by the U.S. Bureau of the Census. Ideally, these indexes should refer to industries that are defined meaningfully from the viewpoint of economic theory. However, the census classifications of industries were developed over a period of years "to

**TABLE 7-1**
PERCENTAGE OF SALES
ACCOUNTED FOR BY THE FIVE
LEADING FIRMS IN INDUSTRIES
A AND B

| Firm | Industry A | Industry B |
|------|------------|------------|
| 1 | 20 | 60 |
| 2 | 20 | 10 |
| 3 | 20 | 5 |
| 4 | 20 | 5 |
| 5 | 20 | 5 |
| Total | 100 | 85 |

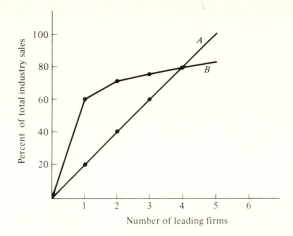

**FIGURE 7-2**
Concentration curves for industries
A and B.

serve the general purposes of the census and other government statistics" and were "not designed to establish categories necessarily denoting coherent or relevant markets in the true competitive sense, or to provide a basis for measuring market power."[7] The census frequently includes products that are not close substitutes, and it sometimes excludes products that are close substitutes. An example of the latter is the existence of two separate "industries" for beet sugar and cane sugar. The census ignores both regional markets (for example, all bakeries are combined into a single national market) and foreign competition (steel imports are excluded from the steel industry).

Since we shall refer to studies that have used census concentration ratios, it should be helpful to provide a brief description of their procedure for classifying industries. Their classification system (known as the Standard Industrial Classification, or SIC) makes use of a series of numbers in which each succeeding digit represents a finer degree of classification. Thus, in the manufacturing sector of the economy, there are only 20 two-digit industries. An example is industry 20, the food and kindred products industry. Within this two-digit industry, there are nine three-digit industries, such as industry 201, the meat products industry. Within this three-digit industry, there are three four-digit industries, such as industry 2015, poultry dressing plants. The Census Bureau has computed concentration ratios for the top 4, 8, and 20 firms for some 450 four-digit industries; these are the ratios most often used in statistical studies of industrial organization.

In Table 7-2 we show four-firm concentration ratios and the total numbers of firms for selected four-digit industries in 1972. The industries were chosen to cover a wide range of concentration ratios. It is immediately apparent that the theoretical market structures of perfect competition and monopoly do not provide useful categories for our real-world industries. Nor is it clear which in-

---

[7] U.S. Bureau of the Census, *Concentration Ratios in Manufacturing Industry, 1963, Part I* (Washington, D.C.: 1966), p. viii.

**TABLE 7-2**
CONCENTRATION OF SELECTED INDUSTRIES, 1972

| Industry | Four-Firm ratio | Number of firms |
|---|---|---|
| Passenger cars (five digit) | 99 | NA |
| Cereal breakfast foods | 90 | 34 |
| Flat glass | 92 | 11 |
| Electric lamps | 90 | 103 |
| Cigarettes | 84 | 13 |
| Tires and inner tubes | 73 | 136 |
| Primary aluminum | 79 | 12 |
| Aircraft | 66 | 141 |
| Soap and detergents | 62 | 577 |
| Beer and malt beverages | 52 | 108 |
| Blast furnaces and steel mills | 45 | 241 |
| Textile machinery | 31 | 535 |
| Petroleum refining | 31 | 152 |
| Cement | 26 | 75 |
| Pharmaceutical preparations | 26 | 680 |
| Fluid milk | 18 | 2026 |
| Bottled   and   canned   soft drinks | 14 | 2271 |
| Screw machine products | 6 | 1780 |

NA = not available.
    *Source:* U.S. Bureau of Census, *1972 Census of Manufacturers, Concentration Ratios in Manufacturing,* MC72 (SR)-2 (Washington, D.C.: 1975).

dustries should be classified as oligopolists or monopolistic competitors. Of course, most would agree that the industries at the top of Table 7-2 (passenger cars, cereals, glass, electric lamps, cigarettes, tires, aluminum, aircraft, and soap and detergents) are oligopolies, but how far down the list should we descend? Even within the oligopolies, there are wide variations in the total numbers of firms. For example, there are only 13 firms in the cigarette industry and 103 in the electric lamp industry, but "electric lamps" is more concentrated than "cigarettes."

If we rather arbitrarily consider industries with concentration ratios of 40 or more to be oligopolistic, then 195 industries out of the 450 total in manufacturing qualify as oligopolies. Given a tendency for Census Bureau industries to be defined too broadly, it is probably correct to conclude that over half of the manufacturing sector in the United States is oligopolistic.

## BARRIERS TO ENTRY

A leader in developing the concept of barriers to entry was Joe Bain. Hence we begin with his definition:

> In loose terms, the condition of entry is ... the "disadvantage" of potential entrant firms as compared to established firms—or, conversely, the "advantage" of established over potential entrant firms.

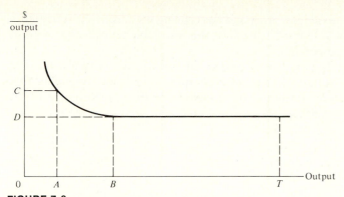

**FIGURE 7-3**
Scale-economy barrier.

Somewhat more precisely, the condition of entry refers to the extent to which, in the long run, established firms can elevate their selling prices above minimal average costs of production and distribution (those costs associated with operation at optimal scales) without inducing potential entrants to enter the industry.[8]

Clearly, Bain's definition is quite broad and covers many diverse factors. These include large economies of scale relative to market demand, absolute-cost advantages (due to patents or superior know-how or control of low-cost supplies of raw materials), strong consumer preferences for the products of established firms, and governmental policies such as tariffs or restrictions to entry. Although some attempts have been made to restrict the term "barriers to entry" to a smaller and more precisely defined set of factors, Bain's original concept seems to be the most commonly accepted one, and we shall follow it here.

**Scale-Economy Barriers**

Consider an industry in which there are barriers to entry of the scale-economy type. Suppose that the long-run average cost curve for a firm (established or potential entrant) in hypothetical industry A is as shown in Figure 7-3.

To achieve minimum average cost, a firm entering industry A must produce an output of at least $0B$. Notice that the curve becomes horizontal at $0B$ instead of rising in the traditional U shape. This is a reflection of the many empirical studies that have failed to find diseconomies at larger and larger outputs. Suppose that total output of industry A is $0T$, and $0B$ is about one-third of $0T$. If there are two firms already in the industry, they must be willing to reduce their market-shares significantly to permit the entrant to attain minimum efficient scale. For example, if each had 50 percent before entry, both would be cut to 33 percent each after entry. The potential entrant would clearly recognize that the two existing firms would not be willing to allow this to happen without a struggle (for example, price and advertising warfare). The recognition of this possibility should serve to discount the attractiveness of entry into industry A at minimum efficient scale.

Of course, the entrant could enter at a smaller scale, say output $0A$ in Figure 7-3. However, at output $0A$ the entrant's unit costs would be higher than the costs of established firms (that is, $0C$ compared with $0D$). Note that the attractiveness of this alternative also depends on the sharpness of the rise of the cost curve at smaller and smaller outputs.

The next question concerns the importance of scale-economy barriers in the economy. While scale economies have been measured in various ways, many economists consider the use of engineering cost estimates the best method for measuring scale economies. This is because engineers' cost estimates usually embody assumptions quite similar to those underlying the long-run average cost curve of economic theory. An engineering study can hold fixed relative factor prices, product homogeneity, location, technology, volume, and so forth, thereby isolating the effect of increases in the rate of output on cost.

The results of one such study which estimated both efficient plant and efficient firm sizes are given in Table 7-3. This 1975 study, conducted by Scherer, Beckenstein, Kaufer, and Murphy, obtained its estimates by interviews with technically qualified personnel working in the industries studied. To obtain the estimates for their 12 industries, they interviewed personnel in 125 companies in six countries.

Taking the figures in Table 7-3 at face value, the second column (which gives efficient *firm* size as a percentage of the total market) indicates that scale-economy barriers are relatively small in most of the 12 industries. Only in the refrigerators and freezers industry is as much as 20 percent of the market necessary for efficiency. The third column indicates that *actual* market-shares of the leading firms are generally considerably greater than necessary to attain efficient size. For example, the average market-share of the four leading firms in the storage battery industry is about 15 percent, yet the efficient firm market-share is only 2 percent.

Two other studies using the engineering approach, one by Bain[9] in 1956 and the other by Pratten[10] in 1971, found similar results for different samples of industries. In only a few industries in each study did the estimated efficient shares approximate the actual shares of the leading firms.

Needless to say, the validity of such studies of economies of scale is not universally accepted. John McGee, for example, argues that there are some serious problems:

> Such estimates cannot be forward-looking and are stale when done. They must implicitly embody some unspecified but homogeneous quality of production management, organization, and control, and must assume that some unspecified but given

---

[9] Joe Bain, *Barriers to New Competition* (Cambridge, Mass.: Harvard University Press, 1956).

[10] C. F. Pratten, *Economies of Scale in Manufacturing Industry* (London: Cambridge University Press, 1971).

**TABLE 7-3**
MINIMUM EFFICIENT SCALE OF PLANTS AND FIRMS AS PERCENTAGE OF U.S. NATIONAL MARKET, 1967

| Industry | Minimum efficient scale plant as percentage of total market | Minimum efficient scale firm as percentage of total market | Four-firm concentration ratio |
|---|---|---|---|
| Beer brewing | 3.4 | 10–14 | 40 |
| Cigarettes | 6.6 | 6–12 | 81 |
| Cotton synthetic fabrics | 0.2 | 1 | 36 |
| Paints, varnishes, and lacquers | 1.4 | 1.4 | 22 |
| Petroleum refining | 1.9 | 4–6 | 33 |
| Shoes, except rubber | 0.2 | 1 | 26 |
| Glass containers | 1.5 | 4–6 | 60 |
| Cement | 1.7 | 2 | 29 |
| Steel works | 2.6 | 3 | 48 |
| Ball and roller bearings | 1.4 | 4–7 | 54 |
| Refrigerators and freezers | 14.1 | 14–20 | 73 |
| Storage batteries | 1.9 | 2 | 61 |

*Source:* F. M. Scherer, A. Beckenstein, E. Kaufer, and R. D. Murphy, *The Economics of Multi-Plant Operation: An International Comparisons Study* (Cambridge, Mass.: Harvard University Press, 1975).

quality of overall management is imagined both to choose and to use the hypothetical physical plant that someone constructed on paper. Also, business problems are not solely engineering problems—which partly explains why not all successful businesses are run by practicing engineers.[11]

McGee lays great stress on the fact that management teams differ greatly in capability. As he puts it: "Can anyone conceive how to evaluate business management apart from how well the enterprise does?"

### Absolute-Cost Barriers

These barriers refer to cases in which the costs for potential entrants are greater than the costs for established firms at every scale of output. One example of such a barrier is the control of all "low-cost" raw material mineral deposits by established firms. Another is the ownership of patent rights, whereby entrants are forced to pay a royalty to the patent holders.

The cost of truly large amounts of capital is often cited as an absolute-cost barrier. As Caves describes this case:

> To enter the steel industry, a new firm might have to collect upwards of a half-billion dollars in capital. If you or I went to the capital market requesting such a loan to start a steel company, we would meet only uproarious laughter. Even a borrower with a much better credit rating, such as a large going firm in another industry, might have to pay more interest to get this capital than would an existing steel firm planning to expand. Again, the entrant's cost curve would lie above the cost curve of the going firm.[12]

### Product Differentiation Barriers

If the established firms in an industry enjoy an advantage over potential entrants because of the preference of consumers for their products, a product differentiation barrier is said to exist. In a pioneering 1967 study, Comanor and Wilson listed three ways in which advertising can erect barriers to entry:

**1** High prevailing levels of advertising create additional costs for new entrants which exist at all levels of output. And more advertising messages per prospective customer must be supplied to induce brand switching as compared with repeat buying because of buyer inertia and loyalty. This results in an absolute-cost advantage for established firms.

**2** Economies of scale in advertising create a barrier to entry. If a new firm should enter at a relatively small scale, the entrant will suffer a cost disadvantage relative to the larger established firms. If the new firm enters at a scale sufficient to realize available economies of scale in advertising, this is likely to in-

---

[11] John S. McGee, "Efficiency and Economies on Size," in H. G. Goldschmid, et al. (eds.), *Industrial Concentration: The New Learning* (Boston: Little, Brown, 1974) p. 102.

[12] Richard Caves, *American Industry: Structure, Conduct, Performance,* 3d ed. (Englewood Cliffs, N.J.: Prentice-Hall, 1972), p. 27

fluence the price or advertising policies of established firms. These possible reactions of established firms increase the costs and risks of entry.

**3** The capital requirements for advertising arising from items 1 or 2 require a higher rate of return than is required on capital for physical plant. This is because the use of capital for advertising does not create tangible assets that can be resold in the event of failure.[13]

This hypothesis about advertising entry barriers has created controversy. In their 1967 study, Comanor and Wilson performed a statistical test of the hypothesis by examining the profitability of industries that had high advertising intensities.[14] The theory was that the higher the advertising intensity, the higher the entry barrier. Since industries with higher entry barriers should have higher profit rates (other factors held constant), a positive correlation between profit rates and advertising intensities should be found. Comanor and Wilson did indeed find such statistical support for the existence of advertising entry barriers, and many later studies have produced similar results.

The controversy, however, has centered largely on the interpretation of the statistics. For example, highly innovative industries tend to be more profitable than others and also tend to advertise more intensively. This might account for the correlation between profit rates and the ratio of advertising to sales. It has also been argued that the direction of causation is wrong. High advertising does not cause high profits; rather, it is high profits that lead to high advertising. Unfortunately, a thorough review of this literature is not possible here; the interested reader should consult the book by F. M. Scherer.[15]

## OLIGOPOLISTIC PRICING BEHAVIOR

Having completed our detailed discussion of two key elements of market structure (concentration and barriers to entry), we turn now to an important type of conduct: oligopolistic pricing behavior.

An oligopoly is an industry with a small number of sellers. The precise upper limit to the number of sellers that may exist in an oligopoly cannot be determined from theory. However, in principle the criterion is whether the sellers take into account their rivals' likely reactions to their own actions. In other words, the essence of oligopoly is recognized interdependence among the firms. General Motors certainly considers the possible responses of Ford and Chrysler when it elects to change its prices. On the other hand, a Kansas wheat farmer never worries about the effect of his or her own sales decisions on the behavior of the farmer next door.

The kinked demand model, though seriously incomplete, is useful in emphasizing this interdependence feature of oligopoly. This model assumes

---

[13] W. S. Comanor and T. Wilson, "Advertising Market Structure, and Performance," *Review of Economics and Statistics,* November 1967.

[14] This study is described in more detail in the final section of this chapter.

[15] F. M. Scherer, *Industrial Market Structure and Economic Performance.*

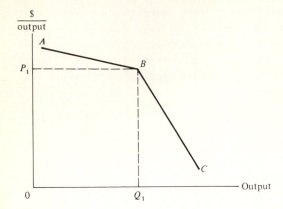

FIGURE 7-4
Kinked demand model.

that the oligopolistic firm's conjectured demand curve is of the general form shown in Figure 7-4.

The rationale underlying the model is as follows. Suppose that the firm's current price is $P_1$. If the firm lowers its price, it is argued that its competitors will respond with equivalent price reductions of their own. Hence, the section of the firm's conjectured demand curve indicated by $BC$ is likely to be relatively inelastic; that is, a price reduction is expected to lead to less-than-proportionate increases in the quantity demanded. On the other hand, if the firm raises its price, its competitors will not follow the increase since they can gain sales from the price leader by not changing price. Thus, section $AB$ of the firm's conjectured demand curve is relatively elastic.

The main implication of the kinked demand model—that oligopolistic prices should tend to be rigid—has been found to yield rather poor results when subjected to empirical analysis. Furthermore, the model has the deficiency of failure to explain how price $P_1$ was reached originally.

We turn now to the Chamberlin model of oligopoly. Although simplified itself, it provides the foundation for a rich and insightful understanding of oligopolistic pricing. Assume that each firm has identical costs in producing the industry's homogeneous product. It follows that maximum profits are attained if the firms act jointly as a monopolist, sharing the monopoly profits equally. Chamberlin argued that such an equilibrium would result even though the firms never conspired explicitly on such a pricing policy. If each of a small number of sellers

seeks his maximum profit rationally and intelligently, he will realize that when there are only two or a few sellers his own move has a considerable effect upon his competitors, and that this makes it idle to suppose they will accept without retaliation the losses he forces upon them. Since the result of a cut by any one is inevitably to decrease his own profits, no one will cut, and, although the sellers are entirely in-

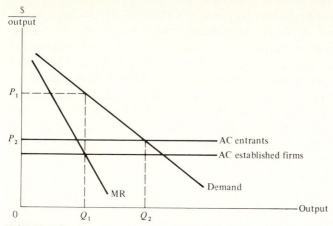

**FIGURE 7-5**
Price determination with absolute cost barrier.

dependent, the equilibrium result is the same as though there were a monopolistic agreement between them.[16]

What will the monopoly price be? If entry is not completely barred, the long-run price will depend on the height of the barriers to entry. To see this, consider the case in Figure 7-5, which assumes that barriers to entry are of the absolute-cost type.

If entry is completely barred, the joint profit-maximizing price would be determined by the intersection of marginal revenue MR and marginal cost (which equals average cost AC since AC is constant). Hence, price would be $P_1$ and output $Q_1$, and each identical seller would share equally in output and profit. But given the assumption that potential entrants could make profits at price $P_1$ (since their AC is below $P_1$), entry would be induced. Entry could be prevented, however, by setting price at $P_2$, the so-called limit price. At the limit price, the established firms would earn positive profits equal to the level of output multiplied by the difference in average costs.

This limit price theory was developed independently by Bain[17] and Sylos-Labini[18] in the late 1950s and was refined by Modigliani.[19] In fact, a key assumption of the theory that should be made explicit is the so-called Sylos

[16] E. H. Chamberlin, *The Theory of Monopolistic Competition* (Cambridge, Mass.: Harvard University Press, 1933), p. 48.

[17] Joe Bain, *Barriers to New Competition.*

[18] P. Sylos-Labini, *Oligopoly and Technical Progress* (Cambridge, Mass.: Harvard University Press, 1962).

[19] F. Modigliani, "New Developments on the Oligopoly Front," *Journal of Political Economy,* June 1958.

postulate. This is the assumption that potential entrants expect existing firms to maintain their output unchanged even though entry takes place. Clearly it is the expected *post*entry output (and price) that is relevant to potential entrants. If potential entrants expect a hostile reaction from established firms, the actual *pre*entry price could be set above the limit price and still not induce entry.

The limit price theory is attractive in its use of constructs suitable for empirical testing. That is, in industries in which the number of sellers is small enough to permit behavior that approximates perfect collusion, the theory predicts that profits will be greater the higher are the barriers to entry. This is, of course, the theory underlying the testing of the hypothesis about advertising entry barriers described earlier in this chapter.

Some evidence on this point was provided in a study by Mann for industries with high concentration ratios. First, we must assume that such collusive behavior is approximated by industries in which the leading eight firms account for 70 percent or more of industry output. Second, we must accept the judgment of Mann in classifying industries by height of entry barriers.[20] Subject to these qualifications, Mann's results, reported in Table 7-4, show that industries with very high barriers do earn higher profit rates than industries with lower barriers. However, there is apparently no difference between the profitability of industries with substantial and moderate-to-low barriers. A further review of empirical studies regarding the effects of barriers to entry will be given later in this chapter.

## Cournot and Warfare Models

The joint profit-maximization theory just presented is only one of numerous theories of oligopoly equilibrium. In our view, that theory, suitably modified to take into account the many factors that can lead to less than perfect collusion, has the best claim to being a general theory of oligopoly. That is, while joint profit-maximizing behavior may miss the mark widely in certain cases, it would appear to best describe the central tendency of oligopoly behavior. In this section we shall contrast perfect collusion with two quite different models, both to provide support for the joint profit-maximization assumption and to explain why deviations are quite plausible. In this section, we shall simplify the exposition by assuming that entry is completely barred.

The Cournot duopoly model can be summarized quickly. Assume that two firms sell a single homogeneous product at the same price $P$. For simplicity, take the cost of production to be zero. If we denote the outputs of firms 1 and 2 by $Q_1$ and $Q_2$, respectively, then

$$Q = Q_1 + Q_2$$

---

[20] Mann relied on Bain's judgment concerning the height of entry barriers in many industries. We might note that the most important types of barriers in the eight industries with very high barriers are as follows (SE = scale economy, PD = product differentiation, AC = absolute cost, and CR = capital requirements): automobiles: SE, PD, CR chewing gum: PD; cigarettes: PD, CR; ethical drugs: PD; flat glass: SE; liquor: PD; nickel: AC; and sulphur: AC.

**TABLE 7-4**
AVERAGE PROFIT RATES FOR HIGHLY CONCENTRATED
INDUSTRIES CLASSIFIED BY BARRIERS TO ENTRY, 1950–1960

| Industry | Average annual profit rate of leading firms, 1950–1960 |
|---|---|
| **Very high barriers** | |
| Automobiles | 15.5 |
| Chewing gum | 17.5 |
| Cigarettes | 11.6 |
| Ethical drugs | 17.9 |
| Flat glass | 18.8 |
| Liquor | 9.0 |
| Nickel | 18.9 |
| Sulphur | 21.6 |
| Average | 16.4 |
| **Substantial barriers** | |
| Aluminum reduction | 10.2 |
| Biscuits | 11.4 |
| Steel | 10.8 |
| Farm machinery and tractors | 8.8 |
| Copper | 11.5 |
| Cement | 15.7 |
| Shoe machinery | 7.4 |
| Average | 11.1 |
| **Moderate-to-low barriers** | |
| Glass containers | 13.1 |
| Tires and tubes | 13.2 |
| Rayon | 8.5 |
| Gypsum products | 14.4 |
| Metal containers | 9.9 |
| Average | 11.9 |

*Source:* H. Michael Mann, "Seller Concentration, Barriers to Entry, and Rates of Return in Thirty Industries, 1950–1960," *Review of Economics and Statistics,* August 1966.

is the combined market output. Let

$$P = 12 - Q = 12 - Q_1 - Q_2$$

be market demand. Then the profit functions for the two firms can be written as

$$\pi_1 = (12 - Q_1 - Q_2)Q_1 \tag{7-1}$$
$$\pi_2 = (12 - Q_1 - Q_2)Q_2 \tag{7-2}$$

The profit functions clearly demonstrate the interdependence that characterizes oligopoly. That is, the profit of firm 1 depends not only on its own output $Q_1$ but also on the output $Q_2$ of firm 2 (and similarly, $\pi_2$ depends on $Q_1$).

The Cournot model assumes that each firm regards its rival's output to be fixed at whatever level it happens to be. Hence, it is assumed that each firm expects its rival not to respond to any changes it makes in its own output.[21] It can be argued that such behavior should not be merely postulated but should be deduced from profit maximization. In fact, it is easy to show that the firms that behave in accordance with this Cournot assumption will not achieve maximum profits.

By partially differentiating equations (7-1) and (7-2) with respect to $Q_1$ and $Q_2$, equating the resulting derivatives to zero, and solving the equations simultaneously, we obtain the Cournot equilibrium.[22]

$$Q_1 = 4 \qquad Q_2 = 4$$
$$\pi_1 = 16 \qquad \pi_2 = 16$$
$$\text{and } \pi_1 + \pi_2 = 32$$

If the firms instead maximize joint profits, sharing the market equally, the equilibrium[23] is given by

$$Q_1 = 3 \qquad Q_2 = 3$$
$$\pi_1 = 18 \qquad \pi_2 = 18$$
$$\text{and } \pi_1 + \pi_2 = 36$$

---

[21] This assumption is usually held to be the most serious deficiency of the Cournot model. Unless the two firms move instantaneously to equilibrium, their adjustment path will embody the implausible assumption that the firms never learn. Even though each firm observes that the other firm *does* change its output in response to its own output change, it continues to believe that the firm will not so respond next time.

[22] Partially differentiating equations (7-1) and (7-2) and setting the resulting derivatives equal to zero yields

$$\frac{\partial \pi_1}{\partial Q_1} = 12 - 2Q_1 - Q_2 = 0$$

$$\frac{\partial \pi_2}{\partial Q_2} = 12 - 2Q_2 - Q_1 = 0$$

These two equations are called the firms' reaction functions. They give the firms' outputs as functions of the other firms' outputs. The simultaneous solution is the Cournot equilibrium given in the text, i.e., $Q_1 = 4$, $Q_2 = 4$.

[23] Jointly maximizing profits amounts to choosing the same total output that would be selected by a monopolist. If $\pi$ is total combined profits, then

$$\pi = (12 - Q)Q$$

and $\pi$ is maximized when

$$\frac{d\pi}{dQ} = 12 - 2Q = 0$$

or for $Q = 6$. If profits are shared equally, $Q = Q_1 + Q_2$ implies $Q_1 = 3$, $Q_2 = 3$.

**TABLE 7-5**
PROFITS MATRIX
(Firm 1's profits given first in each cell)

$Q_2$

|  |  | 3 | 4 | 6 |
|---|---|---|---|---|
| $Q_1$ | 3 | 18, 18 (jt. $\pi$-max.) | 15, 20 | 9, 18 |
|  | 4 | 20, 15 (Warfare) | 16, 16 (Cournot) | 8, 12 |
|  | 6 | 18, 9 | 12, 8 | 0, 0 |

Clearly, the Cournot duopolists could do better by altering their behavior in favor of the collusive, joint profit-maximizing equilibrium. Each firm could increase its profit from 16 to 18. Because of this incentive, we shall generally assume that oligopolists do seek to maximize joint profits, although there are many factors that make this objective hard to achieve. (Some of these factors will be examined in the next section.)

As we observed earlier, it is plausible to expect deviations from behavior that seeks to maximize combined profits. One type of such deviant behavior is price warfare. Everyone is familiar with the gasoline pricing wars that break out from time to time. Sometimes the war is initiated by a service station operator who is dissatisfied with his or her share of the market. Bishop[24] has shown that such behavior cannot be passed off as simply irrational. We can illustrate his warfare theory with the duopoly model described above.

Suppose that firm 1 is run by an ambitious, aggressive management, while the management of firm 2 is more timid and concerned with security. Nevertheless, they are both profit maximizers. Furthermore, suppose that firm 1 is unwilling to settle for half the market.

It will be useful to introduce a profits matrix, which shows the firms' profits for alternative output "strategies." For simplicity, we shall limit each firm to three possible output levels: 3, 4, and 6. The three outputs that firm 1 can elect are listed vertically in Table 7-5, and those of firm 2 are listed horizontally. The entries in the cells of the matrix are the profits (in order: $\pi_1, \pi_2$) associated with the output levels that define that cell location. For example, the Cournot equilibrium is defined by $Q_1 = 4$ and $Q_2 = 4$, or $\pi_1 = 16$, $\pi_2 = 16$. Joint profit maximization is given by $Q_1 = 3$, $Q_2 = 3$.

Now suppose that the aggressive management of firm 1 believes it can force firm 2 to accept less than half of the profits. One way would be to "teach" firm 2

[24] R. L. Bishop, "Duopoly: Collusion or Warfare?" *American Economic Review*, December 1960.

that unless it "agreed," firm 1 would expand its output so that both firms would earn unusually low profits. For example, suppose firm 1 considers the solution $Q_1 = 4$, $Q_2 = 3$ with $\pi_1 = 20$, $\pi_2 = 15$ to be achievable. It could follow the policy of setting $Q_1 = 6$ if $Q_2 = 4$ or $Q_2 = 6$, and setting $Q_1 = 4$ if $Q_2 = 3$. If firm 2 "learned" its lesson as intended, it would note that its own profits would be maximized[25] by setting $Q_2 = 3$. In other words, if firm 2 submitted to firm 1 rather than "waging war," the solution $Q_1 = 4$, $Q_2 = 3$ would be an equilibrium. This warfare equilibrium

$$Q_1 = 4 \qquad Q_2 = 3$$
$$\pi_1 = 20 \qquad \pi_2 = 15$$
$$\text{and } \pi_1 + \pi_2 = 35$$

produces combined profits equal to 35. These, of course, are less than the joint profit-maximization profits of 36. While one could argue that both firms could benefit by colluding and dividing the extra unit of profit, we would maintain that deviations from joint profit maximization are plausible. As Hurwicz has put it, rational behavior is impossible to define in oligopoly:

> There is no adequate solution of the problem of defining "rational economic behavior" on the part of an individual when the very rationality of his actions depends on the probable behavior of other individuals.[26]

We shall now turn to some of the factors in real-world markets that have an impact on the efforts of firms to maximize joint profits.

### Imperfect Collusion

By "imperfect" collusion we simply wish to imply that attaining joint profit-maximizing equilibrium in the real world is nearly impossible. In this section, we shall explore the reasons for this assertion. First, however, we shall examine some of the factors that aid in achieving collusion.

**Factors Helpful to Collusion**  An obvious way to facilitate collusion is by an actual written or oral agreement among the sellers. Such agreements are clearly

---

[25] If firm 2 believes that firm 1 will persist in its policy, then its profits as a function of its own output will be:

| $Q_2$ | $\pi_2$ |
| --- | --- |
| 3 | 15 |
| 4 | 8 |
| 6 | 0 |

Hence, profits are maximized when $Q_2 = 3$.

[26] L. Hurwicz, "The Theory of Economic Behavior," *American Economic Review*, 1945, p. 910.

illegal under the antitrust laws, but they continue to exist secretly in some industries.

We should not assume that joint profits are always maximized in such cases. Fog studied the price negotiations of six Danish cartels and acted as a consultant to a participant in a seventh. (We should note that the cartels were not illegal in Denmark at that time.) He described the negotiations as follows:

> The cartel negotiations I have been informed about have been characterized by reciprocal suspicion and distrust. . . . Each participant seemed to concentrate on gaining advantages at the cost of the others, and to be unwilling to give any concession without due reward, and only paying slight attention to anything like maximizing joint profits.[27]

In one industry in which cartel negotiations failed to reach an agreement, one of the members of the industry offered an explanation:

> Why is a cartel impossible? Because the interests and the viewpoints are too divergent. It is not feasible to have an agreement which limits production because XX has just built a new plant and for that reason they have to utilize their increased capacity. YY also has relatively high fixed costs and hence is interested in a high level of production.[28]

Short of explicit agreement, how might a small number of sellers hope to achieve joint profit maximization? One common institution that is helpful is price leadership. The price leader may be the largest or lowest-cost firm, though this is not always so. The identity of the leader may even change over time. The essential idea is that the leader openly announces its intention to change its price, and the other sellers normally follow with similar price changes. Of course, the leader must assess accurately what price level is likely to be acceptable to its rivals; if the leader is too far off the mark, some rivals may elect not to follow.

The determination of the leader is a learning process. The cigarette industry in the period after the Dissolution Decree of 1911 provides an interesting illustration. In 1910 the Tobacco Trust had 86 percent of the cigarette market in the United States. The trust was found guilty of monopolization and was divided into four successor companies: American, Liggett and Myers, Lorillard, and Reynolds.

During the period 1912–1923, no clear pattern of price leadership existed. Reynolds initiated three price changes which were all followed, but rather slowly. American unsuccessfully initiated one price increase and succeeded in intitiating one price decrease. Liggett and Myers initiated one price increase.

Reynolds, however, was becoming increasingly acceptable to the others as the leader. By 1923 Reynolds was the established price leader. The pricing pattern that prevailed from 1923 to 1931 has been described by Nicholls:

[27] B. Fog, "How Are Cartel Prices Determined?" *Journal of Industrial Economics,* November 1956, p. 20.
[28] Ibid., p. 21.

We find that there were only three price changes (one reduction, two increases) on the major brands of cigarettes between August 1923 and the end of 1931. In each case, Reynolds led in the price change, announced one day before the change became effective. In each case, American followed within 24 hours. Liggett and Myers twice followed within 24 hours, once within three days. Lorillard responded somewhat more tardily at first—within five days in 1928, within three days in 1929—but in 1931 followed within 24 hours. . . . With [two] exceptions, list prices were completely identical throughout the period.[29]

Some well-known price leaders include General Motors in automobiles, Alcoa in aluminum, and U.S. Steel in steel. Scherer has described a fascinating period in the steel industry when Bethlehem Steel assumed the leadership role in order to "teach" its rivals that secret price cutting was not acceptable:

On November 4, 1968, Bethlehem Steel announced a 22 percent cut in the list price of hot-rolled steel sheets, from $113.50 per ton . . . to $88.50 per ton. Its action . . . was evidently provoked by an under-the-counter offer U.S. Steel made to a major Bethlehem customer. . . . Within three days all significant producers joined in the decrease. Three weeks later U.S. Steel in effect sued for peace, quoting a new price of $125.00 per ton. . . .[30]

Price leadership is certainly a mechanism that aids firms in reaching agreement on price without any explicit written or oral communication.

There are other practices and customs in particular industries that aid in reducing the uncertainties of oligopolistic pricing. One example is the use of conventional markup pricing rules. If all firms in an industry become accustomed to calculating prices with the same formula, then pricing changes which reflect industrywide cost changes are more likely to be understood and accepted.

In one study, Hall and Hitch[31] interviewed 38 British firms about their pricing policies. Thirty of the firms indicated that they used some type of full-cost pricing rule. Another study by Kaplan, Dirlam, and Lanzillotti[32] found that many large American corporations also used such rules.

Such a rule might work as follows. The firm chooses a "target" return of, say, 15 percent on capital. It estimates its unit sales for next year as, say, 80 percent of plant capacity. It then estimates the average cost per unit, including both variable costs and overhead costs. Finally, it adds the appropriate margin for profit to produce the desired 15 percent.

Some economists have argued that full-cost pricing is an adequate theory of oligopolistic price determination. Such cost-based pricing rules undoubtedly help reduce uncertainty, thereby promoting coordination. As a complete theory it is unsatisfactory, however, since the demand side is ignored.

[29] W. Nicholls, *Price Policies in the Cigarette Industry* (Nashville: Vanderbilt University Press, 1951), p. 88.

[30] F. M. Scherer, *Industrial Market Structure and Economic Performance,* p. 179.

[31] R. L. Hall and C. J. Hitch, "Price Theory and Business Behavior," *Oxford Economic Papers,* May 1939.

[32] A. D. H. Kaplan, J. B. Dirlam and R. F. Lanzillotti, *Pricing in Big Business: A Case Approach* (Washington: Brookings Institution, 1958).

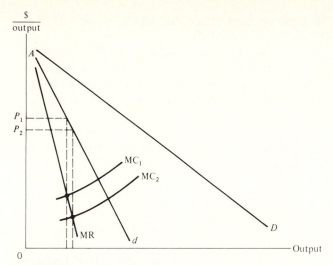

**FIGURE 7-6**
Preferred prices of duopolists sharing market equally.

Virtually all the recent evidence on full cost pricing practices shows that firms do not in fact apply rigid profit-margins, regardless of demand conditions. They vary the margin to suit the product: the more elastic the demand, the lower the margin.[33]

**Factors Harmful to Collusion**   In general, we can state that joint profit maximization will be less likely the greater the number (and the lower the concentration) of sellers; the wider the differences among firms in objectives, costs, and so forth; the greater the number of dimensions of the product that must be agreed on (product specifications, credit terms, delivery times, and so forth); and the greater the incentives for secret price cutting. Other factors that can be important include the concentration of buyers, the degree of product differentiation, and even the cost structure (high fixed costs relative to variable costs).

Many of these factors are self-evident. As the number of sellers rises, the degree of interdependence recognized among them falls. The limit, of course, is the purely competitive model. Also, increased numbers make for more complex problems of coordination. Anyone with experience in committee work knows that reaching agreement is much easier in small committees. The larger the committee, the more likely it is to have at least one "maverick" who will not agree with anyone. The same argument applies to the number of items on which agreement is sought.

To illustrate how cost differences can make joint profit maximization hard to attain, consider a simple duopoly model. Suppose that the two firms sell identical products, but one firm has lower costs. Furthermore, assume that they agree to split the market equally. Figure 7-6 shows the two firms' *preferred*

[33] F. M. Scherer, *Industrial Market Structure and Economic Performance*, p. 187.

prices. Each firm faces the same demand curve $Ad$, which is just half of the market demand curve $AD$.

The profit-maximizing price for the low-cost firm is $P_2$, determined by the intersection of marginal revenue MR and its marginal cost $MC_2$. Similarly, the high-cost firm would prefer $P_1$. Since only one price can exist in the market, there is an obvious conflict. Furthermore, neither of these prices is the joint profit-maximization price.

In order to maximize joint profits, the low-cost firm must produce more than half the total output. Consequently, for the firms to share profits equally, the low-cost firm would have to make payments directly to the high-cost firm. To work out such details would require a considerable amount of coordination. A more likely outcome would be a compromise price which would yield smaller profits than those achieved under joint maximization.

Next, we consider Stigler's [34] theory of oligopoly, which emphasizes the importance of incentives to secretly cut price. Consider a firm in an industry that is currently maximizing joint profits. The market price is $P_1$, and the firm's output is $Q_1$, as shown in Figure 7-7. To make the diagram as simple as possible, we assume constant marginal and average costs.

Two demand curves pass through the current equilibrium price and output. The $DD$ curve is the firm's share of the market demand curve, and it assumes that *all* firms always charge the same price. The $dd$ curve is the firm's demand curve, assuming that all *other* firms maintain their prices at $P_1$.

Clearly, if the firm could secretly drop its price from $P_1$ to $P_2$, thereby moving down the $dd$ curve, it could significantly increase its own profit. That is, the profit before "cheating" (by secretly cutting its price) was the rectangle $P_1CBA$. After cheating, the profit rectangle is $P_2CEF$. Of course, if others discover the price cutter, they may react by dropping their prices also. The result would be to shift the cheater back to the $DD$ curve, where profit would be lower than in either of the two previous equilibria.

In essence, Stigler's theory analyzes the factors that affect the incentives to cheat. The lower the incentives to cheat, the more likely collusion is to be successful. For example, the government sometimes requests bids from various sellers and on a given date announces publicly what each seller bid. The low bidder then gets the contract. Such a process is almost perfect for making collusion successful. Any bidder wanting to cheat by quoting a low price will be publicly exposed to his or her fellow conspirators.

Using a complex mathematical argument, Stigler shows that the aggregate incentive to cheat in an industry is inversely related to an index of concentration.[35] Hence, joint profit maximization should be more closely approximated in industries with higher levels of concentration.

[34] George J. Stigler, "A Theory of Oligopoly," *Journal of Political Economy*, February 1964.
[35] Stigler's analysis uses probability theory. The key ingredient is that a firm's sales can be unusually high in a period either because of purely random events or because of secret price cutting. Hence, the higher the "normal" chance variability of sales, the higher will be a firm's incentive to cheat because of the difficulty its rivals will have in distinguishing price cutting from pure chance. The final link in Stigler's argument is his demonstration that industries with lower concentration have inherently higher normal sales variability.

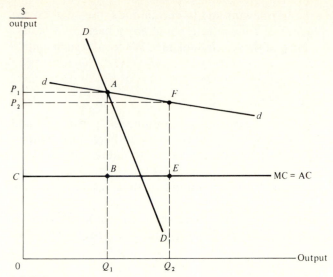

**FIGURE 7-7**
Incentive for secret price-cutting.

To summarize this rather lengthy discussion of oligopoly pricing theory, let us make use of Figure 7-8. In the figure we show the relationships among profitability, concentration, and barriers to entry that on the average appear to be most representative of the theory. Thus, in the long run, profit is predicted to rise with increases in concentration and with the height of barriers to entry. For simplicity in the diagram, we assume only two levels of barriers: low and high. We have also assumed that some threshold level of concentration must be reached before profit will exceed zero.

Again, we must caution that the relationships shown in Figure 7-8 are only representative of the central tendency of the theories of oligopoly pricing. Differences across industries in pricing behavior as well as many of the other fac-

**FIGURE 7-8**
Profitability as a function of concentration and entry barriers.

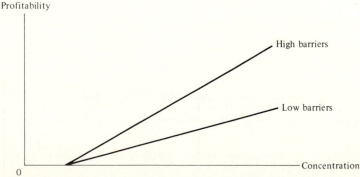

tors discussed above are usually relevant and in certain industries can be expected to outweigh the influence of concentration and entry barriers. Clearly, there is need for empirical testing of these relationships. We turn to such empirical analysis now.

## STATISTICAL TESTS

The number of statistical studies relating concentration, entry barriers, and profits is so large that we cannot possibly discuss them all here. Fortunately, Weiss[36] has made a survey of 54 such studies, and the interested reader is referred to his work. Here we shall report on only two of the better known studies in order to provide some insight into the nature of such research and the problems involved.

The first study examines only the relationship of concentration to profits, while the second is representative of studies that include entry barriers in addition to concentration.

### Bain Study

The 1951 study of Bain[37] was the first test of the concentration-profits hypothesis. Bain used data on 42 industries that had been tabulated by the National Resources Committee and the Securities and Exchange Commission. The eight-firm concentration ratios applied to the year 1935, while the profit data applied to the years 1936–1940. Bain used an accounting measure of profit, *viz,* after-tax profit divided by stockholders' equity. He calculated the measure for each firm in each year. Then he computed a weighted (by equity) annual average *industry* profit rate from the firm data for each industry. Finally, he found the simple average of these annual rates, as shown in Table 7-6. Bain did not find a very good linear relationship between concentration and profit rates. However, he did find that industries with eight-firm concentration above 70 percent tended to have relatively high average profit rates.

> The positive conclusion that does emerge is that there is a rather distinct break in average profit rate showing at the 70 percent concentration line and that there is a significant difference in the average of industry average profit rates above and below this line.[38]

### Comanor and Wilson Study[39]

This study was the first statistical test which used continuous variables to measure entry barriers. The basic statistical hypothesis is that the profit rate $\pi_i$

---

[36] L. W. Weiss, "The Concentration-Profits Relationship and Antitrust," in H. G. Goldschmid, et al. (eds.), *Industrial Concentration: The New Learning.*

[37] Joe Bain, "Relation of Profit Rates to Industry Concentration," *Quarterly Journal of Economics,* August 1951.

[38] Ibid p. 314.

[39] W. S. Comanor and T. Wilson, "Advertising, Market Structure, and Performance."

**TABLE 7-6**
AVERAGE INDUSTRY PROFIT RATES WITHIN
CONCENTRATION DECILES, 1936–1940

| Eight-firm concentration | Number of industries | Average industry profit rate |
|---|---|---|
| 90–100 | 8 | 12.7 |
| 80–89.9 | 10 | 9.8 |
| 70–79.9 | 3 | 16.3 |
| 60–69.9 | 5 | 5.8 |
| 50–59.9 | 4 | 5.8 |
| 40–49.9 | 3 | 8.6 |
| 30–39.9 | 5 | 6.3 |
| 20–29.9 | 2 | 10.4 |
| 10–19.9 | 1 | 17.0 |
| 0–9.9 | 1 | 9.1 |

of the $i$th industry depends on the market structure variables of that industry according to some function

$$\pi_i = f(CR_i,\ B_i,\ e_i) \tag{7-3}$$

where $CR_i$ denotes the concentration ratio of the $i$th industry, $B_i$ a set of entry barrier variables, and $e_i$ an error term representing various unmeasured or random influences.

The particular variables used by Comanor and Wilson were:

*Profit rates* ($\pi$): Profits after taxes as a percentage of stockholders' equity, averaged within each industry for firms with assets over \$500,000. Profit rates are averaged for the period 1954–1957.

*Advertising* (AS): Ratio of advertising to sales averaged over the period 1954–1957.

*Scale economy* (SE): Average plant size among the largest plants accounting for 50 percent of industry output divided by total output in the market.

*Absolute capital requirements* (AK): The average assets needed for a plant as determined for the SE measure.

*Growth of demand* (G): The rate of growth of sales between 1947 and 1957.

*Seller concentration* (CR): The four-firm concentration ratio.

*Regional dummy* (R): A measure to correct for the fact that the data are on a national basis while the soft drinks, dairy, and bakery industries have regional markets.

Restricting their analysis to a sample of 41 consumer goods industries, Comanor and Wilson estimated a large number of multiple regression equations. A leading equation is reproduced below. (Numbers in parentheses are $t$ statistics, and the letter L indicates the logarithm of the variable.)

$$\pi = 0.038 + 0.341\text{AS} + 0.011\text{LAK} + 0.014\text{LG} + 0.028\text{R} \qquad (7\text{-}4)$$
$$\phantom{\pi = 0.038 + 0}(2.3)\phantom{\text{AS} + 0.011}(3.6)\phantom{\text{LAK} + 0.014}(1.4)\phantom{\text{LG} + 0.0}(1.6)$$
$$R^2 = 0.49$$

They concluded that advertising and capital requirements are statistically significant barriers to entry and tend to raise profits. Because of high correlation among capital requirements, scale economies, and seller concentration, they did not discount the last two factors, SE and CR, as influencing profits. For example, they regressed CR on AK, SE, and R:

$$\text{LCR} = 3.85 + 0.244\text{LAK} + 0.238\text{LSE} - 0.294\text{R} \qquad (7\text{-}5)$$
$$\phantom{\text{LCR} = 3.85 + 0.24}(5.1)\phantom{\text{LAK} + 0.2}(3.4)\phantom{\text{LSE} - 0.}(1.2)$$
$$R^2 = 0.81$$

This regression shows that CR, AK, and SE are highly correlated and cannot be expected to yield separate coefficients in the profit equation. The proper interpretation of AK in the profit equation is that it represents the combined effect of concentration, capital requirements, and scale-economy barriers.

While we have been able only to scratch the surface of a large literature on statistical structure-profits studies, enough has been said to indicate the general nature and usefulness of this line of analysis. Readers interested in a more detailed treatment may wish to consult several surveys that have been published.[40]

## COMPETITIVE ANALYSIS AND STRATEGY FORMULATION

In an important recent book,[41] Michael E. Porter has developed in detail a set of techniques for analyzing industries and competitors. The basic conceptual framework is industrial organization analysis. In essence, Porter shows how industrial organization analysis, as developed by economists as a basis for public policy evaluation, can be "turned on its head" and exploited by managers of business firms for strategic planning.

Competitive analysis and strategy formulation are concerned with the way in which a firm can compete more effectively to strengthen its market position. While competitive strategy is only one part of an overall strategic plan, it is clearly an important one.

To appreciate how industrial organization analysis can be applied to strategy formulation, consider Porter's five "structural determinants of the intensity of competition":

**1** Rivalry among existing firms

[40] F. M. Scherer, *Industrial Market Structure and Economic Performance,* chap. 9; John M. Vernon, *Market Structure and Industrial Performance: A Review of Statistical Findings* (Boston: Allyn and Bacon, 1972); and L. W. Weiss, "The Concentration-Profits Relationship and Antitrust."

[41] Michael E. Porter, *Competitive Strategy* (New York: The Free Press, 1980).

**2** Threat of new entrants
**3** Bargaining power of buyers
**4** Bargaining power of suppliers
**5** Threat of substitute products or services

As Porter puts it, the "intensity of competition in an industry is neither a matter of coincidence nor bad luck. Rather, competition in an industry is rooted in its underlying economic structure." Of course, these structural determinants are quite similar to the elements of market structure that we described earlier in this chapter as a key ingredient in industrial organization analysis.

Porter goes on to observe that the "collective strength of these forces determines the ultimate profit potential in the industry. . . . The forces range from intense in industries like tires, paper, and steel—where no firm earns spectacular returns—to relatively mild in industries like oil-field equipment and services, cosmetics, and toiletries—where high returns are quite common."

Once these determinants of competition have been analyzed for a particular industry, the firm should proceed to identify its own strengths and weaknesses relative to each factor. According to Porter, "an effective competitive strategy takes offensive or defensive action in order to create a defendable position against the five competitive forces."

In order to illustrate the ideas more concretely, we now turn to two examples of particular competitive strategies. The first example relates to a strategy of product differentiation in the pharmaceutical industry and the second to a strategy of cost leadership in the automobile industry.

Until the late 1930s, the pharmaceutical industry was relatively static, supplying medicinal chemicals to pharmacists and vaccines to public health programs. Then, during the 1940s, penicillin was developed, largely through government efforts to combat infections in soldiers during World War II. Penicillin, of course, represents one of the most important breakthroughs in the history of medicine.

The largest penicillin supplier was a small chemical manufacturer known as Chas. Pfizer & Company. Surprisingly, the penicillin business quickly became unprofitable. The price of penicillin dropped from $3,955 per pound in 1945 to $282 in 1950. A major reason was that entry was easy. Because government had funded its development, penicillin had not been patented. Also, the suppliers tended to focus on the production aspects of the business, and there was little effort toward product differentiation. Producers generally sold in bulk, and competition was based primarily on price alone.

As a result of the penicillin experience, Pfizer recognized the need to differentiate its products. Hence, in 1950, prompted by its discovery of a new antibiotic, Pfizer made the significant decision to integrate forward into marketing. The new drug, oxytetracycline, was patented and given the brand name Terramycin. Pfizer decided not to license any other firms to produce or sell Terramycin.

In 1950, the Pfizer sales organization was composed of a sales manager, an advertising manager, and eight salespeople (known as detail men). One year later, Pfizer had increased its sales force to about 300 detail men. This enabled the company to promote its new drug directly to physicians and to emphasize its particular advantages over substitute products. Doctors were urged to prescribe by the brand name, Terramycin.

The result was extremely successful for Pfizer. Even after its patent had expired, Pfizer was able to charge a significant premium for Terramycin compared to prices for generic supplies of oxytetracycline. For example, in 1969 Terramycin was priced at $17.80 per 100 capsules compared to generic prices of about $1.70. Sales of Terramycin were over $20 million that year.

Another competitive strategy that is suggested by industrial organization research findings is cost leadership. For example, economies of scale may permit leading firms to develop an entry barrier advantage over rivals. Ford Motor Company in the 1920s provides an example of how this strategy can sometimes backfire. However, it had been a resounding success for over a decade.

In the early 1900s Henry Ford froze the design of the famous Model T and concentrated on mass production at low cost. Motor and chassis parts were completely interchangeable for the entire period 1909–1926. The Model T's price was cut from $950 in 1909 to under $300 in the early 1920s. As a result, Ford's market-share increased from 9 percent in 1909 to a high of 55 percent in 1921. Thereafter, Ford failed to take into account the changing nature of consumer tastes and lost market-share to General Motors.

According to Robert Lanzillotti:

> With the choice between the economical and dependable, but ungainly, Ford and a Chevrolet—which for about $100 more offered not only a more pleasing style, but also greater speed, better transmission, cooling, lubrication, ignition, and springs —the public turned increasingly to the latter. Ford's market share fell from 55 percent in 1921 to 41 percent in 1925, and to slightly more than one-third in 1926.[42]

While the discussion here has been brief, it should demonstrate the potential value of industrial organization analysis to the formulation of effective competitive strategies. It is an interesting application of a line of research originally developed by economists with a strong interest in designing public policies toward business. Readers interested in a more detailed discussion of how to perform competitive analysis should consult the book by Porter.[43]

## QUESTIONS AND PROBLEMS

**7-1** What are the most important elements of market structure? How does each element influence industrial behavior?

**7-2** Do you think that Bain's measures of performance are equally relevant to the firm and society? How might a conflict arise?

**7-3** What are some pitfalls in using the standard four-firm concentration ratio for economic analysis?

---

[42] Robert F. Lanzillotti, "The Automobile Industry," in Walter Adams (ed.), *Structure of American Industry,* 3d ed. (New York: Macmillan, 1961), p. 320.

[43] Michael E. Porter, *Competitive Strategy.*

**7-4** John McGee is quoted in the text as questioning the capability of economists in their studies of economies of scale. Are his reservations valid?

**7-5** How do scale-economy barriers permit existing firms to make above-average profits?

**7-6** Assume two duopolists facing the demand

$$P = 100 - .5\,(Q_1 + Q_2)$$

where the two firms have total cost of

$$C_1 = 5Q_1$$
$$C_2 = .5Q_2^2$$

**a** Find the Cournot equilibrium:

$P =$         Profit of 1 $=$

$Q_1 =$       Profit of 2 $=$

$Q_2 =$       Total profit $=$

**b** Suppose firms 1 and 2 now collude and act jointly to maximize profit. Find

$P =$         Profit of 1 $=$

$Q_1 =$       Profit of 2 $=$

$Q_2 =$       Total profit $=$

**c** Now suppose other firms will enter the market and supply unlimited quantities for prices of $20 and up. What will the colluding duopolists select as their

$P =$         Profit of 1 $=$

$Q_1 =$       Profit of 2 $=$

$Q_2 =$       Total profit $=$

**7-7** The Organization of Petroleum Exporting Countries (OPEC) cartel consists of 12 major oil-producing countries, of which Saudi Arabia is the largest. It has been unusually successful, especially since 1973. Can you offer any explanations for the unusual success of OPEC?

**7-8** How might statistical relationships between structure and performance be useful to management?

## BIBLIOGRAPHY

Bain, Joe: *Barriers to Competition* (Cambridge, Mass.: Harvard University Press, 1956).

Bishop, R. L.: "Duopoly: Collusion or Warfare?" *American Economic Review,* December 1960.

Kaplan, A. D. H., J. B. Dirlam, and R. G. Lanzillotti: *Pricing in Big Business: A Case Approach* (Washington, D. C.: The Brookings Institution, 1958).

Modigliani, F.: "New Developments on the Oligopoly Front," *Journal of Political Economy,* June 1958.

Schmalensee, R.: *The Economics of Advertising* (Amsterdam: North-Holland Press, 1972).

Scherer, F. M.: *Industrial Market Structure and Economic Performance,* 2d ed. (Chicago: Rand McNally, 1980).

Weston, J. Fred: "Pricing Behavior of Large Firms," *Western Economic Journal,* March 1972.

CHAPTER **8**

# ANTITRUST AND REGULATION

**CHAPTER OUTLINE**

INTRODUCTION
ANTITRUST
    Price-Fixing Conspiracies
    Monopolization
    Mergers
REGULATION
    Rationale for Regulation
    Benefits and Costs of Regulation
    FDA Regulation of Pharmaceuticals
QUESTIONS AND PROBLEMS
BIBLIOGRAPHY

**INTRODUCTION**

In this chapter we shall provide an introduction to governmental constraints on corporate decision making. In many cases the primary role of corporate economists is to understand and give advice on the existing and expected effects of various government policies on the corporation. Often the economist is asked to analyze pending government policy changes and to prepare studies setting forth the corporation's position. Examples include oil price decontrol and windfall profit taxes, rate changes for public utilities, patent law reforms,

**269**

labeling requirements for consumer products, laws against conglomerate mergers, safety and fuel-economy requirements for automobiles, and standards for air and water quality. The two major topics in this chapter are antitrust and regulation. Because of space limitations only selected antitrust and regulatory issues can be discussed here. More detailed treatments of these subjects can be found elsewhere.[1]

## ANTITRUST

The major federal antitrust statute in the United States, the Sherman Act of 1890, was the political reaction to the widespread growth of large-scale business combinations, or trusts, formed in the 1880s. Severe business depression had brought about pricing practices that were disastrous to firms in certain industries. To avoid this "cutthroat competition," trusts were formed in many industries, including petroleum, meat-packing, sugar, lead, coal, tobacco, and gunpowder. Farmers' organizations, labor unions, and small businesspeople united in urging passage of a law to protect themselves from the economic power of these new trusts.

There are two main sections of the Sherman Act. Section 1 prohibits contracts, combinations, and conspiracies in restraint of trade. Penalties for violators can be imprisonment and/or a fine. Section 2 prohibits monopolization, attempts to monopolize, and combinations or conspiracies to monopolize "any part of the trade or commerce among the several states, or with foreign nations." Penalties are similar to those for Section 1. The classic target under Section 1 is price-fixing arrangements, while Section 2 is applied to market dominance. We shall consider these two topics in detail shortly.

As a result of dissatisfaction with the Sherman Act during its first few decades, two additional statutes were enacted in 1914. The Clayton Act was designed to define anticompetitive acts more clearly. It outlawed price discrimination, tying clauses and exclusive dealing agreements, interlocking directorates, and mergers between competitors. However, these practices were considered illegal only where they would "substantially lessen competition or tend to create a monopoly." Section 7, which dealt with mergers, was largely ineffective because of a legal loophole. The problem was remedied by the Celler-Kefauver Act of 1950, which amended Section 7. The law toward mergers will be discussed in detail later in this chapter.

The second statute passed in 1914 was the Federal Trade Commission (FTC) Act. The objective was to create a special agency which could perform both investigatory and adjudicative functions. Prior to this time, the Antitrust

---

[1]A good treatment of antitrust policy is contained in the book by F. M. Scherer, *Industrial Market Structure and Economic Performance,* 2d ed. (Chicago: Rand McNally, 1980). A number of books dealing with regulation exist, including Richard Schmalensee, *The Control of Natural Monopolies* (Lexington, Mass.: Heath, 1979); Bruce Owen and Ronald Braeutigam, *The Regulation Game: Strategic Use of the Administrative Process* (Cambridge, Mass.: Ballinger, 1978); and U.S. Congress, Senate Committee on Government Operations, *Study on Federal Regulation,* Vol. 6, 1978

Division of the Justice Department was the sole enforcement agency in antitrust matters. The FTC Act also contained a section which outlawed "unfair methods of competition."

These three laws—the Sherman Act of 1890 and the Clayton and FTC acts of 1914—constitute the substantive framework for antitrust policy in the United States. As indicated in our brief description above, the language is general and the interpretation has been left to the courts. Hence, to really understand what is legal and what is illegal in specific situations, one must be familiar with the important court decisions and the specific rules of law that have been developed in these decisions. We should add that in many situations there remains considerable uncertainty about what a future court might hold to be legal or illegal. This is true, for example, with regard to the term "monopolization." If IBM has 70 percent of the general-purpose computer market, has it been guilty of monopolization? As we shall see, the answer depends on the nature of the tactics IBM followed in winning its large market-share.

Economists tend to view antitrust as a set of laws designed to promote competition and therefore economic efficiency. The basic idea is, of course, that monopoly can lead to an inefficient allocation of resources, as was explained in Chapter 6. At first glance, this view seems to be consistent with the language of the Sherman and Clayton acts. However, it should be observed that while economic analysis can and has influenced the development of antitrust doctrine, there are other important influences as well. One such influence is the political factor of protecting the small businessperson. For example, since competition can lead to the bankruptcy of small, high-cost firms, in certain areas of antitrust the law has been interpreted to protect small businesses even if higher costs result. To illustrate, one important Supreme Court decision contained the following statement:

> It is competition, not competitors, which the Act protects. But we cannot fail to recognize Congress' desire to promote competition through the protection of viable, small, locally owned businesses. Congress appreciated that occasional higher costs and prices might result from the maintenance of fragmented industries and markets. It resolved these competing considerations in favor of decentralization. We must give effect to that decision.[2]

We shall now turn to three major areas of antitrust: price-fixing conspiracies, monopolization, and mergers. Other antitrust topics such as price discrimination and tying contracts are beyond the scope of this chapter.

## Price-Fixing Conspiracies

Section 1 of the Sherman Act outlaws "every contract, combination . . . or conspiracy in restraint of trade." The courts have taken a very clear position with regard to overt conspiracies by competitors to fix prices, share markets, etc. The so-called per se rule toward price fixing was established in the Supreme Court's

[2] *Brown Shoe Company v. U.S.*, 370 U.S. 294, 344 (1962).

*Trenton Potteries* decision in 1927. Some 23 manufacturers of sanitary pottery belonged to an association which attempted to fix the prices of their products. In its decision, the Court concluded:

> The aim and result of every price-fixing agreement, if effective, is the elimination of one form of competition. The power to fix prices, whether reasonably exercised or not, involves power to control the market and to fix arbitrary and unreasonable prices. The reasonable price fixed today may through economic and business changes become the unreasonable price of tomorrow . . . . Agreements which create such potential power may well be held to be in themselves unreasonable or unlawful restraints, without the necessity of minute inquiry whether a particular price is reasonable or unreasonable as fixed and without placing on the Government in enforcing the Sherman Law the burden of ascertaining from day to day whether it has become unreasonable through the mere variation of economic conditions.[3]

The quotation makes clear the distinction between the legal concepts termed per se rules and rules of reason. Under a per se rule, it is only necessary to prove that certain conduct took place; under a rule of reason, which applies in certain areas of antitrust, not only must the conduct be established, but a further judgment as to its "reasonableness" must be made.

Interestingly, the United States stands alone in its per se rule against price fixing. Other industrial nations have adopted a rule of reason approach. For example, the United Kingdom has set forth eight "gateways" which can enable a price-fixing agreement to escape illegality. For example, one gateway is that the agreement can be legal if a court considers the agreement necessary to avoid serious and persistent unemployment effects.

Hence, in the United States a price-fixing agreement is illegal if satisfactory evidence of its existence is uncovered. The penalty can be fines and/or imprisonment. Recently a more potent remedy has become important. Persons damaged by a price-fixing agreement can sue for recovery of 3 times the damages sustained. For example, it is estimated that such payments resulting from the electrical equipment conspiracies of the early 1960s amounted to somewhere between $500 and $600 million.[4]

A much more difficult antitrust problem is what is termed "conscious parallelism." Suppose that there is no evidence that firms got together and made overt agreements to fix prices; however, the firms did behave in parallel fashion by charging identical prices. The key question is whether a conspiracy can be inferred from such conscious parallelism. The importance of this issue is that oligopoly pricing often has characteristics of conscious parallelism.

In an important 1946 decision, the Court seemed to state that the cigarette industry was guilty of conspiracy solely on the basis of its parallel pricing behavior. It observed that "no formal agreement is necessary to constitute an unlawful conspiracy. Often crimes are a matter of inference deduced from the acts of the person accused. . . ."[5]

---

[3] *U.S. v. Trenton Potteries Company et al.,* 273 U.S. 392, 396–398 (1927).
[4] Charles A. Bane, *The Electrical Equipment Conspiracies: The Treble Damage Actions* (New York: Federal Legal Publications, 1973).
[5] *American Tobacco Company et al. v. U.S.,* 328 U.S. 781, 809 (1946).

William H. Nicholls interpreted this decision as a "legal milestone in the social control of oligopoly" because it permitted the "inference of illegal conspiracy from detailed similarity of behavior."[6]

Briefly, the facts in the case which were viewed as particularly significant were as follows:

**1** On June 23, 1931, Reynolds announced an increase in its wholesale cigarette price from $6.40 to $6.85. The other two major firms, American and Liggett & Myers, followed upward to the same price within 24 hours. This increase occurred in the midst of the Great Depression, when leaf prices and labor costs were falling.

**2** In November 1932, after a loss of 23 percent of the market to smaller firms selling "economy brands," the Big Three dropped their prices, almost in unison, to $5.50. This rapidly forced many of the economy-brand suppliers out of the business.

**3** The Big Three bought large amounts of low-grade tobacco, thereby bidding up its price, even though they did not use it for their own cigarettes. It was the type of tobacco used for economy brands.

**4** The Big Three declined to participate in leaf tobacco auctions unless buyers from all three companies were present, and they refrained from buying tobacco grades in which the others had a special interest.

These facts were sufficient for the Court to infer the existence of a conspiracy. However, more recent cases do not seem to support the view that parallel oligopoly pricing alone will be found to be illegal.

In a 1954 decision the Supreme Court concluded:

> The crucial question is whether respondents' conduct toward petitioner stemmed from independent decision or from an agreement, tacit or express. To be sure, business behavior is admissible circumstantial evidence from which the fact finder may infer agreement.... But this Court has never held that proof of parallel business behavior conclusively establishes agreement or, phrased differently, that such behavior itself constitutes a Sherman Act offense. Circumstantial evidence of consciously parallel behavior may have made heavy inroads into the traditional judicial attitude toward conspiracy; but "conscious parallelism" has not yet read conspiracy out of the Sherman Act entirely.[7]

In a widely publicized case involving parallel pricing of tetracycline by five pharmaceutical manufacturers, the Court found the firms innocent. A key fact in this case was that Pfizer, Cyanamid, Bristol, Upjohn, and Squibb each charged the same price of $30.60 for its brand of tetracycline continuously from November 1953 until July 1960. Much attention was given to the low manufacturing cost of around $3.00 and the extremely high profit margins.

In their defense, the companies argued that it would make no sense for any one of them to cut its price. The market demand for tetracycline was price-

---

[6] William H. Nicholls, "The Tobacco Case of 1946," *American Economic Review,* May 1949, p. 296.

[7] *Theater Enterprises, Inc. v. Paramount Film Distributing Corp. et al.* 346 U.S. 537 (1954).

inelastic so that a general price reduction would not expand the total market. Also, a price cut by one would be matched immediately by the others, making such a tactic self-defeating. Furthermore, entry was barred by virtue of Pfizer's patent.[8] Hence, there was no need to lower price to limit entry. Therefore, the maintenance of a common price of $30.60 by the five firms was merely the result of each firm's independent business judgment and did not imply a conspiracy. The Court apparently agreed with this line of argument, concluding that the "parallel pricing among the tetracycline producers, standing alone, does not indicate price fixing."[9]

How can we reconcile these more recent decisions with the earlier *Tobacco* case? More to the point, how are the courts likely to draw the line in determining what circumstantial evidence warrants an inference of conspiracy? According to F. M. Scherer, the accumulated precedents call for "parallelism plus."[10] In the *Tobacco* case he argues that the "plus" could be inferred from the fact that the firms had advance knowledge of impending rival actions that could hardly have been gained without covert communication.

In addition to the legal question of establishing guilt or innocence, conscious parallelism also raises the issue of the appropriate remedy. Clearly, the source of the perceived problem is the interdependence created by the oligopolistic structure of the industry. It seems unlikely, therefore, that this interdependence could be eliminated short of changing the structure of the industry, e.g., by dissolution of the firms into a larger number of independent rivals.[11] It is doubtful that many antitrust experts would favor such drastic remedies, given the present poor state of knowledge linking industry structure and performance.

### Monopolization

Section 2 of the Sherman Act declares it illegal to "monopolize, or attempt to monopolize any part of the trade or commerce among the several states." Again, the language is quite general, and the courts have attempted to interpret it through a long series of cases.

An important early decision concerned the 1911 Standard Oil monopoly of petroleum refining. The Rockefeller brothers put together a combination of more than 120 companies which controlled about 90 percent of the market

---

[8] Pfizer had licensed the other four firms to sell tetracycline. How this came about is a complicated story, but it is a separate issue and need not be described here.

[9] *Charles Pfizer & Company, Inc. et al. v. U.S.,* 367 F. Supp. 91 (1973).

[10] F. M. Scherer, *Industrial Market Structure and Economic Performance,* p. 519.

[11] However, one possible direction that remedies short of dissolution might take is illustrated by the American turbogenerator industry. The two rivals, G.E. and Westinghouse, were able to maintain stable prices for many years through the use of a pricing book and a "price protection" plan. Under the price protection plan, the sellers guaranteed that any discount on new orders would apply retroactively on all orders taken in the past six months. The effect of the plan was to make the incentive to "cheat" through secret price cuts much less. In 1977, the Justice Department got the companies to agree to drop the price protection plan; the hope is, of course, that price competition will be stimulated.

throughout the 1880s and 1890s. The monopoly was alleged to have been achieved largely through the use of predatory tactics, e.g., setting price below cost to force rivals out of business or to soften them up for a takeover.[12]

In its decision, the Supreme Court argued that the crime of monopolization requires the fulfillment of two conditions: the acquisition of monopoly power and the intent to acquire that position and exclude rivals from the industry. Standard Oil, by virtue of its 90 percent market-share, easily met the first condition. Its predatory tactics enabled the Court to infer the necessary intent of the second condition, and Standard Oil was found guilty. The remedy was that Standard Oil was broken up into 33 geographically separated companies.

Over time the definition of the crime of monopolization gradually changed. In the famous *Alcoa* case of 1945, the question of intent to monopolize was inferred not from any predatory tactics but from Alcoa's building up of aluminum capacity in advance of demand.

> It was not inevitable that it should always anticipate increases in the demand for ingot and be prepared to supply them. Nothing compelled it to keep doubling and redoubling its capacity before others entered the field. It insists that it never excluded competitors; but we can think of no more effective exclusion than progressively to embrace each new opportunity as it opened and to face every newcomer with new capacity already geared into a great organization, having the advantage of experience, trade connections and the elite of personnel.[13]

However, the Court did state that Alcoa would have been innocent if its dominant position had merely been "thrust upon" it by the failure of its rivals or because it had demonstrated superior skill, foresight, and industry.

The *Alcoa* case was also important because of its treatment of the problem of market definition. Three alternative definitions of the market were considered, which varied depending on whether secondary aluminum was included in the market and how Alcoa's internal demand for primary aluminum was treated. The three definitions yielded market-shares for Alcoa of 33, 64, and 90 percent. The Court concluded that 90 percent was the correct share and constituted a monopoly. It also stated that 64 percent would be doubtful as enough to qualify as a monopoly, but 33 percent was certainly not enough.

The 1953 *United Shoe Machinery* case provided further insight into the legal meaning of monopolization. United Shoe Machinery supplied between 75 and 85 percent of the market and therefore met the condition of possessing a monopoly. It was found guilty because of various business policies it had followed. United refused to sell its machines and would lease them only for long terms, it included provisions in its leases that made it advantageous for customers to use only United machines, and it provided free repair services.

---

[12] That this was factually true has been disputed by John S. McGee, "Predatory Price Cutting: The Standard Oil (N.J.) Case," *Journal of Law and Economics,* October 1958. McGee also argued that predatory pricing is a costly strategy compared to the alternative takeover strategy of buying out rivals.

[13] *U.S. v. Aluminum Company of America et al.,* 148 F. 2d 416, 432 (1945).

These practices were viewed by the Court as being designed to exclude rivals. In particular, the Court concluded that the causes of United's success

> were neither common law restraints of trade, nor the skill with which the business was conducted, but rather some practice which without being predatory, abusive, or coercive was in economic effect exclusionary.[14]

Important monopolization cases against IBM, AT&T, and three breakfast cereal firms (charged with collective monopolization) were under way as this book was written. The facts are complex and will not be summarized here. It is certain, however, that the final decisions in these cases will be important for this area of antitrust law.

## Mergers

Merger is an important strategy for the corporation, and the motives for merger are numerous. In Chapter 12 we shall discuss the strategy of merger in detail. Antitrust policy is, of course, concerned with mergers that can have anticompetitive effects; hence, we shall focus on these possibilities.

First, it will be useful to classify mergers as either horizontal, vertical, or conglomerate. A horizontal merger is one between two sellers in the same market. An example would be a merger between Texaco and Exxon. Possible anticompetitive effects are quite clear since such mergers increase market concentration directly.

Of course, a horizontal merger may simultaneously increase market power and reduce costs through economies of combined operations. Williamson[15] has developed a simple model which illustrates this case.

In Figure 8-1 initial price is $P_0$ and output is $Q_0$. The degree of competition is assumed to be sufficient to force price down to $AC_0$. Now, assume that a horizontal merger takes place which creates both cost savings and market power. Hence, the postmerger equilibrium results in a price increase to $P_1$ and a cost reduction to $AC_1$. Output falls from $Q_0$ to $Q_1$.

The merger results in a deadweight loss in consumers' surplus equal to triangle $A_1$ in Figure 8-1. (Recall the discussion of deadweight loss in Chapter 6, Figure 6-9.) On the other hand, there is a gain to society as a result of the cost savings, which is shown by the rectangle $A_2$ in Figure 8-1. That is, $A_2$ represents the cost savings in producing output $Q_1$ at an average cost of $AC_1$ rather than $AC_0$.

Hence, the argument could be made that the antitrust authority should compare the loss of $A_1$ with the gain of $A_2$. If $A_2$ exceeds $A_1$, the merger should be permitted, but not otherwise. As we shall see, in the United States antitrust policymakers ignore any possible cost savings and direct their attention solely to the potential anticompetitive effects. We might note that antitrust authorities

---

[14] *U.S. v. United Shoe Manufacturing Corporation,* 110 F. Supp. 295 (1953).
[15] Oliver Williamson, "Economies as an Antitrust Defense: The Welfare Tradeoffs," *American Economic Review,* March 1968.

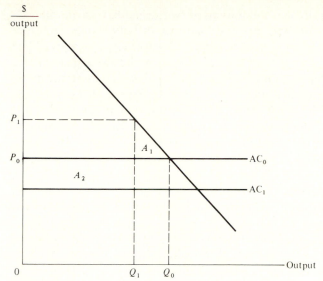

**FIGURE 8-1**
Benefits ($A_2$) and costs ($A_1$) to society of horizontal merger.

in some other countries, such as the United Kingdom, do attempt to weigh the gains against the losses before making a decision on the legality of a merger.

Many experts believe that ignoring the cost savings does not constitute a serious failure of American antitrust policy, however. It is believed that such horizontal mergers rarely yield substantial cost savings. Also, firms that are forbidden to merge can usually achieve the potential economies through internal growth.

Vertical mergers join two firms that have a customer-supplier relationship. A cement manufacturer acquiring a ready-mix concrete company would be an example of a vertical merger. Possible anticompetitive effects are not obvious, although we can mention a few possibilities that have been raised in antitrust proceedings. It has been suggested that a vertical merger can extend market power from one stage of an industry to another. Of course, if such market power exists, one might argue that it should be the antitrust target.

Another anticompetitive possibility is that a series of vertical mergers may raise entry barriers. The idea is that if all cement manufacturers and ready-mix concrete firms merged, a new entrant could no longer enter one business alone but would have to enter both levels simultaneously. This would require larger capital requirements than it would to enter cement or concrete alone.[16]

---

[16] We should also mention the so-called theory of foreclosure. The theory is unclear as to how it harms competition, but it is popular among judges. For example, Chief Justice Warren of the Supreme Court held that a lessening of competition in a vertical merger arises "primarily from a foreclosure." That is to say, does the acquisition of a customer by a supplier foreclose other suppliers from a portion of the market? For a strong criticism of this theory, see Robert H. Bork, "Vertical Integration and Competitive Processes," in J. Fred Weston and Sam Peltzman (eds.), *Public Policy toward Mergers* (Pacific Palisades, Calif.: Goodyear Publishing Co., 1969).

Conglomerate mergers involve the joining of two firms that are completely unrelated to each other. An example would be a merger between an insurance company and a baking company. Possible anticompetitive effects are even less obvious for this case than for vertical mergers. We can cite the argument that appears to be most important in antitrust cases. This is that conglomerate mergers can eliminate potential competition. The merger of Procter & Gamble and Clorox is an example. While Procter & Gamble was not previously in the household bleach market, the government argued that it was a potential entrant, and this threat of entry kept the price of bleach low. When Procter & Gamble acquired Clorox, this threat of potential competition was eliminated.

As noted earlier, the Celler-Kefauver Act of 1950 amended section 7 of the original Clayton Act. The amended Section 7 states that no merger can take place where "the effect of such acquisition may be substantially to lessen competition, or to tend to create a monopoly." The new Section 7, having filled a legal loophole which had made the 1914 version ineffective, has been enforced vigorously, and over 300 cases had been initiated by 1976.

The courts have interpreted the language above to mean that horizontal and vertical mergers involving even relatively small market-shares are unlawful. For example, the first major government victory under new Section 7 concerned two steel producers. A merger between Bethlehem Steel, with 16.3 percent of the national market, and Youngstown Sheet and Tube Company, with 4.6 percent, was held to be illegal.[17]

The first Supreme Court decision under new Section 7, the 1962 *Brown Shoe* case,[18] involved both horizontal and vertical merger elements. Brown Shoe Company was the fourth largest shoe manufacturer in 1955, with about 4 percent of national production. Its partner in the merger, G. R. Kinney Company, had about 0.5 percent. Each had similarly small national shares of shoe retailing.

The Brown-Kinney merger was held to be unlawful. In its opinion, the Court stressed the legislative history of Section 7. The dominant motivation of Congress, according to the Court, was to arrest a "rising tide of economic concentration in the American economy" and to stop mergers at a time when this trend "was still in its incipiency."

Perhaps the simplest way to sum up the law toward horizontal and vertical mergers is to reproduce the Justice Department's 1968 "merger guidelines."[19] These guidelines indicate the market-shares that the Justice Department applies in deciding whether to challenge a merger. Accordingly, horizontal mergers in industries with four-firm concentration ratios of 75 percent or more will be challenged if they involve the following market shares:

[17] *U.S. v. Bethlehem Steel Corp. et al.*, 168 F. Supp. 576 (1958).
[18] *Brown Shoe Company v. U.S.*, 370 U.S. 294 (1962).
[19] U.S. Department of Justice, *Merger Guidelines*, May 30, 1968.

| Acquiring firm, % | Acquired firm, % |
|---|---|
| 4 | 4 or more |
| 10 | 2 or more |
| 15 | 1 or more |

If the concentration ratio is less than 75 percent, the following market shares apply:

| Acquiring firm, % | Acquired firm, % |
|---|---|
| 5 | 5 or more |
| 10 | 4 or more |
| 15 | 3 or more |
| 20 | 2 or more |
| 25 or more | 1 or more |

Vertical mergers involving a supplying firm with 10 percent of the market and purchases of 6 percent or more by the customer will be challenged.

The effect of the tough antitrust policy toward horizontal and vertical mergers is easily seen in American merger trends. Over the period 1948–1953 horizontal and vertical mergers accounted for about 50 percent of all assets acquired in the manufacturing and mining sectors. The corresponding figure for 1973–1977 was only 21 percent.[20] The mirror image of this is, of course, that conglomerate mergers have accounted for a substantially increasing share of all mergers.

As noted earlier, the most important argument against conglomerate mergers has been that they eliminate potential competition.[21] In a 1974 case the Supreme Court tried to define when the elimination of potential competition would render a conglomerate merger unlawful. Thus, a merger may be in violation

if the target market is substantially concentrated, if the acquiring firm has the characteristics, capabilities, and economic incentive to render it a perceived potential *de novo* entrant, and if the acquiring firm's pre-merger presence on the fringe of the target market in fact tempered oligopolistic behavior on the part of existing participants in that market.[22]

The problem of meeting this difficult burden of proof has apparently led to a series of defeats by the government in recent conglomerate merger cases.[23] Hence, antitrust policy toward conglomerate mergers is not nearly as tough as it is toward horizontal and vertical mergers.

[20] F. M. Scherer, *Industrial Market Structure and Economic Performance*, p. 124.
[21] For an analysis of other arguments that have been raised against conglomerates, see Peter O. Steiner, *Mergers* (Ann Arbor: University of Michigan Press, 1975).
[22] *U.S. v. Marine Bancorporation et al.*, 418 U.S. 624 (1974).
[23] Joseph F. Brodley, "Potential Competition Mergers: A Structural Synthesis," *Yale Law Journal*, November 1977.

This concludes our discussion of antitrust policy. Unfortunately, because of space constraints we could only sketch current policy in three areas: price fixing, monopolization, and mergers. We now turn to a short survey of regulation.

### REGULATION[24]

So far we have been concerned with antitrust policy. One can view antitrust policy as a set of rules designed to make the competitive market system work better. Regulation, on the contrary, may be conceived of as a set of direct controls by the government designed to supplant market forces in cases where competition does not appear to work well.

The first significant regulation of business in the United States began in 1887 with the passage of the Act to Regulate Commerce. This act established the Interstate Commerce Commission (ICC) and empowered it to regulate the railroads. An important reason for the creation of the ICC was to curb the monopoly power of the railroads and end the highly discriminatory railroad freight rate structure that existed at that time. The act made it illegal to discriminate among customers, to charge more for short hauls than for long, and to practice secret, collusive price cutting.

In ensuing years the original legislation was amended and broadened. As trucking became an important competitive force in the 1930s, it was brought under ICC jurisdiction. In the 1930s, direct regulation by the federal government spread to other industries, including electric power, telephone and telegraph, natural gas pipelines, and air transportation. This so-called economic regulation was generally concerned with such economic factors as rate levels, rate structures, and entry and exit by firms in those industries. Similar regulation by states began even earlier. For example, Wisconsin and New York began regulating electric power in 1907.

In the past 15 years another kind of regulation has grown rapidly. This social regulation has not been concerned directly with economic factors such as industry profit rates and entry and exit but rather with objectives such as safety, health, and pollution control. Social regulation has existed for selected industries since the turn of the century, beginning with the Food and Drug Act of 1906. In recent years, however, new agencies have been established, e.g., the Environmental Protection Agency, the Occupational Safety and Health Administration, and the Consumer Product Safety Commission. These agencies have been given broad discretionary power to set safety and environmental standards for industrial firms and to undertake other policy actions to further these goals.

In Table 8-1 we have attempted to provide a representative listing of economic and social regulatory agencies and the targets of their regulatory activi-

---

[24] Some of the material in this section is based on Henry G. Grabowski and John M. Vernon, *The Impact of Regulation on Industrial Innovation* (Washington, D.C.: National Academy of Sciences, 1979).

**TABLE 8-1**
REPRESENTATIVE ECONOMIC AND SOCIAL REGULATORY AGENCIES

| Agency (year of establishment) | Regulatory target |
|---|---|
| **Economic regulation** | |
| Interstate Commerce Commission (1887) | Railroads, motor carriers, water carriers, oil pipelines |
| Federal Energy Regulatory Commission (1934) | Electric power, natural gas pipelines and field prices |
| Federal Communications Commission (1934) | Telephone and telegraph, radio and television broadcasting |
| Civil Aeronautics Board (1938) | Airlines |
| State regulatory commissions | Electric power, natural gas, telephone, buses, motor carriers |
| **Social regulation** | |
| Food and Drug Administration (1906) | Food, drug, and medical devices safety |
| Environmental Protection Agency (1970) | Air and water pollution, industrial chemicals and pesticide safety |
| Occupational Safety and Health Administration (1970) | Safety of working conditions |
| Consumer Product Safety Commission(1972) | Safety of consumer products |

ties. The table makes it clear that regulation is a major governmental enterprise and one that cannot be easily described in the space available here. Nevertheless, we hope to provide the reader with an overview of regulation and an appreciation for its variety of forms.

## Rationale for Regulation

In analyzing the rationale for government regulation, it is necessary to consider the nature of the "market failure" which regulation is designed to correct. Hence, we shall review briefly the sources of market failure that have been used to justify regulation.

At one extreme is the case of "natural" monopoly. This involves the situation in which average cost declines over the relevant range of market demand so that a single firm represents the most cost-efficient market solution. Rather than let such a firm achieve monopoly prices and profits, regulation to permit only a "fair" rate of return is often advocated. This is the approach taken in most traditional public utility situations, such as local telephone service, and the distribution of electric power and natural gas.

Figure 8-2 shows the natural monopoly situation. An unregulated monopolist would maximize profit where marginal revenue MR equals long-run marginal cost LRMC, or at price $P_0$. The efficient price for society is, of course, where the demand curve intersects LRMC, or price $P_2$. The problem is that if the regulator required the monopolist to set price at $P_2$, the firm would sustain a loss (long-run average cost LRAC exceeds price when price is set at $P_2$).

To avoid losses, average cost pricing can be used, i.e., setting price at $P_1$. Output is still less than efficiency requires; however, it exceeds the unregulated monopoly output level. Alternatively, price discrimination can be used to approximate more closely the marginal cost pricing result (e.g., charging higher prices for the initial blocks of output than for later blocks).

Sometimes rate regulation and entry restrictions are advocated not to curb excessive monopoly power or overcome inadequate competition but rather to prevent cutthroat competition. It is argued that competition by firms in highly capital-intensive industries with high fixed costs and immobile capital is prone to dynamic instability in which prices and output fluctuate widely, resulting in excessive costs to producers and consumers. This type of market situation was thought by some advocates of regulation to be characteristic of the transportation industries. However, most economists would agree that destructive competition of this sort has been rare historically, and there are few, if any, current circumstances in which regulation is warranted to prevent firms from engaging in too much competition.

Regulation is often instituted to remedy the problem of "externalities." Environmental pollution provides a classic example of external side effects that are not captured directly in market prices. Consider a competitive industry that dumps significant waste products into nearby rivers. In Figure 8-3 two horizontal schedules are shown. The schedule APC represents average private cost, and ASC indicates the level of average social cost. The ASC schedule includes

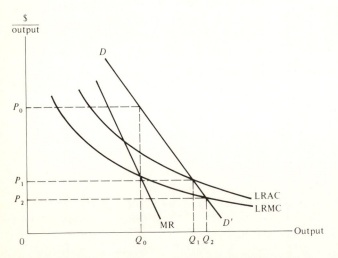

**FIGURE8-2**
Natural monopoly.

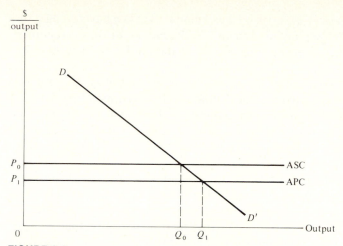

**FIGURE 8-3**
Private and social costs and competitive equilibrium.

APC plus the average cost arising from pollution of the river (costs imposed on downstream water users).

In the absence of governmental intervention the industry's equilibrium will be at price $P_1$ and output $Q_1$. The efficient price and output from society's viewpoint, of course, should be $P_0$ and $Q_0$. In a sense, the industry is selling its products at an artificially cheap price since it does not have to take the pollution costs into account. The government could remedy the situation by imposing a unit tax on the industry equal to the difference between ASC and APC. This would "internalize" the externality.

Another type of market failure that has been used to rationalize government regulation is "information imperfections." This underlies most consumer-protection regulation. For example, the Food and Drug Administration has been given the responsibility to screen all new drugs on grounds of safety and efficacy before they can be made available to the public. In effect, a regulatory agency has been empowered to prohibit or restrict certain voluntary market transactions. Presumably, these transactions are expected to lead to losses in consumer welfare that might occur in the absence of regulation as a result of imperfect information provided to consumers. A similar rationale underlies the activities of the Consumer Product Safety Commission and the Occupational Safety and Health Administration.

In addition to these considerations concerning economic efficiency, government regulation often becomes a mechanism for redistribution of income. Thus, for example, rate regulation often leads to cross-subsidization in which prices are set below costs for some services or markets and the resulting losses are made up by the profits from some other market or services. Telephone service to rural areas provides an example of such cross-subsidization. Common-carrier obligations in transportation furnish another commonly cited example.

Our discussion so far can be criticized as being naive. We have implied that regulation is supplied in response to demand by the public for the correction of market failures. This is sometimes referred to as the public-interest theory of regulation.

While the public-interest theory is undeniably important, it is deficient as a general explanation for the existence of regulation. It is assumed that the existence of market failure is sufficient to generate a demand for regulation, although no mechanism is presented by which the demand is made effective. In effect, the good demanded (regulation) is assumed to be supplied costlessly by the political process.

The failure of the public-interest theory to explain which industries are likely to be regulated has been noted by Posner. He observes that "few, if any, responsible students of the airline industry, for example, believe that there is some intrinsic peculiarity about the market for air transportation that requires prices and entry to be fixed by government. The same may be said for trucking, taxi service, stock brokerage, ocean shipping, and many other heavily regulated industries."[25]

The capture theory of regulation was developed in an attempt to overcome the obvious deficiencies of the public-interest theory. It holds that regulation is supplied in response to the demands of interest groups struggling among themselves to maximize the incomes of their members. Thus, the capture theory treats regulation as a good—the use of government to control entry or fix prices—often demanded by the industry itself for its own benefit and supplied by politicians in return for votes and campaign contributions.

To illustrate the capture theory more concretely, consider Stigler's example of state regulation of weight limits on trucks.[26] Briefly, the trucking industry had emerged as a significant competitor of the railroads by 1930. Stigler hypothesized that the railroads would use their political influence to get states to limit the size of trucks that competed with them and that these limits would vary across states in accordance with the opposing political power of the trucking industry. Thus, for example, in states with many trucks used in agriculture, the farmers would use their influence to obtain higher limits on truck size. Stigler's statistical analysis confirmed this expectation.

Neither theory of regulation is complete. For example, the capture theory does not seem to explain adequately the recent airline deregulation. It also does not appear useful in explaining the emerging new social regulation. Taken together, however, the two theories caution us against taking too simplistic a view of why regulation exists.

---

[25] Richard A. Posner, "Theories of Economic Regulation," *Bell Journal of Economics and Management Science,* Autumn 1974, p. 336.

[26] George J. Stigler, "The Theory of Economic Regulation," *Bell Journal of Economics and Management Science,* Spring 1971.

**Benefits and Costs of Regulation**

The public-interest theory suggests that there are many sound reasons to expect substantial benefits from government regulation. However, regulation obviously entails costs as well as benefits. The most direct and visible costs of regulation are the public expenditures to support the administrative activities of the regulatory agency. Frequently, these are small compared to the value of economic activities under the regulatory agency's control. Because the agency has the power to significantly alter or constrain the decisions made by the regulated firm and its consumers, the overall costs to society resulting from regulation can far exceed the direct administrative costs of operating the regulatory agency.

While earlier advocates of regulation assumed implicitly that government regulation would provide net positive benefits to society, a number of recent studies have demonstrated persuasively that this is not necessarily so. In particular, these studies have pointed to a number of regulatory situations in which the costs to society far exceed the apparent benefits.[27] In some cases, the rationale for regulation appears sound, but regulatory procedures and processes have not been very successful in achieving the intended benefits. In other cases, because of dynamic changes over time in technology or economic factors, the original rationale for regulation no longer applies, but the process continues in an inefficient or imperfect manner. Finally, in other circumstances the application of regulation appears to have been poorly conceived or misguided from the outset.

By the mid-1970s, a considerable movement toward regulatory reform and deregulation had been initiated. A central aspect of this reform movement was federal regulation of transportation: ICC regulation of trucking and Civil Aeronautics Board (CAB) regulation of airlines. The consensus of economists studying these industries is that far from benefiting consumers and the public, the rate-setting and entry-restriction policies of the ICC and CAB had imposed significant net costs on consumers in the form of higher prices for air and surface transportation. One study of surface transportation put the net annual cost of ICC regulation at between $4 billion and $9 billion.[28] Moreover, no convincing market-failure rationale for continued regulation of these industries has been demonstrated by the supporters of regulation. In light of these findings, economists have almost unanimously concluded that society would be better off if regulatory controls over prices and entry were removed from the airline and trucking industries.

Recently, a number of evaluative studies and cost-benefit analyses of regula-

---

[27] A survey of many of these studies is contained in Henry G. Grabowski and John M. Vernon, *The Impact of Regulation on Innovation,* chaps. 3 and 4.

[28] T. G. Moore, "Deregulating Surface Freight Transportation," in A. Phillips (ed.), *Promoting Competition in Regulated Markets* (Washington, D.C.: Brookings Institution, 1975).

tion for safety and environmental goals have been conducted. These have un-covered many instances of unsatisfactory regulatory performance. In particu-lar, they point to the large costs to the private sector as well as lengthy delays in achieving the intended social benefits of regulatory policies. These experiences also have spawned a number of policy recommendations for changes in the cur-rent regulatory process in the safety and environmental areas. One prominent thrust of such proposals is to place greater emphasis on policy measures that at-tempt to utilize economic incentives to achieve social objectives, e.g., effluent fees in pollution control. This approach could be substituted in many circum-stances for current regulatory procedures that rely mainly on bureaucratic con-trols and standards. While such an approach has considerable analytical appeal and the support of certain policymaking groups, it has not yet progressed much beyond the proposal stage.

One of the long-term, more subtle costs of regulation is its possible effect as a disincentive to innovation. In enacting regulations, no consideration is usually given to the effects of the regulations on innovation. This is particularly the case in the Food and Drug Administration (FDA) regulation of pharmaceu-tical products. We conclude our survey of regulation with a detailed case study of FDA regulatory practice to illustrate some of these points.

## FDA Regulation of Pharmaceuticals

Government regulation of pharmaceuticals started in 1906 and has since evolved into a very stringent system of premarket controls over the develop-ment and introduction of new drugs. While early regulation was directed at pat-ent medicine abuses, the sulfanilamide tragedy in 1938 led to passage of the Food, Drug, and Cosmetic Act, which required FDA approval of all new drugs as "safe" before they could be marketed. Then, in 1962, as the disastrous effects of thalidomide were becoming apparent in Europe, the Kefauver-Harris amendments were passed. This law extended FDA controls to the clinical test-ing and development process of new drug compounds. In addition, manufac-turers were required to demonstrate the therapeutic efficacy as well as safety of a new drug prior to obtaining FDA approval.

The fact that new drugs can cause serious unforeseen toxic side effects as well as provide therapeutic benefits is the legislative justification for these strong regulatory controls. At the same time, however, the regulatory decision-making process at the FDA has been characterized by a concern for safety only. As FDA Bureau of Drugs Director Richard Crout has indicated:

> I would emphasize very strongly that the Food and Drug Administration regulates health policy, not economic matters. That is terribly important to understand. We do not pay any attention to the economic consequences of our decisions and the law does not ask us to.[29]

---

[29] J. R. Crout, "Discussion," in R. B. Helms (ed.), *Drug Development and Marketing* (Washing-ton, D.C.: American Enterprise Institute, 1975), p. 196.

While few would question the need for regulatory controls over drug safety and the clinical investigation process, it is important to recognize that society also receives important health benefits from new drug innovation. The pharmaceutical industry has been the source of over 90 percent of the new drug therapies or new chemical entities (NCEs) introduced in the United States since 1950. The industry has also discovered a correspondingly high percentage of those NCEs classified as important therapeutic advances by the FDA and other evaluators.[30]

As the regulatory control of this industry has become more stringent since 1962, a number of adverse trends in pharmaceutical innovation have become increasingly apparent. These include:

**1** *Increased costs and lower yields on new drug introductions:* A recent study by Ronald Hansen indicates that the average cost of introducing an NCE in the United States is now over $50 million.[31] In addition, the average time to develop and gain FDA approval for an NCE is now between 8 and 10 years. This is over an order of magnitude higher than cost estimates for the early 1960s. A number of studies have further analyzed the costs versus sales revenues from recent NCE introductions and have found relatively low average yields on R&D drug investment.[32]

**2** *Declining rates of new product introductions:* The annual rate of new drug introductions in the United States has fallen to less than one-third the rate that existed in the early 1960s. Moreover, an analysis of total market-shares captured by new drug products indicates that these shares have fallen at a comparable rate.[33] This underscores the extent to which new product innovations have declined as a competitive factor in the drug industry.

**3** *Declining growth rates for domestic R&D and shifts in R&D abroad:* In contrast to the very high rates of growth in drug industry R&D activity that characterized the earlier post-World War II period, R&D outlays in real terms have experienced little if any growth in the 1970s. In addition, an increasing percentage of R&D supported by American firms is now done abroad. A recent study shows that roughly one-third of all American-owned NCEs are now first investigated clinically abroad, where clinical investigations are permitted at an earlier stage.[34]

**4** *NCE introductions available abroad before the United States:* Professor William Wardell, a clinical pharmacologist, has documented many cases in

---

[30] David Schwartzman, *Innovation in the Pharmaceutical Industry* (Baltimore: Johns Hopkins University Press, 1976).

[31] Ronald W. Hansen, "The Pharmaceutical Development Process: Estimates of Current Development Costs and Times and the Effects of Regulatory Changes," in R. I. Chien (ed.), *Issues in Pharmaceutical Economics* (Cambridge, Mass.: Lexington, 1979).

[32] David Schwartzman, *The Expected Return from Pharmaceutical Research* (Washington, D.C.: American Enterprise Institute, 1975).

[33] Henry G. Grabowski and John M. Vernon, "Consumer Protection Regulation in Ethical Drugs," *American Economic Review*, February 1977.

[34] William M. Wardell, et al., "The Rate of Development of New Drugs in the United States," *Clinical Pharmacology and Therapeutics*, May 1978.

which new drugs developed abroad (and even many American drugs first introduced abroad) generally take several additional years to gain FDA approval for use in the United States.[35] Wardell's findings are consistent with an analysis of the international diffusion of new drug therapies across four countries (the United States, United Kingdom, France, and Germany). Specifically, Wardell found that a majority of all the new chemical-entity drug introductions into the United States over the period 1965–1975 had a prior introduction in the United Kingdom, France, or Germany. Moreover, if one considers only the 27 new drugs introduced in this period that were specifically classified by the FDA in 1974 as important therapeutic advances, 15 had prior introduction in one of these foreign countries, 8 became available here and abroad in the same year, and only 4 were available here first. This was true despite the fact that the majority of these therapeutically important drugs were discovered in American research laboratories.[36]

Increased regulation has not been responsible for all these adverse trends in the pharmaceutical industry. Other factors, both scientific and economic, have had important effects on pharmaceutical innovation in recent periods. However, a number of studies have concluded that regulation has been one of the more important factors. The most persuasive evidence that this is the case comes from comparative international studies that analyze drug costs and innovation here and abroad over similar periods.

At the present time, FDA officials do not have much incentive to be concerned about possible negative impacts of their policies on innovation. As Dr. Crout's statements above emphasize, the regulatory mandate is drawn in rather narrow terms—to protect consumers against unsafe or ineffective drugs. There is no corresponding mandate dealing with drug innovation or in particular with the need for improved medical therapy.

In addition, the incentive structure confronting the FDA regulator is strongly asymmetric. The regulator stands to bear heavy personal costs if there is a bad outcome associated with the approval of a drug with unforeseen adverse effects. On the other hand, the social costs associated with time delays in obtaining important new drug therapies and lower rates of innovation are less visible and are borne completely by external parties. Hence, the regulator has strong incentives to be risk-averse and err on the side of caution and delay.

In the final analysis, the attitudes of and organizational incentives operating on regulatory officials will have a key influence on how regulation affects drug innovation and the supply of new medicines for treating health problems in this country. Accordingly, if Congress wishes to encourage a more balanced decision-making process, it should consider some institutional mechanisms that give greater weight to the effects of regulation on innovation.

[35] William M. Wardell and L. Lasagna, *Regulation and Drug Development* (Washington, D.C.: American Enterprise Institute, 1975).

[36] Henry G. Grabowski and John M. Vernon, "Consumer Product Safety Regulation," *American Economic Review*, May 1978.

We should stress that while we have discussed FDA regulation of the pharmaceutical industry, there are parallel examples in other industries. For example, the EPA must approve new industrial chemicals and pesticides before they can be marketed. Also, the FDA must approve new medical devices, such as CAT scanners and pacemakers, before marketing.

## QUESTIONS AND PROBLEMS

**8-1** "The conscious parallelism doctrine is fundamentally flawed. The problem is basically a structural one that can be remedied only be dissolution of the oligopolistic firms." Discuss.

**8-2** To be found guilty of monopolization, what is necessary in addition to a large market-share?

**8-3** In a famous antitrust case, a key issue was market definition. Should aluminum foil, waxed paper, and polyethylene be included with cellophane or not? DuPont sold almost all the cellophane, and so a finding that the market was cellophane only would make them guilty of monopolization. The Supreme Court accepted the broader market definition, however, based on testimony that the cross-elasticities of demand at existing prices among cellophane, foil, waxed paper, etc., were "high." Do you agree with the Court in finding DuPont innocent (despite the fact that DuPont had very high profits on cellophane) by accepting the broader market definition?

**8-4** A horizontal merger in the United States is likely to be challenged by antitrust authorities if it involves large market-shares even if large cost savings are expected. Is this approach consistent with economic efficiency?

**8-5** "In an economy devoid of monopoly power, the competitive forces of the capital market should tend to bring the rate of return on investment in all industries into a state of equality, except for risks. In such a workably competitive economy, no firm, irrespective of the number of individual product markets in which it may be engaged, would be in a position to 'unfairly' subsidize one of its products from profits earned on other products." What does this mean in relation to the problem of the conglomerate mergers?

**8-6** "There is a basic dilemma in the public utility regulation. If a regulatory commission is alert and diligent in defense of the consumer, the utility company will have no incentive to increase profits by improving efficiency, for such increases will soon be taken away through mandatory rate reductions. On the other hand, if the commission is passive and ineffectual, the company will have plenty of incentive to increase efficiency, but none of the fruits of increased efficiency will be passed on to consumers." Explain. How might this dilemma be resolved?

**8-7** The United States has recently established a regulatory body, the Consumer Product Safety Commission, to set product safety standards and labeling requirements for any product class in which it finds a "safety" problem. Contrast such a regulatory approach to product safety with a liability system enforced through private legal actions. Discuss the nature of costs and benefits that might be expected from either approach.

## BIBLIOGRAPHY

Averch, H. A., and L. L. Johnson: "Behavior of the Firm under Regulatory Constraint," *American Economic Review,* December 1962.

Demsetz, H.: "Why Regulate Utilities?" *Journal of Law and Economics,* April 1968.

Kahn, A.: *The Economics of Regulation* (New York: John Wiley, 1970).

Posner, R. A.: *Antitrust Law: An Economic Perspective* (Chicago: University of Chicago Press, 1976).

Scherer, F. M.: *Industrial Market Structure and Economic Performance,* 2d ed. (Chicago: Rand McNally, 1980).

Schmalensee, R.: *The Control of Natural Monopolies* (Lexington, Mass.: Heath, 1979).

Stigler, George J.: "The Theory of Economic Regulation," *Bell Journal of Economics and Management Science,* Spring 1971.

PART **FOUR**

# CAPITAL BUDGETING AND RISK ANALYSIS

# CAPITAL BUDGETING

## INTRODUCTION

In this chapter we shall take up investment decisions, or as this topic is usually termed, capital budgeting. Investment decisions may be defined as expenditures for projects that have effects on revenues and costs for periods of at least one year or more. A clear example is the decision to build a new steel plant. However, expenditures for research and development (R&D) and for advertising are often considered as investments. In fact, we shall use R&D investment in the pharmaceutical industry as a detailed example of capital budgeting.

In this chapter we shall restrict ourselves to investment decisions under conditions of complete certainty. In Chapter 10 we shall extend capital budgeting to include risk and uncertainty.

As a specific illustration of a capital budget, the International Telephone and Telegraph Company (ITT) reported in a recent annual report that its capital expenditures amounted to $618 million. A large part of these expenditures went for its major expansion of communication transmission systems and for pulp and cellulose capacity. ITT also reported that approximately $75 million was invested in pollution-abatement equipment. Hence, the major questions to be addressed in this chapter concern the economic principles involved in setting the overall capital budget and selecting the particular projects to be included in the budget.

The key ingredient in capital budgeting is the explicit treatment of time and interest rates. Investment of dollars takes place today, but revenues are not generated until future years. How are we to compare future dollars with present dollars? Of course, the answer has to do with interest rates, and we shall illustrate these points with simple examples in the next section. Following this treatment of fundamentals of present-value calculations, succeeding sections will deal with project selection criteria in greater depth. A final section will discuss the concept and measurement of the firm's cost of capital.

### PRESENT-VALUE FUNDAMENTALS

Consider the hypothetical XYZ Corporation. The following assumptions are made:

**1** The assets of XYZ generate a stream of profits of $1,000 annually with perfect certainty. Taxes, depreciation, etc., do not exist.

**2** The rate of inflation in this economy is zero.

**3** The market rate of interest in this economy is 8 percent.

**4** The XYZ Corporation is financed entirely with common stock, and all profits are paid out as cash dividends.

The first question we ask is, "What is the market value $V$ of the XYZ Corporation?" That is, what is the value of all of the common stock? Think of an investor who owns all the common stock of XYZ. The stock entitles the investor to a stream of $1,000 receipts. In tabular form, the investor is the owner of the following stream of dividends:

| Dollars to be received | At end of year number |
|:----------------------:|:---------------------:|
| 1,000 | 1 |
| 1,000 | 2 |
| 1,000 | 3 |
| 1,000 | 4 |
| 1,000 | 5 |
| • | • |
| • | • |
| • | • |

Why is $V$ not simply the sum of all of the $1,000 dividend payments? Of course, the answer is that one cannot add up dollars receivable at different points in time. It would be like adding up apples and oranges. A dollar to be received next year is worth less than a dollar in hand today, and this is true even though the rate of inflation is zero. The reason is that the dollar in hand today could be placed at interest and would be worth more than $1 next year. In particular, given that the interest rate is 8 percent, $1 today could grow to $1.08 next year. Conversely, 92.6 cents today would grow to $1 next year if placed at interest. In principle, a promise of $1 to be received in one year could be taken to the bank and exchanged for 92.6 cents. This makes it clear why 92.6 cents is referred to as the present value (or present discounted value) of the $1 due in one year. In general, future dollars must be reduced in value, or discounted, to obtain their values in present dollars. We now turn to a discussion of the precise calculations.

Using $D_t$ to represent the dividend amount to be received at the end of the $t$th year and $i$ for the rate of interest, consider first the present value of $D_1$:

*Present Value of $D_1 = D_1/(1 + i)$*

**Proof:** Place $D_1/(1 + i)$ at interest today, and it will grow to

$$\frac{D_1}{1 + i} \cdot (1 + i) = D_1 \text{ in one year}$$

The numerical example is $1,000/(1 + .08) = $925.93. Thus, put $925.93 in the bank at 8 percent, and it will be worth $1,000 at the end of the year.

*Present Value of $D_2 = D_2/(1 + i)^2$*

**Proof:** Place $D_2/(1 + i)^2$ at interest today, and it will be worth

$$\frac{D_2}{(1 + i)^2} \cdot (1 + i) \text{ after one year}$$

Leaving this value at interest for the second year produces

$$\frac{D_2}{(1 + i)^2} \cdot (1 + i) \cdot (1 + i) = D_2$$

Numerically, $1,000/(1 + .08)^2 = $857.34. Deposit $857.34 today, and it will grow to $925.93 after one year. Leaving the $925.93 in the bank for a second year results in the $1,000.

*Present Value of $D_3 = D_3/(1 + i)^3$*
The general argument should be clear. Hence, the formula for the total present value of the stream of dividends can be written as

$$V = \frac{D_1}{1 + i} + \frac{D_2}{(1 + i)^2} + \frac{D_3}{(1 + i)^3} + \ldots \ldots \tag{9-1}$$

$$= \sum_{t=1}^{\infty} \frac{D_t}{(1 + i)^t}$$

Although at first glance it appears that computing $V$ is not possible because of the infinite number of terms, it can be shown[1] that the formula reduces to

$$V = \frac{D}{i} \quad \text{for} \quad D_1 = D_2 = D_3 = \ldots = D \tag{9-2}$$

Hence, for the special case of the dividends all being of the same amount, the value $V$ of the XYZ Corporation is simple to calculate. In particular,

$$V = \frac{\$1,000}{.08} = \$12,500$$

That this is correct can be seen below. Clearly, the present values of dividends get smaller and smaller as the year of receipts gets further and further into the future. One can easily infer that beyond some future year the present values will become zero for all practical purposes.

| Present value of $1,000 (at 8 percent) | Received at end of year number |
|---|---|
| $925.93 | 1 |
| 857.34 | 2 |
| 793.83 | 3 |
| 735.03 | 4 |
| 680.58 | 5 |
| 630.17 | 6 |
| 583.49 | 7 |
| 540.27 | 8 |
| 500.25 | 9 |
| 463.19 | 10 |
| 428.88 | 11 |
| 397.11 | 12 |
| 367.70 | 13 |
| . | . |
| . | . |
| . | . |

Total   $12,500.

There is another way to verify the commonsense meaning of equation (9-2). Observe that an investor should be indifferent between owning XYZ Corporation, entitling the investor to a stream of $1,000 annual receipts, and

---

[1] For proof see W. J. Baumol, *Economic Theory and Operations Analysis*, 4th ed. (Englewood Cliffs, N.J.: Prentice-Hall, 1977), p. 600.

owning a savings account in the bank which pays $1,000 interest per year. Since the interest rate is 8 percent, the investor would need $12,500 on deposit to yield $1,000 annually. Hence, it is clear that in an economy in which the interest rate is 8 percent, competition in the capital market would cause the market value of XYZ to be $12,500 also. Under our strong assumptions, investors would perceive ownership of the XYZ Corporation and ownership of a $12,500 savings account as perfect substitutes.

Table 4 (at end of book) gives the present value of $1 to be received at the end of $n$ periods. To calculate the present value for an amount other than $1, one simply multiplies that amount by the present value of $1.

### Example

Find the present value of $500 to be received at the end of 10 years, where $i = 10$ percent. In Table 4 find the present value of $1 to be .386. Hence, the answer is $(.386)(\$500) = \$193$.

Table 5 (at end of book) gives the present value of a stream of $1 receipts for $n$ periods. To calculate the present value for a stream of receipts other than $1, one simply multiplies that stream by the present value of the stream of $1 receipts.

### Example

Find the present value of a stream of $20 receipts over a period of five years, where $i = 8$ percent. In Table 5 find the present value of a stream of $1 receipts to be 3.993. Hence, the answer is $(3.993)(\$20) = \$79.86$.

Having described how the market value of XYZ is determined, we now consider the basic question of evaluation of a particular investment project. Given the assumption that the objective is to make the market value of the firm as high as possible, the net present value (NPV) criterion becomes quite simple.

An investment project can be conceived of as a stream of cash payments and receipts, or positive and negative cash flows. Since these flows occur over time, we calculate their net present value, or NPV. If NPV is positive, the project should be accepted because it will increase the market value of the firm. Conversely, if NPV is negative, the project would reduce the market value of the firm and should be rejected.

The general formula[2] is

$$\text{NPV} = \sum_{t=0}^{T} \frac{R_t - C_t}{(1 + i)^t} \qquad (9\text{-}3)$$

---

[2] It is assumed that revenues and costs are *cash* receipts and disbursements. This avoids problems of accounting that are beyond the scope of this book. Depreciation expense, for example, is not a cash expenditure, but it does affect the firm's tax payments, which are cash outflows.

Tables 4 and 5 at the end of the book can be used to ease the problem of computing present values.

where NPV = net present value

$R_t$ = revenues received in year $t$

$C_t$ = costs paid for in year $t$

$i$ = rate of interest

$T$ = last year in life of project

As an example, suppose the XYZ Corporation is considering investment in project A, which has the following estimated revenues and costs.

| Revenue, $ | Costs, $ | Year of occurrence |
|---|---|---|
| – | 1,000 | 0 |
| 600 | 500 | 1 |
| 1,200 | – | 2 |

The costs, as is usual for investment activities, take place in the early years, while the revenues take place primarily in the later years. The NPV of project A is easily computed (costs are entered as negative cash flows):

$$\text{NPV} = -1,000 + \frac{100}{1 + .08} + \frac{1,200}{(1 + .08)^2}$$
$$= -1,000 + 93 + 1,029 = \$122$$

Hence, NPV is positive and increases the value of the XYZ Corporation. Notice that the interest rate used is crucial. For example, suppose that the appropriate interest rate is 15 percent. The calculation then becomes

$$\text{NPV} = -1,000 + \frac{100}{1 + .15} + \frac{1,200}{(1 + .15)^2}$$
$$= -1,000 + 86 + 892 = \$-22$$

The higher interest rate would make project A no longer attractive because it would reduce the value of the XYZ Corporation by $22.

**INTERNAL RATE OF RETURN**

Given the simplifying assumptions of our example, the NPV criterion is the correct criterion. However, an alternative criterion known as the internal rate of return (IRR) generally yields the same answer as the NPV and has one advantage over the NPV. The IRR does not require the specification of an interest rate for present-value computation because the IRR is itself defined to be that interest (or discount) rate which makes NPV zero. The definitional equation is therefore

$$\sum_{t=0}^{T} \frac{R_t - C_t}{(1 + r)^t} = 0 \qquad (9\text{-}4)$$

where $r$ = internal rate of return (IRR)
$\quad R_t$ = revenues received in year $t$
$\quad C_t$ = costs paid for in year $t$
$\quad\; i$ = rate of interest
$\quad T$ = last year in life of project

One interpretation of the IRR is that it is that value of the interest rate which would just make the firm indifferent between undertaking and not undertaking the project.

To illustrate the IRR, recall the cash flows of project A. To calculate the IRR for project A, we solve the equation below for $r$:

$$-1,000 + \frac{100}{1 + r} + \frac{1,200}{(1 + r)^2} = 0$$

The answer, which can be found easily by trial and error, is approximately 14.6 percent. Hence, if the market rate of interest was 14.6 percent, NPV would equal zero and the XYZ Corporation would be indifferent about investing in project A.

The IRR is useful in summarizing the economic merit of a project entirely on the basis of its revenues and costs. Whether the project should be undertaken then depends on the comparison of the IRR with the market interest rate. Or as we shall discuss later, in more realistic situations such a market rate of interest does not exist, and the relevant comparison is with the firm's cost of capital. (Estimating the firm's cost of capital is the subject of the last section of this chapter.)

## THE CAPITAL BUDGETING PROCESS

The capital budgeting process of a corporation consists of the generation of ideas for possible investment projects (replacement of old equipment, capacity for new products, etc.), the quantification of the cash flows of those projects, the evaluation of the economic merits of the projects, and finally, the choice of the particular projects to be funded. Hence, the process involves almost every functional area in the corporation.

For example, ideas for projects can be expected to arise in the sales, production, and R&D departments. The engineering and marketing departments would be involved in estimating costs and future sales. The finance and planning departments would monitor the process and evaluate the economic merits of the projects, including how the projects should be financed (new stock issues, borrowing, retained earnings, etc.).

### A Project Evaluation Example

For an example of project evaluation, we shall consider investment in R&D in the pharmaceutical industry. The pharmaceutical industry is one of the most innovative industries and also one of the most highly regulated industries in the United States.

Competition in the pharmaceutical industry takes the form of new product innovation, although in recent years fewer new drugs have been marketed than in past years. This has caused a serious concern among both government policymakers and members of the industry. Many observers argue that a "drug lag" exists in the United States as compared with other countries and that the primary cause is the high costs imposed by the tight regulation of the industry by the Food and Drug Administration (FDA).

These high costs act to lower the IRR on new drug projects, thereby inducing pharmaceutical manufacturers to invest less in R&D in this country. David Schwartzman estimated in a 1975 study[3] that the IRR for average new drug products had fallen significantly between 1960 and 1973. Although his estimates are subject to some dispute, they provide an interesting example of project evaluation. Before turning to his study, however, we should describe briefly how regulation has had an impact on R&D costs.

In contrast to most industries, new pharmaceutical products must be approved for marketing by a government agency, the FDA. The 1962 amendments to the Food, Drug, and Cosmetic Act require that new drugs be approved for both safety and efficacy prior to marketing. This has resulted in an increase in the amount of testing that must be performed before marketing and has also added to the length of the FDA approval process.

Schwartzman's approach to the problem was to estimate what the IRR would be for an average new drug. He used aggregate industry data on R&D expenditures and sales revenues to compute average costs and sales revenues. For example, he calculated that the average 1972 sales in the United States for new drug entities introduced in 1962–1968 were $7.5 million. He then added 47 percent to that figure to obtain an estimate of average international sales. Employing various assumptions about the length of commercial life, profit margins, etc., he estimated the stream of cash flows for an average new drug product. Table 9-1 shows the resulting estimated cash flows for a 30-year period and for the case in which the IRR is calculated to be 7.5 percent. Most of the important assumptions are listed as footnotes to the table.

Although there are 30 years of cash flows in Table 9-1, the 7.5 percent IRR can be computed by a straightforward application of equation (9-4). That is, .075 is the value of $r$ in that equation that makes the sum of the present values for the 30 years precisely equal to zero.[4] Hence, if the cost of capital in the pharmaceutical industry exceeded 7.5 percent, it would not be profitable to invest in R&D.

It is important to note that the 7.5 percent IRR is an estimate of the *average* profitability of R&D, and, of course, particular firms would be expected to make calculations on the basis of detailed knowledge of individual projects.

---

[3] David Schwartzman, *The Expected Return from Pharmaceutical Research* (Washington, D.C.: American Enterprise Institute for Public Policy Research, 1975).

[4] Finding the value of $r$ manually would be an extremely laborious task, although it is in principle a relatively simple trial and error technique. A computer makes the solution quite easy.

**TABLE 9-1**
ESTIMATED STREAM OF COST OF R & D AND NET
INCOME FOR AN AVERAGE NEW DRUG YIELDING A
7.5 PERCENT RETURN
(millions of dollars)

| Year | R&D cost | Year | Net income | Year | Net income |
|------|----------|------|------------|------|------------|
| 1 | −1.22 | 11 | .64 | 21 | 1.91 |
| 2 | −1.22 | 12 | 1.27 | 22 | 1.91 |
| 3 | −1.22 | 13 | 1.91 | 23 | 1.91 |
| 4 | −1.22 | 14 | 1.91 | 24 | 1.91 |
| 5 | −1.22 | 15 | 1.91 | 25 | 1.91 |
| 6 | −1.22 | 16 | 1.91 | 26 | 1.91 |
| 7 | −1.22 | 17 | 1.91 | 27 | 1.91 |
| 8 | −1.22 | 18 | 1.91 | 28 | 1.91 |
| 9 | −1.22 | 19 | 1.91 | 29 | 1.27 |
| 10 | −1.22 | 20 | 1.91 | 30 | .64 |

1 The R&D period is 10 years. Costs are in 1972
dollars and reflect the average costs for all new chemical entities introduced in the 1966–1972 period.

2 Sales revenues are estimated by the average
1972 sales of new chemical entities introduced in the
1962–1968 period. Foreign sales are assumed to be
47 percent of American sales.

3 A 20 percent after-tax profit margin, including
R&D expenditures, is assumed. Subtracting 2.6 percentage points from this figure to cover working capital and investment in plant for the project yields 17.4
percent, which when applied to sales, produces the
net income figures above.

4 A commercial life of 20 years is assumed. Sales
increase to the peak value in the third year and are assumed to be one-third of the peak in the year of introduction and two-thirds of the peak in the next
year. A similar decline is assumed at the end of commercial life.

*Source:* David Schwartzman, *The Expected Return
from Pharmaceutical Research* (Washington, D.C.:
American Enterprise Institute for Public Policy Research, 1975).

The XYZ corporation, for example, might be developing a new tranquilizer
which promises a much higher IRR than the average. Although the average
IRR is low, it does not necessarily follow that all R&D investment will cease.

To illustrate this point further, consider such a project of the XYZ Corporation. Based on the best estimates available for R&D costs, manufacturing
costs, promotional expenditures, and sales revenues, the planning department
has calculated the cash flows expected for its new tranquilizer, drug TQ.[5]

[5] These figures are not entirely hypothetical. The R&D cost figures are taken from a study by
Ronald W. Hansen, "The Pharmaceutical Development Process: Estimates of Development Costs
and Times and the Effects of Proposed Regulatory Changes," in Robert I. Chien (ed.), *Issues in
Pharmaceutical Economics* (Lexington, Mass.: D. C. Heath, 1979).

**TABLE 9-2**
ESTIMATED STREAM OF PRESENT VALUES FOR DRUG TQ AT
VARIOUS DISCOUNT RATES
(thousands of dollars)

| (A)<br>Year<br>number | (B)<br>Present value<br>at 0% | (C)<br>Present value<br>at 20% | (D)<br>Present value<br>at 25% |
|:---:|:---:|:---:|:---:|
| 1 | −1,609 | −1,340 | −1,286 |
| 2 | −2,796 | −1,941 | −1,789 |
| 3 | −3,297 | −1,907 | −1,688 |
| 4 | −2,357 | −1,136 | −965 |
| 5 | −1,809 | −726 | −592 |
| 6 | −2,038 | −682 | −534 |
| 7 | −1,226 | −342 | −257 |
| 8 | −1,061 | −246 | −178 |
| 9 | −769 | −149 | −103 |
| 10 | 0 | 0 | 0 |
| 11 | 350 | 47 | 30 |
| 12 | 9,261 | 1,038 | 636 |
| 13 | 10,842 | 1,013 | 596 |
| 14 | 15,312 | 1,192 | 673 |
| 15 | 19,790 | 1,284 | 696 |
| 16 | 24,758 | 1,339 | 696 |
| 17 | 27,266 | 1,228 | 613 |
| 18 | 32,018 | 1,202 | 576 |
| 19 | 36,726 | 1,149 | 529 |
| 20 | 34,274 | 894 | 395 |
| 21 | 34,274 | 745 | 316 |
| 22 | 34,274 | 620 | 252 |
| 23 | 34,274 | 517 | 202 |
| 24 | 34,274 | 431 | 161 |
| 25 | 34,274 | 359 | 129 |
| 26 | 34,274 | 299 | 103 |
| 27 | 34,274 | 249 | 82 |
| 28 | 34,274 | 207 | 66 |
| 29 | 34,274 | 173 | 53 |
| 30 | 34,274 | 144 | 42 |
| Totals | $536,376 | $5,664 | −$537 |

These cash flows are shown as column B in Table 9-2. Since these figures are prior to any discounting, we label column B as "Present value at 0%" discount rate. As indicated, R&D costs are incurred for the first nine years; year 10 shows a zero cash flow, reflecting the year of FDA approval; and net positive income is expected over the remaining 20 years.

Columns C and D in Table 9-2 show the results of discounting at 20 percent and 25 percent, respectively. The totals at the bottom of each column show the net present value of the project for each discount rate. Hence, if the XYZ Corporation has a 20 percent cost of capital, the NPV is $5.664 million and therefore represents a profitable investment. The reverse is true if its cost of capital is 25 percent, since NPV is negative, implying a reduction in the market value of the firm.

Given that NPV is positive at 20 percent but negative at 25 percent, we can reasonably infer that the IRR is bracketed by these two rates. A good guess would be that the IRR is about 24 percent, since this rate would make NPV approximately equal to zero. Clearly, drug TQ represents a potential "big winner" and is far above the average 7.5 percent IRR of Table 9-1.

This example shows how the IRR can be determined for a single project. We now return to the question of how the choice of the particular projects to be funded is made.

### Investment Opportunity Schedule

A highly simplified view of the project selection process is depicted in Figure 9-1. The firm first arrays its projects by the amount of funds required and by their IRRs. Thus, the project with the highest IRR (*a* percent) requires an investment of $0A$ dollars. The next highest IRR is *b* percent, and this project requires an outlay of $AB$ dollars, and so on. This schedule of investment opportunities is then compared with the firm's cost of capital in order to determine the projects that should be funded.

As an example, suppose that the firm's cost of capital is *g* percent. It then follows that the firm would wish to undertake all five projects, because each project has a higher IRR than its cost of capital. Hence, the capital budget would be $0E$ dollars. A higher cost of capital, say *d* percent, would make only the top three projects economically attractive. This would reduce the capital budget to $0C$ dollars.

**FIGURE 9-1**
Investment opportunity schedule.

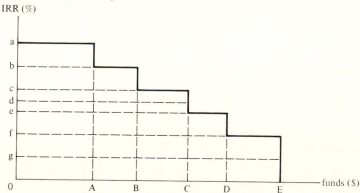

### Complications

Of course, as noted, this is a highly simplified view of the capital budgeting process and ignores some important complications. These complications include cases in which a conflict arises between the NPV and the IRR, the capital rationing problem, and the need for mathematical programming. An especially important complication is the introduction of risk and uncertainty. However, we shall defer the treatment of risk and uncertainty until Chapter 10.

**IRR and NPV Conflict**    Consider two projects being considered by the firm. Project A is the construction of a warehouse in Chicago, and project B is the construction of the same warehouse in St. Louis. The firm needs only one warehouse, however, and so these two projects are said to be mutually exclusive. It should be observed that mutually exclusive projects are by no means rare. For example, even if it were known that St. Louis was the preferred location, the capacity of the warehouse could be viewed as a variable. The firm would be confronted with choosing among warehouses of several possible sizes, and these would be mutually exclusive projects.

Suppose projects A and B have been quantified by their cash flows. Table 9-3 provides the data for these two projects comparable to the data for drug TQ in Table 9-2. However, to conserve space, only the totals of the present values are presented.

Apparently, the IRR for project B exceeds that of project A. That is, the IRR for project A must be less than 25 percent since its NPV at 25 percent is negative. And the IRR for project B must exceed 25 percent because its NPV is positive at 25 percent.

Figure 9-2 makes the point graphically. The IRR for project A is given by the intersection of its NPV curve and the horizontal axis, or 20 percent. That is, a discount rate of 20 percent makes project A's NPV equal to zero, which is the definition of the IRR. Similarly, the IRR for project B is shown to be 28 percent.

Hence, the IRR criterion would indicate that project B should be selected. What does the NPV criterion indicate? Of course, the NPV criterion is to select the project with the highest NPV where the discount rate equals the firm's cost of capital. Clearly, if the firm's cost of capital is greater than 10 per-

**TABLE 9-3**
ESTIMATED PRESENT VALUES FOR PROJECTS A AND B AT VARIOUS
DISCOUNT RATES
(thousands of dollars)

| Present value at 0% | | Present value at 10% | | Present value at 15% | | Present value at 25% | |
|---|---|---|---|---|---|---|---|
| A | B | A | B | A | B | A | B |
| 5,000 | 4,000 | 3,500 | 3,500 | 2,000 | 3,000 | −2,000 | 1,500 |

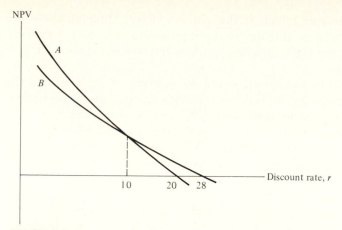

**FIGURE 9-2**
Net present-value curves for two mutually exclusive projects.

cent, both the NPV and the IRR signal project B as the preferred project. However, if the cost of capital is less than 10 percent, there is a conflict. That is, at a cost of capital of, say, 8 percent, project A has the higher NPV but project B still has the higher IRR.

Given that the objective is to maximize the value of the firm, the answer to this conflict is clear. Select the project with the highest NPV (at the discount rate equal to the firm's cost of capital). This follows by definition of NPV. The message is therefore to be wary of the IRR in cases involving choosing between mutually exclusive projects.

A second difficulty with the IRR arises in cases where the stream of cash flows for a project has a series of negative flows, then positive flows, followed by more negative flows. That is, suppose a project is expected to have initial costs, then a series of positive net income terms, followed by more costs. In such cases, the NPV curve can have the appearance of the one shown in Figure 9-3. Clearly, there are two discount rates that make NPV equal to zero:

**FIGURE 9-3**
Multiple values of the IRR.

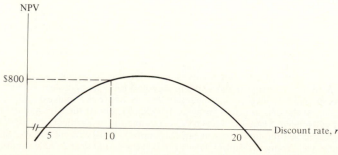

5 percent and 20 percent. Which is the correct IRR? Although there are complex rules that can be used to derive the appropriate IRR in such cases, a safe solution is to use the NPV criterion. Thus, if the cost of capital is 10 percent, the NPV is $800.

A final point should be mentioned in our comparison of the IRR and the NPV criteria. All discounting procedures require a reinvestment assumption. Recall that discounting a future dollar at a given rate is simply the reverse of compounding some amount less than a dollar for the required time at a given rate. Where the discounting takes place over several time periods, the assumption is that during intervening periods any funds made available must be invested at the discount rate. For example, if the IRR for a project with a 10-year economic life is calculated at 30 percent, it is assumed that all funds produced during the first 9 years can be reinvested continually at 30 percent.[6]

While the same basic assumption is required for the NPV approach, the actual reinvestment requirements are not so stringent. Thus if the discount rate in the NPV calculations is the market rate of interest, reinvestment at the same rate can be expected. However, if the internal rate of return is substantially above the market rate, it seems unrealistic to assume that reinvestment can occur continually at this rate.

**Capital Rationing**   In the discussion so far of the selection of projects to be funded, we have assumed that the firm would fund a project if its IRR exceeded the firm's cost of capital. (Of course, there are problems with the IRR when there are mutually exclusive projects, etc. but we shall ignore these for the moment.) The implicit assumption is that there is some rate at which the firm can borrow as large an amount of funds as it wishes. Capital rationing refers to cases in which there is some constraint on the funds available. For example, the firm's board of directors might issue an injunction that no borrowing can take place above some fixed amount.

In such cases, discounting at the cost of capital no longer makes sense. The problem is basically to choose among projects all of which have NPVs and IRRs that would ordinarily indicate that they should be funded.

For simple cases, the answer is that the discount rate should be equal to the IRR for the next best investment opportunity. Consider again Figure 9-1 on

---

[6] An example may be helpful. Consider a firm comparing two mutually exclusive projects, A and B. Both require the same investment and yield the same 30 percent IRR, according to equation (9-4). However, project A has a one-year life, while project B has a two-year life. In terms of cash flows, projects A and B both require $1,000 cash flows initially. Project A provides a cash inflow of $1,300 after one year, and project B yields a cash inflow of $1,690 after two years.

Assuming that the firm's only other alternative is to invest in the bank at 10 percent, which project is preferable? At the end of the second year the firm will receive $1,690 from project B. Now, consider the firm's receipts in year 2 if project A is selected. This is where the reinvestment assumption becomes important. At the end of year 1, project A yields $1,300. If the $1,300 can be reinvested at 30 percent, it will receive $1,690 at the end of year 2, and the two projects are indeed identical. However, by our earlier assumption, the firm can only reinvest at 10 percent. Hence, the strategy of selecting project A yields only ($1,300)(1.1) = $1,430 at the end of year 2, which represents a return of only 19.6 percent for the two years.

page 303. Suppose the firm's cost of capital is $g$ percent, but the firm is re-stricted to a captial budget of only $0B$ dollars. The appropriate discount rate is now $c$ percent rather than $g$ percent, since $c$ percent is the IRR for the next best investment opportunity. The use of $c$ percent precludes the selection of proj-ects with IRRs of less than $c$ percent but more than its cost of capital.

**Mathematical Programming**   The mathematical programming approach[7] is suited for handling not only capital rationing constraints but also complex inter-dependencies among projects over time. Perhaps the best way to illustrate the programming technique is by example.

Consider an electric utility that must construct additional power capacity for its system. The company can invest in one of three alternatives: (1) a nuclear power plant, (2) a coal-fired power plant, or (3) a contract with a neighboring company to provide the needed power. A project to establish a center to train employees in the nuclear technology would, of course, be contingent on the ac-ceptance of the first alternative.

The variant of linear programming known as integer programming can easily handle the types of interdependence described above. (As the name suggests, integer programming[8] differs from linear programming in that the values of the variables in the optimal solution must be integers.) For our example, the follow-ing constraints are needed:

$$X_1 + X_2 + X_3 \leq 1 \tag{9-5}$$

$$X_4 \leq X_1 \quad \text{all } X_i \text{ are nonnegative integers} \tag{9-6}$$

where $X_1$ = nuclear plants
$X_2$ = coal-fired plants
$X_3$ = contracts for power
$X_4$ = nuclear training centers

The interpretation is that if $X_i$ is 0, the project is rejected; and if $X_i$ is 1, the project is accepted. Clearly, by equation (9-5), only one of the three mutually exclusive projects can be accepted. And equation (9-6) makes it possible for the nuclear training center to be accepted only if the nuclear plant is accepted. Of course, the acceptance of the training center is not required even if the nuclear plant is chosen.

Next we consider the problem of budget constraints, namely, that the firm is limited to a fixed amount of investment funds. On the surface, it appears to be relatively easy to incorporate this budget limitation as another integer program-ming constraint. For the same example and symbols as discussed earlier,

$$I_1 X_1 + I_2 X_2 + I_3 X_3 \leq I_0 \tag{9-7}$$

---

[7] The standard reference is H. M. Weingartner, *Mathematical Programming and the Analysis of Capital Budgeting Problems* (Englewood Cliffs, N.J.: Prentice-Hall, 1963).

[8] For an introductory treatment, see Thomas H. Naylor and John M. Vernon, *Microeconomics and Decision Models of the Firm* (New York: Harcourt, Brace & World, 1969), chap. 10.

where $I_i$ = investment funds required for project $i$
$I_0$ = total funds available to the firm

Constraint (9-7) makes it possible to build fund limitations into the integer programming framework. However, the constraint raises an important problem which we must discuss shortly. To understand the problem, though, we must turn to the formulation of the objective function.

Given the objective of maximizing net present value, the objective function can be tentatively written as

$$\text{NPV} = P_1 X_1 + P_2 X_2 + P_3 X_3 + P_4 X_4 \tag{9-8}$$

where $P_i$ = NPV resulting from project $i$.

Now we must consider how the $P_i$'s are obtained. Clearly, the $P_i$'s are supposed to be obtained by discounting the stream of cash flows. But what is the rate of discount?

As noted earlier, it is not meaningful to use the firm's cost of capital as the discount rate if capital rationing exists. In general, the proper discount rate is the IRR on the next best alternative project. But this next best alternative project is not known beforehand and must be determined simultaneously with the optimal configuration of projects. However, this complication[9] is beyond the scope of this book, and while it is not strictly correct to do so, we shall take the $P_i$'s to be constants.

To conclude this discussion, we will formulate a general integer programming model of investment.

The firm seeks to maximize

$$\text{NPV} = P_1 X_1 + P_2 X_2 + \cdots + P_m X_m \tag{9-9}$$

subject to

$$
\begin{aligned}
I_{10} X_1 + I_{20} X_2 + \cdots + I_{m0} X_m &\leq I_0 \\
I_{11} X_1 + I_{21} X_2 + \cdots + I_{m1} X_m &\leq I_1 \\
&\vdots \\
I_{1n} X_1 + I_{2n} X_2 + \cdots + I_{mn} X_m &\leq I_n
\end{aligned}
\tag{9-10}
$$

and

$$X_1, \ldots, X_m \geq 0 \qquad \text{and all integers} \tag{9-11}$$

where $X_i$ = units of project $i$ undertaken
$P_i$ = NPV resulting from project $i$

---

[9] For an analysis of this, see W. J. Baumol and R. E. Quandt, "Mathematical Programming and the Discount Rate under Capital Rationing," *Economic Journal*, June 1965.

$I_t$ = total funds available to firm in period $t$
$I_{it}$ = investment funds required for project $i$ in period $t$

Thus we have added one further dimension to the problem by constraints (9-10). Now the firm can consider the problem of investment in all $n$ time periods simultaneously. Of course, it would be a simple matter to add constraints where groups of projects are mutually exclusive and where projects are contingent upon the acceptance of others. That is, constraints similar to constraints (9-5) and (9-6) could be added as required.

We should not fail to mention one of the most important advantages of the mathematical programming approach. Programming permits the firm to consider all projects in all combinations systematically. Hence the firm is not left to a random process of evaluating projects singly and hoping that good judgment will lead it to the optimal combination.

## THE COST OF CAPITAL

The cost of capital has been used extensively throughout this chapter to refer to the cost of investment funds to a firm. In this section we shall describe briefly the components of the cost of capital and how they can be estimated. However, it should be stressed that this is a major topic in finance, and we can touch only briefly on the main ideas here.[10]

Firms can raise funds in a variety of ways: common stock, preferred stock, long- and short-term debt, and retained earnings. For simplicity, we shall limit our discussion to common stock and debt. The proper cost of capital is then, in reality, a weighted cost of capital, with the cost of common stock, or equity, and the cost of debt being weighted by their respective proportions in the firm's financial structure.

Suppose, for example, that the XYZ Corporation has determined that its optimal debt-to-equity ratio is 40/60. That is, its assets are to be financed with 40 percent debt and 60 percent equity. Its cost of capital should then be calculated as

$$r = .4k_d + .6k_e \qquad (9\text{-}12)$$

where $r$ = cost of capital
$k_d$ = cost of debt
$k_e$ = cost of equity

Before taking up the estimation of $k_d$ and $k_e$, we should observe that the optimal debt-to-equity ratio is itself a complicated subject. It is probably accurate to state, however, that most financial experts agree that there is at least a range

---

[10] A good discussion of this topic is contained in J. Fred Weston and Eugene F. Brigham, *Essentials of Managerial Finance*, 5th ed. (Hinsdale, Ill.: Dryden Press, 1979).

of the debt-to-equity ratio intermediate between the two extremes of all debt and all equity at which the cost of capital is minimized.

The basic argument for an optimal debt-to-equity ratio is that debt costs less than equity because of tax advantages and because investors must be compensated for the greater riskiness of equity. While some debt is a good idea because of its lower cost, the higher the ratio of debt to equity, the higher the cost of equity will become. The reason is that higher debt increases the probability of the firm being unable to meet the required interest expenses and falling into bankruptcy. This, of course, increases the equity owner's risk and leads to the higher $k_e$. The cost of debt $k_d$ rises for the same reason. Figure 9-4 summarizes these relationships.

This discussion also makes it clear why it is not proper to argue, for example, that project M's cost of capital should be $k_d$ *only* because, in fact, it is to be financed entirely with a new debt issue. The all-debt financing of project M means that the *next* project will require all-equity financing in order to move back to the optimal debt-to-equity ratio. But this would mean a sharp jump from $k_d$ to $k_e$ in the cost of capital. To avoid these meaningless aberrations, it is appropriate to view the firm as an ongoing concern and to use the weighted average of $k_d$ and $k_e$.

### The Cost of Debt

The cost of debt $k_d$ is simply the interest rate on *new* debt, adjusted for taxes. Suppose the interest rate is $i$ percent. Since the firm's interest payments are deductible expenses, for income taxes its true after-tax cost is simply

$$k_d = i(1 - t) \tag{9-13}$$

where $i =$ interest rate on debt
$\quad\quad t =$ firm's marginal income tax rate

The reason that $k_d$ is less than $i$ is, of course, the tax saving, which equals $ti$.

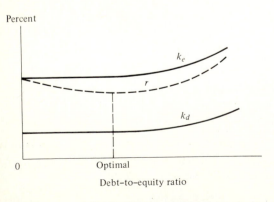

Percent

0          Optimal

Debt–to–equity ratio

**FIGURE 9-4**
Optimal debt-to-equity ratio where cost of capital is minimum.

If $i = 9$ percent and the marginal tax rate $= .40$, the value of $k_d = 5.4$ percent.

### The Cost of Equity

The estimation of the cost of equity $k_e$ is a very complicated subject. It is, in fact, the subject of endless public utility rate cases in which "experts" for the utility argue for high figures and "experts" for consumer groups argue for low rates. While we cannot possibly do justice to the subject here, we shall try to indicate conceptually the value being sought.

Consider a share of common stock of the XYZ Corporation currently traded on the New York Stock Exchange at a price $P$. How is this price determined? One view is that it is equal to the present value of the stream of dividends expected by investors. Recall our earlier discussion of this same point in the first section of this chapter. In equation form,

$$P = \frac{D_1}{1 + k_e} + \frac{D_2}{(1 + k_e)^2} + \dots \tag{9-14}$$

where $P =$ price of stock
$\quad D_1 =$ expected dividend in year 1
$\quad D_2 =$ expected dividend in year $t$
$\quad k_e =$ cost of equity capital

Hence, $k_e$ is simply the discount rate used by investors. Now, if we assume that investors expect dividends to grow at some constant rate $g$, where $g < k_e$, equation (9-14) can be solved for the unknown $k_e$.

$$k_e = \frac{D_1}{P} + g \tag{9-15}$$

Thus, suppose the current dividend yield $D_1/P$ is 8 percent and investors expect that dividends will grow over time at 7 percent. Then equation (9-15) would yield 15 percent as the estimated cost of equity capital.

In practice, the use of equation (9-15) poses obvious problems. What is the current dividend yield? Should it be an average over the past year, or two years, or more? How can we estimate what investors expect the growth rate to be? Past growth rates may have no relation to future growth. In practice, however, the use of past rates is about the only possibility available.

### CONCLUSIONS

In this chapter we have concentrated primarily on single-project investments under complete certainty. (The mathematical programming model did involve multiple projects.) In Chapter 10 we shall consider single-project investment decisions under risk and uncertainty. Multiproject investment decisions under complete certainty and under risk will be treated in Chapter 12.

## QUESTIONS AND PROBLEMS

**9-1** Consider two investments, A and B. The initial cost and expected payoffs are:

|   |      | Payoff at end of years | | |
|---|------|-------|-------|-------|
|   | Cost | 1     | 2     | 3     |
| A | 5,000 | 2,500 | 3,500 | 2,500 |
| B | 3,000 | 2,000 | 4,000 | 0     |

    **a** At a cost of capital of 6 percent, find the net present values of each project. Which investment is preferable?

    **b** At a cost of capital of 12 percent, which project is best?

**9-2** "Capital rationing is not sensible. Why should a firm not invest in a project which promises a return exceeding its cost of capital?" Discuss.

**9-3** What are the major areas of uncertainty in estimating a firm's cost of capital?

**9-4** Edison Power Company is considering adding a power plant to its system. It can add a nuclear plant for an initial cost of $500 million or a coal plant for an initial cost of $300 million. Annual fuel costs of the nuclear plant are estimated to be $20 million, while annual fuel costs for the coal plant are estimated at $40 million. Both plants will last for 30 years and will produce the same outputs of electricity over their lifetimes. Edison Power has a cost of capital of 12 percent. Which plant should be selected?

    *Hint:* Since both plants will produce the same stream of revenues, it is only necessary to determine which plant has the lowest cost. Engineers often solve such problems by converting the plant investments into "equivalent annual costs" which can then be added to other annual costs to get total annual costs. For example, suppose the company borrowed the $500 million for the nuclear plant. At 12 percent interest, what would the annual payments $X$ be in order to repay the loan in 30 years? The answer is to solve for that stream of payments $X$ that will yield a present value of $500 million. That is,

$$\$500 \text{ million} = X \left( \sum_{t=1}^{30} \frac{1}{(1 + .12)^t} \right)$$

Notice that the expression in parentheses has been tabulated in Table 5 at the end of the book. Hence,

$$\$500 \text{ million} = X(8.055)$$

The equivalent annual cost $X$ is $62.1 million, and therefore the total annual cost of the nuclear alternative is $82.1 million. All that is left is to compute a similar figure for the coal plant.

    Of course, one could just as easily have compared the present values of costs for the two alternatives. However, one use often made of the annual-cost method is to compute average cost of output. For example, if the nuclear plant is expected to generate 2 billion kilowatt hours annually, the average cost per kilowatt hour would be 4.1 cents.

**9-5** Calculate the present values of lifetime costs for the two alternatives in problem 9-4.

**9-6** In theoretical work, analysts often make use of "continuous compounding." Rather than formulating the compound value of $P_0$ in $t$ periods as $P_0(1 + i)^t$, the continuous formulation is $P_0 e^{rt}$. The main advantage is that the use of calculus is permitted under continuous compounding. The value of $r$ which produces the same compounded value at any time $t$ is given by $r = 1n(1 + i)$. For example, if $i = .15$, then $r = .14$.

Suppose that a painting appreciates in value over time according to the function (ignore inflation)

$$V = Ae^{\sqrt{t}}$$

If the owner's cost of capital on a continuous compounding basis is $r = .10$, write an expression for the present value of the painting. Find the value of $t$ that maximizes the present value.

## BIBLIOGRAPHY

Baumol, William J.: *Economic Theory and Operations Analysis,* 4th ed. (Englewood Cliffs, N.J.: Prentice-Hall, 1977), chap. 25.

Mossin, Jan: *Theory of Financial Markets* (Englewood Cliffs, N.J.: Prentice-Hall, 1973).

Solomon, Ezra: *The Management of Corporate Capital* (New York: The Free Press of Glencoe, 1959).

Terborgh, G.: *Dynamic Equipment Policy* (New York: McGraw-Hill, 1949).

Van Horne, J. C.: *Financial Management and Policy,* 4th ed. (Englewood Cliffs, N.J.: Prentice-Hall, 1977).

Weston, J. Fred, and E. F. Brigham: *Essentials of Managerial Finance,* 5th ed. (Hinsdale, Ill.: Dryden Press, 1979).

# CHAPTER 10

# RISK ANALYSIS

**CHAPTER OUTLINE**

## DECISION MAKING UNDER RISK AND UNCERTAINTY

Any managerial decision problem can be viewed as a five-step process:

1 Identification of the alternatives available to management
2 Specification of the possible outcomes associated with each alternative
3 Assignment of probabilities to each outcome
4 Formulation of the criteria for choosing among the alternatives
5 Selection of that alternative which satisfies the decision maker's criteria

Thus far we have restricted ourselves to a very special case of this decision-making process. That is, we have considered only those decision problems which are such that for each alternative available, there is one and only one outcome associated with it. This is known as decision making under complete certainty. That is, throughout this book we have assumed that managerial decision makers have perfect information about the firm's demand function, production function, and factor costs. For example, if the firm sets its price, the demand curve is assumed to yield one and only one figure for expected sales volume. Alternatively, for given levels of factor inputs, one and only one output level is specified by the production function.

But in the real world, there may be several possible outcomes associated with each managerial option. For example, if the company embarks on a major advertising campaign, sales may increase, decrease, or not change at all. Our knowledge of the probability distribution of the outcomes associated with each alternative determines whether the problem represents decision making under risk or uncertainty.

In the absence of certainty, the decision maker no longer envisages a one-to-one relationship between alternative courses of action and outcomes. If the decision maker is able to calculate objectively the probability that a given outcome will be associated with a particular alternative, the decision making is said to take place under conditions of objective risk. If, on the other hand, the decision maker has no objective basis for calculating the probabilities associated with the various action-outcome combinations but has some intuitive feeling as to the approximate magnitude of those probabilities, then decision making takes place under conditions of subjective risk. But if the decision maker is unable to calculate (either objectively or subjectively) the probabilities associated with the different action-outcome combinations associated with the situation, then we have decision making under uncertainty.

## DECISION CRITERIA UNDER RISK

Given a decision problem under conditions of risk, what criteria might the decision maker use in choosing among alternative courses of action? Basically, the choice of appropriate decision criteria depends on three important factors: (1) the frequency with which one is confronted with a particular type of decision, (2) the relative magnitude of the risk being considered, and (3) the decision maker's attitude toward risk and uncertainty. In this section, we shall examine six different criteria for decision making under risk:

1 Finite planning horizon
2 Sensitivity analysis
3 Risk discounting
4 Expected value
5 Certainty equivalents
6 Expected utility

### Finite Planning Horizon

The finite planning horizon method is perhaps the simplest way of treating uncertainty. The principle is to alter the length of the period over which returns are expected, depending on the degree of uncertainty. Thus, even though a project is expected to last 40 years, the decision maker may arbitrarily decide to consider only returns over the first 30 years. If positive returns are expected over the last 10 years, the effect of the alteration is to reduce the attractiveness of the project by an amount equal to the present value of the omitted returns. One obvious problem is how the specific alteration is determined. That is, what made the decision maker choose a 30-year life rather than, say, a 32-year life?

Furthermore, as Baumol has pointed out:

> A finite and arbitrary horizon, then, is not really a defensible method for dealing with imperfect foresight. It takes no account of our limited ability to predict events in the more immediate future (which is sometimes as distant as twenty-five years from the present) and forces us to ignore totally what little we can forecast about the more distant future with some degree of confidence.[1]

### Sensitivity Analysis

Sensitivity analysis is quite simple to perform and can provide meaningful information about a project. It involves revising uncertain estimates of projected cash flows and studying the sensitivity of the net present value, or internal rate of return, to such revisions.

As an example, consider a firm that manufactures parts for existing types of computers. Let us assume that an innovation in computers is expected in the future which will seriously reduce the demand for the parts. However, the date of the innovation is uncertain, and the firm is now trying to evaluate the profitability of an addition to its manufacturing capacity. In its profitability calculations the firm has used the year 1988 as its best estimate of the date of introduction of the innovation. The firm could use sensitivity analysis to study the effect of an earlier or later date on profitability. Thus, it might calculate that an in-

---

[1] William J. Baumol, *Economic Theory and Operations Analysis,* 4th ed. (Englewood Cliffs, N.J.: Prentice-Hall, 1977), p. 620.

troduction date of 1986 would make the addition unprofitable, a date of 1987 would make it marginally profitable, and a date of 1988 would make it quite profitable. On the other hand, the firm might discover that the profitability of the addition is relatively insensitive to dates within two years of 1988.

The major advantage of sensitivity analysis is its simplicity. However, it is also subject to rather serious shortcomings.

Sensitivity analysis is quite limited in the amount of information it can provide. For example, it is difficult to draw precise conclusions about the possible effects of combinations of errors in the estimates, even though this is the typical situation of concern. For statistical reasons, it would usually be misleading to consider the case where all the estimates are too optimistic or where all are too pessimistic. In short, sensitivity analysis is useful but its conclusions tend to suffer from a lack of conciseness, precision, and comprehensiveness.[2]

**Risk Discounting**

The present value PV of some future value of cash flow $CASH_t$ is given by the expression

$$PV = \frac{CASH_t}{(1 + r)^t} \tag{10-1}$$

where $r$ denotes the appropriate interest rate or discount rate and $t$ is the time period in which the cash will actually be received. More generally, the present value of a future stream of cash over $n$ time periods can be expressed as

$$PV = \frac{CASH_1}{(1 + r)^1} + \frac{CASH_2}{(1 + r)^2} + \cdots + \frac{CASH_n}{(1 + r)^n} \tag{10-2}$$
$$= \sum_{t=1}^{n} \frac{CASH_t}{(1 + r)^t}$$

In equation (10-2) the stream of cash $CASH_t$ is in reality the expected value of the cash flow in each period $t$. When a decision maker is choosing between two projects, one project may yield higher expected cash flow but also higher risk (standard deviation of cash flow), whereas the other project may yield smaller expected cash flows but at a lower risk. Will the higher expected cash flows be sufficient to offset the higher risk? If not, the less risky project should be adopted; if so, the riskier project is preferred.

The concept of risk discounting is based on the decision maker's trade-off function between risk and return. Figure 10-1 illustrates a risk-return trade-off function for a decision maker. It shows the expected return required to induce the decision maker to accept a risk of a given magnitude (the standard deviation

[2] F. Hillier, "Derivation of Probabilistic Information for the Evaluation of Risky Investments," *Management Science*, April 1963, p. 443.

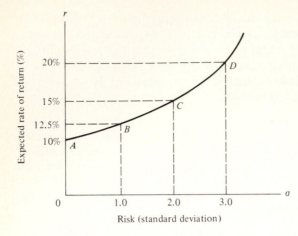

FIGURE 10-1
A risk-return trade-off function.

of cash flow in our example). The decision maker is indifferent among a riskless project with a 10 percent rate of return, a moderately risky project with a 15 percent expected return, and a very risky project with a 20 percent return. As risk increases, higher expected returns are required to motivate the decision maker to accept the increased risk.

The difference between the expected rate of return on a particular risky project and the rate of return on a risk-free project is called the risk premium. In Figure 10-1, the risk-free rate of return is 10 percent. A 5 percent premium is required to induce the decision maker to accept a risk level of $\sigma = 2.0$. A 10 percent risk premium is necessary for a project with a risk level of $\sigma = 3.0$. The average decision maker is indifferent between risk-free project A and risky projects B, C, and D.

Since required returns are linked to the perceived level of risk associated with a given project, equation (10-2) must be modified to take into consideration the effects of risk on the discount rate $r$.

$$PV = \sum_{t=1}^{n} \frac{CASH_t}{(1 + r + \Delta)^t} \qquad (10\text{-}3)$$

where $r$ denotes the risk-free rate of return and $\Delta$ denotes the risk premium. For example, a project with a risk level of $\sigma = 1.0$ would have a discount rate of 12.5 percent, i.e., a risk-free return of 10 percent plus a risk premium of 2.5 percent.

Consider the case of a commercial airline which is considering the purchase of two different types of aircraft. Aircraft 1, which costs $125 million, will seat a maximum of 300 passengers and is expected to generate $30 million in cash each year over the next decade. Aircraft 2 costs $100 million, will seat 250 passengers, and is expected to generate $20 million in cash each year. Aircraft 1 is less fuel-efficient than aircraft 2 and requires a larger crew. Given the uncertainty in the future price of jet fuel and in air traffic demand, the risk levels are estimated to be $\sigma = 3.0$ and $\sigma = 2.0$, respectively, for aircraft 1 and aircraft 2. At these risk levels, management requires a risk premium of 10 percent for aircraft 1 and a 5 percent risk premium for aircraft 2. The adjusted discount rates of 20 percent and 15 percent, respectively, appear in Table 10-1.

To calculate the present value of each aircraft over the 10-year planning horizon we make use of equation (10-3):

$$PV_1 = \sum_{t=1}^{10} \frac{\$30,000,000}{(1 + .20)^t} - \$125,000,000 \qquad (10\text{-}4)$$

$$= \$30,000,000 \times 4.193 - \$125,000,000$$

$$= \$125,790,000 - \$125,000,000$$

$$= \$790,000$$

$$PV_2 = \sum_{t=1}^{10} \frac{\$20,000,000}{(1 + .15)^t} - \$100,000,000 \qquad (10\text{-}5)$$

$$= \$20,000,000 \times 5.019 - \$100,000,000$$

$$= \$100,380,000 - \$100,000,000$$

$$= \$380,000$$

Note that values 4.193 and 5.019 in equations (10-4) and (10-5), respectively, were obtained from Table 5 at end of book.

Therefore, based on the risk-discounting criteria, the company should select aircraft 1 since it yields the highest present value over the 10-year period, even though it involves the largest capital outlay and the greatest risk.

Although the concept of risk discounting has a certain intuitive appeal, its practical implementation is based entirely on the assumption that it is possible to come up with a risk-return trade-off function similar to the one in Figure 10-1. The fact of the matter is that such trade-off functions are usually either completely unknown or extremely difficult to estimate for a particular decision. There is another special assumption involved in the use of risk dis-

**TABLE 10-1**
RISK PROFILE FOR TWO ALTERNATIVE COMMERCIAL
AIRCRAFT

|  | Aircraft 1 | Aircraft 2 |
|---|---|---|
| Initial outlay | $125 million | $100 million |
| Expected annual cash flow | $30 million | $20 million |
| Passenger capacity | 300 | 250 |
| Risk level | 3.0 | 2.0 |
| Risk premium | 10% | 5% |
| Risk-adjusted discount rate | 20% | 15% |

**TABLE 10-2**
RISK PROFILE FOR NUCLEAR AND COAL-FIRED POWER
PLANTS ASSOCIATED WITH ALTERNATIVE ALLOWED RATES
OF RETURN

| Type of rate of return | Probability of rate of return occurring | Profit if rate of return occurs | |
| | | Nuclear, $ | Coal-fired, $ |
| --- | --- | --- | --- |
| Small | .3 | −100,000 | 100,000 |
| Medium | .5 | 250,000 | 250,000 |
| Large | .2 | 600,000 | 300,000 |

counting which should be made explicit. According to Bierman and Smidt, the assumption is that the "probability of a dollar of estimated cash actually materializing will decrease each year by a fixed percentage of the probability in the preceding year." They have given a good example of a project in which risk discounting would be inappropriate because of this special assumption:

> Suppose we consider an investment to build and equip a plant for producing a new product. In some instances the major uncertainty may be related to the cost of constructing the plant, while the demand for the resulting output may be easily predictable in advance with very little uncertainty. . . . The use of atomic energy to generate electric power is a tangible example of this situation. In such a situation the discounting of future revenues, themselves fairly certain, seems a poor way of allowing for the uncertainty about how much the fixed plant will cost.[3]

## Expected Value

An alternative criterion for decision making under risk which does not assume knowledge of the manager's risk-return trade-off function is the concept of expected value.

Consider the case of an electric utility that is trying to decide whether to build an additional nuclear power plant or a coal-fired power plant. As can be seen in Table 10-2, the profitability of these two alternatives depends on the magnitude of the rate of return on investment allowed by the state utility commission. The profitability varies because the rate of return is applied to the amount of investment, and nuclear plants require a greater investment than coal-fired plants for a given plant capacity.

Management is interested in three different rate of return possibilities: a small return, a medium return, and a large return. Based on past experience, management assumes that the probability of a small return in its service area is

[3] Harold Bierman and Seymour Smidt, *The Capital Budgeting Decision* (New York: Macmillan, 1966), p. 54.

.3, the probability of a medium return is .5, and the probability of a large return is .2.

The formula for computing the expected profit associated with a given alternative is

$$\text{Expected profit} = E(\pi) = \sum_{i=1}^{n} P_i \pi_i \qquad (10\text{-}6)$$

where $\pi_i$ denotes the profit associated with outcome $i$ (return $i$), $P_i$ is the probability of outcome $i$ (return $i$) occurring, and $n$ is the number of outcomes (in our case, $n = 3$). The expected profits associated with the nuclear and coal-fired power plants are give by equations (10-7) and (10-8), respectively.

$$E(\pi_N) = \sum_{i=1}^{3} P_i \pi_i \qquad (10\text{-}7)$$
$$= .3(-\$100{,}000) + .5(\$250{,}000) + .2(\$600{,}000)$$
$$= \$215{,}000$$

$$E(\pi_C) = .3(\$100{,}000) + .5(\$250{,}000) + .2(\$300{,}000) \qquad (10\text{-}8)$$
$$= \$215{,}000$$

Thus we observe that although the profitability patterns for the two different types of power plant are really quite different, they have identical expected profits.

On the basis of the expected-value criterion, management would be indifferent between a nuclear plant and a coal-fired plant. But one could question the realism of this possibility. With the nuclear plant there is the possibility of a $100,000 loss as well as a $600,000 gain. With the coal-fired plant the maximum profit is $300,000, but in case of a small rate of return, the company still operates profitably. The point is fairly obvious. The expected-value criterion does not provide the decision maker with much insight into the risk associated with each alternative. To examine the risk involved in these two projects, we must consider the variance and standard deviations of profit as well as the expected value. The variance may be calculated as follows:

$$\text{Variance} = \sigma^2 = \sum_{i=1}^{n} P_i(\pi_i - \bar{\pi})^2 \qquad (10\text{-}9)$$

where $\pi_i - \bar{\pi}$ denotes the deviation about the expected profit $\bar{\pi}$ associated with the outcome $i$ where

$$\bar{\pi} = \sum_{i=1}^{n} P_i \pi_i \qquad (10\text{-}10)$$

The standard deviation $\sigma$ is simply the square root of the variance.

$$\sigma = \sqrt{\sum_{i=1}^{n} P_i(\pi_i - \pi)^2} \tag{10-11}$$

Using the data in Table 10-2, we see that

$$\sigma_N^2 = .3(-100,000 - 215,000)^2 + .5(250,000 - 215,000)^2 \tag{10-12}$$
$$+ .2(600,000 - 215,000)^2$$
$$= 60,025 \times 10^6$$
$$\sigma_C^2 = .3(100,000 - 215,000)^2 + .5(250,000 - 215,000)^2 \tag{10-13}$$
$$+ .2(300,000 - 215,000)^2$$
$$= 6,025 \times 10^6$$

Taking the square root of the respective variances yields

$$\sigma_N = \$245,000 \tag{10-14}$$
$$\sigma_C = \$77,621 \tag{10-15}$$

Using the standard deviation as a measure of risk, we see that although the nuclear plant and the coal-fired plant have identical expected profits, the nuclear plant is 3.2 times as risky as the coal-fired plant ($\sigma_N/\sigma_C = 3.2$). The coefficient of variation is another way of comparing the risks associated with two or more projects. The coefficient of variation CV is defined as the ratio of the standard deviation to the expected value of a random variable. In our example,

$$CV_N = \frac{\sigma_N}{\pi_N} = 1.14 \tag{10-16}$$

$$CV_C = \frac{\sigma_C}{\pi_C} = .36 \tag{10-17}$$

With this alternative measure of risk, the nuclear plant is still 3 times as risky as the coal-fired plant.

In addition to the fact that the expected-value criterion does not deal adequately with the extreme values of a random variable in a risky situation, it has another major limitation. The reader will note in our example of an electric power plant that neither $E(\pi_N)$ nor $E(\pi_C)$ corresponds to any of the actual observed profit values $\pi_i$. This is not surprising since the concept of expected value is not defined in terms of any single outcome. In fact, the calculation of expected value and the use of expected-value maximization as a decision criterion depends substantially on the law of large numbers, whereby the expected value is reduced to a quasi-certain value over a large number of replications. The law of large numbers states that if in $n$ identical replications of an experiment $X_i$ occurs $k$ times, and if $n$ is very large, then $k/n$ approaches the probability $P_i$ that $X_i$ will occur.

The expected-value criterion was designed for use in a repetitive environment such as gambling or insurance. In some cases, the law of large numbers, and hence the expected-value criterion, is an inappropriate decision rule. Such a case is the "one-shot" decision in which a single decision must be made in an environment which cannot be replicated. Consider our example of an electric utility in which the management of the utility desires to make a single decision about nuclear versus coal-fired power plants based on the a priori probability distribution of allowed rates of return in its service area over, say, the past 10 years. To some extent, it can be argued that the probability distribution of rates of return based on past experience is of limited use for a particular time period in the future, say the next 10 years. The probability distribution in Table 10-2 simply indicates the proportion of small, medium, and large rates of return which occurred in the past 10 years. For these data to be useful, we would want to be able to replicate this situation for a large number of 10-year periods, not just for a single 10-year span.

The use of the expected-value criterion has also been critized because the law of large numbers requires successive replications to be statistically independent. This is virtually impossible to achieve in a business environment.

However, it is the failure of the expected-value criterion to consider extreme values of random variables that involves the greatest dissatisfaction. That is, there are chance prospects for which the expected value is theoretically infinite, and yet no reasonable decision maker will accept the risk unless he or she is paid a very large sum of money.

### Certainty Equivalents

Assume that a decision maker is confronted by a probability distribution of profit from a given project. As was the case with risk-return trade-off functions (Figure 10-1), the decision maker is assumed to want a balance between the expected profit and some measure of the dispersion of profits. Let the mean of the probability distribution represent the expected return and the standard deviation represent the dispersion of risk associated with the project. A decision maker is said to be risk-averse if for the same expected return he or she prefers a smaller value for the standard deviation to a larger one or if for the same value of the standard deviation he or she prefers a larger expected return to a smaller one. Furthermore, according to whether one's aversion to risk is strong or weak, either one may prefer a low expected return combined with a smaller standard deviation to a higher expected return combined with a large standard deviation or one may prefer the opposite.

Based on these assumptions, we can formulate a set of expected return ($M$) and standard deviation ($\sigma$) risk indifference curves. Assuming that as the standard deviation increases, a larger compensating increase in expected return ($M$) is required, the risk indifference curves would be expected to be concave to the *M* axis, as in Figure 10-2. Note the similarity between risk indifference curves and risk-return trade-off functions (Figure 10-1). The axes on Figure 10-2 are the reverse of those in Figure 10-1, with expected return *M* substituted for expected rate of return *r* on the horizontal axis.

Figure 10-2 also depicts a boundary line or efficient set of risk-return combinations, based on the assumption that the decision maker is risk-averse. The boundary line can be derived by noting that the $\sigma$-*M* plan contains numerous points, each one corresponding to a different project. Comparing any point between the boundary line and the vertical axis with any point on the boundary line reveals that points on the boundary line have maximum expected return for a given value of $\sigma$ and minimum $\sigma$ for a given value of *M*. Thus, if there is any point not on a proposed boundary line which has a greater *M* for the given value of $\sigma$ or a smaller $\sigma$ for the same *M*, then this point becomes a point on the boundary.

In Figure 10-2, the risk-return combination represented by point *P* is optimal. Point *N* with $M = 0N$ is the equivalent certain return since $\sigma = 0$ at this point. Of course, a different set of risk indifference curves will change the optimal point *P* and its equivalent.

A number of objections can be raised against the certainty equivalence approach or the manner in which it is used. The first objection, which is also the most destructive, concerns the exact manner in which a choice is made among risk-return combinations on the boundary line. The usual assumption regarding the attitude toward risk is that of risk aversion and a decreasing marginal rate of substitution of $\sigma$ for *M*. This implies concave risk indifference curves and a boundary line as in Figure 10-2.

However much agreement there is on the shape of the curves, no attempt is made to specify methods for deriving a set of $\sigma$-*M* risk indifference curves for an individual decision maker. In effect, there is no way to choose among the

**Figure 10-2**
Risk indifference curves.

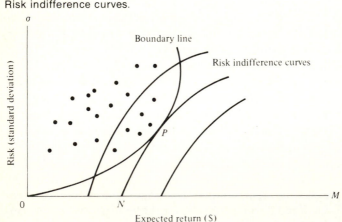

risk-return combinations on the boundary line. The usual choice of risk aversion as the attitude toward risk is itself questionable and constitutes one objection to the manner in which the certainty equivalence approach is most often used. There appears to be quite general agreement that decision makers commonly possess an attitude toward risk which can best be described as a combination of preference for and aversion to risk. That is, for some ranges of outcomes a decision maker may exhibit risk preference, while for others there may be risk aversion.

Another objection to the certainty equivalence approach is that it does not give adequate attention to the case in which there are multiple projects rather than just a single project. Chapter 12 treats the question of decision making under risk when multiple projects are being evaluated.

### Expected Utility

In Appendix B to Chapter 2 we introduced the concept of utility theory in conjunction with demand analysis. Utility theory has also been proposed as the basis for choosing among alternative projects in situations involving risk. Indeed, there is an extensive literature surrounding the use of utility theory as a criterion for making decisions under risk. Unfortunately, the practical application of utility theory to decision making under risk is almost nonexistent. It simply is not used by managerial decision makers to make actual business decisions. We have included it in this section merely for the sake of completeness. The following example will serve to illustrate the concept.

Suppose that a decision maker must choose between two projects X and Y. The monetary outcomes associated with projects X and Y appear in column 1 of Tables 10-3 and 10-4, respectively. Assume further that the probabilities associated with each of the outcomes of projects X and Y are given by column 2 of Tables 10-3 and 10-4. Next we assume that the utility to the decision maker associated with each outcome can be measured and appears in column 3 of the two tables.[4]

The key assumption underlying the assignment of utility levels for this example is that the decision maker is risk-averse and has a diminishing marginal utility for money. For example, in Table 10-4 note that the marginal utility of the additional \$250,000 in moving from outcome $Y_3$ to $Y_2$ is $94 - 85 = 9$, while the marginal utility associated with the additional \$250,000 between $Y_2$ and $Y_1$ is only $97 - 94 = 3$. Of course, as we noted in the previous section, decision makers need not be risk-averse.

Expected utility for a particular project is defined as the sum of the product of the probabilities and utilities associated with each outcome. If $P_i$ denotes the probability of outcome $i$ occurring and $U_i$ denotes the utility associated with

---

[4] At least in theory, it is possible to derive an individual's utility function through the use of five axioms of cardinal utility proposed by Von Neumann and Morgenstern in *Theory of Games and Economic Behavior* (Princeton, N.J.: Princeton University Press, 1947).

**TABLE 10-3**
EXPECTED UTILITY OF PROJECT X

| Outcome | Monetary outcome, $ (1) | Probability (2) | Utility (3) | Expected utility (4) |
|---------|---------|---------|---------|---------|
| $X_1$ | 500,000 | .1 | 85 | 8.5 |
| $X_2$ | 300,000 | .2 | 60 | 12.0 |
| $X_3$ | 250,000 | .4 | 53 | 21.2 |
| $X_4$ | 150,000 | .3 | 30 | 9.0 |
| | | | | 50.7 |

outcome $i$, then the expected utility $E(U)$ is given by

$$E(U) = \sum_{i=1}^{n} P_i U_i \qquad (10\text{-}18)$$

where $n$ equals the number of possible outcomes.

Thus we see from Tables 10-3 and 10-4 that the expected utility of project X is 50.7 and the expected utility of project Y is 42.1. According to the expected-utility criterion, project X should be selected. (On the other hand, if the expected monetary value is the decision criterion, it is easy to show that project Y should be selected.)

This procedure seems to be rather straightforward and easy to implement. Indeed, one simply follows some simple rules to arrive at a decision. There is only one hitch. Economists and management scientists do not know how to come up with objective measures of utility for individual decision makers. In spite of the vast literature available on the use of utility theory for decision making under risk, we do not know of a single case in which a major corporate decision has been made where the decision maker's utility function was specified and quantified. The techniques which have been proposed in the literature for quantifying are impossible to implement in the real world. They are

**TABLE 10-4**
EXPECTED UTILITY OF PROJECT Y

| Outcome | Monetary outcome, $ (1) | Probability (2) | Utility (3) | Expected utility (4) |
|---------|---------|---------|---------|---------|
| $Y_1$ | 1,000,000 | .1 | 97 | 9.7 |
| $Y_2$ | 750,000 | .1 | 94 | 9.4 |
| $Y_3$ | 500,000 | .2 | 85 | 17.0 |
| $Y_4$ | 100,000 | .6 | 10 | 6.0 |
| | | | | 42.1 |

based either on information that is not available or on information that can be obtained only at an inordinate cost in terms of the decision maker's time.

In summary, utility theory is an abstract concept of limited practical value.

## DECISION TREES

A number of texts on managerial economics have proposed the use of decision trees for multistage or multiperiod decision problems involving risk. In reality, decision trees constitute a special case of the application of the expected-value criterion that has been described in this chapter. Figure 10-3 describes the decision tree for a firm which must decide whether to embark on a major advertising campaign and spend $25 million or settle for a lesser campaign which will cost only $10 million.

As can be seen in columns 2, 3, and 4 in Figure 10-3, by investing in the major advertising campaign, the probability distribution of sales revenue is affected quite positively relative to the probability distribution of sales associated with the small advertising campaign. Column 5 shows the expected sales which results from the product of columns 3 and 4. If we net out the cost of the respective advertising campaigns, then the major campaign yields expected net sales of $295 million, while the small campaign produces expected net revenues of $215 million.

Obviously, our decision tree here is quite simple, but it can easily be extended to a multiperiod problem. Suppose that Figure 10-3 represents the situation for year 1 only. Depending on which advertising campaign is actually employed and whether demand is low, medium, or high, we can envisage similar decisions for years 2, 3, 4, etc. Associated with each type of advertising campaign would be an assumed probability distribution for demand. To further complicate matters, one might retain a market research firm to make recommendations as to which type of advertising campaign to employ. Market research might also be used to evaluate the effects of the campaign.

**FIGURE 10-3**
Decision tree for an advertising campaign.

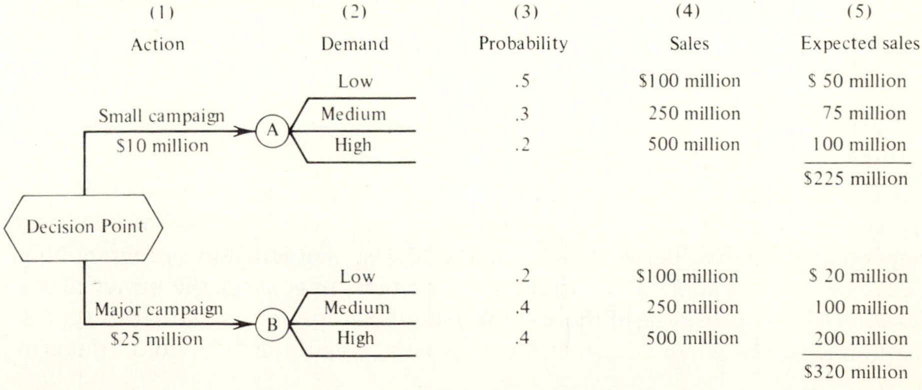

| (1) Action | (2) Demand | (3) Probability | (4) Sales | (5) Expected sales |
|---|---|---|---|---|
| Small campaign $10 million (A) | Low | .5 | $100 million | $ 50 million |
| | Medium | .3 | 250 million | 75 million |
| | High | .2 | 500 million | 100 million |
| | | | | $225 million |
| Decision Point | | | | |
| Major campaign $25 million (B) | Low | .2 | $100 million | $ 20 million |
| | Medium | .4 | 250 million | 100 million |
| | High | .4 | 500 million | 200 million |
| | | | | $320 million |

In summary, it would not take much effort to produce an extremely complex decision tree for a typical multistage, multi-time period decision problem. Therein lies the principal reason why decision trees are seldom used in actual practice. Not unlike utility theory, decision trees seem to have been created primarily for readers of textbooks on managerial economics. Their practical value as a decision maker's tool is minimal.

## COMPUTER SIMULATION

Perhaps the most widely used technique for analyzing decision problems under risk is computer simulation. The verb "to simulate" is a term which has come into vogue in a number of scientific disciplines to describe the ancient art of model building. Although simulation has been applied to some extremely diverse forms of model building, ranging from Renaissance paintings and sculpture to scale models of supersonic jet airliners and computer models of cognitive processes, it has come to mean something quite specific to both physical scientists and social scientists. The modern use of the word traces its origin to the work of Von Neumann in the late 1940s, who coined the term "Monte Carlo analysis" to apply to a numerical technique used to solve certain nuclear-shielding problems which were either too expensive for experimental solutions or too complicated for analytical treatment. Monte Carlo analysis refers to the solution of deterministic mathematical problems by simulating a probability distribution which has properties that satisfy the mathematical relations of the deterministic problem.

With the advent of computers in the 1950s, simulation took on yet another meaning, for it became possible to experiment with mathematical models (describing some system of interest) on a computer. For the first time in history, social scientists found that it was possible to perform controlled, laboratory-type experiments in a manner similar to that employed by physicists, but using a computer rather than some physical process such as a nuclear reactor.

We shall define "simulation" as a numerical technique for conducting experiments with mathematical and logical models which describe the behavior of an economic system on a computer over extended periods of time. The principal difference between a simulation experiment and a real-world experiment is that with simulation the experiment is conducted with a model of the economic system rather than with the actual system itself.

### Rationale

To outline the rationale underlying the use of simulation as a vehicle of analysis for decision making under risk it is necessary to point out an obvious but very important similarity between marginal analysis, mathematical programming, and simulation as applied to corporate economics. In general, the principal motivation for using any one of these three analytical tools with regard to corporate economics is the pursuit of scientific knowledge about the behavior of the firm.

When applied to corporate economics the scientific method takes the form of the following well-known four-stage procedure: (1) observation of the economic system, (2) formulation of a mathematical model which attempts to explain the observations of the system, (3) prediction of the behavior of the system on the basis of the model by using mathematical or logical deduction, that is, by obtaining solutions to the model, and (4) performance of experiments to test the validity of the model.

For the most part, the emphasis of marginal analysis, linear programming, and the other analytical tools discussed in this book has been on the second and third steps of the scientific method. That is, with each of the previously mentioned analytical approaches, a mathematical model describing some aspect of the behavior of the firm is formulated, and some type of optimum solution is derived through a specific analytical technique. With marginal analysis and linear programming, major emphasis is placed on the deductive rather than the inductive processes of the scientific method.

However, the orientation of simulation is somewhat different. The methodological view taken by users of simulation is that when one is dealing with corporate economics, it is often not plausible to carry out one or more of the four steps of the scientific method. Although this position is similar to the methodological position in economics which asserts that it is impossible to conduct controlled experiments in economics, it is not exactly the same. The position of those who advocate the use of simulation as a mode of analysis is that some form of simulation may prove to be an acceptable substitute for the step (or steps) in the scientific method which is causing the difficulty. That is, simulation may permit the possibility of conducting a type of pseudoexperiment on an economic system.

Looking first at the observation stage of the scientific method, we find frequently that it is either impossible or extremely expensive to observe the actual behavior of the firm in response to changes in business strategies or in the external environment. For example, certain data on competitors, cost data, production data, etc., may not exist for a particular business. However, we may have sufficient information to formulate "meaningful" hypotheses about the probability distributions of some of these variables over time or to estimate their trends over time.

We may then use a computer to generate data (pseudoobservations) for the business system of interest on the basis of the assumed probability distributions or frequency distributions. The pseudoobservations may in turn be used by the corporate economist in formulating, manipulating, and testing models describing the behavior of the system as a whole. That is, we merely substitute the computer-generated data for the missing actual observations of the business system. In many cases these simulated data may prove to be completely adequate, particularly if the model of the system under study is sensitive only to large changes in the values of the simulated input data.

To be sure, in the second step of the scientific method we would want to avoid formulating models that describe the behavior of some company solely on the basis of simulated data. However, we may be willing to place considerable confidence in business planning models formulated with the aid of data collected from empirical observations which have been supplemented by simulated data (in the case of missing data), provided that the model has been subjected to extensive statistical testing in the fourth step of the scientific method.

It is the third step of this methodology that has provided most of the impetus for using simulation as a tool of analysis in corporate economics. Even though a mathematical model can be formulated to describe a dynamic company operating under conditions of risk or uncertainty, it may not be possible to obtain a solution for the model by standard analytical techniques such as differential calculus or linear programming and in turn make predictions about the behavior of the business. Most of the problems in corporate economics are of such a complex nature that solution techniques do not exist for solving them, or if the techniques do exist, they may very well exceed the capacity of present-day computers. Models used in the development of theories of the business cycle and market behavior both give rise to diffculties of this type. Since the 1930s, economists have relied on solutions to differential and difference equations as the standard analytical technique for investigating the behavior of business cycles and competitive markets. But as nonlinearities, higher-order equations, and random (probabilistic) variables are introduced into these models, solutions by straightforward analytical techniques become increasingly difficult if not impossible. Although it may be conceptually possible to formulate a model describing the behavior of a dynamic, multiprocess firm operating under risk, present-day mathematical techniques are incapable of yielding solutions to a problem of this magnitude. Under these circumstances corporate economists have almost been forced to turn to numerical analysis or simulation as an alternative mode of analysis.

With the computer hardware and software available today, simulation models can be made as complex and realistic as our imagination will permit, for analytical solutions to these models are not necessary. Regardless of how complicated the model is, simulation enables us to trace out the time paths of the model.

Finally, it may be either impossible or very costly to perform experiments to test the validity of mathematical models that describe the behavior of a business. Obviously, this problem is merely a mirror image of the first problem we discussed regarding the implementation of the scientific method. In both cases there exists a problem of insufficient data. In the first case, data available for formulating hypotheses about the system were insufficient. However, in the fourth step of the scientific method the problem lies in obtaining numerical data to verify the model and its solution. In fact, the only difference between these two problems is the use to which the simulated data are to be put. For example, in the first case we may be interested in simulating next year's sales data to facilitate the formulation of a mathematical model describing the behavior of a firm which uses sales data as one of its inputs. However, in the fourth case we

**TABLE 10-5**
ESTIMATES OF RELEVANT VARIABLES

|  | **Expected value** | **Standard deviation** |
|---|---|---|
| Operating expenses OE | $200,000 | $20,000 |
| Market-share MS | 18% | 3% |
| Market sales SL | $5 million | $500,000 |

may be interested in simulating next year's sales data for an entirely different reason. That is, simulated data may be used to test alternative hypotheses concerning the operation of the firm during the forthcoming year. Such hypotheses are usually called decision rules. In other words, simulation provides us with a tool for tracing out the effects of alternative decision rules on the behavior of the firm within the confines of a tightly controlled laboratory experiment. To be sure, it may be assumed that we can do the same thing with some of the other analytical tools described in this book, but with simulation we can experiment with more variables, more decision rules, more complex models, and models which more nearly approximate the actual behavior of business firms. And we can do all these things with great speed on computers.

Chapter 3 contained an application of computer simulation to an econometric model of the textile industry. The model was solved and validated with computer simulation techniques. Chapter 12 will treat a special case of simulation: corporate simulation models. To illustrate the applicability of simulation under the assumptions of risk analysis, we shall briefly describe a capital budgeting application.

### A Capital Budgeting Application

David B. Hertz[5] has developed an interesting approach to capital budgeting which involves simulating the probability distributions of the important variables which determine the profitability of investment projects.

We shall use a manufacturing firm as an example to illustrate the Hertz model. The problem is to construct the probability distribution of the present value of the firm's proposal to build a new plant.

First we must select those variables which are important to the present-value calculation. Let us choose only three for simplicity: (1) operating expenses OE, (2) market-share MS, and (3) market sales SL. Next we must obtain estimates of these three variables. These estimates are listed in Table 10-5. It will be useful to think of the following general function for calculating the present value PV of a project:

$$PV = f(OE, MS, SL, \ldots) \tag{10-19}$$

[5] David B. Hertz, "Risk Analysis in Capital Investment," *Harvard Business Review,* January–February 1964.

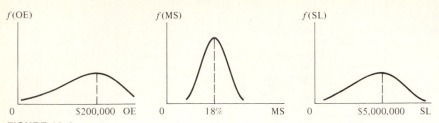

**FIGURE 10-4**
Probability density functions of relevant variables.

That is, the PV of the project is a function of the three random variables listed in Table 10-5. The dots indicate that there are many other variables which we have ignored here. Of course, we should be interested only in critical variables anyway, i.e., those variables to which PV is sensitive and about which much uncertainty exists.

We should point out again that a normal investment evaluation procedure involves simply substituting the values in the expected-value column of Table 10-5 into equation (10-19). However, in this case, the information in the standard deviation column would be ignored. As to the source of the standard deviation estimates, they are guesses made by the individual doing the expected-value estimates.

In Figure 10-4 we show the probability density functions of the three variables in Table 10-5. The probability functions can, of course, take any shape and are by no means restricted to symmetrical ones. For the moment we shall make the assumption that the three random variables are mutually independent. Later this assumption will be relaxed.

By using the computer to generate random variables from the three distributions,[6] we can generate a probability density function of PV by simulation. That is, the computer generates a random variable from each distribution in Figure 10-4. These three values are substituted into equation (10-19), and PV is computed and stored. Then three more random variables are generated, and PV is computed and stored again. Repeating this process, say 1,000 times, would provide us with enough observations on PV to construct the desired distribution. That is, the end result would be a distribution of PV such as is shown in Figure 10-5.

It is important to note that the PV equation (10-19) is likely to be nonlinear in the variables OE, MS, and SL. Thus, the mean of the PV distribution in Figure 10-5, *viz,* $500,000, is unlikely to be the same value of PV that would be obtained by simply substituting the expected values from Table 10-5 into equation (10-19).

Hertz used an internal rate of return criterion in his model rather than the PV criterion we have used. In reporting the results of his example, he observed

---

[6] For a discussion of this technique see T. H. Naylor and J. M. Vernon, *Microeconomics and Decision Models of the Firm* (New York: Harcourt Brace, 1969).

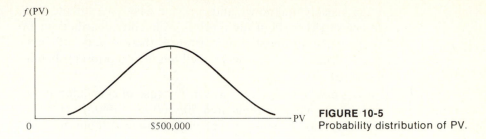

**FIGURE 10-5**
Probability distribution of PV.

a rather large difference between the rate calculated with expected values only and the rate determined via simulation.

> Management had been informed, on the basis of the "one best estimate" approach, that the expected return was 25.2% before taxes. When we ran the new set of data through the computer program, however, we got an expected return of only 14.6% before taxes. This surprising difference not only is due to the fact that under the new approach we use a range of values; it also reflects the fact that we have weighted each value in the range by the chances of its occurrence.[7]

Finally, the Hertz model is capable of handling dependency among the random variables. For example, it is reasonable to view variables OE and MS as being interdependent. That is, it could be argued that the lower the firm's operating expenses OE, the higher will be its market-share MS.

The method for handling this interdependence of MS and OE is straightforward. The firm would develop a number of probability distributions of MS, each corresponding to a different range of values of OE. As an example, say only two distributions of MS are constructed, one with an expected value of 15 percent and the other with a value of 20 percent. The computer generates a random variable from the OE distribution first. If it happens to fall in the lower half of the range of OE values, the computer then generates a random variable from the MS distribution with the 20 percent expected value. The rest of the procedure is the same as was described earlier.

## PRACTICAL LIMITATIONS OF RISK ANALYSIS

As we have mentioned, even though risk analysis is a popular topic in many graduate schools of business, in reality formal risk analysis is not used very often as a practical decision-making tool. We shall outline some of the reasons for this.

First, most of the approaches described thus far assume that the decision maker has either empirical knowledge or a priori knowledge of the probability distribution of the random variable(s) of interest. The fact of the matter is that the probability distributions of the key random variables of interest in a

---

[7] Hertz, "Risk Analysis in Capital Investment," p. 183.

decision problem are usually unknown and are not easy to estimate empirically. A lot has been written about the a priori probability distributions of executives. Although we do not doubt their existence, there is very little evidence that corporate executives know how to spell out their a priori probabilities in any formal manner.

Second, risk analysis can be very expensive in the case of simulation models. Simulation experiments must be replicated 50, 100, or 1,000 times. (The example model in the previous section was replicated 50 times.) If our model is large and complex, these replications require enormous amounts of computer time if we examine many alternative policies or external assumptions.

Third, simulation models with risk analysis involve a host of very serious methodological problems, including validation, experimental design, and analysis of data generated by the simulation model. These are difficult problems which are beyond the scope of this book.[8]

Fourth, formal risk analysis is difficult to sell to top management. The number of managers who are comfortable with probability distributions, random variables, and standard deviations constitutes a very small subset of managers.

Of the techniques described thus far, sensitivity analysis with computer simulation models may very well be the most commonly used formal tool for risk analysis. Suppose, for example, we have a model of an oligopolistic market. We do not know what price our principal competitor will charge. Therefore, we run the simulation experiment on the basis of several different assumed pricing policies on the part of the competition: high, low, and most likely prices. We then examine the impact of these different competitive strategies on the sales of our own firm. Thus we are able to evaluate the sensitivity of our sales to competitive pricing policies. Computer simulation is widely used by corporate decision makers to perform sensitivity analyses.

## DECISION RULES UNDER UNCERTAINTY

Having considered the problem of decision making under risk, we now turn to the problem of decision making under uncertainty, i.e., the case in which the probabilities associated with future outcomes are unknown. To illustrate the problem of decision making under uncertainty, consider a firm which is planning to embark on a major television advertising campaign. Three television networks are available for use by the firm in carrying out its campaign. These alternative networks are denoted by $A_1$, $A_2$, and $A_3$, respectively. Associated with each television network are three possible outcomes $O_1$, $O_2$, and $O_3$. These outcomes represent increments in total profit for the firm which result from the use of a particular television network for the advertising campaign. (Incremental profits are measured in millions of dollars.) The payoff matrix

[8] See Thomas H. Naylor, *Computer Simulation Experiments with Models of Economic Systems* (New York: John Wiley, 1971).

**TABLE 10-6**
A PAYOFF MATRIX

| Outcomes / Alternatives | $O_1$ | $O_2$ | $O_3$ |
|---|---|---|---|
| $A_1$ | $12 | −$6 | $24 |
| $A_2$ | $36 | $12 | $48 |
| $A_3$ | −$3 | $60 | $30 |

which the firm faces is given by Table 10-6. Note that the payoff matrix consists of three rows, one for each alternative television network. There are also three columns, one for each possible outcome. The elements of the payoff matrix represent the increase in profit to the firm associated with every possible outcome which may occur as the result of using one of the three network alternatives. Which alternative (or alternatives) should the firm choose?

In this section we shall outline five possible rules which decision makers may use in making a decision of this type. These criteria include:

1 Bayes rule
2 Maximin rule
3 Maximax rule
4 Hurwicz rule
5 Minimax regret rule

### Bayes Rule

The Bayes rule states that if we have absolutely no information about the probabilities associated with future outcomes, we should assign equal probabilities to each of the possible outcomes and use these probabilities to compute the expected value of each alternative course of action. In our example, we would assign a probability of 1/3 to each of the three outcomes $O_1$, $O_2$, and $O_3$. The expected profit for each alternative would be

$$E\pi_1 = 1/3(12) - 1/3(6) + 1/3(24) = \$10$$
$$E\pi_2 = 1/3(36) + 1/3(12) + 1/3(48) = \$32$$
$$E\pi_3 = 1/3(-3) + 1/3(60) + 1/3(30) = \$29$$

According to the Bayes rule, the firm would select alternative 2; that is, it would choose television network 2, which yields an expected profit of $32.

The Bayes rule possesses a number of obvious shortcomings. The most serious of these deficiencies is the fact that it is usually not clear in advance to the decision maker which unknown outcomes are equally probable. If in fact there are $n$ possible outcomes and the decision maker is aware of only $m$ of these, his or her decision will be influenced considerably by the magnitude of $m$. Suppose that 10 possible outcomes may occur, and the decision maker is aware of 5 of them. Applying Bayes rule, the decision maker would assign a probability of 1/5 to each outcome. On the other hand, if the decision maker had known there were actually 10 outcomes, he or she would have assigned a probability of 1/10 to each outcome.

Since the Bayes rule makes use of the expected-value concept, it also suffers from the inadequacies associated with the expected-value approach discussed earlier in this chapter.

### Maximin Rule

The maximin rule represents a very conservative approach to decision making. For each possible alternative the decision maker determines the worst possible outcome, i.e., the one with the lowest payoff. The decision maker then selects that alternative whose minimum payoff is highest. In other words, the objective is to maximize one's minimum possible gains.

In our example the minimum possible payoffs associated with alternatives $A_1$, $A_2$, and $A_3$ are $-\$6$, $\$12$, and $-\$3$, respectively. The minimum profit of $A_2$ is larger than that of $A_1$ and $A_3$. Therefore, the maximin criterion would also call for the use of television network 2.

### Maximax Rule

Whereas the maximin rule offers considerable appeal to the conservative decision maker, the maximax rule is best suited for the proverbial "optimist" who looks only at the best possible outcome. This criterion can be illustrated by examining the behavior of someone who plays the horses and in placing his or her bet to win on a given horse looks only at the fact that the horse has won 2 races in the past while completely overlooking the fact that the horse did not win 73 of the 75 races which he or she ran.

In our example problem (again referring to Table 10-6) the decision maker using a maximax criterion would select alternative $A_3$, because it is possible to obtain a payoff of $\$60$ by choosing this alternative. The decision maker completely disregards the fact that he or she might also lose $\$3$ by selecting $A_3$. The maximax rule, which is a decision rule well suited to a gambler, considers only the most glittering payoff associated with any strategy and is blind to any other possibilities.

### Hurwicz Rule

Hurwicz has proposed a rule which lies somewhere between the conservative extreme of the maximin rule and the optimistic extreme of the maximax rule. According to the Hurwicz rule, the decision maker should use a weighted average of the minimum and maximum payoffs of each alternative in making a decision. In our example, suppose that we assign a weight of $\alpha = 1/3$ to the minimum payoff of each alternative and a weight of $1 - \alpha = 2/3$ to the maximum payoff associated with each alternative. The three alternatives would be evaluated as follows:

$$A_1 = 1/3(-6) + 2/3(24) = \$14$$
$$A_2 = 1/3(12) + 2/3(48) = \$36$$
$$A_3 = 1/3(-3) + 2/3(60) = \$39$$

Applying the Hurwicz rule, the firm would select alternative $A_3$. Of course, if the decision maker were somewhat more conservative and $\alpha$ was assigned a value of 2/3 and $1 - \alpha$ was 1/3, then $A_2$ would be chosen rather than $A_3$. Like the maximin and the maximax rules, the Hurwicz rule ignores information about the less extreme values of the payoffs associated with each strategy or alternative.

### Minimax Regret Rule

The minimax regret rule focuses on the opportunity cost of an incorrect decision on the part of the decision maker. From the payoff matrix in Table 10-6 we construct a new matrix in Table 10-7, called a regret matrix. The elements in the regret matrix are computed in the following manner. The element in the $i$th row and the $j$th column of the regret matrix is the opportunity cost of choosing the $i$th alternative when the $j$th outcome is realized. For example, if the decision maker selects the first alternative $A_1$ and outcome $O_1$ actually occurs, then the decision maker forgoes $24, i.e., the difference between the $12 the decision maker actually receives and the $36 he or she could have received after selecting $A_2$. Note that the element in row 2 and column 1 is equal to $0 because $A_2$ is the best alternative to have chosen if outcome $O_1$ occurs. The other elements in the regret matrix are calculated in a similar manner.

The philosophy underlying this approach is the protection of the decision maker against excessive opportunity costs. To protect against excessive oppor-

**TABLE 10-7**
A REGRET MATRIX

| Outcomes / Alternatives | $O_1$ | $O_2$ | $O_3$ |
|---|---|---|---|
| $A_1$ | $24 | $66* | $24 |
| $A_2$ | $0 | $48* | $0 |
| $A_3$ | $39* | $0 | $18 |

tunity costs, the decision maker applies a minimax rule to the regret matrix. The maximum possible loss in each row is denoted by an asterisk in Table 10-7. That alternative whose row contains the smallest of the three maximum regret elements is chosen by the decision maker. In our example, $A_3$ will be chosen. $A_3$ is said to be a minimax strategy, since it minimizes the decision maker's maximum possible loss. Since the minimax regret rule considers only the largest regret element in each row of Table 10-7, it, not unlike the maximin, maximax, and Hurwicz rules, ignores a substantial amount of the data in the payoff matrix.

## QUESTIONS AND PROBLEMS

**10-1** Compare and contrast decision making under conditions of certainty, risk, and uncertainty.

**10-2** Discuss the advantages and limitations of the following criteria for decision making under risk:
  **a** Finite planning horizon
  **b** Sensitivity analysis
  **c** Risk discounting
  **d** Expected value
  **e** Certainty equivalents
  **f** Expected utility

**10-3** List some examples where decision trees have proved to be useful decision-making tools.

**10-4** Discuss the relationship between computer simulation techniques and the scientific method.

**10-5** Explain how computer simulation may be used as a capital budgeting tool.

**10-6** Discuss some of the practical limitations of the use of formal risk analysis as a managerial decision-making tool.

**10-7** Define and explain each of the following decision rules for decision making under uncertainty:
  **a** Bayes rule
  **b** Maximin rule
  **c** Maximax rule
  **d** Hurwicz rule
  **e** Minimax regret rule

**10-8** The XYZ Corporation is considering two projects, A and B. Both projects are concerned with an expansion of the firm's activities in the state of Washington. Project A would accomplish this by the purchase of an existing small company, while project B would involve construction of a new plant and the hiring of new personnel. After making the best estimates possible of the streams of net cash flows for the two projects, the question becomes one of how the greater uncertainty of project B should be taken into account.

Suppose management has decided that project A is to be evaluated at the firm's cost of capital, i.e., 10 percent, while project B's discount rate is to be 15 percent, i.e., to include a 5 percent risk premium. The following data summarize the two projects:

| Year | Net cash flows | |
| --- | --- | --- |
| | Project A, $ | Project B, $ |
| 1 | 100,000 | 125,000 |
| 2 | 100,000 | 125,000 |
| 3 | 100,000 | 125,000 |
| 4 | 100,000 | 125,000 |
| 5 | 100,000 | 125,000 |
| 6 | 100,000 | 125,000 |

Calculate the present values of the two projects.

**10-9** The director of corporate development of a conglomerate has been asked to evaluate three alternative investments, each requiring an initial outlay of about $50 million. The director has obtained the following rough estimates of the probability distributions of the net present value NPV of each of these investments:

| Investment 1 | | Investment 2 | | Investment 3 | |
| --- | --- | --- | --- | --- | --- |
| P(NPV) | NPV, $ | P(NPV) | NPV, $ | P(NPV) | NPV, $ |
| .2 | 10 million | .2 | 5 million | .2 | 25 million |
| .1 | 25 million | .1 | 30 million | .3 | 50 million |
| .5 | 40 million | .4 | 50 million | .5 | 75 million |
| .2 | 100 million | .3 | 125 million | | |

Using the expected-value criterion, how should the director of corporate development rank the three investments?

**10-10** Suppose that the CEO of the company described in problem 10-9 is thought to have a constant marginal utility of income which can be approximated by the utility function $U = 25 + 3\text{NPV}$ when NPV is net present value in millions of dollars. Which investment will the CEO choose? What if the CEO's utility function for income is characterized by diminishing marginal utility and is of the form $U = 250\text{NPV} - \text{NPV}^2$? Which investment will be selected in the latter case?

**10-11** The vice president of exploration and development for an independent oil and gas drilling company has been given the following payoff matrix by the company's geologist regarding a well that is about to be drilled.

PAYOFF MATRIX

| Well depth, feet | States of Nature | | | |
| --- | --- | --- | --- | --- |
| | Oil, $ | Gas, $ | Both, $ | Neither, $ |
| 10,000 | 25,000 | 10,000 | 30,000 | −100,000 |
| 15,000 | 100,000 | 20,000 | 100,000 | −150,000 |
| 20,000 | 500,000 | 50,000 | 400,000 | −250,000 |

The geologist has advised the vice president that three alternative drilling strategies appear to be viable. The well may be drilled to depths of 10,000,

15,000, or 20,000 feet. There is the possibility of finding oil, gas, both, or nothing. The cost of drilling the well increases with the depth of the well. The quality of the oil and gas which may be found is also influenced by the depth of the well. The drilling company must contract for equipment and labor in advance. If it decides to drill a 10,000-foot well, it is not possible for the company to increase the depth of the well to say 15,000 feet after it reaches a depth of 10,000 feet without increasing its costs drastically.

What advice would you have for the vice president of exploration and development in choosing a drilling strategy? What additional information would be useful in making such a decision?

**10-12** The management of the Key Largo Shipyard will soon be negotiating a new contract with the union that represents the company's employees, the International Brotherhood of Ship Carpenters, Caulkers, and Joiners. (The union's contract is renegotiated each year.) The one issue involved at this time is the wage rate. As has been the case for the past 20 years, both the company and the union have agreed to submit their dispute to an arbitration board.

The tripartite arbitration board consists of three members: a company representative, a union representative, and an impartial member appointed by the American Arbitration Association who acts as chairperson.* In most cases the final decision is made by the chairperson, since the union representative seldom feels compelled to vote with management, and vice versa.

The selection of a management representative is of utmost importance since that representative's actions may well influence the final outcome of the dispute, even though the chairperson is actually impartial. The chairperson's decision may well be influenced by the choices made by both the union and management as to their respective representatives. For example, if management selects as its representative an individual who is a radical company person, and the union chooses an individual who is either unbiased or does not express favoritism toward the union vocally, the chairperson may have a negative reaction against the company and favor the union in his or her final decision.

Management is considering five different types of individuals to represent the company on the arbitration board. These individuals are indicated below by the symbols $M_1$, $M_2$, $M_3$, $M_4$, and $M_5$.

| Management representative | Characteristics |
| --- | --- |
| $M_1$ | An unbiased individual |
| $M_2$ | An individual whose voting record in arbitration cases indicates a slight bias in favor of management but who on occasion has voted against management |
| $M_3$ | A company person who utilizes a soft-sell approach |
| $M_4$ | An outspoken company person |
| $M_5$ | A radical company person |

---

* The American Arbitration Association maintains a national panel of more than 13,000 persons, each of whom is an expert in his or her chosen field or profession and is qualified to render impartial decisions in arbitration cases.

The union has a similar set of individuals whom it is considering to represent it in the dispute. The individuals are indicated below by $U_1$, $U_2$, $U_3$, $U_4$, and $U_5$.

| Union representative | Characteristics |
|---|---|
| $U_1$ | An unbiased individual |
| $U_2$ | An individual whose voting record in arbitration cases indicates a slight bias in favor of the union but who on occasion has voted against the union |
| $U_3$ | A union person who utilizes a soft-sell approach |
| $U_4$ | An outspoken union person |
| $U_5$ | A radical union person |

Past experience in arbitration cases has indicated that the average hourly wage increase (in cents per hour) associated with the type of representative whom management employs at the bargaining table is completely dependent on the type of representative whom the union chooses. Likewise, the average hourly wage increase (in cents per hour) associated with the type of representative the union employs is dependent on the type of representative whom management chooses. (It is convenient to refer to the choices available to the union and management as strategies.)

It should be emphasized that neither the union nor management knows the other's final strategy decision until the arbitration hearing actually begins. Neither party can alter its choice of a representative once the representative's name has been submitted to the chairperson of the arbitration board.

Twenty years of arbitration experience indicates that the following table is an approximate indication of the expected average wage increases (in cents per hour) associated with the different possible combinations of union and management representatives chosen to serve on the arbitration board.

|       | $M_1$ | $M_2$ | $M_3$ | $M_4$ | $M_5$ |
|-------|-------|-------|-------|-------|-------|
| $U_1$ | 0     | 5     | 10    | 10    | 30    |
| $U_2$ | 10    | 5     | 15    | 15    | 35    |
| $U_3$ | 25    | 15    | 10    | 20    | 40    |
| $U_4$ | 15    | 5     | 5     | 15    | 20    |
| $U_5$ | −5    | 0     | 5     | 10    | 10    |

Although the average wage increases in this table are not an exact representation of the wage increases associated with the different union-management strategies utilized over the past 20 years, management feels that it will prove to be a useful guide in selecting the type of individual to represent the company in future wage negotiations. Furthermore, both the union and management know the approximate wage increases associated with each union-management strategy combination.

Using the criteria for decision making under uncertainty described in this chapter, devise a set of strategies for the company's management in negotiating with the union.

*Hint:* This problem is an example of what economists call a two-person, zero-sum, competitive game. It can be expressed as a linear programming problem.

**10-13** An editorial in *The Wall Street Journal* of August 18, 1981, offered the following analysis. Do you agree with the analysis?

> This morning's mail brought an appeal for funds from Columbia University. While this isn't unusual, the special appeal enclosed by the Department of History was. The basis for their solicitation was not that training historians is critical to society, but that recruiting students is critical for the reputation of the department.
>
> Eyebrows raised, we wondered about other points made in their letter; like, "The price of a Columbia degree in history is the assumption of an alarming heavy burden of debt," and the department's admission that it has been able to place only 60% to 70% of its graduates.
>
> Which started us wondering about the value of an investment in a Ph.D. Say it takes six years of schooling, at $6,000 a year in direct costs and $15,000 forgone in salary someone is likely to earn with a bachelor's degree. A Ph.D. is likely to raise the salary to $17,500, which amounts to something over a 34-year career. The gain, however, has to be adjusted for the risk of unemployment, which the Columbia History Department puts at .35.
>
> To do this right, a businessperson would add up these income flows and discount them to present value, so we unzipped our calculator and punched some numbers, casting everything in 1981 dollars and using 3% as the real cost of funds. It comes out that the present value of the direct and opportunity costs is $113,761. The present value of the higher salary would be $309,708, but this drops to $201,309 when adjusted for risk. So with the $108,398 risk adjustment and $113,761 in costs, the true opportunity cost of an investment in a Columbia history Ph.D. looks like $222,159.
>
> Thus, taxpayers and donors ought to ask themselves just how many Ph.D.s in history they want to buy for the nation at $222,000 a crack. Students, and parents, ought to ask if the price is right: Is a Ph.D. worth $222,000 of utility? Because it is sure not worth it as an investment.[9]

*Note:* For space reasons we omitted a 3% interest rate in our Table 5 at the back of the book. The relevant entries in the 3% column for this problem are: period 6, 5.417; period 40, 23.115.

---

[9]Reprinted by permission of *The Wall Street Journal*, © Dow Jones & Company, Inc., 1981. All Rights Reserved.

# PART FIVE

# STRATEGIC PLANNING

# CHAPTER 11

# MICROECONOMICS: THE LANGUAGE OF STRATEGIC PLANNING

In Chapter 1 we suggested that strategic planning is perhaps the single most important application of microeconomics to managerial decision making. We also

**345**

noted that the essence of strategic planning is long-term resource allocation for the firm. Given the importance of strategic planning to the long-term profitability of a company, it seems appropriate to devote a section of this book to strategic planning.

In this chapter we shall summarize the elements of strategic planning, develop an economic paradigm for strategic decision making, and attempt to demonstrate the appropriateness of employing microeconomics as the language of strategic planning. In Chapter 12 we shall examine two specific analytic tools of strategic planning: analytical portfolio models and corporate simulation models. The concluding chapter, Chapter 13, will be concerned with the politics of corporate economics. The rationale underlying this chapter is based in part on the fact that corporate economics is increasingly being used as a strategic planning tool. In many companies there are intense internal political conflicts concerning who controls the company's planning process. To the extent that corporate economics is an important tool of strategic planning, it behooves corporate economists and users of corporate economics to understand some of the behavioral implications of the use of corporate economics within a corporation.

## MICROECONOMIC FOUNDATIONS OF STRATEGIC PLANNING

In all too many corporations, accounting, almost by default, is used as the language of strategic planning. Financial reports, budgets, and long-term financial plans are expressed in accounting terms. Indeed, in many companies the chief financial officer, who usually is an accountant, controls not only accounting and budgeting but strategic planning as well. One of the results of strategic plans based primarily on accounting as a conceptual framework is a preoccupation with financial details and inadequate attention to such issues as goals, objectives, the external environment, and business strategies.

Although accounting may be a useful language for evaluating a business's historical performance, it may not be the most effective language for strategic planning. Strategic planning is forward-looking; accounting is by definition backward-looking. It is not surprising that one language is not suitable for two such dissimilar needs. Perhaps it is appropriate to consider replacing accounting with economics as the relevant language of strategic planning. Microeconomics tends to be more forward-looking than accounting, focusing on goals and objectives and the decisions that are necessary to achieve them.

Macroeconomists, concerned with the economy as a whole, have done a marvelous job of raising the awareness level of corporate management as to the importance of macroeconomic information in strategic planning. Unfortunately, microeconomists have not done nearly as good a job of pointing out that the economic theory of the firm is an extremely useful conceptual framework for viewing a company as a whole. This is particularly true if the company consists of a collection or portfolio of businesses, some of which may be interdependent with regard to production, marketing, or distribution. Under the assumptions of microeconomics, the firm attempts to make a set of product-output decisions and factor-input decisions which are consistent with its overall objectives in light of the information available on product demand, factor supply, and production technology. But that is precisely what strategic planning is all about. It deals with the selection of business strategies that will enable management to achieve its long-term objectives on the basis of limited information about the company's macroeconomic, competitive, regulatory, technological, factor-supply, and international environments. Corporate economists and corporate planners should spend more time listening to each other; both might benefit from the experience. The aim of this chapter and Chapters 12 and 13 is to facilitate the exchange of information between corporate economists and corporate planners.

## STRATEGIC PLANNING

In the previous section we indicated that the economic theory of the firm consists of three basic elements: (1) goals and objectives, (2) information about the firm's internal and external environments, and (3) decisions about resource allocation. In this section we shall demonstrate that strategic planning consists of essentially the same three elements. We shall examine each element within the framework of strategic planning.

To illustrate strategic planning methodology we shall use Northwest Industries as an example. Northwest Industries is a diversified conglomerate which, as is shown in Figure 11-1, owns nine different businesses, ranging from industrial products to chemical products and consumer products. (Two of these businesses, Buckingham and Coca-Cola Los Angeles, were sold in late 1981.) Since it was organized as the holding company of the Chicago Northwestern Railroad in 1968, Northwest Industries has compiled one of the most impres-

**FIGURE 11-1**
Operating companies of Northwest Industries.

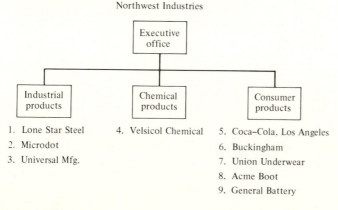

sive growth rates in earnings of any of the diversified conglomerates. Its earnings per share of common stock increased from $.53 per share in 1968 to $9.40 per share in 1981. According to the annual report of Northwest Industries, the ultimate objective of the company is "to maximize total return (market appreciation plus dividends) over a period of time to its stockholders." For the ten years ended December 31, 1981, the compound annual total return to common stockholders was 21.4 percent.

Northwest Industries is an example of a highly decentralized firm in which each business or operating company enjoys a high degree of autonomy. Northwest has utilized formal strategic planning since its inception in 1968. It is a prime example of the benefits which can be derived from effective strategic planning.

### Goals and Objectives

In Chapter 1 we defined corporate objectives as a general statement of the sense of direction in which senior management wants to see a company move over the long term. Once overall corporate objectives have been specified, divisional and departmental objectives must be defined, reviewed, and approved by the next level of management. Corporate objectives, of course, must be approved by the board of directors.

Not unlike government policymakers, corporate executives face multiple constituencies: investors, management, employees, consumers, government, and the general public. These diverse groups are likely to have conflicting objectives. The role of the CEO is to somehow come up with a stable set of objectives which minimizes the degree of conflict and enables the company to survive.

Many companies have no formal objectives whatsoever. Other companies have implicit objectives which are understood by all but may not ever have been written down. One well-known company achieved a remarkable degree of success during the past 30 years without any semblance of formal objectives or, for that matter, formal planning. Yet everyone in the company understood very well that there were three major corporate objectives: (1) remain number one in the industry, (2) continue to increase sales and profits, and (3) remain a single-product business.

In the case of Northwest Industries, the company does not have formal corporate objectives. However, the general managers of the nine operating companies are provided with guidelines which they are expected to follow in preparing their strategic plans. For example, the philosophy of Northwest Industries is first to operate in fields which are basic—in the sense that Northwest's products are commonplace and will always be purchased—and diverse, and second to be the leader in each of these industries. In addition, corporate management stresses the importance of well-known brands in each field.

Below is a list of representative corporate financial, marketing, and production objectives.

### Financial

1 Survive and avoid bankruptcy.
2 Become and remain profitable.
3 Maximize return on investment.
4 Increase cash flow.
5 Become free of debt.
6 Pay dividends.
7 Increase the dividend payout.
8 Avoid a financial takeover.

### Marketing

1 Increase market-share.
2 Become the market leader.
3 Achieve an international reputation for service and quality.
4 Overtake a competitor.
5 Drive a potential competitor out of the market.

### Production

1 Improve our efficiency in manufacturing.
2 Reduce operating costs.
3 Improve capacity utilization.
4 Smooth out production swings.
5 Maintain full employment.

Whereas corporate objectives describe a future state of being for the company to work toward, corporate goals are much more specific. They refer to a specific achievement to be realized within a definite time period. Goals are often quantifiable.

Corporate goals follow from corporate objectives. Once corporate goals have been defined, divisional and departmental goals may be formulated as well.

Below is a set of specific corporate goals which correspond to the classes of objectives we have just described.

### Financial

1 Achieve a return on sales of 15 percent by 1982.
2 Achieve a return on investment (ROI) of 10 percent by 1981.

**3** Achieve a current ratio of at least 2.0.
**4** Increase earnings per share by at least 25 percent per year.
**5** Pay a dividend of $1 per share beginning in 1981.
**6** Acquire a particular company in 1982.

**Marketing**

**1** Obtain a market-share of at least 50 percent by 1982.
**2** Introduce our products into the United Kingdom and Scandinavia in 1981.
**3** Reduce the number of client complaints by 20 percent.
**4** Increase total sales volume by 15 percent next year.

**Production**

**1** Reduce excess capacity by 5 percent.
**2** Reduce inventories by 10 percent.
**3** Reduce operating costs by 15 percent.
**4** Reduce the cost of raw materials by 10 percent.

In the case of Northwest Industries, even though corporate financial goals are not spelled out explicitly, the company has managed to achieve sales and earnings growth rates of approximately 20 percent per year.

**Information**

An integral part of any strategic plan is a review of the company's external environment and an assessment of its internal strengths and weaknesses.

**External Environment**   There are at least six major areas of concern which should be addressed by senior management in reviewing the firm's external environment:

**1** Macroeconomic environment
**2** Competitive environment
**3** Regulatory environment
**4** Technological environment
**5** Factor-supply environment
**6** International environment

*Macroeconomic Environment*   Among the questions to be asked about the long-term macroeconomic environment are the following: Will the economy continue to grow or will there be periods of slower growth or possibly no growth at all? What can we say about the rate of inflation over the next few years? What about the availability and prices of basic inputs into the company's production process? Will there be shortages of oil, and how high will the price of fossil fuels go?

These are not easy questions to answer. Corporate executives should be wary of econometricians and futurists who promise more than they can deliver in terms of long-term economic forecasts. Forecasting the future is a tough business, and econometricians have not compiled an impressive record of accuracy with their long-term forecasting models.

*Competitive Environment* Bruce Henderson of the Boston Consulting Group has suggested that the underlying principle of good corporate strategy is, "Concentrate your strength against your competitor's relative weakness." But to do this one must understand the competition thoroughly. How much is known about the competitor's financial strength? What pricing policies are being used by the competitor? What do we know about the cost structure of competitors and their advertising budgets for next year? These are tough questions to answer, but any long-term strategic plan must be based on realistic assumptions about the likely behavior of competitors.

*Regulatory Environment* Obviously, management must carefully monitor the political and regulatory environment of the company in terms of pending legislation, changes in government regulations, and changes in public opinion. In a democracy private corporations exist because they have been granted a charter by the government to do business. Just as the government grants charters to corporations, it may also impose severe constraints on corporate operations in the form of inflexible regulations.

*Technological Environment* For high-technology firms such as computer hardware and software vendors, electric utilities, and electronics firms, changes in technology are an extremely important element in the external environment. With the rapid changes taking place in the field of microprocessors, a company which does not stay abreast of these changes can be rendered completely obsolete overnight.

*Factor-supply Environment* Since the 1979 worldwide oil crisis, firms have become much more sensitive to the availability and cost of critical raw materials such as oil, coal, natural gas, and other natural resources. Increasingly, companies must have contingency strategies to implement if the supply of a critical raw material is curtailed.

*International Environment* For multinational firms there are a host of external factors to be considered in developing a strategic plan. In addition to all the factors listed above, multinational companies must also consider such questions as political stability, the possibility of a change in government, nationalization of certain industries, and currency fluctuations.

If a long-term strategic plan is to be useful, it must be based on very explicit assumptions about these factors. These are not the types of assumptions which can be delegated to analysts. They represent the heart of the business, and top management must ultimately participate in their formulation and accept the associated risks.

**Internal Environment**   Once corporate management has reviewed the external environment and has transmitted this information to all divisions and all departments, each level of management is ready to begin its own situation assessment on the basis of the corporate assumptions about the external environment. The situation assessment consists of a description of opportunities and problems which the firm is likely to encounter over the planning horizon. Opportunities may take many different forms, including:

1  Financial strength
2  Market-share
3  Experience
4  A favorable public image
5  Technical expertise
6  Patents
7  Skilled personnel
8  Trade names
9  Good products
10  Low costs
11  Distribution system
12  Economies of scale

On the other hand, there may be significant problems on the horizon which will serve as obstacles or constraints to future corporate growth. It is essential that these problems be reviewed and appraised realistically. Corporate problems can take many different forms:

1  Economic uncertainty
2  Inflation
3  Shortages in factor-input supplies
4  Energy prices
5  Competition
6  Market saturation
7  Changes in consumer tastes
8  Government regulations
9  Supply of skilled labor
10  Political uncertainty in international markets
11  Demographic shifts
12  Health hazards associated with certain products

### Resource Allocation Decisions

For a multidivisional firm such as Northwest Industries there are three different types of long-term decisions about resource allocation which must be made by corporate management in conjunction with the annual strategic plan: (1) portfolio decisions, (2) investment decisions, and (3) project decisions.

**Portfolio Decisions**   Portfolio decisions concern the question of which businesses the company should be in. In the case of Northwest Industries, the question might be posed as follows: "Should we continue to hold a portfolio (collection) of businesses which includes Lone Star Steel, Microdot, Velsicol Chemical, etc., or should we consider divesting ourselves of one or more of the operating companies and possibly acquiring additional businesses?" Criteria for making strategic portfolio decisions and analytical tools to assist in the decision-making process are discussed in Chapter 12.

**Investment Decisions**   The second long-term strategic decision which the firm must consider is the level of commitment, usually measured in dollars of investment, to be made to each of the company's businesses or operating companies. Criteria for investment decisions were presented in Chapter 9. Some additional analytical tools for choosing among alternative investments will be discussed in Chapter 12.

**Project Decisions**   Project decisions are concerned with how investment dollars are allocated by the company for a particular business. For example, if Northwest Industries chooses to invest $100 million in Lone Star Steel, should all the money be spent on a new steel mill or should some of it be spent on research and development? If so, how much should be spent on research and development? In reality, project decisions are merely a subset of investment decisions.

**Interdependence**   Thus far we have treated portfolio decisions, investment decisions, and project decisions as though they were independent decisions, yet we know very well that they are completely interdependent. Whether Northwest Industries retains a particular business depends on the expected return generated by that business by comparison with other available alternatives. But the profitability of the business will depend on the level of investment in the business and the profitability of specific projects within that business.

Theoretically, one might argue that the solution of these three decision problems should be obtained simultaneously. Unfortunately, in the real world this turns out to be extremely difficult to achieve. An iterative approach is often used in which operating company managers propose a set of projects to corporate management for approval. These projects compete for investment dollars with those proposed by the other operating companies. Portfolio decisions and investment decisions are based on the set of projects proposed by each operating company. Rarely are portfolio decisions made which consider all logical combinations of projects and investment levels.

Although it is beyond the scope of this book, it should be obvious to the reader that microeconomics represents an appropriate conceptual framework for analyzing the interdependence of the firm's three decisions about allocation of strategic resources.

### The Problem of Strategic Planning

Each of these three problems can be formulated in three different ways: (1) optimization, (2) systems analysis, and (3) "what if?" analysis. We shall briefly describe each of these approaches to strategic planning and explain why the "what if?" approach appears to be the most viable of the three.

**Optimization**   The optimization approach toward strategic planning assumes that the goal of the CEO is to maximize with respect to a single objective, where the objective is typically expressed as net profit, return on investment (ROI), or discounted cash flow. That is, the problem of top management is to select that set of strategies which will yield a maximum return to the stockholder subject to constraints imposed by (1) the availability of production inputs (labor, raw materials, equipment, etc.), (2) production technology, (3) the financial resources available to the company, and (4) the external economic, regulatory, and competitive environments.

This is the approach to strategic planning which is implicit in the economic theory of the firm. Most textbooks on microeconomic theory and managerial economics subscribe to this view of the strategic problem of the firm.

Unfortunately, it has some rather serious limitations. It is rarely, if ever, used by the senior management of real-world companies as a framework for strategic problems. Strategic planning is a multidimensional problem. To be sure, management is interested in profit, discounted cash flow, and ROI. But if the CEO wants the company to survive in the kind of world described in Chapter 1, he or she must be concerned with a multiplicity of output variables including sales, operating costs, market-share, growth liquidity, and cash flow, to mention only a few.

The problem of strategic planning is to some extent an ill-defined problem and does not lend itself to the narrow view of optimization presented in some economics textbooks.

**Systems Analysis**   An alternative formulation of the problem of strategic planning eliminates the necessity of optimizing with respect to a single objective. This approach assumes that the CEO has assigned a specified numerical value to each important output variable describing the performance of the company. For example, numerical targets might be set for ROI, sales growth, market-share, and cash flow. Given the same set of constraints described in the formulation of the optimization problem, the strategic planning problem is to determine a set of strategies which are consistent with the numerical values assigned to the target variables. If the constraints can be represented as a set of mathematical equations, the solution to the strategic planning problem involves solving the set of equations for the strategic variables in terms of given values of the numerical targets.

This approach has great intuitive appeal and would appear to have considerable potential as a framework for strategic planning. Not unlike the optimization approach, this methodology also has severe limitations.

If there are fewer strategic decision variables than there are target variables, a solution to the problem may be mathematically impossible except in special cases. On the other hand, if the number of strategy variables exceeds the number of target variables, an infinite number of solutions will be possible. Within the systems analysis framework, the first of these two problems can be resolved only by increasing the number of strategic decision variables or reducing the number of target variables until there is an equal number of target variables and strategic variables.

Unfortunately, neither of these alternatives is particularly appealing. It is frequently the case that when one formulates the strategic problem of the firm, one will have already included all the strategic decision variables that are meaningful for the decision maker. Therefore, increasing the number of strategy options may, in fact, be impossible. On the other hand, discarding some of the target variables is not a very appealing alternative, either. That is, the decision to change the set of target variables is tantamount to redefining the scope of the strategic planning problem. Presumably, a particular target variable or set of target variables has been included in the problem definition because the CEO feels that it is an important performance measure for the company. In the case where there are more strategy variables than target variables, the decision maker can assign arbitrary values to the surplus decision variables and solve for the remaining ones.

Although the problem of balancing the number of target variables and the number of strategic decision variables is likely to constitute a serious limitation of the systems analysis approach to strategic planning, there is another problem that may be of even greater importance. The assumption that the CEO is going to make a commitment to a specific set of numerical targets for the output variables is at best highly questionable. There are relatively few senior executives of major corporations who are likely to be willing to put in writing specific target values of a set of performance variables such as profit, ROI, revenue, market-share, growth, etc. A methodology based on information (e.g., values of target variables) that simply is not available cannot be expected to yield particularly useful results to the decision maker. However, it may be possible for planning analysts to propose alternative sets of target variables for consideration by management and run a series of "what if?" experiments to provide management with a set of alternative strategies that are capable of yielding different sets of target values.

Although the systems analysis approach has some merit, the approach described in the next section offers strategic planners the greatest latitude and flexibility in experimenting with alternative managerial policies.

**"What If?" Analysis**    A third approach to the problem of strategic planning involves obtaining answers to a number of strategic "what if?" questions. With this approach to strategic planning it is not necessary to assume prior knowledge of the objective function or numerical targets of the CEO or other senior executives.

As was the case with the optimization approach and the systems analysis approach, it is extremely helpful if the relevant constraints can be expressed as a set of mathematical equations. The mathematical formulation of these constraints is called a planning model. Planning models will be described in more detail in Chapter 12.

For any given set of managerial strategies, one generates the time paths of the relevant output variables. In other words, when one approaches the CEO, one asks two questions: "What output (target) variables are of particular interest to you?" and "What sets of decision variables appear to be relevant and feasible?" With the "what if?" approach one can show the corporate executive the consequences of proposed managerial strategies. In addition, planning analysts may also suggest a few strategies or policies for consideration by senior management, and these strategies can be put to a similar test. The decision maker then selects the strategies that are most compatible with his or her long-term objectives.

There are a number of advantages to the "what if?" approach relative to the optimization approach and the systems analysis approach. First, it is not necessary to assume the availability of information about the senior management's preferences that is either impossible or extremely difficult to obtain. Second, the "what if?" approach provides management with the type of information required to make decisions. Third, the number of strategy variables and target variables need not be equal. Fourth, the "what if?" approach seems to come very close to capturing the essence of the way in which corporate executives actually view strategic decisions.

Indeed, in most companies which have made a serious commitment to strategic planning, strategic planning is synonymous with the ability to answer "what if?" questions.

The "what if?" approach to strategic planning is by far the most widely used of the three alternative approaches to the problem of strategic planning.

## AN ECONOMIC PARADIGM
## FOR STRATEGIC DECISION MAKING

In this section, we shall describe an eight-step process for strategic decision making which we believe is generally applicable to multidivisional and multinational strategic planning. Although this economic paradigm is quite simplistic, it may nevertheless prove to be a useful conceptual framework for assisting corporate executives in asking the "right" questions about strategic planning. This strategic planning process can be applied at either the corporate, operating company, or departmental level within a particular company.

Of course, academic purists who are always looking for the "answer" or the "perfect" solution may not be satisfied with a heuristic approach which does not promise to deliver the optimum solution in all cases. However, this process will enable senior executives to sort out the relevant factors in a strategic decision and to use their own judgment in choosing among alternative strategies.

The eight steps are listed below:

1 Identify stakeholders.
2 Review goals and objectives.
3 Specify corporate constraints.
4 Review existing strategic options.
5 Search for additional strategic options.
6 Sort out strategic options worthy of serious consideration.
7 Evaluate strategic options.
8 Select a set of strategic options.

### 1  Identify Stakeholders

Strategic decisions, whether at the corporate, divisional, or departmental level, are not made in a vacuum. Managers of corporations exist in an environment which is characterized by multiple constituencies: investors, other managers, employees, consumers, government, and the general public. More often than not, these different stakeholders have conflicting objectives with regard to how the corporation should be managed.

Investors want high earnings per share and a satisfactory dividend payout rate. Other managers are concerned with their own salaries, the size of their staffs, and territorial rights within the company. Employees will press for high salaries and wages, liberal fringe benefits, and stable employment. Consumers want high quality, excellent service and support, and low prices. Finally, to the extent that the government represents the general public, it is interested in the overall implications for social welfare of strategic decisions.

The problem lies in the absence of practical analytical tools for assigning weights or priorities to these conflicting goals and objectives. To be sure, there is no shortage of academic approaches such as utility theory, social welfare theory, and goal programming which have been proposed by academic economists and management scientists. But the fact of the matter is that without exception all these techniques are based on assumptions or data requirements which are impossible to satisfy.

The upshot of all this is that one of the principal roles of corporate managers is to be able to somehow balance these conflicting objectives so that the company not only survives but actually grows and provides a useful service to its various constituencies. In other words, all the computer models in the world are not likely to replace this important function of management any time soon.

The point is that while it is not possible to solve the problem of multiple constituencies scientifically, managers must be acutely aware of the objectives of all the key players who are affected by strategic decisions.

### 2  Review Goals and Objectives

In the previous section we outlined the importance of formulating corporate, divisional, and departmental goals and objectives. Obviously, the selection of corporate strategies is void of meaning if it is not preceded by the definition of goals and objectives for each level of the company.

### 3  Specify Corporate Constraints

Corporate growth and development is often impeded by a variety of constraints which may be imposed by government, outside financiers, technology, availability of inputs into the production process, and the personal whims of managers or owners of the corporation. These constraints must be understood and dealt with by management as they go through the strategic decision process.

For example, banks, financial institutions, and public utilities are restricted by law as to the types of businesses they may go into. For example, a bank cannot open a department store or even a management consulting firm. Expansion in certain foreign countries may be risky or impossible as a result of a broad spectrum of political constraints ranging from the threat of nationalization to the possibility of a military takeover of the government. Outside financiers may impose limitations on debt, dividend payout, executive salaries, and capital expenditures.

Strategic planning may prove to be a useful vehicle for ascertaining the costs associated with some of these constraints in order to determine whether it will be worthwhile for management to invest the time and money required to eliminate a particular constraint or alleviate the negative impact of the constraint. Information of this type can be extremely valuable to management in attempting to make strategic decisions.

### 4  Review Existing Strategic Options

The next step in the strategic decision-making process is to review those strategic options which are already being exercised or are known to be available. This is usually done annually as part of the strategic planning process, but many companies find it useful to repeat this process on a quarterly or semiannual basis.

The purpose of this review is to at least make a preliminary judgment on the adequacy of the existing set of strategic options. Among the questions to be answered at this stage are the following: Will the strategic options available to us provide for an adequate return on investment? Are we protected from currency devaluations? Can we survive another major recession with our present mix of businesses? Can we improve our market-share sufficiently to produce enough cash to finance the construction of a more efficient plant?

The results of this review of the current inventory of strategic options will play a major role in determining whether the company should consider a corporate development strategy to acquire new businesses or instead pursue international markets and businesses.

### 5  Search for Additional Strategic Options

The search for additional strategic options is perhaps the most creative part of the entire strategic decision-making process. Although there are varying opinions on this subject and countless books have been written on how to be creative, we are not of the view that creativity is something that can be easily described or taught. To be sure, brainstorming sessions, sensitivity groups, and other forms of group dynamics may have a place in the executive suite. Furthermore, the interaction of executives in small groups may tend to stimulate their creative instincts. But in the final analysis, it is the individual corporate executive who must come up with new strategic options which seem to make sense.

The successful search for new business strategies can certainly be enhanced by modern scientific analysis, data retrieval, and search procedures. But this is one aspect of management where the executive must be free to consider the impossible and respond to his or her entrepreneurial instincts which say that a particular deal has a chance of success or not. An attempt to overformalize the search for new strategic options can stifle creativity and fail to produce the types of strategies which are really needed to run the company.

### 6  Sort out Strategic Options Worthy of Serious Consideration

The next step in the process involves reducing the number of strategic options under consideration to a relatively small number of options which merit more rigorous evaluation and consideration. Not unlike several other parts of the decision process, step 6 is an intuitive step.

Basically what is involved is a subjective evaluation of all the strategic options which have been defined in light of given goals and objectives and given corporate constraints and policies. Strategies which clearly violate corporate policies and constraints are eliminated at this stage. Likewise, strategies which contribute only marginally to major goals and objectives should be dropped from further consideration. Only those strategies which survive this critical, intuitive stage will be subjected to the kind of rigorous analysis described in Chapter 12.

### 7  Evaluate Strategic Options

This step in the decision-making process involves the objective evaluation of alternative strategies, using the type of portfolio models and "what if?" models described in Chapter 12. Those strategies which were not rejected in step 6 must now be subjected to serious analysis and evaluation. Portfolio models can be used to determine "optimum" portfolios of strategies. Computer-based planning models can simulate the effects of alternative financial, marketing, and production strategies on the behavior of the company, division, or department.

This step in the decision process represents an important interface between modern tools of economic analysis and the intuition and good judgment of an experienced manager. The information generated by the analysis produced in this step will provide the basis for strategic decisions in step 8.

### 8   Select a Set of Strategic Options

The eighth and final step of the decision process represents the moment of truth on the part of the manager. A decision must be made on the set of business strategies which will actually be implemented.

The toughest part of the strategic decision problem is that the evaluations produced in step 7 generate a multiplicity of output measures. In other words, we are once again confronted with multiple stakeholders who have conflicting objectives, but now we have multiple measures of performance on which to base a decision.

The analytical planning tools available to managers permit them to evaluate the effects of alternative strategies either on a single output measure or on a host of output variables.

Neither this book nor any other book can tell a manager how to make a final strategic decision. Those who claim otherwise are promising something which is impossible to deliver. Economists can show managers the likely impact of their strategic decisions on a host of business output variables, but that is all they can do. The managers alone must actually make the strategic decisions. But this is as it should be, because that is what managers are paid to do in the first place.

### QUESTIONS AND PROBLEMS

**11-1**  Why should a book on corporate economics be concerned with strategic planning?

**11-2**  What is the difference between a goal and an objective? To what extent do goals reflect the degree of commitment of senior management to long-term strategic planning?

**11-3**  What is the difference between strategic planning and forecasting?

**11-4**  Explain the relationship among portfolio decisions, investment decisions, and project decisions.

**11-5**  Why is optimization seldom used as a strategic planning tool?

**11-6**  What are some of the practical problems involved in implementing the so-called systems analysis approach to strategic planning?

**11-7**  Relate the discussion of innovative and positive economics in Chapter 1 to strategic planning methodology.

**11-8**  Why is the "what if?" approach to strategic planning the most widely used methodology?

**11-9**  Why is microeconomics an appropriate language for strategic planning?

**11-10**  Who are the stakeholders of a company?

## BIBLIOGRAPHY

Abel, Derek F., and John S. Hammond: *Strategic Market Planning* (Englewood Cliffs, N.J.: Prentice-Hall, 1979).

Ackoff, Russell L.: *A Concept of Corporate Planning* (New York: John Wiley, 1972).

Ansoff, H. Igor: *Strategic Management* (New York: John Wiley, 1979).

Baumol, William J.: *Economic Theory and Operations Analysis* (Englewood Cliffs, N.J.: Prentice-Hall, 1977).

Bonini, Charles P.: *Simulation of Information and Decisions Systems of the Firm* (Englewood Cliffs, N.J.: Prentice-Hall, 1963).

Boulding, Kenneth E.: "The Present Position of the Theory of the Firm," in Kenneth E. Boulding and W. Allen Spivey (eds.), *Linear Programming and the Theory of the Firm* (New York: Macmillan, 1960).

Boulding, Kenneth E., and W. Allen Spivey (eds.): *Linear Programming and the Theory of the Firm* (New York: Macmillan, 1960).

Chamberlin, E. H.: *The Theory of Monopolistic Competition* (Cambridge, Mass.: Harvard University Press, 1933).

Clarkson, G. P. E.: *Portfolio Selection: A Simulation of Trust Investment* (Englewood Cliffs, N.J.: Prentice-Hall, 1962).

Coate, Malcolm B.: *The Boston Consulting Group's Portfolio Planning Model: An Economic Analysis.* Unpublished Ph.D. dissertation. (Duke University, 1980).

Cohen, Kalman J., et al.: *The Carnegie Tech Management Game* (Homewood, Ill.: Irwin, 1964).

Cyert, Richard M., and James G. March: *A Behavioral Theory of the Firm* (Englewood Cliffs, N.J.: Prentice-Hall, 1963).

Dorfman, Robert: *Application of Linear Programming to the Theory of the Firm* (Berkeley: University of California Press, 1951).

Dorfman, Robert, Paul A. Samuelson, and Robert M. Solow: *Linear Programming and Economic Analysis* (New York: McGraw-Hill, 1958).

Gale, D.: *The Theory of Linear Economic Models* (New York: McGraw-Hill, 1960).

Hamilton, W. F., and M. A. Moses: "An Optimization Model for Corporate Financial Planning," *Operations Research*, May–June 1973, 21, 677–692.

Hayes, Robert H., and William J. Abernathy: "Managing Our Way to Economic Decline," *Harvard Business Review*, July–August 1980, 67–77.

Henderson, Bruce D.: *Henderson on Corporate Strategy* (Cambridge, Mass.: Abt, 1979).

Henderson, James M., and Richard E. Quandt: *Microeconomic Theory* (New York: McGraw-Hill, 1958).

Hicks, J. R.: *Value and Capital* (Oxford: Clarendon, 1939).

Lester, Richard A.: "Shortcomings of Marginal Analysis for Wage-Employment Problems," *American Economic Review,* March 1946, 36, 63–82.

Lester, Richard A.: "Marginalism, Minimum Wages, and Labor Markets," *American Economic Review,* March 1947, 37, 135–148.

Lintner, John: "The Valuation of Risk Assets and the Selection of Risky Investments in Stock Portfolios and Capital Budgets," *Review of Economics and Statistics,* February 1965, 47, 13–37.

Lorange, Peter, and Richard F. Vancil: *Strategic Planning Systems* (Englewood Cliffs, N.J.: Prentice-Hall, 1977).

Luce, R. Duncan, and Howard Raiffa: *Games and Decisions* (New York: John Wiley, 1957).

Machlup, Fritz: "Marginal Analysis and Empirical Research," *American Economic Review,* September 1946, 36, 519–554.

Machlup, Fritz: "Rejoinder to an Antimarginalist," *American Economic Review,* March 1947, 37, 148–154.

Markowitz, H.: *Portfolio Selection.* Cowles Foundation Monograph No. 16. (New York: John Wiley, 1959).

Naylor, Thomas H.: "The Theory of the Firm: A Comparison of Marginal Analysis and Linear Programming," *Southern Economic Journal,* January 1966, 32, 263–274.

Naylor, Thomas H.: *Corporate Planning Models* (Reading, Mass.: Addison-Wesley, 1979).

Naylor, Thomas H.: *Strategic Planning Management* (Oxford, Ohio: Planning Executives Institute, 1980).

Naylor, Thomas H. (ed.): *Corporate Strategy: The Integration of Corporate Planning Models and Economics* (Amsterdam: North-Holland, 1981).

Naylor, Thomas H., and John M. Vernon: *Microeconomics and Decision Models of the Firm* (New York: Harcourt Brace, 1969).

Orcutt, Guy H.: "Simulation of Economic Systems," *American Economic Review.* December 1960, 50, 893–907.

Orcutt, Guy H., et al.: *Microanalysis of Socioeconomic Systems: A Simulation Study* (New York: Harper, 1961).

Porter, Michael E.: *Competitive Strategy* (New York: Free Press, 1980).

Robinson, Joan: *The Economics of Imperfect Competition* (London: Macmillan, 1933).

Rosenkranz, Friedrich: *An Introduction to Corporate Modeling* (Durham, N.C.: Duke University Press, 1978).

Samuelson, Paul A.: *Foundations of Economic Analysis* (Cambridge, Mass.: Harvard University Press, 1947).

Schoeffler, Sidney, R. Buzzell, and R. Heany: "Impact of Strategic Planning on Profit Planning," *Harvard Business Review,* March–April 1974, 52, 137–145.

Schrieber, Albert N. (ed.): *Corporate Simulation Models* (Seattle: University of Washington Press, 1970).

Sharpe, William F.: "Capital Asset Prices: A Theory of Market Equilibrium under Conditions of Risk," *Journal of Finance,* September 1964, 19, 425–442.

Shubik, Martin: "A Curmudgeon's Guide to Microeconomics," *Journal of Economic Literature,* June 1970, 8, 405–434.

Shubik, Martin: *Games for Society, Business, and War* (Amsterdam: Elsevier, 1975).

Shubik, Martin: *The Uses and Methods of Gaming* (New York: Elsevier, 1975).

Shubik, Martin, and Richard Levitan: *Market Structure and Behavior* (Cambridge, Mass: Harvard University Press, 1980).

Simon, Herbert A.: "Rationality as Process and as Product of Thought," *American Economic Review,* May 1978, 68, 1–16.

Steiner, George A.: *Strategic Managerial Planning* (Oxford, Ohio: Planning Executives Institute, 1977).

Sutton, C. J.: *Economics and Corporate Strategy* (Cambridge: Cambridge University Press, 1980).

Theil, H.: *Optimal Decision Rules for Government and Industry* (Amsterdam: North-Holland, 1964).

Tinbergen, J.: *On the Theory of Economic Policy* (Amsterdam: North-Holland, 1955).

Van Horne, James C.: *Financial Management and Policy* (Englewood Cliffs, N.J.: Prentice-Hall, 1980).

Von Neumann, John, and Oskar Morgenstern: *Theory of Games and Economic Behavior* (Princeton, N.J.: Princeton University Press, 1944).

Williamson, Oliver E.: *The Economics of Discretionary Behavior: Managerial Objectives in a Theory of the Firm* (Englewood Cliffs, N.J.: Prentice-Hall, 1964).

Williamson, Oliver E.: *Corporate Control and Business Behavior* (Englewood Cliffs, N.J.: Prentice-Hall, 1970).

Williamson, Oliver E.: *Markets and Hierarchies* (New York: Free Press, 1975).

CHAPTER **12**

---

# STRATEGIC PLANNING MODELS

---

**CHAPTER OUTLINE**

## OVERVIEW OF STRATEGIC PLANNING MODELS

In Chapter 11 we defined strategic planning and pointed out the relevance of microeconomics as a conceptual framework on which strategic planning can be grounded. Also included in Chapter 11 was an economic paradigm for strategic decision making. Step 7 in our paradigm for strategic decision making was concerned with the evaluation of the firm's strategic options. In this chapter we shall examine three specific analytical tools for evaluating strategic decisions: (1) competitive strategy models, (2) portfolio optimization models, and (3) corporate simulation models.

Assume that a company has a collection, or portfolio, of businesses, products, or divisions and must decide how to allocate its scarce financial resources across the portfolio. Which businesses should be stimulated by investment in the hopes of producing growth and eventually increased cash flow? Which businesses should be retained but maintained at present levels of investment? Which businesses should be purged from the portfolio altogether since they offer little promise of either growth or cash? These are all examples of the problem of portfolio planning.

In the early 1960s under the leadership of Fred J. Borsch, the General Electric Company pioneered in the development of an analytical framework to facilitate this type of strategic decision making. Collectively, these tools are called portfolio models. Essentially there are two different types of portfolio models available for evaluating strategic plans: competitive strategy models and optimization models. In the following two sections we shall describe the Boston Consulting Group (BCG) model and the PIMS model, two of the best known competitive strategy models available. Next we shall outline five different portfolio optimization models and conclude the chapter with an overview of corporate simulation models.

Although some economists may not be familiar with all the strategic planning models described in this chapter, we believe it is important for corporate economists to have at least a cursory knowledge of the analytical tools currently being used for strategic planning.

## THE BOSTON CONSULTING GROUP MODEL

By far the most popular of the competitive strategy models is the BCG model. The BCG approach is based on two relatively simple concepts: the growth-share matrix and the experience curve. In this section we shall describe each of these concepts separately as well as the growth and financial strategies which result from combining them.

### The Growth-Share Matrix

The basis of the growth-share matrix (Figure 12-1) is the concept that where a product or business falls in a two-dimensional matrix of market growth and market-share and where it might fall in the future may have significant strategic implications. Among the strategic implications are corporate resource allocation, product or business strategies, and management recruiting strategies.

The growth-share matrix subdivides a company into component products or businesses, each of which is separable from the others. For each business, the market growth rate is defined along with the product's relative market-share or dominance and plotted on the growth-share matrix.

The definition of market-share employed by BCG is based on the concept of market dominance, which is defined as the ratio of the company's market-share to the market-share of the largest competitor in the market. The emphasis on the largest competitor is based on the relative cost implications of BCG's theory of experience effects, which hypothesizes that the firm with the largest market-share will often have the greatest accumulated experience and thereby

**FIGURE 12-1**
The growth-share matrix.

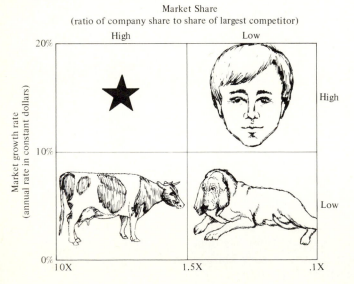

Market Share
(ratio of company share to share of largest competitor)

the lowest unit costs. In the growth-share matrix, the relative competitive position or market-share is plotted on a logarithmic scale. This allows for another implication of the experience effect which suggests that differences in the rate of cash generation or return on investment between competitors are related to the ratio of their relative competitive positions.

The second dimension of the growth-share matrix is a measure of business attractiveness. The measure of business attractiveness used by BCG is the market growth rate, which is defined as the annual rate of growth of sales in constant dollars. The strategic importance of growth to a business is so well known that we need not elaborate on it here. Suffice it to say that economies of scale, reduced unit costs, and an improved competitive position provide strong incentives to motivate firms to aspire to increased sales growth. To be sure, sales growth is by no means the only measure of business attractiveness which may be considered.

The growth-share matrix in Figure 12-1 is divided into four cash quadrants, each of which will be defined and illustrated below. The boundaries separating the quadrants are to some extent arbitrary. The market growth boundary is usually set at 10 percent and the market-share boundary at 1.5 times the market-share of the largest competitor. The BCG originally set the market-share boundary at 1.0, but subsequent analysis has suggested that 1.5 reflects a more stable condition than 1.0, which represents parity. Of course, it is possible to define a growth-share matrix with a finer grid than the one used by BCG. The directional policy matrix developed by the Royal Dutch Shell Group represents an attempt to employ a finer grid. We shall now define each of the four quadrants of the BCG growth-share matrix and comment on the strategic implications of each category.

**Cash Cow**  Products with high market-share and slow growth frequently generate large amounts of cash—more cash than is required to maintain market-share. The excess cash generated by such products should not be reinvested in the products. Indeed, if the ROI is greater than the market growth rate, the cash cannot be reinvested indefinitely without reducing ROI. The appropriate strategy is to protect the current position of the cash cow while generating cash to invest in selected stars, problem children, research and development, and other long-term projects.

**Star**  The star is the high-growth, high-market-share product. It usually shows positive profits, but it may or may not produce positive cash flow. (Perhaps one of the most spectacular stars of all times is the hamburger business of McDonald's.) If the star remains a market leader, it will eventually evolve into a cash cow when growth is reduced and reinvestment requirements decline.

**Problem Child**  The upper-right-hand quadrant of Figure 12-1 represents a business characterized by high market growth and low market-share. Originally

BCG described this type of business as a "question mark," but more recently the term "problem child" has become more popular. The problem child has an inferior market position and typically requires more cash than it can generate. If cash is not provided, a problem child may fall behind and drop out of the market. However, even if cash is provided, the product may become a "dog" when the growth slows. Problem children require large injections of cash to buy market-share. Such products are likely to be liabilities unless they can become market leaders.

Apparently General Electric's decision to leave the computer industry in the late 1960s was based heavily on analysis that showed that GE's computer business was a problem child with little hope of becoming a star, given the competition from IBM, without massive amounts of additional cash. GE was simply not willing to take such a large risk and opted to sell its computer business to Honeywell. Unfortunately, in selling off its computer mainframe business, GE also sold the technology needed to develop microprocessors, which would become vital to many of its other businesses in the 1980s. As a result of a decision made over 10 years ago, GE is having to invest millions of dollars in the 1980s to reacquire some of the technology it sold in the early 1970s. This example serves to emphasize the importance of properly defining what business one is in and the possible consequences of misdefining the business in the first place.

**Dog**   Finally, products or businesses with low market-share and slow growth are called dogs. Although dogs may show a positive profit, the profit must consistently be reinvested simply to maintain market-share. Dogs are worthless and are evidence of the failure to achieve a position of market leadership or to cut one's losses when faced with a "no win" situation.

In summary, the BCG growth-share matrix represents a conceptual framework on which portfolio investment decisions can be based. A balanced portfolio of businesses calls for:

**1** Heavy investment in stars whose high share and high growth assure the future
   **2** Protection of cash cows that supply the funds for future growth
   **3** Selective investment in problem children to be converted into stars
   **4** Liquidation of dogs

### The Experience Curve

Based on the learning curve, which was first developed in 1925 at the Wright-Patterson Air Force Base, the Boston Consulting Group has popularized an extension of the learning curve known as the experience curve. According to the BCG, the unit costs (in real terms) of manufacturing a product decline approximately 20 to 30 percent each time accumulated experience is doubled.

Learning curves typically express direct labor costs per unit on the vertical axis and total units produced on the horizontal axis. Figure 12-2 illustrates

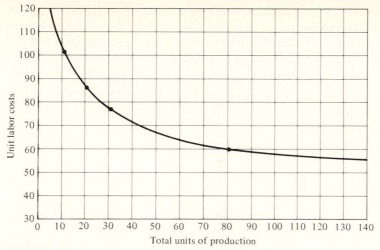

**FIGURE 12-2**
An 85 percent learning curve.

what is called an 85 percent learning curve. Every time total production doubles, direct labor costs per unit drop to 85 percent of the original level. Stated alternatively, direct labor costs per unit decrease 15 percent each time output doubles. Transforming both the horizontal and vertical dimensions of the learning curve to logarithms (using double-log graph paper) produces a straight-line relationship, as we see in Figure 12-3.

Whereas the learning curve concentrates exclusively on direct labor costs, the BCG has generalized the concept to include all manufacturing costs. The literature abounds with empirical examples of situations in which the experi-

**FIGURE 12-3**
An 85 percent learning curve expressed on a log-log scale.

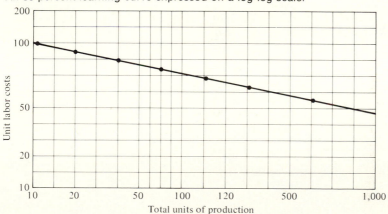
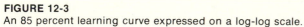

ence curve seems to apply. Examples of the experience effect include semiconductors, crushed limestone, gas ranges, polyvinylchloride, and steam turbine generators. Figure 12-4 contains an experience curve for integrated circuits.

Among the factors which are thought to explain the experience effect are:

1 Improved labor efficiency (learning)
2 New processes and improved methods (specialization)
3 Product redesign
4 Product standardization
5 Economies of scale
6 Factor-input substitution

In summary, according to Bruce D. Henderson of the BCG, "The experience curve cost effects are an observable fact. They can be confirmed by observation. The principal problems encountered in application are those of defining cost elements and defining the measuring unit of experience."

Some economists have expressed strong objections to the experience curve on the grounds that it implies that the firm's long-run average cost function is always decreasing. In Chapter 4 the possibility of the long-run average cost function decreasing initially, reaching a minimum point, and eventually increasing was discussed. The experience curve is inconsistent with economists' view of the long-run average cost function.

The strategic implications of the experience curve are numerous. Below we shall summarize ten of the more important business effects as outlined by Bruce D. Henderson in his 1974 paper entitled "The Experience Curve—Reviewed."

1 *Market-share:* Costs are inversely proportional to market-share. High market-share should produce low cost.

**FIGURE 12-4**
The experience curve for integrated circuits.

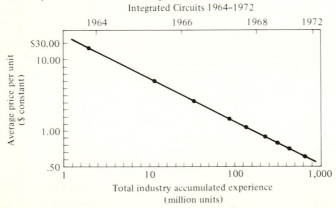

Integrated Circuits 1964–1972

Total industry accumulated experience
(million units)

**2** *Growth:* Relative costs should improve if growth is faster than that of competitors.

**3** *Debt capacity:* Relative debt capacity should increase with no loss of safety if market-share increases.

**4** *Shared experience:* Cost will decline proportionally faster or slower when cost elements are shared between more than one product.

**5** *Cost control:* Cost declines are predictable and therefore should be the basis for cost control and management evaluation.

**6** *Product design:* Choice of design element alternatives can be determined by whether initial experience is high or low compared with future volume expected.

**7** *Make or buy:* Choice of make or buy should be determined by the relative difference between your experience and supplier experience differential if you make.

**8** *Procurement negotiation:* The value to the supplier of large-scale procurement can be calculated. Also, the rate of normal cost change for the supplier can be calculated.

**9** *Market potential:* By comparing market elasticity with cost decline, the market potential can be approximated.

**10** *Product line breadth:* The total economic effect of product line extension can be evaluated by interaction of the experience and volume of combined cost elements.

### Growth and Financial Strategies

The primary focus of the growth-share matrix is on the portfolio aspects of business strategy. On the other hand, the competitive aspects of strategy are the principal concerns of experience curve theory. The third aspect of business strategy treated by the BCG is finance.

To the extent that growth is perceived as a critical measure of corporate performance, the role of finance takes on considerable importance. The company that grows the fastest is the company that generates enough cash to add to its assets at the fastest rate. According to the BCG, "The firm that grows the fastest is the one which sustains the highest rate of return on its equity capital (and reinvests these funds). The firm that grows the fastest is the one that brings to bear the greatest force of resources in the face of its competitors." The BCG argues further that a firm's "sustainable rate of growth depends in part on and is limited by the rate at which it can generate funds available for commitment to the growth target, and the return it can expect to earn on these funds." The sources of these funds are, of course, retained earnings, debt, and new equity. The rate of return and the risk profile of alternative products will determine their effectiveness. "The critical issue is sustaining the optimum mix of strategic resources in the proper place at the proper time in the proper amounts."

Finally, summarizing the importance of financing in the selection of business and competitive strategies, Alan J. Zakon of the BCG has concluded:

> It is the responsibility of the financial officer to develop a set of goals and policies in *financial* terms that will support the corporate goals. In fact, it is his responsibility to develop financial opportunities to attain these objectives. To do this he, and top management, must clearly understand the interrelation of the financial parameters that contribute to growth and the effect of their manipulation.

Competitive strategy must necessarily be based on the following interdependent set of elements: (1) debt policies, (2) dividend policies, (3) price policies, (4) industry growth, and (5) competitive cost positions. Financial strategy is integrally linked to the company's cost position and ability to remain competitive. Again according to Dr. Zakon, "Failure to approach competitive strategy through an integration of financial and operating insights must result in failure to understand the real competitive system."

Two rules of thumb summarize the BCG's approach to the integration of financial strategy, competitive strategy, and portfolio selection. First, a business must generate either growth or cash to remain in the corporate portfolio. Second, businesses with high growth will use more cash than businesses with low growth.

Returning to the growth-share matrix, we shall attempt to integrate financial strategy, competitive strategy, and portfolio selection strategy. By examining the growth-share matrix displayed in Figure 12-1, the BCG has set forth the following conclusions:

**1** Today's growth should be taken from the stars (high share, high growth). Stars are typically almost self-financing, but care must be taken not to allow other competitors to erode market-share.

**2** Today's financing should be taken from the cash cow (high share, low growth). All stars eventually become cash cows when growth slows and share is maintained.

**3** Tomorrow's growth should be taken from the problem children (high growth, low share). Unless it attains high market-share, a problem child will never supply cash or meaningful growth. Problem children require heavy funding to attain high share while growth remains.

**4** Nothing worthwhile can be expected from dogs (low share, low growth). Divestiture is the recommended strategy.

To put financial strategy in its proper perspective, the BCG has concluded:

> Financial strategy is a powerful competitive force. This does not mean a simplistic conclusion of use of debt and do not pay dividends. Rather, it means the construction of a portfolio of businesses to maximize debt capacity and *overall cash generation ability* and to redirect cash flow into areas of opportunity. The net result is a continual postponement of corporate maturity and the combination of growing earnings, minimum profit margins in growth areas, and maximum financially sustainable growth.

## Some Practical Problems

In spite of the popularity of competitive strategy models in general and the BCG methodology in particular, there are some practical problems involved in applying these tools.

**1** The fundamental concept underlying the growth-share matrix is that it is possible to segment markets and businesses into well-defined, meaningful subsets. In reality, this often turns out to be either extremely difficult or impossible. Indeed, the entire notion of market-share is frequently quite elusive.

**2** The usefulness of the growth-share matrix is highly correlated with the accuracy of the growth and market-share projections for a given business. The BCG literature seems to assume that the growth-share projections are accurate.

**3** To some extent the growth-share matrix represents an oversimplification of the strategic problem of the firm. It fails to take into consideration the likely interdependencies among different products and businesses, and it cannot possibly deal with the effects of changes in the company's external environment.

**4** Although the idea of expressing unit costs as a function of "experience" has a certain appeal, it too represents an oversimplification, because costs depend on the scale of operations and the factor-input combinations employed by the firm as well as a host of other variables.

**5** The BCG methodology as described in the literature does not tell the decision maker which strategy to select or show the consequences of selecting alternative strategy options.

## THE PIMS MODEL

The PIMS (profit impact of market strategy) program of the Strategic Planning Institute (SPI) represents a second type of competitive strategy model which is used by a number of large companies in the United States and Europe. It too has its historical origins in the General Electric Company.

Utilizing a data base of strategic information on over 2,000 product line businesses, the PIMS program has as its objectives "to discover the general 'laws' that determine what business strategy, in what kind of competitive environment, produces what profit results" and "to produce reports for the managers of each business unit which they can use as a basis for decision making."

## Methodology

The basic methodology underlying most of the research findings of PIMS is multiple regression analysis. Using the PIMS data base on approximately 1,000 businesses, SPI has developed a single-equation econometric model which explains about 75 percent of the variation in return on investment among these businesses in terms of 28 "profit-influencing" factors. A similar model has also been developed which explains 70 percent of the variation in cash flow among these same businesses in terms of 19 "cash flow-influencing" factors. In each of these models, the profit-influencing and cash flow-influencing factors are identified (on the basis of statistical significance) and discussed in some detail. Among the factors identified as influencing profitability are rate of growth, degree of market concentration, market-share, product quality, and productivity of capital and labor. The PIMS methodology is based on the assumption that while there are differences among businesses, it is possible to identify common factors that cut across all businesses.

## PIMS Reports

Participants in the PIMS program receive a number of reports. These reports include Par reports, strategy reports, and portfolio reviews.

The Par ROI report specifies the return on investment that is normal for a business, given its market attractiveness, competitive position, degree of differentiation from competitors, and production structure. The report also quantifies individual strategic strengths and weaknesses, as indicated by the impacts of key profit-influencing factors.

The strategy reports are said to answer the following questions: (1) If this business continues on its current track, what will its future operating results be? and (2) What changes in market-share, investment intensity, and vertical integration are likely to produce better results?

Finally, the PIMS portfolio reviews represent an attempt to answer the following kinds of questions: (1) Has the strategic position of the portfolio improved over the last few years? (2) Is the portfolio performing well or badly, given its strategic position? (3) Will proposed business plans strengthen the portfolio? How much? (4) Which plans deserve the most detailed review? (5) Which businesses are potential divestment candidates?

## Research Findings

Derek F. Abel and John S. Hammond in their book *Strategic Market Planning* have succinctly summarized the important research findings of the PIMS project. They are listed below as determinants of ROI and of cash flow.

### Determinants of ROI

1 *Investment intensity:*
   a Large investment and high marketing intensity equals poor ROI.
   b Capacity utilization is vital when fixed-capital intensity is high.
   c High capital intensity and small market-share equals disaster.
2 *Market-share:*
   a Market-share is most profitable in vertically integrated industries.
   b High research and development spending depresses ROI when market-share is weak.

*c* Capacity utilization is most important for low-share businesses.

*d* Heavy marketing depresses ROI for low-share businesses.

*e* Market-share and quality are partial substitutes for each other.

**3** *Market growth rate:*

*a* A rapid rate of new product introduction in fast-growing markets depresses ROI.

*b* Research and development is most profitable in mature, slow-growth markets.

**4** *Life cycle stage:*

*a* A narrow product line in the early or middle stage of the product life cycle is less profitable than at the later stage.

**5** *Marketing expenses:*

*a* High research and development expenses plus high marketing expenses depress ROI.

*b* High marketing expenses depress ROI, especially when quality is low.

### Determinants of Cash Flow

**1** *Investment intensity:*

*a* Low or medium growth coupled with low investment intensity produces cash; high growth coupled with high investment intensity is a cash drain.

*b* Harvesting share when investment intensity is low produces cash; building share when investment intensity is high is a cash drain.

*c* Investment plus marketing intensity results in cash drains.

*d* Few new product introductions coupled with low investment intensity produce cash.

**2** *Relative market-share:*

*a* High relative share improves cash flow; high growth decreases it.

*b* High share and low investment intensity produce cash; low share and high investment intensity result in cash drain.

*c* High relative share produces cash, especially when marketing intensity is low.

### A Critical Appraisal of PIMS

Although some economists have criticized the methodology of PIMS on the grounds that it places too much faith in single-equation econometric models, the real value of PIMS lies in its data base containing extensive time series and cross-sectional data on finance, marketing, and productive operations for over 2,000 strategic business units. The research potential of the PIMS data base remains virtually untapped by corporate and academic economists.

### OPTIMIZATION MODELS

For many years economists and management scientists have been proposing optimization models similar to the ones described in Chapter 5 to solve the firm's portfolio planning problem. The dream of a CEO sitting in his or her office managing a portfolio of businesses according to some formal optimization model has yet to occur in the real world. Although the decade of the 1970s witnessed growth in the use of portfolio models such as the BCG model and the PIMS model as well as corporate simulation models, very few companies have considered optimization as a portfolio planning tool. The main obstacle to the use of optimization models for strategic planning, as was pointed out in Chapter 11, is one of problem definition.

However, we believe that the experience gained by firms in the 1970s with portfolio planning models and simulation models has laid the groundwork for the introduction of optimization models as strategic planning tools in the 1980s. In this section we shall describe some of the options available for extending some of the concepts of the BCG and others to include optimization. We shall begin by describing two relatively simple portfolio optimization models proposed by Weingartner. These are followed by a linear programming model developed by the BCG which incorporates their concepts of the growth-share matrix and the experience curve. We shall then describe the relatively advanced model of Hamilton and Moses and point out how some of the notions of risk analysis (Chapter 10) can be extended to portfolio analysis through the use of capital-asset pricing models.

### A Simple Portfolio Optimization Model

The firm is assumed to have a portfolio of different businesses available to it for investment purposes. The problem of the firm is to select that combination of businesses in which to invest its funds so as to maximize the net present value of the total portfolio over the planning horizon $T$ subject to a set of budget constraints. The model consists of the following variables:

$X_i$ = fraction of business $i$ to be undertaken
$PV_i$ = net present value of business $i$
$I_{ti}$ = present value of investment required in business $i$ in time year $t$
$B_t$ = present value of budget ceiling for year $t$
$UF_t$ = amount of unused funds in year $t$

The objective is to maximize total net present value NPV

$$NPV = \sum_{i=1}^{n} PV_i X_i \qquad (12\text{-}1)$$

subject to a set of budgeting constraints

$$\sum_{i=1}^{n} I_{1i} X_i + UF_1 = B_1 \qquad (12\text{-}2)$$

$$\sum_{i=1}^{n} I_{ti}X_i - \mathrm{UF}_{t-1} + \mathrm{UF}_t = B_t \tag{12-3}$$

$$t = 2, \ldots, T$$

and
$$0 \leq X_i \leq 1 \qquad i = 1, \ldots, n \tag{12-4}$$
$$\mathrm{UF}_t \geq 0 \qquad t = 1, \ldots, T \tag{12-5}$$

Equation (12-2) states that the amount invested in all $n$ businesses plus the amount of unused funds available in year 1 should be equal to the budget constraint of the first year. For all future years, equation (12-3) holds. It states that the amount invested in all businesses during year $t$ minus the amount of unused funds carried over from the previous year plus the amount of unused funds in the current year must equal the budget for that year. Inequality (12-4) indicates that the commitment to a particular business can vary from 0 to 1. If $X_i$ is equal to zero, then the business is in effect being dropped from the portfolio. If $X_i$ is equal to 1, then investment is being carried out at its full potential for that business. Of course, it is possible to require $X_i$ to be an integer, thus transforming the portfolio problem into an integer programming problem. Finally, equation (12-5) simply requires nonnegative cash balances. That is, no debt is permitted in this model.

Although this model is quite simple, it illustrates the fact that the firm's portfolio planning problem is essentially a problem of resource allocation. In the models which follow we shall gradually increase the number of factors taken into consideration, thus making the models more realistic and more useful in particular situations.

### A Portfolio Optimization Model with Debt

A second portfolio optimization model proposed by Weingartner is somewhat more realistic than the first in that it permits the possibility of debt. Again we assume a portfolio of $n$ businesses, and the problem of the firm is to determine which businesses are worthy of investment and what level of commitment to make to each business, if any, to maximize the net present value of the portfolio. The variables in the model are defined below:

$X_i =$ fraction of business $i$ to be undertaken

$\overline{\mathrm{PV}}_i =$ net present value of all flows subsequent to time horizon $T$, if any, discounted to the horizon at a give rate of interest $r$

$\mathrm{PV}_{ti} =$ net present value in year $t$ associated with decision to include business $i$ in the portfolio. ($\mathrm{PV}_{ti}$ may be either positive or negative depending on whether it represents an increment in revenue. We shall assume $\mathrm{PV}_{ti}$ to be positive if it represents an expenditure and negative if it represents revenue.)

$CASH_t$ = funds which are anticipated to be generated by the firm from operations in year $t$ and which may be attributed to the resources the firm currently controls. (They are the anticipated future cash throw-off based on continuation of the firm but excluding revenues to be derived from investments which the model was designed to determine.)

$DEBT_t$ = amount borrowed in year $t$ at interest rate $r$

$UF_t$ = amount available for lending, that is, carrying over to the next period at interest rate $r$. (Lending and borrowing are accomplished by means of "renewable" one-year contracts, where for simplicity in exposition, all interest is payable at the end of the year.)

As before, the objective is to determine the values of $X_i$ to maximize net present value NPV.

$$NPV = \sum_{i=1}^{n} \overline{PV}_i X_i + UF_T - DEBT_T \qquad (12\text{-}6)$$

subject to constraints (12-7) and (12-8), which state that the firm cannot spend more in year 1 or any year through year $T$ than the amount of funds anticipated to be generated in that year from operations

$$\sum_{i=1}^{n} PV_{1i} X_i + UF_1 - DEBT_1 \leq CASH_1 \qquad (12\text{-}7)$$

$$\sum_{i=1}^{n} PV_{ti} X_i - (1+r)UF_{t-1} + UF_t \qquad (12\text{-}8)$$
$$+ (1+r)DEBT_{t-1} - DEBT_t \leq CASH_t \qquad t = 2, \ldots, T$$

As before $X_i (i = 1, \ldots, n)$ must lie on the unit internal and $UF_t$ and $DEBT_t$ must be nonnegative $t = 1, \ldots, T$.

In their present form, both the optimization models described in this section are linear programming models. If we impose the additional constraint that the $X_i$'s must be integers, the models become integer programming problems.

### A Strategy-Based Model for Resource Allocation

In this section and the following section we shall describe two somewhat more comprehensive portfolio optimization models, one proposed by the BCG and another developed by Hamilton and Moses. Since the algebra in each of these models becomes somewhat tedious, we shall provide a verbal summary description of each model rather than a complete mathematical treatment.

The BCG has defined a set of six major decisions which are the heart of a company's problem of allocation of strategic resources:

1 What businesses should be supported for growth?

2 Which businesses should be managed for greater cash generation?

3 What should the level of dividends to shareholders be?

4 How much debt should the company use to finance its growth?

5 Should the company divest specific businesses or divisions?

6 Should the company seek acquisitions, and if so, what should the nature of these acquisitions be?

To aid in the difficult task of managing a large number of different businesses in a complex competitive environment, the BCG has developed a strategy-based model for resource allocation. The model is a linear programming model which helps management choose either a growth strategy or a cash strategy for each business in the company's portfolio, thus allocating the company's scarce resources as optimally as possible.

For each business, the model indicates which strategic option maximizes the company's growth or long-run earnings subject to a set of financial constraints. The strategic option selected takes into consideration the necessary trade-offs between growth and return over a specific planning horizon, say five years. Both the cash plan and the growth plan for each business are based on the following financial forecasts for each business: return on assets, growth in sales, growth in assets, and growth in earnings.

In the process of formulating growth and cash plans for the specific businesses, the model maintains a balance between cash inflows and outflows. The major sources and uses of funds to express these cash balances include:

**Sources of funds**

1 Operating income

2 New debt

3 Reduction of working capital assets or sale of fixed assets

4 Other cash inflows

**Uses of funds**

1 Interest payments

2 Dividends

3 Investment in new assets

4 Other cash outflows

In summary, there are two alternative versions of the BCG model for resource allocation. In the first case the objective is to select a portfolio of cash and/or growth plans to maximize growth, which is defined as assets at the end of the planning horizon. In the second case the objective is to maximize earnings, which are defined as net income after interest at the beginning of the planning period. In both cases the selection of strategic options is constrained by the following three cash constraints, assuming a five-year planning horizon:

1 Five yearly cash balances reflecting yearly minimum cash requirements and maximum cash availabilities (other than from operations and financial policies)

**2** Four minimum yearly growth rates in earnings per share

**3** A five-year minimum cash balance requirement, averaging over the entire planning period the cash flows from operations and financial decisions

There are several obvious limitations to the BCG optimization model which may explain why it is not widely used by corporate executives. First, the assumption that all strategic decisions can be reduced to the dichotomy of cash versus growth is an oversimplification of the planning problem. Second, the BCG model unduly restricts the firm's investment options. Third, the methodology is completely incapable of handling interdependent businesses. Fourth, to some extent this model assumes away the problem of strategic planning by virtue of the information required to feed the model. Although the BCG model is a step in the right direction, it is understandable why so few firms have embraced this approach to portfolio planning.

### An Optimization Model for Corporate Financial Planning

Perhaps the best known portfolio optimization model was published by Hamilton and Moses in 1973. The model was designed specifically for strategic planning in a large diversified company. The model includes a full range of financial decisions including internal capital budgeting, acquisitions, divestments, debt creation/repayment, stock issue/repurchase, and dividend payout. The model employs mixed integer programming to select optimal investment and financing strategies over a multiperiod planning horizon.

Like the BCG optimization model, this model also permits two different types of strategy options: momentum strategies and development strategies. Momentum strategies represent a continuation of present activities in current lines of business. Development strategies reflect proposed changes in the nature or level of present activities.

The objective of the firm is to maximize earnings per share subject to a set of goal constraints, corporate constraints, and group constraints. Earnings are defined as

$$\text{Earnings} = \text{(income from strategies)} - \text{(cost of corporate long-} \quad (12\text{-}9)$$
$$\text{term debt)} - \text{(cost of long-term debt tied to strat-}$$
$$\text{egies)} - \text{(cost of short-term debt)} - \text{(dividend cost}$$
$$\text{of preferred securities)} + \text{(credit for early corpor-}$$
$$\text{ate debt repayment)}$$

The different types of financial constraints included in the model are outlined below:

**I** Goal constraints:
  **A** Stable growth in earnings per share
  **B** Return on assets
  **C** Return on equity

**II** Corporate constraints:
  **A** Funds flow
    **1** Inflow
      **a** Selected strategies
      **b** Divestments
      **c** Equity sales
      **d** Net debt proceeds
    **2** Outflow
      **a** Dividend payments
      **b** Debt expenses
      **c** Debt retirement
      **d** Stock repurchases
  **B** Interest coverage
  **C** Leverage ratio: ratio of long-term debt to the sum of long-term debt plus equity
  **D** Short-term debt
  **E** Additions to common stock
  **F** Minimum corporate income
**III** Group constraints:
  **A** Business mix: Restrictions on the mix of corporate activities in order to retain or promote a specified corporate character or to help reduce risk.
  **B** Strategy/source constraints: Constraints related to strategy and funds; source selection.
  **C** Divestment: Momentum strategy for each business must be accepted or divested but not both.
  **D** Development/momentum strategies: Selection of an incremental development strategy has meaning only if the corresponding momentum strategy is accepted.
  **E** Tied financing: Limited to some maximum value associated with each strategy.
  **F** Early debt repayment: Total repayments over the planning horizon must not exceed the amount of debt outstanding at the end of the period.
  **G** Funds/source limits: Funds drawn from any source in a given time period may be limited to some range.

Unfortunately, there is little evidence to suggest that either the BCG model or the Hamilton and Moses model has been used extensively as a strategic planning tool. However, these models represent interesting conceptual frameworks from which to view the problem of strategic portfolio planning.

**Capital-Asset Pricing Models**

The modern literature on finance abounds with applications of the capital-asset pricing model (CAPM) which was first developed by Sharpe and Lintner and is based on the earlier work of Markowitz. Until recently, most of the applications of the CAPM were oriented toward the problem of an individual investor involved in the selection of a portfolio of securities under conditions of risk.

Markowitz showed that the variance of the return on a portfolio of financial securities depends not only on the riskiness of the individual securities in the portfolio but also on the relationship among these securities, i.e., on the covariances between the respective securities in the portfolio. He showed that the variance of a portfolio of securities may be less than the smallest variance of an individual security if there are sufficient negative covariances among the securities. (A negative covariance between two securities can be interpreted to mean that when the return from one security is above its average value, the return from the other is below its average value.) The optimum portfolio involves selecting that combination of securities which yields the best combination of expected return and risk, which, of course, depends on the investor's utility function.

It can be shown that there is an implied equilibrium relationship between risk and return for each security. In equilibrium, a security will be expected to yield a return commensurate with its unavoidable risk. This is simply the risk that cannot be avoided by diversification. The greater the unavoidable risk of a security, the greater the return that the investor will expect from the security. The relationship between expected return and unavoidable risk and the valuation of securities in this context constitutes the essence of the capital-asset pricing model.

Among the numerous financial applications of the CAPM described in the literature are (1) valuation of a firm's common stock, (2) capital budgeting, (3) merger and acquisition analysis, and (4) valuation of warrants and convertible securities. Recently, two management consulting firms, Marakon Associates and Strategic Planning Associates, have proposed the possibility of employing the CAPM not only as a decision-making tool for investors with a portfolio of financial assets but also as a planning tool for corporations that manage a portfolio of businesses, divisions, strategic business units, etc. In the latter case the portfolio consists of tangible assets, while in the former case it consists only of financial assets. The CAPM is based on the following seven assumptions:

**1** All investors in securities are single-period (say one year), expected-utility wealth maximizers who choose securities on the basis of mean and variance of return.

**2** Investors can borrow or lend funds at a risk-free interest rate.

**3** Investors have identical subjective estimates of the means, variances, and covariances of all securities.

**4** The market for financial securities is perfectly competitive, and all investors are price takers.

**5** The quantity of securities is fixed.

**6** All securities are perfectly divisible and liquid; i.e., they are marketable without significant transaction costs.

**7** There are no taxes.

The CAPM attempts to determine how an investor's financial assets are valued when the behavior of all investors in the stock market is taken into consideration. To extend the CAPM to the case of a corporation that owns a portfolio of businesses, we must assume that the businesses have the same properties as securities.

A complete treatise on capital-asset pricing models is beyond the scope of this chapter. For a more complete treatment of the possible application of capital-asset pricing models as a strategic planning tool, see the recent paper by Naylor and Tapon which is referenced in the bibliography at the end of this chapter.

## CORPORATE SIMULATION MODELS

During the 1970s most of the 1,000 largest companies in the United States were also using a somewhat different yet complementary analytical tool for strategic planning: corporate simulation models. (The reader may recall that simulation was first introduced in Chapter 10 in our discussion of risk analysis.) Many companies use both competitive strategy models and corporate simulation models to evaluate business strategies.

The major reason why corporate managers turned to corporate simulation models in the 1970s was the need to obtain answers to some of the difficult "what if?" questions which arose as a result of some of the problems and opportunities generated by (1) the energy crisis, (2) shortages, (3) international liquidity problems, (4) increased competition, and (5) economic uncertainty. Top management has become increasingly aware that the old ways of muddling through are not adequate to meet the complex problems that will face corporations in the future. The need for a more systematic approach for evaluating the consequences of alternative managerial policies and socioeconomic and political events on the future of the corporation is self-evident. A change in pricing or advertising policies affects production operations, cash flow, and the profit-and-loss statement. Difficulty in borrowing additional funds to finance inventories leads to reverberations not only in the balance sheet but also in marketing strategies and production plans. The problem is that everything is related to everything else. Ad hoc plans which focus on only one functional area of the business are likely to be myopic and ineffective and can lead the firm into troubled waters. In order to survive during these turbulent days, corporate plans must be both comprehensive and systematic.

Corporate simulation models provide management with the analytical capability to achieve both of these objectives. They represent an attractive, viable alternative to informal, ad hoc planning procedures. The uses of these models vary from company to company depending on managerial objectives. *The New York Times,* for example, uses its planning model to evaluate the effects of alternative marketing strategies for the newspaper as well as its other operating companies including radio and television stations and magazines. United Air Lines based its decision to acquire Boeing 767 aircraft on the results obtained from its financial planning model. A major division of Abbott Laboratories recently decided to build a new plant; again the planning model provided the analytical basis for the decision.

For the most part, the methodology underlying corporate simulation models has been developed by practitioners in the corporate world rather than by academic researchers. To be quite specific, accountants and financial analysts in all too many companies have been the driving force behind the use of these models. As a result, the linkages between corporate simulation models and microeconomic theory have tended to be minimal. To a great extent, accounting has provided the conceptual framework underlying most of the corporate simulation models which have been developed to date. For this reason, many of the existing corporate models contain an excessive degree of detail and are of limited usefulness as strategic planning tools.

Only recently have economists become seriously interested in corporate simulation models. It is to be hoped that this development will result in the melding of economics and accounting as the conceptual framework for corporate modeling. However, the reader will note that in the corporate models described in this chapter, the balance is still weighted heavily on the accounting side. We will attempt to emphasize the potential contributions of corporate economics as an analytical framework for corporate modeling.

Figure 12-5 contains a flowchart of a corporate simulation model that is driven by a series of business planning models for the individual businesses of the company. These models may be used on a stand-alone basis at the business unit level or consolidated and used by the corporate planning department, senior financial officers, or the chief executive officer. Each business unit model consists of a front-end financial model driven by a marketing model and a production model.

**FIGURE 12-5**
A conceptual framework for corporate simulation models.

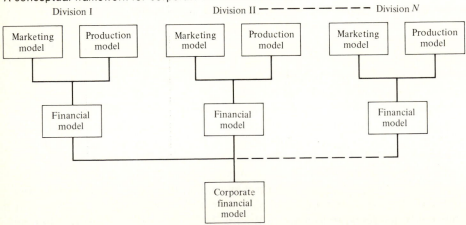

The objectives of the business unit models are to generate alternative scenarios and business plans on the basis of varying assumptions about business unit policies and assumptions about the external environment of the businesses. The plan which is actually chosen should be robust in the sense that it will yield reasonably good results (profits, return on investment, etc.) under a wide variety of circumstances which may plausibly arise in the future.

## Financial Planning Models

Each business planning model produces as output data a pro forma income statement for the business unit. In cases in which the business unit is actually a subsidiary of the parent company, pro forma balance sheets and sources and uses of funds statements may be produced as well. Basically, these business financial models can be used to simulate the effects on net profit of alternative business strategies for a given business unit. The validity of the results generated by a business unit financial model will be no better or worse than the assumptions underlying the revenue and production cost projections which feed the model.

Typically, the availability of financial data is not an obstacle to the development of a corporate simulation model. Large and small firms alike have sufficient financial data to build a financial planning model.

For example, an annual financial planning model for a corporation can be developed with last year's balance sheet and annual report data for the previous three or four years. Stand-alone financial models simply do not require substantial amounts of historical data. The first corporate financial model developed by Hercules, Inc., was based entirely on annual report data from the preceding four years.

Of course, it is important to differentiate between a financial planning model and a model of the company's accounting structure. A model of the firm's accounting system may consist of thousands of equations, one for each accounting line item. Several electric utility companies have developed models of their accounting systems. These models produce hundreds of pages of output and are almost completely worthless as financial planning models. The human mind cannot comprehend that much information. A financial planning model should contain only information which is essential to plan and to control the organization. Obviously, which information is essential for these purposes is a matter of managerial judgment.

## Marketing Planning Models

Marketing planning models provide the revenue projections which drive the business planning models. Two alternatives are available: forecasting models and econometric marketing models. The former may be merely a set of extrapolations of the trends implicit in a historical set of data, with each trend developed for one variable independently of others. The latter may refer to a more complex extrapolation of trends in which the interdependence among variables is considered. Short-term forecasting models are naive, mechanistic models, devoid of explanatory power. They cannot be used to do "what if?" analysis. On the other hand, econometric models are rich in explanatory power and may be used to link sales to the national economy and to conduct marketing policy simulation experiments. With econometric marketing models, it is possible to simulate the effects on sales and market-shares of alternative advertising, pricing, and promotional policies. Marketing models provide the sales revenue forecasts which are required to drive both the financial and production models shown in Figure 12-5. The specification, estimation, and validation of econometric marketing models is based heavily on demand theory (Chapter 2), empirical demand analysis, and econometrics (Chapter 3). Econometric marketing models require a considerable amount of expertise on the part of the analyst. To build successful econometric marketing models the analyst must be well versed in microeconomic theory, econometrics, and statistics and knowledgeable about the product market to be modeled.

### Production Planning Models

Given a sales forecast for a particular business unit, how much will it cost to produce at a level which will satisfy the demand forecast? That is the raison d'être for production planning models. A number of companies, including Northwest Industries and Texaco, use a type of activity analysis approach to production planning modeling which generates the cost of goods sold associated with a given demand forecast. A reasonable extension of this approach is for the production model to generate the minimum cost associated with a given level of demand for the products of the business unit. This latter alternative represents a logical interface between mathematical programming and other optimization techniques and corporate simulation models.

The ability to model the production activities of a company is entirely dependent on the quality of the cost accounting data generated by the company's production operations. Continuous-process types of industries such as petroleum refineries and chemical plants usually have reasonably good production cost data; the same is true of steel mills and automobile assembly lines. But the closer the manufacturing operations of a plant come to being a "job shop" type of operation, the less likely the chances of having adequate production cost data. Production planning models draw heavily on the theory of production and cost that was outlined in Chapters 4 and 5.

### Integrated Planning Models

It is important to be able to integrate marketing and production models into financial planning models at the business unit level. That is, revenue forecasts and operating costs are generated by the marketing and production models, respectively. The integration of the latter two models into the former will greatly facilitate the use of the business planning model. In Figure 12-5, the individual business models are examples of integrated business planning models. The TVL case at the end of this chapter is also an example of an integrated planning model.

## Consolidated Planning Models

As previously indicated, the individual business planning models in Figure 12-5 may be used as planning tools for the separate business units or consolidated at the corporate level to form consolidated corporate plans. The corporate planning department should have the option to perform "what if?" experiments with any of the business unit models either on a stand-alone basis or as part of a totally integrated planning and modeling system. The output reports of a consolidated corporate planning model typically include pro forma income statements, balance sheets, and sources and uses of funds statements.

## Three Example Models

To further illustrate the application of corporate simulation models as a strategic planning tool, we shall briefly describe three existing corporate simulation models: the *New York Times,* the Tennessee Valley Authority, and Northwest Industries. These will be followed by detailed descriptions of two hypothetical models: the TVL model and the Standard International model.

**The *New York Times* Model**   The *New York Times* corporate modeling efforts begin in 1974 in response to the publisher's concerns over the newspaper's declining market-share and uncertainty about the future impact of the economy of New York City on circulation and advertising. At that time, the New York Times Company had no formal planning system whatsoever. Since 1974 business planning models have been built by the corporate planning staff for the *New York Times* newspaper, 15 other smaller newspapers owned by the company, *Family Circle* magazine, and two cable television companies recently acquired by the company. The rigor and discipline imposed by the development of the computer-based planning models led to the development of a formal strategic planning system which is now in use by corporate management and top management of the various newspapers, publishing companies, and radio and television stations owned by the New York Times Company.

The *New York Times* model is used exclusively as a corporate planning tool to evaluate corporate goals, objectives, and strategies as well as the strategic plans of the operating companies. It makes no pretense of being an operational tool for the operating companies. Although the model of the *New York Times* newspaper contains over 300 equations, the models of the other newspapers and related businesses each contain only 25 to 30 equations.

The model of the lead newspaper has been particularly effective in forecasting circulation and advertising expenditures. As was mentioned previously, the model was used as one of the inputs which led to the change in the format, layout, and type style of the *New York Times* newspaper. The *New York Times* model is completely integrated into the company's annual strategic planning process and enjoys the support of the highest levels of management within the lead newspaper and the parent company. The model of the lead newspaper is unique by virtue of the extent to which it links advertising and circulation to the national economy and the economy of New York City through the use of sophisticated econometric relationships. Figures 12-6 and 12-7 contain

**FIGURE 12-6**
The *New York Times* corporate planning model.

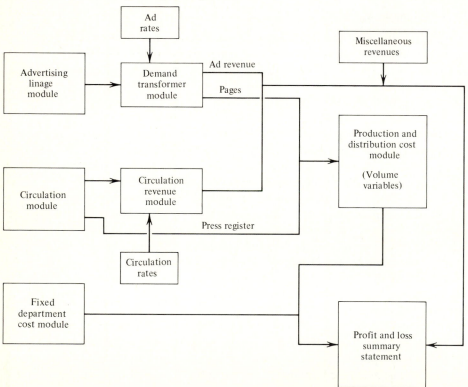

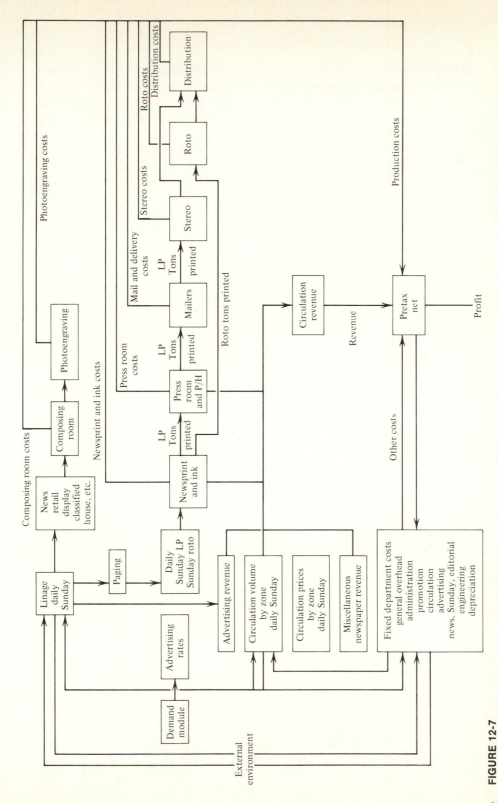

**FIGURE 12-7**
Production-distribution cost module of the *New York Times* model.

flowcharts of the logic of the *New York Times* model. Below we have outlined some of the dependent variables and external variables and reproduced several representative equations from an earlier version of the advertising-circulation econometric model for *The New York Times* developed by Dr. Leonard Forman.

**Circulation variables**

| | |
|---|---|
| CIRCD | Daily circulation |
| CIRCS | Sunday circulation |
| SC4 | National daily |
| SC9 | National Sunday |
| SC11 | City daily home delivery |
| SC12 | Suburban daily home delivery |
| SC14 | City Sunday home delivery |
| SC15 | Suburban Sunday home delivery |
| SC16 | City daily newsstand |
| SC17 | Suburban daily newsstand |
| SC18 | City Sunday newsstand |
| SC19 | Suburban Sunday newsstand |

**Advertising linage variables**

| | |
|---|---|
| AMUSE | Total amusements |
| AMUSESUN% | Sunday amusements as a percentage of total amusements |
| EMP | Total help-wanted classified |
| SL2101 | Department store daily |
| SL2102 | Amusements daily |
| SL2103 | Real estate display daily |
| SL2103A | Classified apartments daily |
| SL2103B | Classified real estate daily |
| SL2107 | Retail other daily |
| SL2202 | General daily |
| SL2202A | Other general daily |
| SL2399 | Automotive daily |
| SL2400 | Financial daily |
| SL2501 | Help-wanted classified daily |
| SL2503 | Other classified daily |
| SL2503A | Other classified except real estate daily |
| SL2600 | Help-wanted display daily |
| SL3102 | Amusements Sunday |
| SL3103 | Real estate display Sunday |
| SL3103A | Classified apartments Sunday |
| SL3103B | Classified real estate Sunday |
| SL3501 | Help-wanted classified Sunday |
| SL3600 | Help-wanted display Sunday |
| SL4101 | Department store Sunday |
| SL4107 | Retail other Sunday |
| SL4202 | General Sunday |
| SL4202A | Other general Sunday |
| SL4399 | Automotive Sunday |
| SL4400 | Financial Sunday |
| SL4503 | Other classified Sunday |
| SL4503A | Other classified except real estate Sunday |

| SL5999 | Sunday magazine |
| SL6999 | Book review |
| SL7999 | Special sections |
| SUN% | Sunday help-wanted display as percentage of total display |
| SUN%3501 | Sunday help-wanted classified as a percentage of total classified |
| TOTAPT | Total classified apartments |
| TOTDISP | Total help-wanted display |

**External variables**

| CDMV&P | Personal consumption expenditures, motor vehicles, and parts |
| CNDUM | Dummy for loss of NYC newspapers |
| CPI | Consumer price index |
| EEA | Employment nonagricultural establishments |
| EHH | Total employment household survey |
| GNP | Gross national product |
| GNPK72 | Real potential GNP |
| HHNETWORTH | Household net worth |
| HUSTS | Housing starts |
| MONEY | Money supply |
| NEST22& | Noninstitutional population 22 and over |
| PGNP | GNP deflator |
| P3 | Suburban and city daily price |
| P4 | National daily price |
| P8 | Suburban and city Sunday price |
| P9 | National Sunday price |
| RMMBCAAANS | Moody's AAA corporate bond rate |
| RU | Unemployment rate |
| STRIKE2 | Strike dummy variable |
| STRIKE 2A | Strike dummy variable |
| STRIKE 3 | Strike dummy variable |
| TIME | Trend variable |

**Circulation equations**

National daily

$$SC4 = -142.16 + .22144 * SC9 + .0057300 * (SL2022 + SL2501 + SL2503)$$
$$+ .34473 * SC4(-1) + 1.6413 * EHH + .84302 * P9 - 4.0371 * P4$$
$$+ 17.978 * STRIKE2 + 12.532 * STRIKE2A - 19.878 * STRIKE3$$

National Sunday

$$SC9 = 395.42 + 526.78 * (CPI - CPI(-1)) + .60837 * SC4 - 1.8062 * EHH$$
$$- 1.1354 * P9 + 2.4923 * P4 + .33235 * SC9(-1)$$

City daily home delivery

$$SC11 = -94.053 - .80112 * P3HD - .023381 * SC16 + .49019 * SC14$$
$$+ 1.9608 * EHH - .99487 * CNDUM - 5.9084 * STRIKE2 - 12.503$$
$$* STRIKE3$$

City Sunday home delivery

$$SC14 = -1.3539 + .30103 * (SC11 + SC16) - 2.0433 * RU + 1.8727 * P3HD$$
$$- .62865 * P8HD + 3.8678 * CNDUM - 29.899 * STRIKE3 - 31.330$$
$$* STRIKE2 - 11.321 * STRIKE2A$$

City daily newsstand

$$SC16 = 283.27 + .031376 * (SC18 + SC19) - .19847 * (SC11 + SC12)$$
$$- 6.4878 * P3 + 1.1469 * P8 + .018695 * (SL2107 + SL2501)$$
$$- 10.697 * CNDUM + 30.447 * STRIKE2 - .029908 * STRIKE3$$

City Sunday newsstand

$$SC18 = 112.66 + 271.01 * (CPI - CPI(-1)) + .42557 * SC18(-1) + .35497$$
$$* (SC11 + SC16) + 4.4971 * P3 - 1.8154 * P8 - .47245 * RU$$
$$+ 40.325 * STRIKE2 + 33.891 * STRIKE3$$

### Advertising linage equations

Total help wanted classified

$$EMP = EXP(10.010 - 1.5761 * LOG(CIRCS/CIRCD) * 6.3240$$
$$* LOG(GNP72/GNP72(-1)) - .93403 * LOG((RU + RU(-1)$$
$$+ RU(-2) + RU(-3))/4.0000) - .33148 * STRIKE2 - 11.247$$
$$* STRIKE2A - .071687 * SLOW - .13253 * EMPDUM)$$

Department store daily

$$SL2101 = EXP(-.092991 + .16772 * LOG(SL4101) + .65982$$
$$* LOG(CIRCD) - .30405 * LOG((RU + RU(-1) + RU(-2)$$
$$+ RU(-3) + RU(-4) + RU(-5) + RU(-6))/7.0000) + .051172$$
$$* XTIME - .0002/970 * XTIME ** 2.0000 - .31390 * STRIKE2$$
$$- 9.3630 * STRIKE2A - .19057 * STRIKE3)$$

Real estate display daily

$$SL2103 = 30.681 + .20147 * SL2103(-1) + .26794 * SL2103(-2) + 7.4149$$
$$* HUSTS - 23.494 * STRIKE3 - 83.243 * STRIKE2A + 27.424$$
$$* SLOW$$

Retail other daily

$$SL2107 = EXP(-.88690 - .64886 * LOG(CIRCS/CIRCD) + .78388$$
$$* LOG(GNP72) + .028473 * TIME - .00018934 * TIME ** 2.0000$$
$$* STRIKE3 - 8.0614 * STRIKE2A)$$

Automotive daily

$$SL2399 = 416.03 + .08971 * CIRCD - 417.80$$
$$* (CDMV\&P/NEST22\&)/PGNP - 24.652 * RU - 158.92$$
$$* (HHNETWORTH - HHNETWORTH(-4))/HHNETWORTH(-4))$$
$$+ .27780 * SL2399(-1) - 60.022 * STRIKE2 - 101.30$$
$$* STRIKE3 - 263.05 * STRIKE2A$$

Financial daily

$$SL2400 = 31.338 + .0016017 * SL4400 * (CIRCD + CIRCD(-1)$$
$$+ CIRCD(-2) + CIRCD(-3))/4.0000 + 917.19 * MONEY(-1)$$
$$- MONEY(-3))/MONEY(-3) - 1.5328 * (GNPK72 - GNP72)$$
$$+ 88.970 * RMMBCAAANS - 68.632 * STRIKE2 - 99.541$$
$$* STRIKE3 - 346.16 * STRIKE2A$$

Amusements Sunday

$$SL3102 = AMUSESUN\% * AMUSE + ADDSL3102$$

Sunday magazine

$$SL5999 = EXP(7.7758 - .63788 * LOG((RU + RU(-1) + RU(-2)$$
$$+ RU(-3))/4.00000 - 11.222)STRIKE2A - .12729$$
$$* STRIKE2 - .34779 * STRIKE3)$$

Book review

$$SL6999 = 410.92 + 1.6349 * TIME - 32.612 * P6999 - 17.120 * RU$$
$$- 39.492 * STRIKE2 - 36.418 * STRIKE3 - 319.96 * STRIKE2A$$
$$+ 22.374 * SLOW$$

Special sections

$$SL7999 = - 369.51 + 8.9244 * EEA + .24963 * SL7999(-1) - 165.70$$
$$* STRIKE2A$$

**Tennessee Valley Authority Model**  The TVA model is one of the most sophisticated corporate models ever built in the United States. It includes a forecasting model, a power system simulation model, various forecast models, a pricing model, a system expansion model, and a financial planning model. It took over 30 worker-years to develop this complicated model. Although the TVA model is impressive in its technical detail, its lack of user orientation is a severe limitation. The flowchart for the TVA model appears in Figure 12-8.

**Northwest Industries Model**  Probably the most advanced computer-based planning, modeling, and management information system in place today is at Northwest Industries in Chicago. Although its formal strategic planning system goes all the way back to 1968, its corporate modeling system was not implemented until 1977.

The company developed integrated (financial, marketing, and production) models for eight of its nine operating companies, including Lone Star Steel, Acme Boot, Union Underwear, Coca-Cola Los Angeles, and General Battery. These models were developed by the corporate planning department. Each model is a quarterly model consisting of around 30 equations. The planning horizon is four years. The business planning models are used primarily to evaluate the strategic plans of the operating companies. Two examples will serve to illustrate the use of these models by senior management. Recently, corporate management developed an expanded model of Lone Star Steel to evaluate an $800 million capital expenditure project to expand the production capacity of Lone Star. The results generated by the model were a key element in causing corporate management to reject the project and consider other alternatives. In 1980, both General Battery and Union Underwear were projecting continued expansion of their sales and profits on the basis of recent trends. However, the business planning models for each of these operating companies pointed to a serious recession in 1980, with significant negative effects on the profitability of the two businesses. The models were correct. In addition to the previously mentioned business planning models, Northwest Industries has the capability to do merger-acquisition analysis and cash management with its computer-based planning and modeling system.

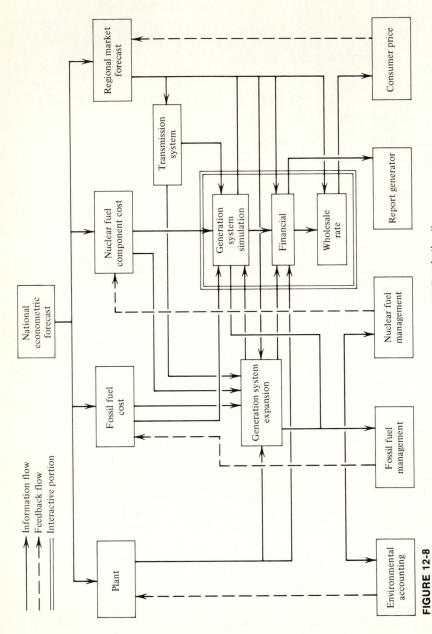

Information flow
Feedback flow
Interactive portion

**FIGURE 12-8**
Flowchart of the integrated planning model of the Tennessee Valley Authority.

## THE TVL CASE

TV Limited is the American subsidiary of the multinational Swiss electronic firm known as Zeta Electronics, Ltd. TV Limited (TVL) is a manufacturer of television sets. In early 1976, TVL had just received its year-end financial reports for 1975. The director of corporate planning at TVL was interested in developing a corporate simulation model to facilitate the formulation of the next five-year plan for the company. At present the company has a manual strategic planning system, but it has proved to be somewhat rigid and inflexible. Specifically, the director of corporate planning was interested in acquiring the capability to answer "what if?" questions to evaluate alternative marketing and financial policies in light of possible scenarios which might evolve for the economy of the United States. TVL is heavily dependent on the American economy, since over 80 percent of its market is in the United States.

### Goals and Objectives

The director of corporate planning at TVL envisaged a fully integrated business planning model for TVL based on certain guidelines provided by the vice president of corporate planning for the parent company, Zeta Electronics, Ltd.

The model was to consist of a front-end financial model driven by a marketing model and a production model, as illustrated in Figure 12-9. Based on historical data since 1966, the financial model was to produce annual financial reports for the period 1976–1980. The financial reports would include an income statement and a balance sheet. In addition, the model was expected to generate a five-year market forecast and a five-year production forecast.

After a careful review of the planning requirements for TVL, the director of corporate planning determined that it was important for management to monitor a total of 32 different output variables. These variables would become the major indicators by which management would judge the performance of the company. It followed that these variables would also serve as the output of the TVL corporate planning model.

After consultation with the president, vice president of finance, treasurer, vice president of marketing, and vice president of manufacturing, the director of corporate planning decided that it would be desirable to attempt to link the

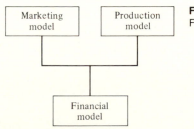

**FIGURE 12-9**
Flowchart for the TVL corporate planning model.

TVL model to the economy of the United States. It was felt that both long- and short-term interest rates as well as several other measures of overall economic activity were important external financial variables that should be treated as input into the model. After repeated experimentation, national income was selected as a good leading indicator for television sales in the United States. These external variables were included in the model.

Since the primary objective of the model was to evaluate the impact of alternative management strategies on the performance of the company, a great deal of attention was given to the selection of the policy variables to be included in the model. Nine policy variables were integrated into the model. These variables included three marketing policy variables: advertising expenses, the price of color TV sets, and the price of black-and-white (b&w) TV sets.

On the financial side, management could control the number of shares of stock outstanding, the price to be charged if additional shares were to be sold, and whether dividends were declared. Management could also establish a minimum cash balance such that if cash dropped below this minimum, the cash gap could be made up by drawing on the company's short-term line of credit. TVL could also elect whether to acquire additional long-term debt or retire some of its existing debt.

In planning for the next five years, management wanted to be able to consider different financial and marketing strategies and anticipate their likely impact on TVL's market performance and financial condition. Among the kinds of "what if?" questions of interest to management were the following: What will be the impact on total revenue if we raise prices and hold advertising expenditures constant? If we double our advertising budget, how much cash will we need? Should we sell additional stock to finance our expansion and growth or should we acquire additional long-term debt? Is our cash management policy effective? What if interest rates go up? What if the American economy goes into recession again?

### Definition of Variables

Following is a list of the 32 output variables, 3 external variables, and 9 management policy variables which appear in the TVL model. We define each variable and specify the units associated with it.

### Output variables

| Variable | Name (units) |
| --- | --- |
| AP | Accounts payable ($1,000) |
| AR | Accounts receivable ($1,000) |
| BW | B&w TV sales ($1,000) |
| CA | Current assets ($1,000) |
| CASH | Cash ($1,000) |
| CGS | Cost of goods sold ($1,000) |
| CL | Current liabilities ($1,000) |

| COLOR | Color TV sales ($1,000) |
|---|---|
| CR | Current ratio (ratio) |
| CS | Common stock ($1,000) |
| DIV | Dividends ($1,000) |
| EPS | Earnings per share ($/share) |
| ES | Earned surplus ($1,000) |
| INTEREST | Interest ($1,000) |
| INV | Inventory ($1,000) |
| LTD | Long-term debt ($1,000) |
| MA | Miscellaneous accruals ($1,000) |
| NET | Net profit ($1,000) |
| NPLANT | Net plant and equipment ($1,000) |
| NPTSR | Net profit to sales ratio (ratio) |
| NSHARES | Number of shares ($1,000) |
| OA | Other assets ($1,000) |
| OE | Operating expenses ($1,000) |
| PBT | Profit before taxes ($1,000) |
| RTAX | Reserve for federal income taxes ($1,000) |
| RTE | Retained earnings ($1,000) |
| SALES | Sales revenue ($1,000) |
| STD | Short-term debt ($1,000) |
| TA | Total assets ($1,000) |
| TAX | Federal income taxes ($1,000) |
| TE | Total expenses ($1,000) |
| TL | Total liabilities ($1,000) |

**Input variables**

**External**

| Variable | Name (units) |
|---|---|
| LTR | Long-term interest rate |
| STR | Short-term interest rate |
| Y | National income ($billion) |

**Policy**

| Variable | Name (units) |
|---|---|
| ADV | Advertising expenses ($1,000) |
| DPS | Dividends per share ($1) |
| MIN | Minimum cash balance ($1,000) |
| NDEBT | New long-term debt ($1,000) |
| NOMINAL | Nominal value per share ($1) |
| NSHARES | Number of shares ($1,000) |
| PBW | Price of b&w TV sets ($1) |
| PC | Price of color TV sets ($1) |
| REPAY | Repayment of long-term debt ($1,000) |

## Historical Data

Three types of historical data were available to TVL for the development of its corporate planning model: marketing, production, and financial data.

Table 12-1 contains marketing data over the 1966–1975 period. The data include price and volume data by product as well as advertising expenditures and national income for the United States.

**TABLE 12-1**
TVL HISTORICAL MARKETING DATA, 1966–1975

| Year | Color TV sales Volume, 1,000 | Price, $ | B&W TV sales Volume, 1,000 | Price, $ | Advertising expenses, $1,000 | National income, $billion |
|------|------|------|------|------|------|------|
| 1966 | 17.1 | 260 | 12.3 | 138 | 1,600 | 414.5 |
| 1967 | 19.9 | 264 | 15.3 | 138 | 1,760 | 427.3 |
| 1968 | 20.4 | 270 | 15.2 | 146 | 1,792 | 457.7 |
| 1969 | 21.7 | 270 | 15.4 | 150 | 1,840 | 481.9 |
| 1970 | 24.4 | 276 | 18.5 | 150 | 2,000 | 518.1 |
| 1971 | 27.9 | 280 | 20.0 | 160 | 2,160 | 564.3 |
| 1972 | 30.4 | 280 | 21.3 | 160 | 2,240 | 620.6 |
| 1973 | 31.5 | 280 | 21.8 | 160 | 2,272 | 653.6 |
| 1974 | 33.6 | 283 | 23.0 | 164 | 2,368 | 701.3 |
| 1975 | 34.2 | 285 | 23.7 | 164 | 2,400 | 723.5 |

Unfortunately, TVL's manufacturing cost accounting data were somewhat limited. Production volume (assumed to be equal to sales volume) by product, cost of goods sold, and inventory data appear in Table 12-2.

Relatively complete financial data were available, including annual income statement data (Table 12-3) and balance sheet data (Table 12-4).

## External Assumptions

The TVL model was based on a set of assumptions about the external environment of the firm. These assumptions were assumed to be beyond the control of TVL's management but of vital importance to the future of the company.

**TABLE 12-2**
TVL HISTORICAL PRODUCTION DATA, 1966–1975

| Year | Color TV volume, 1,000 | B&W TV volume, 1,000 | Total volume, 1,000 | Cost of goods sold, $1,000 | Inventory, $1,000 |
|------|------|------|------|------|------|
| 1966 | 17.1 | 12.3 | 29.4 | 3,010.3 | 1,167.2 |
| 1967 | 19.9 | 15.3 | 35.2 | 3,829.8 | 1,546.7 |
| 1968 | 20.4 | 15.2 | 35.6 | 3,709.1 | 1,545.4 |
| 1969 | 21.7 | 15.4 | 37.1 | 4,084.5 | 1,470.4 |
| 1970 | 24.4 | 18.5 | 42.9 | 5,040.0 | 2,092.1 |
| 1971 | 27.9 | 20.0 | 47.9 | 5,616.1 | 2,202.4 |
| 1972 | 30.4 | 21.3 | 51.7 | 6,556.0 | 2,026.4 |
| 1973 | 31.5 | 21.8 | 53.3 | 6,277.1 | 2,584.7 |
| 1974 | 33.6 | 23.0 | 56.6 | 6,640.0 | 2,656.2 |
| 1975 | 34.2 | 23.7 | 57.9 | 6,953.2 | 2,863.1 |

**TABLE 12-3**
TVL HISTORICAL INCOME STATEMENT DATA, 1966–1975

| | 1966 | 1967 | 1968 | 1969 | 1970 | 1971 | 1972 | 1973 | 1974 | 1975 |
|---|---|---|---|---|---|---|---|---|---|---|
| Sales revenue | 6,143.4 | 7,365.0 | 7,727.2 | 8,169.0 | 9,509.4 | 11,012.0 | 11,920.0 | 12,308.0 | 13,280.8 | 13,633.8 |
| Expenses | | | | | | | | | | |
| Cost of goods sold | 3,010.3 | 3,829.8 | 3,709.1 | 4,084.5 | 5,040.0 | 5,616.1 | 6,556.0 | 6,277.1 | 6,640.0 | 6,953.2 |
| Advertising expenses | 1,600.0 | 1,760.0 | 1,792.0 | 1,840.0 | 2,000.0 | 2,160.0 | 2,240.0 | 2,272.0 | 2,368.0 | 2,400.0 |
| Operating expenses | 233.4 | 287.2 | 293.6 | 326.8 | 399.4 | 451.5 | 512.6 | 516.6 | 531.2 | 545.4 |
| Interest | 354.4 | 343.9 | 720.4 | 636.3 | 563.6 | 1,022.4 | 704.2 | 1,273.1 | 1,616.7 | 1,553.8 |
| Total expenses | 5,198.2 | 6,220.9 | 6,515.1 | 6,887.6 | 8,003.0 | 9,250.0 | 10,012.8 | 10,338.8 | 11,155.9 | 11,452.4 |
| Profit before taxes | 945.2 | 1,144.1 | 1,212.1 | 1,281.4 | 1,506.4 | 1,762.0 | 1,907.2 | 1,969.2 | 2,124.9 | 2,181.4 |
| Federal income taxes | 453.7 | 554.9 | 593.9 | 627.9 | 745.8 | 881.0 | 953.6 | 984.6 | 1,062.4 | 1,090.7 |
| Net profit | 491.5 | 589.2 | 618.2 | 653.5 | 760.6 | 881.0 | 953.6 | 984.6 | 1,062.5 | 1,090.7 |
| Dividends | 360.2 | 362.3 | 363.4 | 367.8 | 371.6 | 372.5 | 370.6 | 369.5 | 370.1 | 375.6 |
| Retained earnings | 131.3 | 226.9 | 254.8 | 285.7 | 389.0 | 508.5 | 583.0 | 615.1 | 692.4 | 715.1 |

**TABLE 12-4**
TVL HISTORICAL BALANCE SHEET DATA, 1966–1975

| | 1966 | 1967 | 1968 | 1969 | 1970 | 1971 | 1972 | 1973 | 1974 | 1975 |
|---|---|---|---|---|---|---|---|---|---|---|
| Assets | | | | | | | | | | |
| Cash | 800.2 | 421.3 | 1,354.4 | 2,344.4 | 2,071.2 | 3,111.3 | 2,078.1 | 2,554.4 | 4,215.0 | 5,168.1 |
| Accounts receivable | 491.5 | 626.0 | 734.1 | 939.4 | 950.9 | 991.1 | 1,192.0 | 1,232.3 | 1,300.1 | 1,363.4 |
| Inventory | 1,167.2 | 1,546.7 | 1,545.4 | 1,470.4 | 2,092.1 | 2,202.4 | 2,026.4 | 2,584.7 | 2,656.2 | 2,863.1 |
| Current assets | 2,458.9 | 2,594.0 | 3,633.9 | 4,754.2 | 5,114.2 | 6,304.8 | 5,296.5 | 6,371.4 | 8,171.3 | 9,394.6 |
| Net plant and equipment | 5,212.9 | 5,715.3 | 7,316.8 | 7,747.6 | 7,906.6 | 9,867.8 | 9,126.7 | 11,244.1 | 13,436.0 | 14,635.2 |
| Other assets | 102.3 | 140.9 | 181.5 | 220.7 | 259.2 | 300.8 | 341.0 | 384.4 | 424.3 | 464.9 |
| Total assets | 7,774.1 | 8,450.2 | 11,132.2 | 12,722.5 | 13,280.0 | 16,473.4 | 14,764.2 | 17,999.9 | 22,031.6 | 24,494.7 |
| Liabilities | | | | | | | | | | |
| Accounts payable | 150.5 | 210.6 | 222.5 | 265.5 | 352.8 | 365.0 | 393.4 | 345.2 | 398.4 | 417.2 |
| Short-term debt | 1,107.8 | 975.0 | 1,610.0 | 2,272.5 | 2,261.3 | 2,840.0 | 1,956.1 | 2,652.3 | 3,674.3 | 4,316.1 |
| Reserve for federal taxes | 450.0 | 560.0 | 600.0 | 625.0 | 740.0 | 890.0 | 1,000.0 | 1,010.0 | 1,025.0 | 1,050.0 |
| Miscellaneous accruals | 22.5 | 28.1 | 34.6 | 43.6 | 53.2 | 64.9 | 81.1 | 101.4 | 127.7 | 159.7 |
| Debt repayment | 90.6 | 92.5 | 92.0 | 94.9 | 95.6 | 100.1 | 100.4 | 110.6 | 115.3 | 118.0 |
| Current liabilities | 1,821.4 | 1,866.2 | 2,559.1 | 3,301.5 | 3,502.9 | 4,260.0 | 3,531.0 | 4,219.5 | 5,340.7 | 6,061.0 |
| Long-term debt | 2,417.0 | 2,417.0 | 4,179.2 | 4,772.3 | 4,342.7 | 6,390.0 | 4,401.3 | 6,365.5 | 8,660.9 | 9,711.3 |
| Common stock | 2,000.0 | 2,500.0 | 2,500.0 | 2,500.0 | 3,000.0 | 3,000.0 | 3,500.0 | 3,500.0 | 3,500.0 | 3,500.0 |
| Earned surplus | 1,535.7 | 1,667.0 | 1,893.9 | 2,148.7 | 2,434.4 | 2,823.4 | 3,331.9 | 3,914.9 | 4,530.0 | 5,222.4 |
| Total liabilities | 7,774.1 | 8,450.2 | 11,132.2 | 12,722.5 | 13,280.0 | 16,473.4 | 14,764.2 | 17,999.9 | 22,031.6 | 24,494.7 |

**TABLE 12-5**
EXTERNAL MARKETING
ASSUMPTIONS

| Year | National income Y, $billion |
|------|------------------------------|
| 1976 | 750.20 |
| 1977 | 775.40 |
| 1978 | 788.90 |
| 1979 | 800.00 |
| 1980 | 822.50 |

In forecasting sales volume for color and b&w TV sets, national income in the United States was found to be a good leading indicator. For this reason national income data were tabulated in Table 12-5.

The production model employed by TVL was relatively primitive and reflected the dearth of accurate cost accounting data available to build such a model and the fact that management was more concerned with marketing and financial problems than with production problems. Both cost of goods sold and work-in-process inventory were assumed to be driven entirely by sales. No data were available on specific factor-input costs. The external production assumptions are spelled out in Table 12-6.

Finally, the financial module of the TVL model was based on a set of rather detailed assumptions explaining the relationship between TVL's financial structure and its external environment. These assumptions appear in Table 12-7 and include assumptions about interest rates, expenses, tax rates, depreciation, accounts receivable, and accounts payable. In each case, the external financial assumptions were made over the period 1976–1980.

## Policy Assumptions

In addition to a set of external assumptions, the TVL model was also based on a set of managerial policy assumptions for the coming five-year period. Marketing policies included price and advertising (Table 12-8). The policy assumptions underlying the production model were relatively simplistic (Table 12-9). However, it should be pointed out that with adequate technical and cost accounting data, an in-depth activity analysis production model could have been specified. Such a model would have linked production volume to resource requirements

**TABLE 12-6**
EXTERNAL PRODUCTION ASSUMPTIONS

1. Cost of goods sold (CGS) equals 60% of sales (SALES)
2. Work-in-process inventory (INV) equals 20% of sales (SALES)

**TABLE 12-7**
EXTERNAL FINANCIAL ASSUMPTIONS

1. Long-term interest rate (LTR) equals 10%
2. Short-term interest rate (STR) equals 12%
3. Operating expenses (OE) equal 10% of sales (SALES)
4. Federal income tax rate equals 50%
5. Accounts receivable (AR) equal 10% of sales (SALES)
6. Depreciation for plant and equipment is assumed to be 5% per year
7. Other assets (OA) increase by $40,000 each year
8. Accounts payable (AP) equal 6% of cost of goods sold (CGS)
9. Miscellaneous accruals (MA) increase by 25% per year

(raw materials, labor, capital, etc.). Given a sales forecast, an activity analysis model would generate a resource demand forecast and the cost of the resource needed to satisfy demand. Companies such as Inland Steel, Potlatch, and Monsanto utilize a production modeling technique of this type.

Consistent with the emphasis placed on financial analysis by TVL's management, Table 12-10 contains a set of seven financial policy assumptions on which the model is based.

### Model Specification

#### Marketing Model
*Specification*  To explain the behavior of color and b&w TV sales volume, the following two-equation econometric model was formulated:

$$COLOR = a + bPC + cBW + dADV + eY \qquad (12\text{-}10)$$

$$BW = f + gPBW + hCOLOR + iADV + jY \qquad (12\text{-}11)$$

In reality, many different behavioral equations were specified. Equations (12-10) and (12-11) represent the result of screening out numerous unaccepta-

**TABLE 12-8**
MARKETING POLICY ASSUMPTIONS

| Year | Color TV price, $ | B&W TV price, $ | Advertising expenses, $1,000 |
|------|-------------------|-----------------|------------------------------|
| 1976 | 300 | 180 | 3,000 |
| 1977 | 310 | 190 | 3,000 |
| 1978 | 320 | 200 | 3,000 |
| 1979 | 330 | 210 | 3,000 |
| 1980 | 340 | 220 | 3,000 |

**TABLE 12-9**
PRODUCTION POLICY ASSUMPTIONS

1. Two products: color TV sets (COLOR) and black and white TV sets (BW).
2. Production output approximately equals sales volume for both color TV sets (COLOR) and (BW) sets
3. No adjustments made in sales (SALES), output, or cost of goods sold (CGS) to reflect changes in work-in-process inventory (INV)

ble equation specifications. Equation (12-10) states that volume of color TV sales (COLOR) is related to the price of color sets (PC); the number of b&w sets sold (BW), since they are substitutes for color sets; total advertising expenditures (ADV); and national income ($Y$). On the other hand, in equation (12-10) we observe that volume of b&w TV sales (BW) is assumed to be linked to the price of b&w sets (PBW), the number of color sets sold (COLOR), advertising expenditures (ADV), and national income ($Y$). Many other national macroeconomic indicators were considered, but national income proved to yield the best statistical fit.

In summary, equations (12-10) and (12-11) represent a hypothesis about the sales behavior of the two kinds of TV sets manufactured by TVL. But in Table 12-1 we have 10 years of historical data on each of the variables included in equations (12-10) and (12-11). Armed with these data, it is possible to estimate the coefficients $a, b, c, \ldots, f, g, h, \ldots$, of the two models, subject these parameter estimates to a series of statistical tests, and evaluate the dynamic properties of the model. Once an acceptable model has been specified and estimated, it can be used to generate forecasts for each type of TV set.

*Estimation* Table 12-11 contains the printout of the estimation of the parameters of the COLOR equation, using ordinary least squares to estimate each equation separately. The estimated equation is given by

$$COLOR = 11.271 - .133PC - .228BW + .024ADV \qquad (12\text{-}12)$$
$$+ .013Y$$

**TABLE 12-10**
FINANCIAL POLICY ASSUMPTIONS

1. Dividends per share (DPS) equal $2.15
2. If cash (CASH) is less than the required minimum cash balance (MIN), additional short-term debt (STD) equal to 1.33 times the cash deficit is generated; otherwise, STD equals STD of last period
3. No new long-term debt (NDEBT) is contemplated
4. Nominal value per share (NOMINAL) based on average value of previous shares sold equals $20 per share
5. Number of common shares outstanding (NSHARES) equals 225,000
6. Annual repayment of long-term debt (REPAY) equals $100,000
7. No additional plant and equipment (NPLANT)

**TABLE 12-11**
ESTIMATION OF COLOR TV EQUATION

Least-squares regression estimated equation is
$COLOR = -0.1334*PC - 0.2283*BW + 0.0237*ADV + 0.0132*Y + 11.2709$

| Independent variables | Estimated coefficient | Standard error | t test |
|---|---|---|---|
| PC | −0.1334 | 0.0200 | −6.6704 |
| BW | −0.2283 | 0.1122 | −2.0336 |
| ADV | 0.0237 | 0.0022 | 10.7829 |
| Y | 0.0132 | 0.0017 | 7.7233 |
| CONSTANT | 11.2709 | 3.9949 | 2.8213 |

Number of observations used = 10
$R^2 = 0.9999$
Standard error = 0.0966
F statistic (4, 5) = 9302.4648

The first thing we note in equation (12-12) is the signs of the coefficients. The signs of PC and PBW are both negative, as would be expected. The negative signs respectively imply that the law of demand is at work in the color TV market and that color TV sets and b&w sets are substitutes. In Table 12-11, we also examine the $R^2$'s and the $t$ statistics. The exceptionally high $R^2$'s indicate that the right-hand variables have explained most of the variance in COLOR. The $t$ statistics indicate that all the right-hand-side variables are statistically significant at the .05 level.

The econometric coefficient estimates for equation (12-11) are given by

$$BW = -7.360 - .121PBW - .499COLOR + .027ADV \quad (12-13)$$
$$+ .005Y$$

The interpretation of equation (12-13) is similar to that of equation (12-12). Since equations (12-12) and (12-13) represent a system of simultaneous equations, the final estimates of the parameters of these equations should probably be done with two-stage least squares rather than ordinary least squares.

Although equations (12-12) and (12-13) both produced excellent statistical fits, the reader should be aware that these equations are the results of numerous other specifications and estimations that were rejected either because the models did not make sense or because of unacceptable $R^2$'s or $t$ statistics.

***Validation*** The model set forth in equations (12-10) and (12-11) appears to be based on rational economic theories. According to economic theory, we would expect the signs of coefficients $b$ and $g$ to be negative. The law of demand provides the rationale for this assertion. Since COLOR and BW are substitute products, we would assume that coefficients $c$ and $h$ would also be negative. Economic theory would also lead us to assume that increased advertising expenditures and increased income would increase the quantity demanded of a given product. Therefore, we would anticipate that coefficients $d$, $e$, $i$, and $j$ would all be positive.

As we have previously indicated, equations (12-12) and (12-13) have good $R^2$'s and good $t$ statistics, and the signs of the coefficient are consistent with our a priori understanding of the TV market. In other words, we can have confidence in the model's explanatory power.

Finally, the most severe test of the validity of our model is its ability to accurately forecast the behavior of the system it was designed to emulate. This implies that the model must be solved simultaneously for COLOR and BW over time, based on given values for PC, PBW, ADV, and $Y$. We can then compare the simulated values of the two output variables COLOR and BW with their actual observed historical values.

Actual and simulated values of COLOR and BW are tabulated in Table 12-12, and the mean percent absolute errors are computed as well. As we can see from the mean percent errors, the model tracks the actual values of COLOR and BW very well.

The fact that the model tracks well historically is no guarantee that it will forecast accurately between 1976 and 1980. Unless there is additional information to the contrary, this is probably the best we can do. We shall now proceed to use equations (12-12) and (12-13) in the integrated TVL corporate planning model.

**Production Model**  There are only two production equations in the TVL model. Equation 40 in the income statement model (Table 12-13) states that cost of goods sold (CGS) will on the average be equal to approximately 60 percent of sales revenues (SALES). Equation 200 in the balance sheet model

**TABLE 12-12**
VALIDATION OF MARKETING MODEL

| | Color TV sales volume | | | B&W TV sales volume | | |
|------|--------|-----------|------------|--------|-----------|------------|
| Year | Actual | Simulated | Difference | Actual | Simulated | Difference |
| 1966 | 17,100 | 17,555.5 | 55.5 | 12,300 | 12,335.0 | 35.0 |
| 1967 | 19,900 | 19,903.6 | 3.6 | 15,300 | 15,303.9 | 3.9 |
| 1968 | 20,400 | 20,295.7 | −104.3 | 15,200 | 15,159.0 | −41.0 |
| 1969 | 21,700 | 21,700.4 | 0.4 | 15,400 | 15,386.3 | −13.7 |
| 1970 | 24,400 | 24,463.5 | 63.5 | 18,500 | 18,474.1 | −25.9 |
| 1971 | 27,900 | 27,974.3 | 74.3 | 20,000 | 20,033.3 | 33.3 |
| 1972 | 30,400 | 30,323.1 | −76.9 | 21,300 | 21,301.0 | 1.0 |
| 1973 | 31,500 | 31,404.0 | −96.0 | 21,800 | 21,794.0 | −6.0 |
| 1974 | 33,600 | 33,627.6 | 27.6 | 23,000 | 23,021.0 | 21.0 |
| 1975 | 34,200 | 34,261.4 | 61.4 | 23,700 | 23,678.8 | −21.2 |

Mean absolute error = 56.4
Mean percentage error = 0.2203

Mean absolute error = 20.2
Mean percentage error = 0.1188

**TABLE 12-13**
TVL INCOME STATEMENT MODEL

---

```
 10 COLOR = 11.270 − .133 * PC − .228 * BW + .24 * ADV + .013 * Y
 20 BW = − 7.360 − .121 * PBW − .499 * COLOR + .027 * ADV + .005 * Y
 30 SALES = PC * COLOR + PBW * BW
 40 CGS = .60 * SALES
 50 OE = .10 * SALES
 60 INTEREST = STR * STD + LTR * LTD
 70 TE = CGS + ADV + OE + INTEREST
 80 PBT = SALES − TE
 90 TAX = .5 * PBT
100 NET = PBT − TAX
110 DIV = DPS * NSHARES
120 RTE = NET − DIV
```

---

(Table 12-14) assumes that the value of the company's work-in-process inventory (INV) will be approximately 20 percent of the sales revenue (SALES).

**Financial Model**    The financial model consists of two separate models: (1) an income statement model and (2) a balance sheet model. To specifiy a financial model, an analyst must sit with someone within the company who is very familiar with the company's financial structure and examine each line item of the two financial reports to be generated by the model. The assumptions on

**TABLE 12-14**
TVL BALANCE SHEET MODEL

---

```
130 CASH = TL − AR − INV − NPLANT − OA
140 IF CASH < MIN
150 STD = STD + 1.33 * (MIN − CASH)
160 ELSE
170 STD = STD(−1)
180 END
190 AR = .10 * SALES
200 INV = .20 * SALES
210 CA = CASH + AR + INV
220 NPLANT = .95 * NPLANT(−1)
230 OA = OA(−1) + 40
240 TA = CA + NPLANT + OA
250 AP = .06 * CGS
260 RTAX = TAX
270 MA = 1.25 * MA(−1)
280 CL = AP + STD + RTAX + MA + REPAY
290 LTD = LTD(−1) + NDEBT − REPAY
300 CS = NOMINAL * NSHARES
310 ES = ES(−1) + RTE
320 TL = CL + LTD + CS + ES
```

---

which each of the two models was based were summarized in Tables 12-7 and 12-10.

*Income Statement*   Table 12-13 contains the equations for the income statement model. The model contains 12 equations—one equation for each line item in the income statement.

Statements 10 and 20 in Table 12-13 correspond respectively to equations (12-12) and (12-13) of the marketing model. The asterisks denote multiplication. Otherwise, the two statements are identical to the two previously estimated econometric equations for COLOR and BW sales volume. Total sales revenue SALES is the sum of the revenue from color TV sets and b&w TV sets.

The equation for cost of goods sold, statement 40, was previously specified in conjunction with the production model. Advertising expense (ADV) is a policy variable. Its values are given in Table 12-8 for the period 1976–1980.

Short-term interest is the product of the short-term interest rate (STR) and short-term debt (STD). Long-term interest is the product of the long-term interest rate (LTD) and long-term debt (LTD). Total interest (INTEREST) is calculated in statement 60 and is the sum of short-term interest and long-term interest.

Total expenses (TE) and profit before taxes (PBT) are accounting identities and are defined by statements 70 and 80, respectively. Federal income taxes (TAX) are computed in statement 90, assuming a tax rate of 50 percent. Net profit (NET) is defined by statement 100. Total dividends paid (DIV) is the product of dividends per share (DPS) and the number of shares outstanding (NSHARES). Finally, retained earnings (RTE) are calculated in statement 120.

*Balance sheet*   The equations for the balance sheet model are specified in Table 12-14.

The balance sheet is balanced with the cash account. In statement 130 cash (CASH) is defined as the sum of liabilities and equity (TL) minus all assets other than cash. If cash (CASH) is less than the required minimum cash balance (MIN), additional short-term debt equal to 1.33 times the cash deficit (MIN-CASH) is generated by statement 150. Otherwise, short-term debt remains unchanged.

In statements 190 and 200 accounts receivable (AR) and work-in-process inventory value (INV) are expressed as 10 percent and 20 percent of sales revenue (SALES), respectively. Current assets (CA) are defined as the sum of cash (CASH), accounts receivable (AR), and inventory (INV) in statement 210.

Depreciation is subtracted from net plant and equipment (NPLANT) in statement 220 at the rate of 5 percent per year. Other assets (OA) are incremented by $40,000 in statement 230, and total assets (TA) are defined by statement 240.

Turning to the liabilities side of the balance sheet, accounts payable (AP) are computed in statement 250 as a fixed percentage (6 percent) of cost of goods

**TABLE 12-15**
TVL MARKET FORECAST, 1976–1980

| Year | Net profit, $1,000 | Total revenue, $1,000 | Color TV volume, 1,000 | Sales price, $ | B&W TV volume, 1,000 | Sales price, $ | Advertising expenses, $1,000 | National income, $billion |
|---|---|---|---|---|---|---|---|---|
| 1976 | 658.2 | 19,318.0 | 44.80 | 300.00 | 32.66 | 180.00 | 3,000.00 | 750.20 |
| 1977 | 721.2 | 19,704.8 | 43.94 | 310.00 | 32.02 | 190.00 | 3,000.00 | 775.40 |
| 1978 | 772.6 | 20,014.2 | 42.93 | 320.00 | 31.38 | 200.00 | 3,000.00 | 788.90 |
| 1979 | 817.6 | 20,280.7 | 41.89 | 330.00 | 30.75 | 210.00 | 3,000.00 | 800.00 |
| 1980 | 864.9 | 20,562.6 | 41.00 | 340.00 | 30.11 | 220.00 | 3,000.00 | 822.50 |

sold (CGS). Short-term debt (STD) was previously calculated in statement 170. The reserve for federal income taxes (RTAX) is equal to federal taxes for the year (TAX).

Miscellaneous accruals (MA) in statement 270 are assumed to increase by 25 percent each year. Retirement of long-term debt (REPAY) is a policy variable. Current liabilities (CL) are summed in statement 280. Long-term debt (LTD) is defined as last year's long-term debt plus any new debt (NDEBT) minus payments of the debt (REPAY).

If we assume that the nominal value per share of stock is the average price paid to the company for all outstanding shares, the total paid in value of the common stock (CS) is the product of the nominal value per share (NOMINAL) and the number of outstanding shares (NSHARES). This relationship appears in statement 300.

Finally, earned surplus (ES) is updated in statement 310, and total liabilities (TL) are computed in statement 320.

### Policy Simulation Experiments

**Scenario 1**   Given the external assumptions of Tables 12-5 through 12-7 and the policy assumptions of Tables 12-8 through 12-10, we now employ the corporate model listed in Tables 12-13 and 12-14 to produce a five-year plan for TVL. The plan will produce a total of four output reports over the period 1976–1980. The reports include a market forecast (Table 12-15), a production forecast (Table 12-16), a projected income statement (Table 12-17), and a projected balance sheet (Table 12-18).

From a financial standpoint, this scenario assumes no change in the financial relationships of the past. Advertising expenses will be held fixed at $3 million per year, and the prices of color and b&w TV sets will be increased each year. TVL subscribes to an econometric forecasting service which has provided it with five-year projections of national income, short-term interest rates, and long-term interest rates. The simulated results of scenario 1 which are

**TABLE 12-16**
TVL PRODUCTION FORECAST, 1976–1980

| Year | Net profit, $1,000 | Color TV volume, 1,000 | B&W TV volume, 1,000 | Total volume, 1,000 | Cost of goods sold, $1,000 | Inventory, $1,000 |
|---|---|---|---|---|---|---|
| 1976 | 658.2 | 44.80 | 32.66 | 77.46 | 11,590.8 | 3,863.6 |
| 1977 | 721.2 | 43.94 | 32.02 | 75.96 | 11,822.9 | 3,941.0 |
| 1978 | 772.6 | 42.93 | 31.38 | 74.31 | 12,008.5 | 4,002.8 |
| 1979 | 817.6 | 41.89 | 30.75 | 72.64 | 12,168.4 | 4,056.1 |
| 1980 | 864.9 | 41.00 | 30.11 | 71.11 | 12,337.6 | 4,112.5 |

**TABLE 12-17**
TVL PROJECTED INCOME STATEMENT: SCENARIO 1, 1976–1980 ($)

|  | 1976 | 1977 | 1978 | 1979 | 1980 |
|---|---|---|---|---|---|
| Sales revenue | 19,318.0 | 19,704.8 | 20,014.2 | 20,280.7 | 20,562.6 |
| Expenses |  |  |  |  |  |
| Cost of goods sold | 11,590.8 | 11,822.9 | 12,008.5 | 12,168.4 | 12,337.6 |
| Advertising expenses | 3,000.0 | 3,000.0 | 3,000.0 | 3,000.0 | 3,000.0 |
| Operating expenses | 1,931.8 | 1,970.5 | 2,001.4 | 2,028.1 | 2,056.2 |
| Interest | 1,479.0 | 1,469.0 | 1,459.1 | 1,449.0 | 1,439.0 |
| Total Expenses | 18,001.6 | 18,262.4 | 18,469.0 | 18,645.5 | 18,832.8 |
| Profit before taxes | 1,316.4 | 1,442.4 | 1,545.2 | 1,635.2 | 1,729.8 |
| Tax | 658.2 | 721.2 | 772.6 | 817.6 | 864.9 |
| Federal income taxes | 658.2 | 721.2 | 772.6 | 817.6 | 864.9 |
| Dividends | 483.7 | 483.7 | 483.7 | 483.7 | 483.7 |
| Retained earnings | 174.5 | 237.5 | 288.9 | 333.9 | 381.2 |

generated by solving the 32 equations in Tables 12-13 and 12-14 appear in Tables 12-15 through 12-18.

**Scenario 2** The second scenario generated by the TVL model assumes that the price of the color set will be $285 and the price of a b&w set $164 for the

**TABLE 12-18**
TVL PROJECTED BALANCE SHEET: SCENARIO 1, 1976–1980 ($)

|  | 1976 | 1977 | 1978 | 1979 | 1980 |
|---|---|---|---|---|---|
| Assets |  |  |  |  |  |
| Cash | 5,273.7 | 6,077.1 | 6,918.5 | 7,792.3 | 8,699.9 |
| Accounts receivable | 1,931.8 | 1,970.5 | 2,001.4 | 2,028.1 | 2,056.3 |
| Inventory | 3,863.6 | 3,941.0 | 4,002.8 | 4,056.1 | 4,112.5 |
| Current assets | 11,069.1 | 11,988.6 | 12,922.7 | 13,876.5 | 14,868.7 |
| Net plant and equipment | 13,903.4 | 13,208.3 | 12,547.8 | 11,920.5 | 11,324.5 |
| Other assets | 504.9 | 544.9 | 584.9 | 624.9 | 664.9 |
| Total assets | 25,477.4 | 25,741.8 | 26,055.5 | 26,421.9 | 26,858.1 |
| Liabilities |  |  |  |  |  |
| Accounts payable | 695.4 | 709.4 | 720.5 | 730.1 | 740.3 |
| Short-term debt | 4,316.1 | 4,316.1 | 4,316.1 | 4,316.1 | 4,316.1 |
| Reserve for federal taxes | 658.2 | 721.2 | 772.6 | 817.6 | 864.9 |
| Miscellaneous accruals | 199.6 | 249.5 | 311.9 | 389.9 | 487.4 |
| Debt repayment | 100.0 | 100.0 | 100.0 | 100.0 | 100.0 |
| Current liabilities | 5,969.3 | 6,096.2 | 6,221.1 | 6,353.7 | 6,508.7 |
| Long-term debt | 9,611.3 | 9,511.3 | 9,411.3 | 9,311.3 | 9,211.3 |
| Common stock | 4,500.0 | 4,500.0 | 4,500.0 | 4,500.0 | 4,500.0 |
| Earned surplus | 5,396.8 | 5,634.3 | 5,923.1 | 6,256.9 | 6,638.1 |
| Total liabilities | 25,477.4 | 25,741.8 | 26,055.5 | 26,421.9 | 26,858.1 |

**TABLE 12-19**
TVL REVISED MARKETING POLICY ASSUMPTIONS:
SCENARIO 2

| Year | Color TV price, $ | B&W TV price, $ | Advertising expenses, $1,000 |
|------|-------------------|-----------------|------------------------------|
| 1976 | 285 | 164 | 3,200 |
| 1977 | 285 | 164 | 3,350 |
| 1978 | 285 | 164 | 3,550 |
| 1979 | 285 | 164 | 3,700 |
| 1980 | 285 | 164 | 4,000 |

five-year period beginning in 1976. Advertising expenditures will rise according to the schedule in Table 12-19. Otherwise, there are no changes in the original financial, marketing, and production assumptions which were spelled out in Tables 12-5 through 12-10. For scenario 2, we display only the income statement projections in Table 12-20.

**Other Scenarios**   There are countless other scenarios which could be run with the TVL model, ranging from experiments with alternative forms of external financing to different assumptions about interest rates and the national economy. Scenarios could also be generated for alternative cash management policies, depreciation policies, and federal tax policies. For each scenario, we can produce any combination of the output reports which were produced by scenario 1 or easily specify only certain variables to be printed after the model has been solved.

**TABLE 12-20**
TVL PROJECTED INCOME STATEMENT FORECAST: SCENARIO 2, 1976–1980 ($)

|  | 1976 | 1977 | 1978 | 1979 | 1980 |
|---|------|------|------|------|------|
| Sales revenue | 20,481.9 | 21,835.5 | 23,567.6 | 24,870.2 | 27,476.6 |
| Expenses |  |  |  |  |  |
|   Cost of goods sold | 12,289.0 | 13,101.3 | 14,140.6 | 14,922.1 | 16,486.0 |
|   Advertising expenses | 3,200.0 | 3,550.0 | 3,550.0 | 3,700.0 | 4,000.0 |
|   Operating expenses | 2,048.2 | 2,183.5 | 2,356.8 | 2,487.0 | 2,747.7 |
|   Interest | 1,479.1 | 1,469.1 | 1,459.0 | 1,449.1 | 1,439.0 |
| Total expenses | 19,016.3 | 20,103.9 | 21,506.4 | 22,558.2 | 24,672.7 |
| Profit before taxes | 1,465.4 | 1,731.6 | 2,061.2 | 2,312.0 | 2,803.9 |
| Federal income taxes | 732.7 | 865.8 | 1,030.6 | 1,156.0 | 1,401.9 |
| Net profit | 732.7 | 865.8 | 1,030.6 | 1,156.0 | 1,402.0 |
| Dividends | 483.7 | 483.7 | 483.7 | 483.7 | 483.7 |
| Retained earnings | 249.0 | 382.1 | 546.9 | 672.3 | 918.2 |

### Limitations of the TVL Model

Clearly, the economic underpinnings of the TVL model leave a great deal to be desired. Although it is typical of most of the corporate simulation models being used today, its demand, production, and cost relationships could at best be described as somewhat primitive. Below we shall outline some ways in which the economic content of the model could be improved subject to the availability of relevant historical data.

**Demand** First, the two-equation demand model could be extended to include more products. Second, it may be possible to find other managerial decision variables such as research and development expenditures or special promotional campaigns which are statistically significant in some equations. Third, for some products it may be necessary to consider the pricing and advertising policies of TVL's principal competitors. Fourth, other national economic indicators may be important in some of the demand equations. Fifth, the final model should be reestimated, using two-stage least squares.

**Production Cost** For all practical purposes, the TVL model does not really have a production function embedded in it. It is essentially a sales-driven model in which the cost of goods sold is a constant multiple of sales. Numerous options are available, including some of the models proposed in Chapters 4 and 5, to link production output to the factor inputs required to sustain a given level of business. Given a demand forecast for a particular product, we should be able to say how much labor, capital, and raw materials will be required to produce sufficient output to satisfy demand. This implies the need for a detailed description of the input-output relationships for each product $j$ and the need to know how much of input $i$ is required to produce a unit of $j$. We need to have this information for all inputs and outputs. If we have the prices of the factor inputs, we can then compute operating costs and costs of goods sold. Obviously, some allowance must be made for raw materials, work-in-process, and finished goods inventories to make the model more realistic.

**Financial** There are several directions we could go with the financial model. First, it could be converted into a much more detailed and sophisticated cash management model. Second, the tax component could be expanded considerably. Third, inflation and changes in foreign currency exchange rates could also be introduced. Fourth, the model could be modified for short-term profit planning rather than five-year strategic planning. Fifth, several of the assumed-value models including accounts receivable and accounts payable could be replaced by econometric relationships. Sixth, the debt structure of most large companies is more complex than that of TVL. A more realistic model would take this factor into consideration.

**Corporate** Since TVL is a subsidiary of Zeta Electronics in Switzerland, the management of Zeta might want to have similar models constructed for each of its subsidiaries. These separate business planning models could then be consolidated into an integrated corporate planning model for Zeta Electronics. In other words, each business would develop its own planning model and use it to develop its own five-year plan. However, the vice president of corporate planning for Zeta Electronics could maintain a duplicate data base and model for each business and perform his or her own "what if?" experiments with the separate business models or with the consolidated corporate model.

## THE STANDARD INTERNATIONAL CASE

Roger Smith, vice president of finance of Standard International, wants to determine the financial requirements of the company over the four-year period 1976–1979. Among the problems with which he is concerned is whether additional debt or equity financing will be required over that period.

The president of Standard has also asked him to produce pro forma financial statements and financial ratios for the next four years, as he is considering several possible acquisitions and wants some reliable financial projections to determine whether Standard will be in a position to pursue such matters. Historical income statement data, balance sheet data, and financial ratios are contained in Tables 12-21 through 12-24, respectively, for the period 1969–1975. (Income statement and balance sheet figures are expressed in thousands of dollars.)

Mr. Smith proposes to develop a financial planning model in response to the president's queries. In order to construct such a model, it is necessary to make a number of assumptions. Mr. Smith assumes that the sales trend manifested by 1969–1975 data will continue through 1979. He further assumes that the cost of goods sold will be about 82 percent of sales. The federal income tax rate is expected to remain constant at 50 percent. In 1975 dividends were increased to $1.30 per share. There are 500,000 shares of common stock outstanding. The directors have indicated that since sales have increased by more than 5 percent for two consecutive years, dividends will continue at $1.30 per share.

Accounts receivable are expected to run about 10 percent of sales, and Standard will continue its policy of maintaining inventories at 20 percent of sales.

Since Standard just completed a major plant-expansion program, plant and equipment will remain constant during the next four years. Depreciation ($630,000) is computed on a straight-line basis with a life of 20 years and no salvage value at the end. Other assets are assumed to increase at the rate of $40,000 per year net.

Accounts payable are assumed to be 6 percent of cost of goods sold, and miscellaneous accruals will increase 25 percent per year. Mortgage payments will remain constant at $300,000 per year. No additional equity financing has been planned at this time. Earned surplus increased each year by the increment in retained earnings.

Cash will be treated as a residual in the model. That is, cash is the variable which balances the balance sheet. A positive cash balance implies a cash

**TABLE 12-21**

HISTORICAL INCOME STATEMENT FOR STANDARD INTERNATIONAL, $1,000

| | 1969 | 1970 | 1971 | 1972 | 1973 | 1974 | 1975 |
|---|---|---|---|---|---|---|---|
| Sales | 11,546 | 12,791 | 14,492 | 16,420 | 18,603 | 21,078 | 23,881 |
| Cost of goods sold | 9,875 | 10,870 | 11,884 | 13,464 | 15,255 | 17,284 | 19,582 |
| Gross profit | 1,671 | 1,921 | 2,609 | 2,956 | 3,349 | 3,794 | 4,299 |
| Operating expenses | 727 | 755 | 580 | 657 | 744 | 843 | 955 |
| Profit before taxes | 944 | 1,166 | 2,029 | 2,299 | 2,604 | 2,951 | 3,343 |
| Federal income taxes | 472 | 583 | 1,014 | 1,149 | 1,302 | 1,475 | 1,672 |
| Net profit | 472 | 583 | 1,014 | 1,149 | 1,302 | 1,475 | 1,672 |
| Dividends | 350 | 350 | 350 | 350 | 350 | 350 | 650 |
| Retained earnings | 122 | 233 | 664 | 799 | 952 | 1,125 | 1,022 |

**TABLE 12-22**
HISTORICAL BALANCE SHEET FOR STANDARD INTERNATIONAL, $1,000

| Assets | 1969 | 1970 | 1971 | 1972 | 1973 | 1974 | 1975 |
|---|---|---|---|---|---|---|---|
| Cash | 5,517 | 5,730 | 6,314 | 7,041 | 7,886 | 6,962 | 5,942 |
| Accounts receivable | 1,170 | 1,292 | 1,449 | 1,642 | 1,860 | 2,108 | 2,388 |
| Inventory | 1,972 | 2,280 | 2,898 | 3,284 | 3,721 | 4,216 | 4,776 |
| Current assets | 8,659 | 9,302 | 10,661 | 11,967 | 13,467 | 13,286 | 13,106 |
| Net plant and equipment | 5,320 | 4,940 | 4,560 | 4,180 | 3,800 | 5,320 | 7,690 |
| Other assets | 302 | 355 | 395 | 435 | 475 | 515 | 555 |
| Total assets | 14,281 | 14,597 | 15,616 | 16,582 | 17,742 | 19,121 | 21,351 |

| Liabilities | 1969 | 1970 | 1971 | 1972 | 1973 | 1974 | 1975 |
|---|---|---|---|---|---|---|---|
| Accounts payable | 690 | 720 | 713 | 808 | 915 | 1,037 | 1,175 |
| Reserve for federal taxes | 472 | 583 | 1,014 | 1,149 | 1,302 | 1,475 | 1,672 |
| Miscellaneous accruals | 79 | 121 | 151 | 189 | 236 | 295 | 369 |
| Current mortgage payment | 100 | 100 | 100 | 100 | 100 | 200 | 300 |
| Current liabilities | 1,341 | 1,524 | 1,979 | 2,246 | 2,554 | 3,008 | 3,516 |
| Mortage payable | 3,750 | 3,650 | 3,550 | 3,450 | 3,350 | 4,150 | 4,850 |
| Common stock | 6,000 | 6,000 | 6,000 | 6,000 | 6,000 | 6,000 | 6,000 |
| Earned surplus | 3,190 | 3,423 | 4,087 | 4,886 | 5,838 | 5,963 | 6,985 |
| Total liabilities | 14,281 | 14,597 | 15,616 | 16,582 | 17,742 | 19,121 | 21,351 |

**TABLE 12-23**
HISTORICAL FINANCIAL RATIOS FOR STANDARD INTERNATIONAL

|  | 1969 | 1970 | 1971 | 1972 | 1973 | 1974 | 1975 |
|---|---|---|---|---|---|---|---|
| Earnings per share | .94 | 1.17 | 2.03 | 2.30 | 2.60 | 2.95 | 3.34 |
| Current ratio | 6.46 | 6.10 | 5.39 | 5.33 | 5.27 | 4.42 | 3.73 |
| Net profit-to-sales ratio | 0.04 | 0.05 | 0.07 | 0.07 | 0.07 | 0.07 | 0.07 |

surplus; a negative cash balance implies a cash deficit. A major feature of the model is its ability to project cash. The assumptions underlying the proposed financial model are summarized in Table 12-24.

The reader is encouraged to build a financial planning model based on the assumptions underlying this case. Suppose the company is considering a $7,500,000 acquisition in 1977. Will the company need to obtain additional cash to finance such a project?

## QUESTIONS AND PROBLEMS

**12-1** Discuss some of the limitations of the concept of the strategic business unit.
**12-2** List some of the assumptions underlying the growth-share matrix and the experience curve.
**12-3** How would one go about applying the BCG and PIMS methodologies to businesses that are interdependent?
**12-4** Based on your knowledge of econometrics and economic theory, suggest some ways to improve the PIMS methodology.

**TABLE 12-24**
STANDARD INTERNATIONAL ASSUMPTIONS

Historical data: 1969–1975
Planning period: 1976–1979
Historical sales trend continues
Cost of goods sold: 82% of sales
Operating expenses: 4% of sales
Federal income tax rate: 50%
Dividends: $1.30 per share of common
Accounts receivable: 10% of sales
Inventories: 20% of sales
No additions to plant and equipment
Depreciation: $630,000 per year
Other assets: $40,000 net increase per year
Accounts payable: 6% of cost of goods sold
Miscellaneous accruals: 25% increase per year
Mortgage payments: $300,000 per year
Cash is residual

**12-5** Why do you think the Hamilton and Moses model and the BCG optimization model have not been used very much as strategic planning tools? Be specific.

**12-6** Discuss the limitations of the capital-asset pricing model as a strategic planning tool.

**12-7** Discuss some of the differences that may emerge if corporate simulation models are developed by corporate economists rather than accountants and financial analysts.

**12-8** Discuss the applicability of demand theory to the formulation of integrated corporate simulation models.

**12-9** To what extent can the theories of production and cost described in Chapters 4 and 5, respectively, be integrated into corporate simulation models?

**12-10** Outline several ways in which linear programming might be interfaced with corporate simulation models, particularly with regard to the production component of business simulation models.

**12-11** Discuss the possible linkage of corporate simulation models with analytical portfolio models such as those of the Boston Consulting Group and PIMS.

**12-12** Indicate how corporate simulation models can be used as a capital budgeting tool.

**12-13** Discuss some of the practical problems involved in incorporating formal risk analysis into corporate simulation models.

## BIBLIOGRAPHY

Abel, Derek F., and John S. Hammond: *Strategic Market Planning* (Englewood Cliffs, N.J.: Prentice-Hall, 1979).

Boston Consulting Group: "A Strategy-Based Resource Allocation Model." Unpublished, undated report. (Boston, Mass.: The Boston Consulting Group).

Cohen, Kalman J.: "Dynamic Balance Sheet Management: A Management Science Approach," *Journal of Bank Research,* Winter 1972, 9–19.

Cohen, Kalman J., and Frederick S. Hammer: "Linear Programming and Optimal Bank Asset Management Decisions," *Journal of Finance,* May 1967, 22, 2, 147–165.

Cox, William E.: "Product Portfolio Strategy, Market Structure and Performance," in Hans B. Thorelli (ed.), *Strategy Plus Structure Equals Performance* (Bloomington, Ind.: University of Indiana Press, 1977).

Fama, Eugene F.: *Foundations of Finance* (New York: Basic Books, 1976).

Fama, Eugene F., and Merton H. Miller: *The Theory of Finance* (New York: Holt, Rinehart & Winston, 1972).

Gale, Bradley T.: "Planning for Profit," *Planning Review,* January 1978.

Hamilton, William F., and Michael A. Moses: "An Optimization Model for Corporate Financial Planning," *Operations Research,* May–June 1973, 21, 677–692.

Henderson, Bruce D.: *Henderson on Corporate Strategy* (Cambridge, Mass.: Abt, 1979).

Lintner, John: "The Valuation of Risk Assets and the Selection of Risky Investments in Stock Portfolios and Capital Budgets," *Review of Economics and Statistics,* February 1965, 47, 13–37.

Lorange, Peter, and Richard F. Vancil: *Strategic Planning Systems* (Englewood Cliffs, N.J.: Prentice-Hall, 1977).

Markowitz, H.: *Portfolio Selection.* Cowles Foundation Monograph No. 16 (New York: John Wiley, 1959).

Mayo, R. Britton: *Corporate Planning and Modeling with SIMPLAN* (Reading, Mass.: Addison-Wesley, 1979).

Naylor, Thomas H.: *The Politics of Corporate Planning and Modeling* (Oxford, Ohio: Planning Executives Institute, 1978).

Naylor, Thomas H.: *Corporate Planning Models* (Reading, Mass.: Addison-Wesley, 1979).

Naylor, Thomas H. (ed.): *Simulation Models in Corporate Planning* (New York: Praeger, 1979).

Naylor, Thomas H.: *Strategic Planning Management* (Oxford, Ohio: Planning Executives Institute, 1980).

Naylor, Thomas H. (ed.): *Corporate Strategy: The Integration of Corporate Planning Models and Economics.* (Amsterdam: North Holland, 1982).

Naylor, Thomas H., and Francis Tapon: "The Capital Asset Pricing Model: An Evaluation of its Potential as a Strategic Planning Tool." Corporate Economics Program Working Paper Number 6. Duke University, April 1, 1981.

Ross, Stephen A.: "The Current Status of the Capital Asset Pricing Model," *Journal of Finance,* June 1978, 33, 885–901.

Schoeffler, Sidney: "Cross-Sectional Study of Strategy, Structure, and Performance: Aspects of the PIMS Program," in Hans B. Thorelli (ed.), *Strategy Plus Structure Equals Performance* (Bloomington, Ind.: University of Indiana Press, 1977).

Sharpe, William F.: "Capital Asset Prices: A Theory of Market Equilibrium under Conditions of Risk," *Journal of Finance,* September 1964, 19, 425–442.

Sharpe, William F.: *Investments* (Englewood Cliffs, N.J.: Prentice-Hall, 1978).

Tobin, James: "Liquidity Preference as Behavior towards Risk," *Review of Economic Studies,* February 1958, 25, 65–86.

Van Horne, James C.: *Financial Management and Policy* (Englewood Cliffs, N.J.: Prentice-Hall, 1980).

Weingartner, H. Martin: *Mathematical Programming and the Analysis of Capital Budgeting Problems* (Englewood Cliffs, N.J.: Prentice-Hall, 1963).

# CHAPTER 13

# THE POLITICS OF CORPORATE ECONOMICS

**CHAPTER OUTLINE**

Failure to Produce Useful Results
Inaccurate Forecasts
Failure to Meet Deadlines
Inadequate Political Support from Top Management
POLITICAL ADVICE TO CORPORATE ECONOMISTS
QUESTIONS AND PROBLEMS


Although the interest in corporate economics among large corporations has
increased exponentially during the past 10 years, corporate economists often
find themselves in the middle of serious internal political controversies with
other corporate executives. Indeed, their effectiveness is often impaired by a
hostile political environment within the company.

There appear to be a number of specific reasons why corporate economists
encounter difficulty in doing their jobs within the corporate environment. First,
their academic training fails to prepare them for the political realities of life in a
large, complex corporation. Second, the fact that the role of forecasting and
econometric modeling is often misunderstood by senior management may put
corporate economists in a completely untenable position. Third, the place
where they are situated within the organization structure of the company may
not be viable and may give rise to considerable conflict with managers of other
departments. Fourth, very few senior executives know how to use corporate
economists properly. Fifth, corporate executives may not know how to ask
corporate economists the "right" questions. We shall examine these problems
and propose alternative solutions to each of them.


### THE TRAINING OF CORPORATE ECONOMISTS

Corporate economists who hold graduate degrees in economics typically have
been exposed to a heavy dose of economic theory, econometrics, statistics, and
mathematics. Although these tools are necessary to support the type of analysis done by corporate economists, they do little or nothing to help corporate
economists communicate with pragmatic corporate executives who often have
a complete disdain for anything that smacks of economic theory. Many corporate economists have great difficulty translating theories learned at the university into practical results. They often encounter even more severe problems
attempting to communicate these ideas to skeptical managers.

There is increasing evidence that the really serious obstacles to the effective
use of corporate economics have little to do with the limitations of existing corporate economic tools such as forecasting techniques, econometric models, and
computer-based planning models. The real problems seem to lie in the interface
between these tools and the people who are needed to make them work.

With the advent of econometric models, the political problems surrounding
corporate economics have become even more complex. The heart of the
problem is that corporate economists who attempted to develop these models

in the past frequently did not possess the necessary political and human relations skills required to make senior management feel comfortable with such sophisticated tools. In the early 1970s econometric modeling was oversold to senior management. Promises were made for which economists could not deliver results. Due dates and schedules were not met. Managerial expectations inflated by overzealous outside consultants were not fulfilled. Frustration, anger, and complete disillusionment on the part of management followed in the wake of these events. It was, therefore, not surprising to find many senior executives backing off from corporate economics in the mid-1970s or at least viewing corporate economists with a jaundiced eye.

As we indicated before, it is not really surprising to find that corporate economists are not effective politicians, for there is little or nothing in their formal academic training to prepare them to cope with the many practical, political problems one typically encounters in implementing economic models in the real world. Most university courses in economics these days provide minimal guidance in dealing with the politics of corporate economics. All too often academic economics courses are little more than courses in applied mathematics. Too little attention is given to the human side of corporate economics. Yet countless corporate economists have learned the hard way that sophisticated mathematics and econometric modeling techniques are neither necessary nor sufficient to provide top management with an effective decision-making tool. The politics of corporate economics may be the single most important factor in determining the success or failure of a particular corporate economics project.

On the other hand, some corporate executives view the work of corporate economists with a type of naive optimism. Having transcended the period of skepticism and distrust of economists and econometric models, some senior executives perceive economic models as a panacea. This type of corporate officer is potentially quite dangerous. If the corporate economist is not aware of unrealistic expectations on the part of such executives, he or she may be incurring a substantial risk. The day of reckoning arrives when the econometric model does not produce the results expected by the naive user—results which were totally beyond the reach of the model in the first place.

Users and providers of corporate economic services may have quite diverse goals, and sometimes these goals may even be in conflict with each other. Both senior executives and corporate economists would be well advised to be on the lookout for hidden agenda which may be more important than stated agenda. To protect themselves, corporate managers should make certain that they understand their own goals as well as the stated and implied goals of the corporate economists. On the other hand, the corporate economist must necessarily try to ascertain all of the manager's goals, whether they be openly stated or otherwise.

One reason why corporate economists sometimes have difficulty in the corporate environment is that they have frequently received their training in traditional academic economics departments. Although turnpike theorems, three-stage least squares, and full-information maximum-likelihood methods have their place, knowledge of these topics will probably do little to determine whether an economist is successful in a large corporation.

Corporate economists trained in academic economics departments need to supplement the usual courses in theory, econometrics, and statistics with courses in accounting, finance, strategic planning, and organization behavior. More importantly, Ph.D. dissertations and M.A. theses should be based on applications of economics to real-world problems rather than irrelevant, obscure, academic topics. Finally economists who plan to work in industry should seek out summer employment in corporations to gain exposure to the dynamic world of corporate economics.

## MISUNDERSTANDINGS OF ECONOMIC FORECASTING

The role of economic forecasting is perhaps one of the least understood activities of corporate economists. The failure of senior management to understand the limitations of economic forecasting has led to the demise of many an economist when actual operating results did not conform to the forecast.

Corporate economic forecasts are based on assumptions about the company's external environment. The forecasts are no more accurate than the least accurate assumption on which they rest. Incorrect assumptions may lead to substantial forecasting errors. Forecasts generated by econometric models are "what if?" forecasts based on external assumptions and policy assumptions provided by the corporate economist. Above all, the name of the forecasting game is "what if?"

### Unrealistic Expectations

The president of a very successful conglomerate in the midwest initiated a corporate econometric modeling project several years ago. As outside consultants on the project, our role was to help formulate the project plan for the modeling project. Initially the president said that he wanted to be able to sit in his Chicago office and on a monthly basis, four years into the future, produce forecasts that would be more accurate than those currently produced by the 10 operating companies. Our role was to let him know that what he had in mind was simply impossible. It was beyond the state of the art to produce such forecasts at corporate headquarters without the direct participation of the operating companies. Furthermore, he had to be persuaded that any forecasting model which might be developed should not be relied on to produce *the* forecast but rather should be used to generate alternative forecasts based on different assumptions about the external environment.

One of the more ambitious econometric marketing modeling projects to date is a model developed by a Texas manufacturing company. During the early stages of development of the model, after the objectives had been aired thoroughly, the director of corporate planning raised an amazing question about the model. He wanted to know whether the model could forecast the market-share of each of the company's competitors in each of 30 different markets. To give you some indication of the magnitude of his question, the company sells nearly 1,000 products in each market, each of which has anywhere from 5 to 50 competitors. The planning director was quickly informed that even if the company used the services of the Central Intelligence Agency to collect data on each of its competitors, there was no way that the econometric model could forecast the market-share of each of the company's competitors. He was further informed that forecasting the company's market-share by product was in itself a monumental task and that the corporate economics staff would consider itself fortunate if it could achieve this goal.

This anecdote illustrates an important point. Not only is it desirable to communicate to management the expected benefits to be derived from using an econometric model, it is equally important to inform management of the limitations of the model. In other words, for the mutual protection of both corporate economists and corporate executives, we recommend the preparation of two lists at the outset of the project: (1) a list of what the model can be expected to achieve and (2) a list of things the model cannot possibly do. Following the aforementioned episode, the director of planning was provided with the two lists outlined below:

### The model can

**1** Take variables over which management has direct control (price, sales force, etc.) and project variables over which management has no control (sales, market-share, etc.)
**2** Test the effects of different market strategies without having to experience them
**3** Provide a systematic approach for forecasting in which the influence of each management strategy can be isolated for review and action
**4** Project industry sales and price and company sales by major product group
**5** Improve the accuracy of all forecasts
**6** Explain "why" for the forecasts

### The model cannot

**1** Evaluate individual competitive reactions on market-share
**2** Forecast specific market volume
**3** Forecast sales by region
**4** Predict events which occur discountinuously, such as wars, strikes, etc.

It is important for management to understand that although it is impossible to predict or model such phenomena as wars, strikes, floods, earthquakes, and political upheavals, it may indeed be possible to model the effects of such events on the behavior of the company. Although we cannot predict whether there will be another Watergate affair or when a particular OPEC country will cut off the supply of crude oil, we can simulate the likely consequences of such events for the financial performance of the company.

### One-Scenario Forecasting

In 1973, a large regional bank in the United States (the largest in its region) based its 1974 financial forecast on only one assumption, that the prime rate of interest would go down in 1974. Unfortunately, the prime rate of interest did not go down in 1974. Instead, it reached 12 percent. As a result of one-scenario forecasting, the bank became the second largest bank in its region. Many firms engage in one-scenario forecasting because the cost of manually evaluating alternative scenarios is so high in terms of personnel time that management is frequently presented with only one forecast or one scenario. A simple financial forecasting model would have made it possible for the bank's management to compute the cost of being wrong in its assumption about the prime rate of interest. In other words, suppose we bet that the prime would drop to 7 percent in 1974 and it actually went to 10 percent or possibly even 12 percent. What risks would we take by assuming the prime will go down if, in fact, it goes up? Forecasting the prime is a difficult business, and econometric model builders are not noted for their success in attempting to predict it. Would the bank's management have made a different decision if it had known the downside risk associated with its one-scenario forecast?

Economic planning models enable management to examine alternative futures and look at multiple scenarios. Indeed, it can be argued that economic planning models make planning possible. Without the ability to look at alternative futures, planning is impossible.

### Planning versus Forecasting

It is not uncommon among many corporate executives to confuse long-term planning and forecasting. They will argue that long-term forecasting is impossible because of the difficulty of predicting wars, political events, and the behavior of competitors. This, of course, precisely misses the point of planning. It is only when there is uncertainty in the external environment that planning becomes important. The fact that we cannot forecast the future with any degree of precision provides the rationale underlying the "what if?" approach to strategic planning.

### Participatory Forecasting

Just as senior executive participation is a necessary prerequisite for successful strategic planning, it is also a requirement for effective economic forecasting. First, the analyst must fully understand the forecasting objective. Why is the forecast important? What types of decisions will be based on the forecast?

What are the costs associated with an inaccurate forecast? Second, the analyst should not be willing to take the entire risk of erroneous assumptions. That is, the users of the forecast should participate in the formulation of the external assumptions on which the forecast is based. An analyst who loses his or her job because the assumptions on which a forecast was based proved to be incorrect deserves that fate if the assumptions were made entirely by the analyst. Forecasting must be a joint venture between the analyst and the user of the forecast, with the user participating in the formulation of the external assumptions.

### Multiple Forecasts

Some companies such as electric utilities produce different forecasts for different purposes. One electric utility got itself in difficulty by producing one forecast for the stockholders, one for internal management, one for the state regulatory agency, and one for the Federal Power Commission. On several occasions the company managed to mix its forecasts and present the wrong forecast to a particular group.

The idea of multiple forecasts to suit alternative forecasting needs has merit. However, one should manage to keep the forecasts separate and be explicit about the differences in objectives among the forecasts.

## ECONOMETRIC MODELING

### Folklore versus Fact

The forecasting track record of national econometric models in the United States since 1974 has not been particularly impressive. In an article in the *Journal of Business* (1978, Vol. 51, No. 4) entitled "Forecasting with Econometric Methods," J. Scott Armstrong argues that "evidence from social psychology suggests that econometricians will avoid evidence that disconfirms their beliefs." Two specific beliefs of econometricians were examined by Armstrong.

The first belief is that econometric methods provide more accurate short-term forecasts than other methods. Of the experts surveyed by Armstrong, 95 percent argued that econometric methods are superior for short-range forecasting. However, an examination of the literature by Armstrong did not support this belief. "Econometric forecasts were not shown to be significantly better in any of the 14 *ex post* and 16 *ex ante* tests. There was no tendency towards greater accuracy over these tests."

The second belief is that more complex econometric methods yield more accurate forecasts. Armstrong found that 72 percent of the experts in his sample felt that complexity contributed to accuracy. According to Armstrong, the literature does not support this belief, either. "Complex models were not significantly better in any of the 5 indirect tests and 11 direct tests."

### Econometric Service Bureaus

As previously mentioned, the 1970s witnessed the advent of a number of econometric service bureaus offering econometric models and data bases. In a number of cases, overly ambitious salespeople from these bureaus have seriously oversold the merits and forecasting accuracy of econometric models. In addition, some of these services are available only on very expensive computer timesharing networks, thus adding significantly to their cost. A principal role of corporate economists is to help management utilize econometric service bureaus more efficiently.

### Undersell Forecasting

Given the practical realities of forecasting with econometric models, we feel that it makes a great deal of sense for the corporate economist to play the role of devil's advocate with regard to the forecasting accuracy of econometric models. It is better to undersell econometrics than to risk overselling and not be able to deliver the results which have been promised. A number of corporate economists have found that providing management with a complete list of caveats regarding econometrics will greatly enhance their credibility in the eyes of senior management.

## SPECIFIC POLITICAL CONFLICTS

A number of potential conflicts may emerge between corporate economists and the following departments: corporate planning, management science, line managers, and data processing. If the CEO is not paying attention to what is going on, such conflicts may persist. It is impossible to utilize corporate economic information effectively if political conflicts of this type are tolerated by the CEO.

### Corporate Planning

Corporate economists have come to realize that the corporate planning department represents a reasonable place within the corporate organization structure for economists to function effectively. Indeed, a number of corporate economists now find themselves heading up corporate planning departments. In other companies the corporate economist and the head of corporate planning engage in open warfare, thus seriously reducing each other's effectiveness.

Although economists are capable of producing studies and analyses with immediate, short-term implications, their comparative advantage seems to lie in long-term strategic planning. For this reason, we strongly endorse the current trend among corporations to place corporate economics in the corporate planning department. An obvious side benefit of such an organizational strategy is that it will tend to minimize the chances of conflict between the director of planning and the corporate economist.

## Management Science

Although management science continues to gain in stature as an important concept in corporations, its role as a stand-alone department seems to be on the decline. That is, management has come to realize that management science tools are most effective when they are integrated throughout the company rather than residing in a highly specialized group known as the management science department.

If a company has a separate management science department and a separate corporate economics staff, the potential for conflict is enormous. The reason is fairly obvious. The differences in methodology employed by corporate economists and management scientists are negligible. The tools are the same. The only difference is in the applications of the analytical tools.

There are numerous departments within the company which should have strong management science skills: corporate planning, finance, production, etc. We believe this is the appropriate way to utilize management science. On the other hand, we do not see the need to have a corporate economist in every operating department. Many departments will need information provided by corporate economics, but they will not need their own corporate economists. Under this arrangement, management scientists interspersed throughout the various staff and operating departments may become the principal users of the services of corporate economics.

## Line Managers

In some companies economists have been seriously misunderstood by pragmatic line managers who have little or no patience with what they perceive to be academic theories produced by economists. Line managers are also likely to resent any signals whatsoever that the corporate economist is trying to tell them how to do their job.

To minimize conflict between the corporate economics group and line managers, corporate economists should restrict their relationship with line managers to only two activities. First, as part of the strategic plan of the company, corporate economists should provide line managers with an overall assessment of the economic environment they are likely to face over the planning horizon. Second, corporate economists should be available to provide consulting services to line managers in the form of forecasts, econometric modeling, and economic analyses. These services should be initiated by line managers. To be sure, there is nothing wrong with the corporate economics group embarking on an educational program to make line managers more aware of the benefits to be derived from the use of their services.

## Data Processing

Failure to achieve good communications with the in-house, corporate data processing group has often meant that economists have had to rely entirely on expensive outside service bureaus for economic data bases, software, and econometric forecasts. This is indeed unfortunate, for many companies could reduce the cost of these services significantly by utilizing the in-house computer rather than doing it all through an outside service bureau.

## HOW TO ASK THE RIGHT QUESTIONS OF THE CORPORATE ECONOMIST

Although many corporate economists have been guilty of a failure to communicate effectively with top management by being too theoretical or using economic jargon rather than plain English, senior executives bear at least part of the responsibility for the poor communication. The problem of senior executives is not that they do not understand the technical details of Keynesian economic theory or heteroscedasticity but rather that they do not know how to ask economists the right questions. Unfortunately, all too many senior executives appear to be intimidated by economists. They approve expensive econometric modeling projects proposed by outside econometric service bureaus without any knowledge of the expected benefits or lack of benefits from the project.

The following questions need to be asked more often by top management to keep corporate economists honest. What is this model or study going to do for me? How much will it cost? When can I expect to see some results from the study? What can be said about the validity and credibility of the results? How can the company put the information gained from the study to effective use? If top management keeps hammering away at issues of this type, it then becomes possible to have a real dialogue between top management and corporate economists.

## WHY SOME CORPORATE ECONOMISTS HAVE FAILED

### Ill-Defined Problem

Perhaps the single most important aspect of corporate economics is problem definition. Once the management problem has been defined clearly, much of the analysis which follows represents a series of technical details. But formalizing problem definition for corporate management can be an elusive process. It is the aspect of corporate economics which most resembles an art rather than a science. Many a corporate economics project has gone astray because of vagueness in setting goals and objectives. If six months to a year after the project is under way, the corporate economists discover that they have misunderstood management's goals and objectives, the entire project may be in deep trouble. Valuable corporate resources may have been spent trying to solve the wrong problem. The following example may serve to illustrate the issue of problem definition.

In 1972, a large manufacturer of computer hardware decided to embark on a project involving the use of corporate economic modeling to determine the effect of fourth-generation computer hardware/software on corporate revenue even though fourth-generation computers had not been designed yet. In other words, the company wanted to use the model to facilitate the design of its fourth-generation computer line, admittedly not an easy task.

Led by an economist, the eight-person modeling team consisted of six insiders and two consultants. The fundamental hypothesis underlying the project was that one should attempt to model the behavior of vice presidents of finance of large companies, since they are the individuals who typically make the final decisions on major computer hardware/software acquisitions. This was a reasonable assumption on which to begin work on the model. Unfortunately, that was the point where good judgment ceased.

The team leader had the preconceived notion that computer acquisition decisions are based entirely on rational considerations. He further assumed that vice presidents of finance have perfect information on the marginal costs and marginal benefits of alternative computer hardware and software. Finally, he proposed that a very sophisticated modeling technique known as Pontryagin's maximum principle be used to model the behavior of vice presidents of finance. Although Pontryagin's maximum principle played a useful role in the Soviet and American space programs, to the best of our knowledge it has never been used to model the behavior of vice presidents of finance. The use of the maximum principle required information that simply was not available in this case. Furthermore, the assumptions underlying the maximum principle bore no resemblance to the situation being modeled.

The consultants on the project kept insisting that some actual computer users be interviewed to gain empirical data on why people acquire computers. This suggestion was consistently rejected by the team leader.

The situation was a classic example of a corporate economist knowing too much mathematics for his or her own good. Furthermore, the corporate economist carefully shielded the modeling team from contact with anyone in management, particularly those individuals who were supposed to have perceived the problem in the first place. This alone is sufficient to guarantee disaster.

Nearly eight worker-years of effort went into the project over a period of 12 months. No data were collected, no model was ever specified, no equations were estimated, and no simulation was run. The net output of the project consisted of a 45-minute flipchart presentation. No conclusions or policy recommendations were generated by the project. That so little tangible output could be produced from such a substantial effort is truly amazing. But when you consider that the definition of the project goals changed at least six times in less than six months, the results are not really surprising.

## Unfulfilled Expectations

Related to the pitfalls of ill-defined problems is the issue of unrealistic expectations on the part of management. As previously mentioned, some corporate executives have adopted the very risky posture of viewing corporate economics as a panacea. Although it is desirable to have management's confidence in corporate economics, their overconfidence can be a dangerous thing. There comes a day of reckoning when management expects to see results. If their expectations are unrealistic but the corporate economists are unaware of the extent of the problem, there is a good chance that the expectations will not be satisfied. Unfulfilled managerial expectations can lead to serious consequences and the demise of corporate economics departments.

### Excessive Use of Technical Jargon

The burden of responsibility for communications rests in the hands of corporate economists, not in the hands of management. It is not incumbent on management to familiarize themselves with the technical jargon of economic theory and econometrics. Corporate economists must not only understand management's problems, they must learn to speak the language of management as well. The politics of corporate economics involves continuous selling and reselling of concepts which may seem alien and unrealistic to management. One of the quickest ways to turn management off to corporate economics is to present corporate economics in a highly abstract, technical manner. The use of economics jargon is cited as having contributed to the death of more than one corporate economics department.

### Failure to Produce Useful Results

Obviously, if an econometric model does not produce the types of results for which it was intended or if nonanalytic techniques yield more useful results than the model, no amount of political savvy will be sufficient to bail out the project. There are at least two ways in which this situation can arise. First, the model may prove to be ineffective as a forecasting tool because of some misunderstanding concerning problem definition and project objectives; that is, maybe the model was designed to be an effective tool for solving a particular problem, but the problem turned out not to be the "right" problem. Second, sometimes corporate economists encounter serious practical problems in developing an econometric model which does precisely what it was intended to do. With econometric marketing models there is no guarantee that one will be able to come up with an acceptable model. Insufficient data, theoretical problems, and statistical problems can all lead to serious problems in the development of econometric models. With econometric models, science and technology can take you only so far. In the final analysis, experience, judgment, and even a little luck are required to produce operational, policy-analytic econometric models.

### Inaccurate Forecasts

In spite of recent improvements in econometric modeling techniques, forecasting accuracy remains one of the most elusive goals of corporate economics. If the only objective of an econometric model is forecasting accuracy, the model should not be developed in the first place. Although econometric models can lead to improved forecasting accuracy, there are other uses of these models which are more important, such as policy analysis, scenario generation, and "what if?" simulations.

If one is interested only in forecasting accuracy, one may not need to go to the trouble of building an econometric model. Naive forecasting techniques such as time trends and exponential smoothing may suffice. Alternatively, judgmental forecasts may be more accurate than any forecasts produced by econometric models. One of the problems with a model developed by Wells Fargo Bank several years ago was that the judgmental forecasts of security analysts turned out to be more accurate than the forecasts produced by the model. This is an awkward position in which to find oneself.

We are reminded of the early forecasting objectives set for the Dresser Industries model. It was stated emphatically that management would not tolerate forecasting errors greater than 5 percent. Needless to say, with hundreds of different products involved, this target was later revised upward.

No matter how you slice it, forecasting is a tough business.


### Failure to Meet Deadlines

One should never forget that managing a planning model is like managing a large research and development project. The fact that the economic planning model of a major oil company required 23 worker-years to complete strongly implies that there was a serious slippage in the schedule for the model. Unmet deadlines and schedules are the joint responsibility of the corporate economist and his or her analysts. Schedules should be set, and if deadlines are consistently not met, corrective management action must be taken. Specific target outputs should be established for delivery on specific dates. Management should expect to receive definite results according to a preannounced schedule.

In preparing an econometric modeling schedule, one should anticipate problems and delays and make allowance for them in the schedule. For example, econometric models frequently require repeated specifications, estimation, and validation. To obtain a single good equation may require as many as 25 alternative specifications of the model.


### Inadequate Political Support from Top Management

The evidence is substantial that the most successful corporate economics departments have not necessarily been the most sophisticated. Among the more successful corporate economics groups are included *The New York Times,* McGraw-Hill, Standard Oil of Indiana, and Northwest Industries. In each case they have enjoyed the strongest possible political support from the CEO.

Without the support of top management, corporate economics is likely to become impotent and ineffective. Ultimately, what the politics of corporate economics is all about is obtaining and maintaining the political support of top management for the continued development of corporate economics projects.

## POLITICAL ADVICE TO CORPORATE ECONOMISTS

Having previously suggested that senior executives need to learn how to ask economists the right questions, we now turn our attention to the economists. Below we shall outline several courses of action which may enable corporate economists to improve their political effectiveness with corporate executives.

First, any corporate economist who is detached from the corporate planning department should work toward an alliance with that group. If corporate planning has the support of the CEO, it is potentially a very important power base within the company and is therefore worthy of pursuit by the corporate economist. As we have already implied, the directorship of the company's strategic planning department is not an inappropriate target for an ambitious corporate economist.

Second, corporate economists need to learn the art of underselling economic forecasts and economic models. Such a strategy can do wonders for the credibility of the corporate economist.

Third, economic theories and models should be kept as simple as possible to enhance the likelihood of management's understanding and support.

Fourth, considerable effort should be directed toward encouraging top management to be very explicit in formulating their objectives for economic forecasts and models. An important role of the economist is to draw this information out of management.

Fifth, the rewards from economic forecasting should be commensurate with the risks. An economic analyst who earns $25,000 per year cannot be expected to shoulder all the risks associated with an economic forecast based on a series of external assumptions over which he or she has no influence or control. Corporate executives who are paid 3 and 4 times that amount should participate in the process of formulating the assumptions on which forecasts are based.

## QUESTIONS AND PROBLEMS

**13-1** What can corporate executives do to improve communications with corporate economists?

**13-2** Explain the difference between planning and forecasting.

**13-3** Why do econometricians continue to have such a high degree of confidence in large-scale econometric models, particularly in light of their abysmal track record in forecasting the economy of the United States during the 1974–1975 and 1979–1980 recessions?

**13-4** Discuss some of the reasons why corporate economists have not always been successful in the corporate world.

**13-5** What are some of the major political obstacles that may impede the work of corporate economists?

**13-6** Compare and contrast the role of the corporate economist and that of the corporate attorney in monitoring the firm's external environment.

# PART SIX

# STATISTICAL TABLES

**TABLE 1**

*t* VALUES

| Degrees of freedom | Probability | | | | |
|---|---|---|---|---|---|
| | .10 | .05 | .025 | .01 | .005 |
| 1 | 3.078 | 6.314 | 12.706 | 31.821 | 63.657 |
| 2 | 1.886 | 2.920 | 4.303 | 6.965 | 9.925 |
| 3 | 1.638 | 2.353 | 3.182 | 4.541 | 5.841 |
| 4 | 1.533 | 2.132 | 2.776 | 3.747 | 4.604 |
| 5 | 1.476 | 2.015 | 2.571 | 3.365 | 4.032 |
| 6 | 1.440 | 1.943 | 2.447 | 3.143 | 3.707 |
| 7 | 1.415 | 1.895 | 2.365 | 2.998 | 3.499 |
| 8 | 1.397 | 1.860 | 2.306 | 2.896 | 3.355 |
| 9 | 1.383 | 1.833 | 2.262 | 2.821 | 3.250 |
| 10 | 1.372 | 1.812 | 2.228 | 2.764 | 3.169 |
| 11 | 1.363 | 1.796 | 2.201 | 2.718 | 3.106 |
| 12 | 1.356 | 1.782 | 2.179 | 2.681 | 3.055 |
| 13 | 1.350 | 1.771 | 2.160 | 2.650 | 3.012 |
| 14 | 1.345 | 1.761 | 2.145 | 2.624 | 2.977 |
| 15 | 1.341 | 1.753 | 2.131 | 2.602 | 2.947 |
| 16 | 1.337 | 1.746 | 2.120 | 2.583 | 2.921 |
| 17 | 1.333 | 1.740 | 2.110 | 2.567 | 2.898 |
| 18 | 1.330 | 1.734 | 2.101 | 2.552 | 2.878 |
| 19 | 1.328 | 1.729 | 2.093 | 2.539 | 2.861 |
| 20 | 1.325 | 1.725 | 2.086 | 2.528 | 2.845 |
| 21 | 1.323 | 1.721 | 2.080 | 2.518 | 2.831 |
| 22 | 1.321 | 1.717 | 2.074 | 2.508 | 2.819 |
| 23 | 1.319 | 1.714 | 2.069 | 2.500 | 2.807 |
| 24 | 1.318 | 1.711 | 2.064 | 2.492 | 2.797 |
| 25 | 1.316 | 1.708 | 2.060 | 2.485 | 2.787 |
| 26 | 1.315 | 1.706 | 2.056 | 2.479 | 2.779 |
| 27 | 1.314 | 1.703 | 2.052 | 2.473 | 2.771 |
| 28 | 1.313 | 1.701 | 2.048 | 2.467 | 2.763 |
| 29 | 1.311 | 1.699 | 2.045 | 2.462 | 2.756 |
| 30 | 1.310 | 1.697 | 2.042 | 2.457 | 2.750 |
| 40 | 1.303 | 1.684 | 2.021 | 2.423 | 2.704 |
| 60 | 1.296 | 1.671 | 2.000 | 2.390 | 2.660 |
| 120 | 1.289 | 1.658 | 1.980 | 2.358 | 2.617 |
| ∞ | 1.282 | 1.645 | 1.960 | 2.326 | 2.576 |

*Source:* Reproduced from Table III (Distribution of *t*) on page 46 of Fisher and Yates: *Statistical Tables for Biological, Agricultural and Medical Research* (London: Longman Group Ltd.). Previously published by Oliver Boyd, Edinburgh, and by permission of the authors and publishers.

**TABLE 2**

*F* VALUES

(5 percent)

| Degrees of freedom for denominator | Degrees of freedom for numerator | | | | | |
|---|---|---|---|---|---|---|
| | 1 | 2 | 3 | 4 | 5 | 6 |
| 1 | 161 | 200 | 216 | 225 | 230 | 234 |
| 2 | 18.51 | 19.00 | 19.16 | 19.25 | 19.30 | 19.33 |
| 3 | 10.13 | 9.55 | 9.28 | 9.12 | 9.01 | 8.94 |
| 4 | 7.71 | 6.94 | 6.59 | 6.39 | 6.26 | 6.16 |
| 5 | 6.61 | 5.79 | 5.41 | 5.19 | 5.05 | 4.95 |
| 6 | 5.99 | 5.14 | 4.76 | 4.53 | 4.39 | 4.28 |
| 7 | 5.59 | 4.74 | 4.35 | 4.12 | 3.97 | 3.87 |
| 8 | 5.32 | 4.46 | 4.07 | 3.84 | 3.69 | 3.58 |
| 9 | 5.12 | 4.26 | 3.86 | 3.63 | 3.48 | 3.37 |
| 10 | 4.96 | 4.10 | 3.71 | 3.48 | 3.33 | 3.22 |
| 11 | 4.84 | 3.98 | 3.59 | 3.36 | 3.20 | 3.09 |
| 12 | 4.75 | 3.89 | 3.49 | 3.26 | 3.11 | 3.00 |
| 13 | 4.67 | 3.80 | 3.41 | 3.18 | 3.02 | 2.92 |
| 14 | 4.60 | 3.74 | 3.34 | 3.11 | 2.96 | 2.85 |
| 15 | 4.54 | 3.68 | 3.29 | 3.06 | 2.90 | 2.79 |
| 16 | 4.49 | 3.63 | 3.24 | 3.01 | 2.85 | 2.74 |
| 17 | 4.45 | 3.59 | 3.20 | 2.96 | 2.81 | 2.70 |
| 18 | 4.41 | 3.55 | 3.16 | 2.93 | 2.77 | 2.66 |
| 19 | 4.38 | 3.52 | 3.13 | 2.90 | 2.74 | 2.63 |
| 20 | 4.35 | 3.49 | 3.10 | 2.87 | 2.71 | 2.60 |
| 21 | 4.32 | 3.47 | 3.07 | 2.84 | 2.68 | 2.57 |
| 22 | 4.30 | 3.44 | 3.05 | 2.82 | 2.66 | 2.55 |
| 23 | 4.28 | 3.42 | 3.03 | 2.80 | 2.64 | 2.53 |
| 24 | 4.26 | 3.40 | 3.01 | 2.78 | 2.62 | 2.51 |
| 25 | 4.24 | 3.38 | 2.99 | 2.76 | 2.60 | 2.49 |
| 26 | 4.22 | 3.37 | 2.98 | 2.74 | 2.59 | 2.47 |
| 27 | 4.21 | 3.35 | 2.96 | 2.73 | 2.57 | 2.46 |
| 28 | 4.20 | 3.34 | 2.95 | 2.71 | 2.56 | 2.44 |
| 29 | 4.18 | 3.33 | 2.93 | 2.70 | 2.54 | 2.43 |
| 30 | 4.17 | 3.32 | 2.92 | 2.69 | 2.53 | 2.43 |
| 32 | 4.15 | 3.30 | 2.90 | 2.67 | 2.51 | 2.40 |
| 34 | 4.13 | 3.28 | 2.88 | 2.65 | 2.49 | 2.38 |
| 36 | 4.11 | 3.26 | 2.86 | 2.63 | 2.48 | 2.36 |
| 38 | 4.10 | 3.25 | 2.85 | 2.62 | 2.46 | 2.35 |
| 40 | 4.08 | 3.23 | 2.84 | 2.61 | 2.45 | 2.34 |
| 42 | 4.07 | 3.22 | 2.83 | 2.59 | 2.44 | 2.32 |
| 44 | 4.06 | 3.21 | 2.82 | 2.58 | 2.43 | 2.31 |
| 46 | 4.05 | 3.20 | 2.81 | 2.57 | 2.42 | 2.30 |
| 48 | 4.04 | 3.19 | 2.80 | 2.56 | 2.41 | 2.30 |
| 50 | 4.03 | 3.18 | 2.79 | 2.56 | 2.40 | 2.29 |
| 55 | 4.02 | 3.17 | 2.78 | 2.54 | 2.38 | 2.27 |
| 60 | 4.00 | 3.15 | 2.76 | 2.52 | 2.37 | 2.25 |
| 65 | 3.99 | 3.14 | 2.75 | 2.51 | 2.36 | 2.24 |
| 70 | 3.98 | 3.13 | 2.74 | 2.50 | 2.35 | 2.22 |
| 80 | 3.96 | 3.11 | 2.72 | 2.48 | 2.33 | 2.21 |
| 100 | 3.94 | 3.09 | 2.70 | 2.46 | 2.30 | 2.19 |
| 200 | 3.89 | 3.04 | 2.65 | 2.41 | 2.26 | 2.14 |
| 400 | 3.86 | 3.02 | 2.62 | 2.39 | 2.23 | 2.12 |

*Source:* Reprinted by permission from *Statistical Methods,* 6th ed., by George W. Snedecor and William G. Cochran, © 1967 by the Iowa State University Press, Ames, Iowa.

**TABLE 3**

*F* VALUES

(1 percent)

| Degrees of freedom for denominator | Degrees of freedom for numerator | | | | | |
|---|---|---|---|---|---|---|
| | 1 | 2 | 3 | 4 | 5 | 6 |
| 1 | 4052 | 4999 | 5403 | 5625 | 5764 | 5859 |
| 2 | 98.49 | 99.01 | 99.17 | 99.25 | 99.30 | 99.33 |
| 3 | 34.12 | 30.81 | 29.46 | 28.71 | 28.24 | 27.91 |
| 4 | 21.20 | 18.00 | 16.69 | 15.98 | 15.52 | 15.21 |
| 5 | 16.26 | 13.27 | 12.06 | 11.39 | 10.97 | 10.67 |
| 6 | 13.74 | 10.92 | 9.78 | 9.15 | 8.75 | 8.47 |
| 7 | 12.25 | 9.55 | 8.45 | 7.85 | 7.46 | 7.19 |
| 8 | 11.26 | 8.65 | 7.59 | 7.01 | 6.63 | 6.37 |
| 9 | 10.56 | 8.02 | 6.99 | 6.42 | 6.06 | 5.80 |
| 10 | 10.04 | 7.56 | 6.55 | 5.99 | 5.64 | 5.39 |
| 11 | 9.65 | 7.20 | 6.22 | 5.67 | 5.32 | 5.07 |
| 12 | 9.33 | 6.93 | 5.95 | 5.41 | 5.06 | 4.82 |
| 13 | 9.07 | 6.70 | 5.74 | 5.20 | 4.86 | 4.62 |
| 14 | 8.86 | 6.51 | 5.56 | 5.03 | 4.69 | 4.46 |
| 15 | 8.68 | 6.36 | 5.42 | 4.89 | 4.56 | 4.32 |
| 16 | 8.53 | 6.23 | 5.29 | 4.77 | 4.44 | 4.20 |
| 17 | 8.40 | 6.11 | 5.18 | 4.67 | 4.34 | 4.10 |
| 18 | 8.28 | 6.01 | 5.09 | 4.58 | 4.25 | 4.01 |
| 19 | 8.18 | 5.93 | 5.01 | 4.50 | 4.17 | 3.94 |
| 20 | 8.10 | 5.85 | 4.94 | 4.43 | 4.10 | 3.87 |
| 21 | 8.02 | 5.78 | 4.87 | 4.37 | 4.04 | 3.81 |
| 22 | 7.94 | 5.72 | 4.82 | 4.31 | 3.99 | 3.76 |
| 23 | 7.88 | 5.66 | 4.76 | 4.26 | 3.94 | 3.71 |
| 24 | 7.82 | 5.61 | 4.72 | 4.22 | 3.90 | 3.67 |
| 25 | 7.77 | 5.57 | 4.68 | 4.18 | 3.86 | 3.63 |
| 26 | 7.72 | 5.53 | 4.64 | 4.14 | 3.82 | 3.59 |
| 27 | 7.68 | 5.49 | 4.60 | 4.11 | 3.79 | 3.56 |
| 28 | 7.64 | 5.45 | 4.57 | 4.07 | 3.76 | 3.53 |
| 29 | 7.60 | 5.42 | 4.54 | 4.04 | 3.73 | 3.50 |
| 30 | 7.56 | 5.39 | 4.51 | 4.02 | 3.70 | 3.47 |
| 32 | 7.50 | 5.34 | 4.46 | 3.97 | 3.66 | 3.42 |
| 34 | 7.44 | 5.29 | 4.42 | 3.93 | 3.61 | 3.38 |
| 36 | 7.39 | 5.25 | 4.38 | 3.89 | 3.58 | 3.35 |
| 38 | 7.35 | 5.21 | 4.34 | 3.86 | 3.54 | 3.32 |
| 40 | 7.31 | 5.18 | 4.31 | 3.83 | 3.51 | 3.29 |
| 42 | 7.27 | 5.15 | 4.29 | 3.80 | 3.49 | 3.26 |
| 44 | 7.24 | 5.12 | 4.26 | 3.78 | 3.46 | 3.24 |
| 46 | 7.21 | 5.10 | 4.24 | 3.76 | 3.44 | 3.22 |
| 48 | 7.19 | 5.08 | 4.22 | 3.74 | 3.42 | 3.20 |
| 50 | 7.17 | 5.06 | 4.20 | 3.72 | 3.41 | 3.18 |
| 55 | 7.12 | 5.01 | 4.16 | 3.68 | 3.37 | 3.15 |
| 60 | 7.08 | 4.98 | 4.13 | 3.65 | 3.34 | 3.12 |
| 65 | 7.04 | 4.95 | 4.10 | 3.62 | 3.31 | 3.09 |
| 70 | 7.01 | 4.92 | 4.08 | 3.60 | 3.29 | 3.07 |
| 80 | 6.95 | 4.88 | 4.04 | 3.56 | 3.25 | 3.04 |
| 100 | 6.90 | 4.82 | 3.98 | 3.51 | 3.20 | 2.99 |
| 200 | 6.76 | 4.71 | 3.88 | 3.41 | 3.11 | 2.90 |
| 400 | 6.70 | 4.66 | 3.83 | 3.36 | 3.06 | 2.85 |

*Source:* Reprinted by permission from *Statistical Methods*, 6th ed., by George W. Snedecor and William G. Cochran, © 1967 by the Iowa State University Press, Ames Iowa.

**TABLE 4**
PRESENT VALUE OF $1 TO BE RECEIVED AT END OF PERIOD $n$

Present value $= 1/(1 + i)^n$

| Period | 1% | 5% | 6% | 7% | 8% | 9% | 10% | 12% | 14% | 15% | 16% | 18% | 20% |
|---|---|---|---|---|---|---|---|---|---|---|---|---|---|
| 1 | .990 | .952 | .943 | .935 | .926 | .917 | .909 | .893 | .877 | .870 | .862 | .847 | .833 |
| 2 | .980 | .907 | .890 | .873 | .857 | .842 | .826 | .797 | .769 | .756 | .743 | .718 | .694 |
| 3 | .971 | .864 | .840 | .816 | .794 | .772 | .751 | .712 | .675 | .658 | .641 | .609 | .579 |
| 4 | .961 | .823 | .792 | .763 | .735 | .708 | .683 | .636 | .592 | .572 | .552 | .516 | .482 |
| 5 | .951 | .784 | .747 | .713 | .681 | .650 | .621 | .567 | .519 | .497 | .476 | .437 | .402 |
| 6 | .942 | .746 | .705 | .666 | .630 | .596 | .564 | .507 | .456 | .432 | .410 | .370 | .335 |
| 7 | .933 | .711 | .665 | .623 | .583 | .547 | .513 | .452 | .400 | .376 | .354 | .314 | .279 |
| 8 | .923 | .677 | .627 | .582 | .540 | .502 | .467 | .404 | .351 | .327 | .305 | .266 | .233 |
| 9 | .914 | .645 | .592 | .544 | .500 | .460 | .424 | .361 | .308 | .284 | .263 | .226 | .194 |
| 10 | .905 | .614 | .558 | .508 | .463 | .422 | .386 | .322 | .270 | .247 | .227 | .191 | .162 |
| 15 | .861 | .481 | .417 | .362 | .315 | .275 | .239 | .183 | .140 | .123 | .108 | .084 | .065 |
| 20 | .820 | .377 | .312 | .258 | .215 | .178 | .149 | .104 | .073 | .061 | .051 | .037 | .026 |
| 25 | .780 | .295 | .233 | .184 | .146 | .116 | .092 | .059 | .038 | .030 | .024 | .016 | .010 |
| 30 | .742 | .231 | .174 | .131 | .099 | .075 | .057 | .033 | .020 | .015 | .012 | .007 | .004 |
| 40 | .672 | .142 | .097 | .067 | .046 | .032 | .022 | .011 | .005 | .004 | .003 | .001 | .001 |

**TABLE 5**
PRESENT VALUE OF A STREAM OF $1 RECEIPTS FOR $n$ PERIODS

$$\text{Present value} = \sum_{t=1}^{n} (1/(1 + i)^t)$$

| Period | 1% | 5% | 6% | 7% | 8% | 9% | 10% | 12% | 14% | 15% | 16% | 18% | 20% |
|---|---|---|---|---|---|---|---|---|---|---|---|---|---|
| 1 | 0.990 | 0.952 | 0.943 | 0.935 | 0.926 | 0.917 | 0.909 | 0.893 | 0.877 | 0.870 | 0.862 | 0.847 | 0.833 |
| 2 | 1.970 | 1.859 | 1.833 | 1.808 | 1.783 | 1.759 | 1.736 | 1.690 | 1.647 | 1.626 | 1.605 | 1.566 | 1.528 |
| 3 | 2.941 | 2.723 | 2.673 | 2.624 | 2.577 | 2.531 | 2.487 | 2.402 | 2.322 | 2.283 | 2.246 | 2.174 | 2.106 |
| 4 | 3.902 | 3.546 | 3.465 | 3.387 | 3.312 | 3.240 | 3.170 | 3.037 | 2.914 | 2.855 | 2.798 | 2.690 | 2.589 |
| 5 | 4.853 | 4.329 | 4.212 | 4.100 | 3.993 | 3.890 | 3.791 | 3.605 | 3.433 | 3.352 | 3.274 | 3.127 | 2.991 |
| 6 | 5.795 | 5.076 | 4.917 | 4.766 | 4.623 | 4.486 | 4.355 | 4.111 | 3.889 | 3.784 | 3.685 | 3.498 | 3.326 |
| 7 | 6.728 | 5.786 | 5.582 | 5.389 | 5.206 | 5.033 | 4.868 | 4.564 | 4.288 | 4.160 | 4.039 | 3.812 | 3.605 |
| 8 | 7.652 | 6.463 | 6.210 | 5.971 | 5.747 | 5.535 | 5.335 | 4.968 | 4.639 | 4.487 | 4.344 | 4.078 | 3.837 |
| 9 | 8.566 | 7.108 | 6.802 | 6.515 | 6.247 | 5.995 | 5.759 | 5.328 | 4.946 | 4.772 | 4.607 | 4.303 | 4.031 |
| 10 | 9.471 | 7.722 | 7.360 | 7.024 | 6.710 | 6.418 | 6.145 | 5.650 | 5.216 | 5.019 | 4.833 | 4.494 | 4.193 |
| 15 | 13.865 | 10.380 | 9.712 | 9.108 | 8.559 | 8.060 | 7.606 | 6.811 | 6.142 | 5.847 | 5.575 | 5.092 | 4.675 |
| 20 | 18.046 | 12.462 | 11.470 | 10.594 | 9.818 | 9.128 | 8.514 | 7.469 | 6.623 | 6.259 | 5.929 | 5.353 | 4.870 |
| 25 | 22.023 | 14.094 | 12.783 | 11.654 | 10.675 | 9.823 | 9.077 | 7.843 | 6.873 | 6.464 | 6.097 | 5.467 | 4.948 |
| 30 | 25.808 | 15.373 | 13.765 | 12.409 | 11.258 | 10.274 | 9.427 | 8.055 | 7.003 | 6.566 | 6.177 | 5.517 | 4.979 |
| 40 | 32.835 | 17.159 | 15.046 | 13.332 | 11.925 | 10.757 | 9.779 | 8.244 | 7.105 | 6.642 | 6.234 | 5.548 | 4.997 |

# INDEX